Paul Daffey is a Melbourne journalist who has written three books:
Local Rites
Beyond the Big Sticks
Behind the Goals

He has also contributed chapters towards several books, including:
This Game of Ours
Black and Blue
The Barrackers Are Shouting
The Australian Game of Football since 1858
Glory and Fame
The Grand Finals, Volume 1
The Grand Finals, Volume 2
The Footy Almanac
Footy Town

Paul Daffey is also a tour guide in Melbourne and throughout Victoria.

The Totem Poles of Ouyen United

TRAVELS IN COUNTRY FOOTY

Paul Daffey

The Totem Poles of Ouyen United: Travels in Country Footy

ISBN 978-0-646-80416-3

Daffey Publications
P.O. Box 172
Northcote
Vic 3070

pauldaffey27@gmail.com
daffeytours.com.au

Cover art: John Harrison
Cover design: Megan Ellis
Book design: Megan Ellis
Printed by McPherson's Printing Group
Distribution by Australian Fishing Network

Contents

The Grand Tour

The Last Quarter

Appendix 1

Appendix 2

Appendix 3

Appendix 4

Glossary

Club	**Pronunciation**
Bealiba	*Bee-alli-ba*
Boinka	*Bow-inka*
Boulka	*Bool-ka*
Condobolin	*Con-dobe-alin*
Corack	*Core-rack*
Cowangie	*Cow-anjee*
Danyo	*Dan-yo*
Dering	*Derr-ing*
Gorya	*Gaw-ya*
Irymple	*Eye-rymple*
Kattyoong	*Katty-ong*
Kiamal	*Ky-ammal*
Kulwin	*Kull-win*
Linga	*Ling-ga*
Merbein	*Mer-been*
Mitiamo	*Mitty-ammo*
Nangiloc	*Nan-jee-loc*
Nunga	*Nung-ga*
Orroroo	*Orra-roo*
Ouyen	*Oh-yen*
Patchewollock	*Patchy-wollock*
Pirro	*Pirr-o*
Tiega	*Ty-eeja*
Torrita	*Tor-reeta*
Trinita	*Trinn-ita*
Turriff	*Turr-iff*
Tutye	*Tutt-ee*
Ungarie	*Ung-gair-ee*
Wathe	*Way-thee*
Walpeup	*Wal-pee-up*

Map 1: Victoria

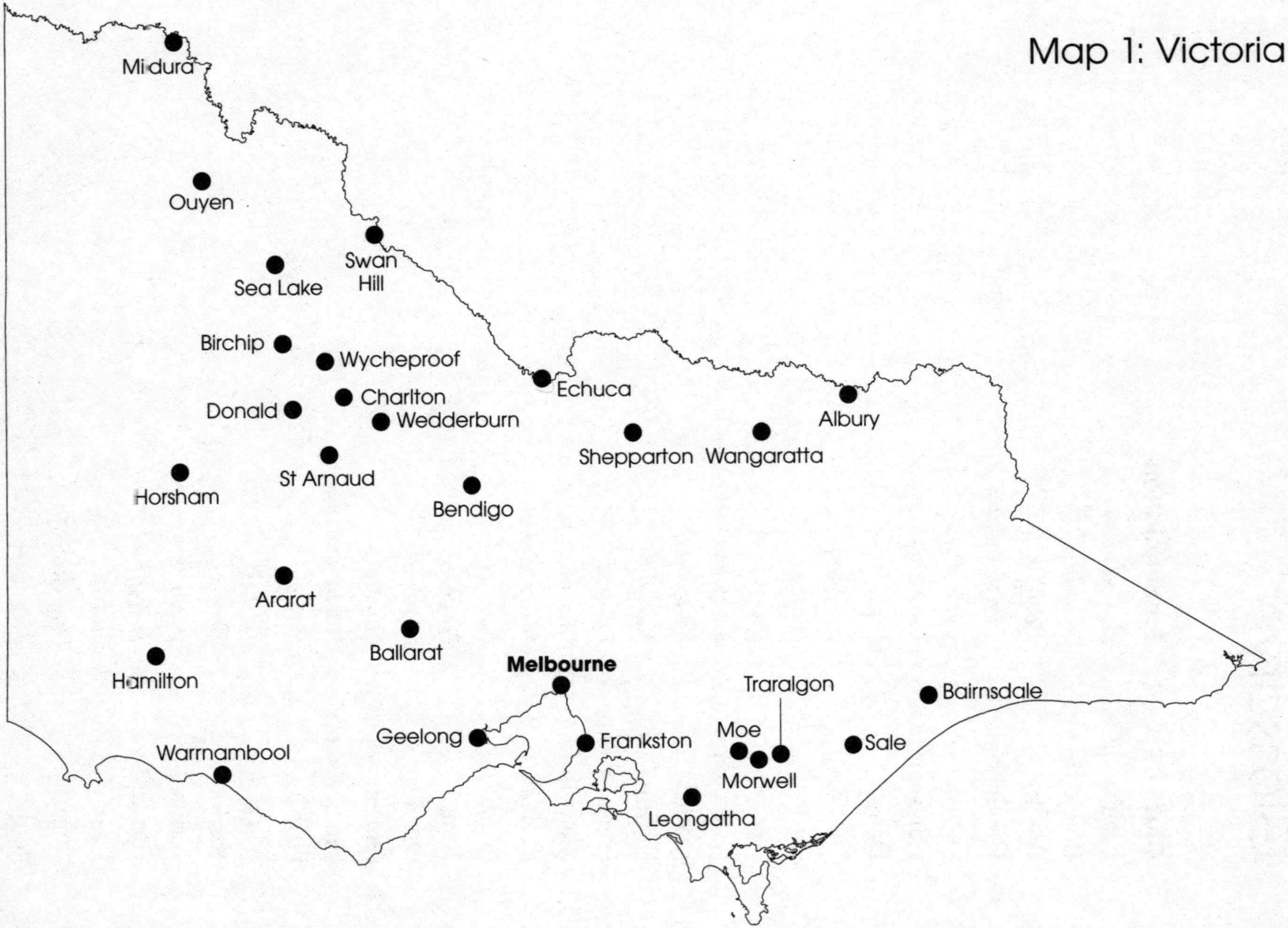

Foreword

When I was growing up, there were two main institutions in country towns, the football ground and the church. Like most kids, I loved one of those and tolerated the other.

When I was growing up in Ouyen, the place of worship I fell in love with was Blackburn Park. Every Saturday morning, I felt a sense of wonder and possibility when I jumped out of bed and put on my woolly Tiega jumper (if I hadn't slept in it the night before). The itchiness of the jumper on my bare skin was a minor inconvenience considering the excitement of the day ahead.

I have a photo of the moment I "got" football. I was five or six years of age. My parents owned the Fairy Dell Café in Ouyen. We were on a road trip to Nangiloc to buy fruit and vegetables for the café.

When we pulled over for a snack stop, the well-worn Sherrin came out along with the Thermos. I kicked the ball, and for the first time in my life it spun correctly. When I bounced the ball, it didn't dribble along the ground as usual; it returned to me. There was something magical about that day on a dusty road near Nangiloc.

When I was that age, football for me was about going to watch my two older brothers Peter and David play for Tiega at some ground in the Mallee. It might have been at Underbool or Walpeup, or one of those other towns with a name that rolls so nicely off the tongue. After the footy, we made it home to watch the footy replay on television and eat fried dim sims, which was Mum's meal of choice on Saturday nights.

One Saturday, we were particularly excited about going to the footy because Tiega were playing at Sea Lake. The bush telegraph had led us to believe that, over the summer, Sea Lake had moved to a new, MCG-sized oval with an indoor warm-up area.

MCG-sized!

Never had a ten-year-old boy heard a more thrilling phrase. When we got to the ground, we walked on it as if we were walking on Lord's for the first time. We didn't say anything; we just drank it in. The indoor warm-up area was simply a basketball court. But, hey, who cared about that!

My father John was a Scottish immigrant whose family had moved to Melbourne. Later, he moved to Ouyen with his job in the railways department. He met my mother, Margaret, who was part of the Vallance family from Kulwin. They went to dances at the VRI, and then Dad asked Mum's father Hector for her hand in marriage. He firmly declined.

Dad played for Tiega, and Hector was Kiamal through and through. There were rivalries like Collingwood and Carlton, Manchester United and Manchester City, and the Ashes. And then there was Tiega v Kiamal. The old man had a bit of work to do to win Hec's approval.

My first memory of playing in a game is a grand final in the under-thirteens between Tiega and Manangatang. The under-thirteens, or minis, as they were called, played at half-time of the senior game – two halves of seven minutes each. "Manang" hadn't lost a game all year. We were underdogs, but we felt we had a chance because their ruckman and best player was out.

I have a vivid memory of the one kick I had for the match. I can still see the exact spot on the hallowed Blackburn Park where I got the kick. I gave it everything, and it went approximately nine metres – right to our best player, Martin "Mouse" Floyd. Mouse cut back to the middle, where I was positioned, and ran straight over the top of me. The embarrassment of being run over by my teammate lives in me to this day. And Mouse brings it up every time I see him.

We got out to a score of 1.1 (7), a score that was almost unassailable considering it took five kicks to get the ball from the centre to the goalsquare. But, being football, there was a twist. Somehow, when the siren went, the score was all square at 1.1 (7) apiece.

There was talk of a rematch after the senior game. Our coach thought we'd overachieved by getting the draw, so he told us to scurry off to the trotting track where we couldn't be found.

The draw stood.

In 1982, Tiega and Kiamal merged. There was talk of how big this was, but I was too young to understand the significance of it all. The merged club was called Ouyen Rovers, and they adopted the Demons colours. While I barracked for Richmond, I also loved Robbie Flower, the champion wingman who wore No.2 for Melbourne. So the No.2 sat proudly on my back when I played for the Rovers.

One of the many rituals in country footy was how you found out who was playing in the team. Some found out in the clubrooms after the main training session, but in Ouyen, most of us found out by looking up the teams on the window of the local shop. Many times we were waiting there while the A4 sheet of paper with the football oval printed on to it was Durexed up on the window.

I remember seeing my name on a dotted line on the oval for the first time when I was eleven years old. I was named in a forward pocket in the under-sixteen team. It gave me butterflies in the stomach.

When I was growing up in Ouyen, a boy called Trevor Poole captured not just local attention, but the attention of scouts from the Big Smoke. He was fifteen or sixteen, and playing senior football for Tempy-Gorya-Patchewollock at the Tempy ground. TGP wore the Tigers colours. The teenager moved in a way that suggested he would continue to wear the Tigers colours in Melbourne. Under the zoning system in place at that time, Mallee footballers were zoned to Richmond. I found myself transfixed when I watched Trevor Poole.

I've always thought I had a perfect upbringing when it came to exposure to cities and towns. I grew up in Ouyen, a town of 1600 where, on my first day in Prep, I walked to school. My cousins, the McMonnies, had a farm at Wemen on the Murray, just along from Robinvale, where I spent every school holidays riding motorbikes and swimming in the river. My family left Ouyen and moved to Bendigo when I was twelve. Bendigo had 58,000 people and a pizza shop that was open on more than just Friday nights.

The next move was to Melbourne as an eighteen-year-old. I was ready to take on all that the city had to offer, but I feel for those who have only ever known the city. I reckon they've missed out on something special.

Like most people, I'm incredibly proud of where I'm from. I enjoy telling people I was born in a little town in the Mallee called Ouyen, which is famous for two things: being the hottest town on the Victorian weather map; and its vanilla-slice competition.

I love those things about it, but for me, the romance of the town is entwined with football. The names of the O'Callaghan, Healy and Robertson families conjure up emotions that remind me of a time when footy was everything to me, but in a different way to the way it is everything to me today.

A few years ago, I was travelling up to Robinvale when I stopped off in Wedderburn for a coffee. While I was wandering along the town's main street, I stumbled into the local Men's Shed. From my understanding, the Men's Shed program has been set up to enable country people to come together to talk. It's an innovative program, but essentially it aims to do what country football has been doing for many years.

Long may it be the case that country football brings people together. And well done to Paul Daffey and *The Totem Poles of Ouyen United* for celebrating the contribution that football has made to life in the Mallee and all around Victoria.

Wayne Campbell, 2019

Wayne Campbell played 297 games for Richmond. Trevor Poole was the Richmond football manager towards the end of Wayne's career. Wayne is now the general manager of football operations at the GWS Giants.

Introduction

During the writing of this book, I was visiting family in Swan Hill with my mother Marie when we took a diversion to the Swan Hill Regional Art Gallery. Two local artists, one a dentist, the other an accountant, had an exhibition. The dentist, John Harrison, had a painting that took my fancy.

John Harrison grew up in England, and studied dentistry in London. On graduation, he wanted to work and travel. So he applied for jobs in Australia. When he was offered a position in Broken Hill, he said, "Why not?" When he first got off the train at Broken Hill, he said, "What have I done?"

But he stayed. On a trip to Adelaide with friends, he met a woman called Laurel Jilbert, who had grown up near Ultima, a town in the Mallee region of Victoria, near Swan Hill. They married and moved to Swan Hill, where John was a dentist for forty years. As a hobby, he took up painting. His works often depicted the striking colours of the Mallee.

The painting that took my eye in the Swan Hill gallery depicted a sunset over Ultima, which, besides being the town of John's wife, is the town where my mother is from. John's colours reminded me of the sunsets that I saw in Ultima when I was visiting my grandparents and wider family. I rang John and asked whether he would be interested in heading up the road to take a look at the totem poles inside the entrance at Blackburn Park in Ouyen. I asked whether he might like to paint the poles for an image to be used on a book cover. My request sparked in John the sense of adventure that he had shown when he first went to Broken Hill.

"Why not?"

This book might well be the first in Australian publishing to have utilised the talents of an English dentist at large by a footy oval in the Mallee with an easel and a bush-vivid palette. I have approached the book with a similar sense of adventure. I hope to bring to life in words the colour and verve of footy in country Victoria as depicted by John Harrison in his image of Blackburn Park in Ouyen.

Part 1

Mallee Voices

1

The Land of the Twig

It is a still winter's evening when I pull into the grounds of the Hilltop Motel on the southern outskirts of Ouyen, the town at the heart of the Mallee region in the north-west corner of Victoria. To the west, the sun is blazing pink and orange as it drops below the flat horizon. Bernie Kelly, my host for the evening, emerges at the door of my motel room to take me into town. We are going for a meal at the Ouyen Club before we head to Blackburn Park, the home of the Ouyen United Football Club, for an evening of footy banter. It is an evening that, for me, will spark a new journey into the heart of country footy.

During that evening in Ouyen, I will hear many great tales, both tall and true. Some of the tales will remind me of going to footy matches in the Mallee when I was a boy. Others will open the door to a story that is like a modern fable. It is a story of the drift from the farms to the cities and towns. It is a story of displacement as young footballers with dirt under their fingernails take up jobs behind desks, where earning opportunities abound but life is somehow less rich.

I discover that the Ouyen United footy club is the result of an extraordinary number of clubs that have merged into one. It will set me off a journey in which I look at country footy as a whole, but with particular reference to the Mallee, to the red soil and the hardy eucalypts that withstand bushfire and drought, like the families who have remained on the land.

After my explorations in the Mallee, I continue my footy travels to other parts of the state during the remainder of the 2018 season. I go to the foot of the Strzelecki Ranges in Gippsland, to an abandoned oval near Wedderburn, and to the old gold town of Inglewood. I see a grand final of high drama at Frankston Park before I finish up on the balcony of the Horsham City Oval, where I case out the career of a country footballer who has played in an unfeasible number of senior premiership teams. His premierships are listed in the extensive appendices at the back of the book, along with a list of all the country footballers I could find who have played in six or more senior flags.

The appendices are taken up mainly with the details of my research into just how many clubs have contributed towards the formation of the Ouyen United Football Club. Through these figures and the stories behind the figures, in the Mallee and elsewhere around Victoria and beyond, I hope to create a snapshot of the game of Australian football in its country heartland.

The seeds of my initial evening at Blackburn Park in Ouyen were planted in my home in Northcote, in inner Melbourne. I was a journalist with a penchant for writing about local footy, sometimes amateur footy and suburban footy, but mostly country footy because, I found, that's where the best stories were. Writing about men on the land whose boots crunched the dirt as they walked into the change rooms carried more punch than writing about men in the suburbs who stacked shelves at the supermarket before driving through a lattice of streets to get to training.

The youngest of our three children, Leo, had a friend at school called Samuel Healy. One night, Sam's father Peter pulled up a chair at our kitchen bench after arriving to pick up his son. We shared a drink while Peter told me about his background in country footy. He said he was from Ouyen. His home club was Tiega, a club I had heard about once or twice through an old teammate at Golden Square but a club that, really, I knew nothing about.

Peter explained that Tiega was a club that was formed by farmers just west of Ouyen. His father, Frank Healy, played in the backline until he was forty-two years of age. Then he served the club as president for many years. Frank's brothers, including his twin brother Kevin, were among the great characters of Mallee footy. In all, there were seven boys and five girls in that generation of the Healy family. The members of a few large families provided the backbone of a highly successful era for Tiega.

One night when Peter was a boy, he was stunned when two officials from Collingwood arrived at the family home to get the signature of his father, as the Tiega club president, on a clearance form for a Tiega player. Peter could not believe that officials from Collingwood, the most famous club in the land, were in his home attending to a football matter with Tiega, a small club in the Mallee.

The young Tiega player in question, Denis O'Callaghan, had played senior football with Collingwood the previous season, only to return to Tiega for family reasons. That night, he signed on to resume his career with Collingwood, and he went on to play in defence for the Magpies in the 1970 Grand Final. Denis O'Callaghan's brothers, meanwhile, would remain key players with Tiega.

In 1971, Tiega were in the midst of their run of fourteen consecutive grand finals. They went through the season undefeated, and in the lead-up to the 1971 Grand Final, they were highly favoured to win another premiership. Their rivals in the Grand Final were Kiamal, a club formed by farmers just north of Ouyen. Kiamal, the Magpies from the Mallee, had been going for fifty years. They won two premierships in their first twenty years, but they had not won any flags at senior level for thirty years.

After a controversy before the opening bounce, Kiamal got the jump. Their captain-coach, Don Pohlner, one of the toughest players to pull on a boot in the Mallee, kicked three early goals as the Magpies established a lead of six goals at half-time. Tiega then fought back.

Seated at our kitchen bench, Peter Healy described the match as a "ding-dong battle". He said his cousins, Des and Rob Healy, and the Pohlner brothers, Don and Ray, were relentless in their quest for the ball for four gruelling quarters, but unfortunately for Tiega, it was Kiamal who won the day.

Then he added something unexpected.

"They celebrated for about six weeks afterwards with a twig just out of town."

I frowned.

Peter smiled, and began an explanation that Mallee people must occasionally provide. A "twig" is a Mallee term for a small bonfire around which men and women gather to have a drink and a chat under the stars. You can get a twig going in a paddock or by a river. Someone might throw a hotplate on to the fire and cook up a steak or two. The beer is cold, but the company is warm. For Mallee people, a twig is a cherished custom.

After the 1971 Mallee league Grand Final, the Kiamal players built a twig by a road near their home ground just north of Ouyen and kept it alight until November. Players would drop by at any time and find a teammate with whom they could share a tale or two about their triumph. On weekends, the number of players swelled and the party resumed. The protracted nature of the Kiamal twig was a source of irritation for the people of Tiega.

Leaving aside the events surrounding the footy match, I was struck by the use of the word "twig" itself. In the original sense of the word, a twig is a small branch that has been broken from a tree. The word carries a sense of something that is slender and delicate. In this case, however, the word "twig" denotes a social gathering that is rich and robust, which seems to me a subtle stroke of genius, and yet another reason to see the Mallee as a region apart.

For several years, I was part of a show on ABC Radio in which we took calls from footy grounds around Australia. During September, it became part of the fabric of the finals to hear about Alvie's win in the wet or the quality of the tawny port that was being sold from the booth at Tanunda. For our biggest moment, my on-air colleague Ian Cover persuaded the president from Stony Creek to get his players to belt out the club song on national radio after his team had pulled off an unlikely triumph at an oval in South Gippsland.

After talking to Peter Healy about the 1971 Mallee league Grand Final, I went on radio and mentioned the Kiamal twig, and the fact that it had crackled away for six weeks in the glowing aftermath of the breakthrough premiership. The response from listeners was immediate. While Mallee people rang in to confirm the delights of standing on red earth around a small fire, one or two listeners from other regions rang in to tell of their terms for such gatherings. Unfortunately, I am unable to remember the alternatives because they were not nearly as good as "twig". I would always link Kiamal's premiership with one of the great terms in the Australian vernacular.

In subsequent chats, Peter Healy told me more about Mallee footy. He himself started playing in the forward pocket for the Tiega under-sixteen team in 1972, when he was twelve years of age. The Tiega juniors failed to score in Peter's first season, but four years later he was still in the juniors and they won the flag.

Throughout his school years, Peter watched the Tiega senior team play every week. He rated his cousin Des Healy as the best country footballer he has seen. Des, like several male members of the Healy clan, boarded at St Patrick's College in Ballarat before returning home to the Mallee and taking up life on the land. Des was a bullocking ruck-rover who rarely emerged from a pack without the ball. "He was so strong through the core," Peter said. "No one could tackle him."

Over the course of his long career, Des Healy became renowned for one interleague match almost as much his many honours at club level. In 1973, the Sunraysia league was due to host the North Central league in Mildura in their zone match in the annual interleague carnival known as the Victorian country championships. Sunraysia league officials asked Mallee league officials whether they would like to field a team to play against a second Sunraysia team. Their match would be the curtain-raiser before the country championships match.

In the lead-up to the curtain-raiser, word got to the Mallee players that their hosts from the Sunraysia league regarded them as hicks, not to be taken seriously. In the first quarter, Des Healy cannoned through so many rivals in his pursuit of the ball that Sunraysia players lay strewn across the turf like skittles in a bowling alley. Des went for the ball with the same vigour for the rest of the match. His performance left a large impression on rivals and teammates alike.

I later met Des, and he revealed himself to be a shy and humble man. When I asked whether I could take his photo, the look on his face suggested he had rarely heard such an unfortunate request. Des played like a wrecking ball, but off the field he was as a gentle man. Through Des, I gained a sense of the nuance of Mallee football beyond the renowned toughness and isolation.

In that era of Tiega's success, it was common for Tiega footballers who were boarding at St Pat's to return home for the Mallee league finals. Wayne Carmichael was sixteen years of age when he returned home to play for Tiega's senior team during the finals in 1976. Peter Healy said the teenaged Carmichael had brilliant skills, and he could hit leading forwards on the chest with searing stab kicks. His performances on a wing helped Tiega towards the 1976 premiership. In 1980, Carmichael was living and working in Mildura; on weekends, he drove an hour down the Calder Highway to play with Tiega. Despite an aversion to training, he played so well that he won the league best and fairest award.

Peter Healy, like hundreds of Mallee footballers, remembers playing against Les Latta, who was a mainstay on Mallee ovals for fifty years. Les Latta was born in 1920. At fourteen years of age, he defied his parents' orders against playing football and began cycling ten kilometres along sandy back roads to get to training at the Torrita Football Club. Later, with his parents now aware of his football proclivities, he moved clubs to Walpeup. In 1960, Les Latta was forty years of age when he played at half-back in Walpeup's premiership team. At forty-five, he responded to his demotion from the Walpeup senior team by gaining a transfer to Underbool. He later transferred back to Walpeup, and in 1980, at sixty years of age, he was still playing at full-back for the reserves. His superb judgement of the ball in the air enabled him to outpoint opponents who were less than half his age.

Peter Healy said the Tiega reserve players came to believe that they were prolonging Les Latta's career. "No one wanted to tackle him and perhaps go down in history as the one who put him out of the game," he said.

For three seasons, Les Latta played alongside his son Bob in the Walpeup senior team. He also played alongside his sons Fred and Roy in the Walpeup reserves. Les Latta's sons and grandsons added to his legend with their own highly decorated careers. Peter said Les was still looking as strong as a Mallee bull until just before he died in 2014 at the age of ninety-four.

Peter recalled the feats of a couple of players from the Ouyen Football Club, one a champion, the other less so. Rodney "Bushy" Vallance won two league medals with his striking performances as a centreman. But Peter's recollection was strongest when he recalled Peter "Sparks" Darley, the Ouyen full-back, whom he described as solidly built.

"Sparks could kick a ball like no one I've ever seen," Peter said. "He would regularly kick torpedoes from full-back past the centre circle.

"On a good day, with the wind behind him, he could kick from full-back to centre half-forward at Blackburn Park. My father thought I was exaggerating when I mentioned this, but I don't think so."

I now think Peter Healy and I should have chatted about Mallee footy while we were standing around a small fire in the backyard, or maybe by the Merri Creek, but I am thankful for the part of those chats in stoking my interest in footy in Victoria's north-west. I grew up going to the occasional game in the Mallee because I had family there. After I began to write about country footy for newspapers as a journalist, I enjoyed seeking out stories from what I knew to be a colourful corner of the state. But during the period when I met Peter Healy I was also learning about Mallee footy through my work on a history of the administration of Victorian country football. The ruling body of country footy, the Victorian Country Football League, had commissioned me to write its history before it was wound up. Through my research, I was able to put Mallee football in the context of the game at large. I realised that, while Mallee football was extremely tough, it was also brittle. The Mallee as a region has suffered more than most from the drift of families from farms to the cities and towns.

In the 1970s, footy in the Mallee experienced an enormous high point and a corresponding low point. In 1974, five players from the Mallee Football League were included in the North Central league team that won the final of the Victorian country championships. The inclusion of the Mallee Five – as I'll call them – in the victorious North Central league team confirmed to Mallee football people the strength of their competition in the least populated region of the state.

Yet, within twelve months of that triumph, a process was in place that would threaten to tear the competition apart. Two of the seven clubs in the Mallee league, the Ouyen and Murrayville football clubs, were trying to leave. Ouyen wanted to go to the Sunraysia league, which was based in Mildura, because it was considered a major league, while Murrayville wanted to transfer to the Lameroo and District league, over the border in South Australia, because it would cut down on travelling time. The wishes of the two clubs prompted the ruling body of country football, the VCFL, to conduct an investigation into Mallee football.

The VCFL restructured the make-up of competitions in the north-west of the state in late 1978, but the declining fortunes of clubs in the most isolated regions prompted a series of mergers and closures in the coming years in any case. By 1997, following two decades of upheaval in football around Ouyen, there was only one club left in the town, called Ouyen United.

A decade later, under the direction of a teacher from the town of Ouyen's sole remaining public school, Ouyen P-12 College, a handful of Year 9 students created a unique homage to the disparate strands of the Ouyen United Football Club by painting totem poles that had been erected inside the entrance to the club's home ground, Blackburn Park. The students painted nine poles in the colours of the clubs that had folded into one another over a course of years to form Ouyen United. Soon after the erection of the poles in 2009, the unlikely sight of them prompted drivers to interrupt their journey along the Calder Highway and check the out the poles and their details of multiple mergers. The story behind the poles invoked equal measures of horror and fascination. No one, however, expected the poles to become a tourist attraction.

AFL Victoria, the body that took over the operations of the VCFL, published the book on the history of the VCFL in 2017. After publication, I thought it might be an idea to get a couple of speaking engagements at county footy clubs as a means of selling some books. I was due to host a lunch in Bendigo, so I approached a few clubs from in the north of the state about the possibility of a gathering in their clubrooms while I was up that way. My contact in Ouyen was Bernie Kelly, who had been the secretary of the Mallee league during the Mallee restructure in the 1970s. Bernie was most helpful when I was writing the book, and he was even more helpful after I had written it. Bernie said that if I would be prepared to drive five hours from Melbourne, he would make sure it was worth my while.

Bernie is the postman in Ouyen. On his morning postal rounds during the winter of 2017, he made it his business to rouse interest in my visit. He encouraged any football person whose path he crossed to get to the clubrooms at Blackburn Park for the function. He even took money for books before I had arrived in town. In twenty years of writing about country footy, I had never had a sales agent. I had never known such hospitality.

It is a Wednesday evening in late July 2017 when Bernie Kelly allows me to deposit my bag in my room at the Hilltop Motel before he whisks me back out the door to go to the Ouyen Club for our counter tea. At the club, we enjoy a lovely meal of steak and vegies after which Bernie makes sure I meet Andy Jardine, the playing-coach of Ouyen United, who is here for a meal with family and friends. Andy's lineage as a footballer in this town goes back for almost a century. Some of his forebears played for Kiamal after the formation of the club in 1920. Some of them ran the club as president and secretary and others as coach. Andy clearly shares these leadership qualities. He's seated at a large rectangular table, but it is as if the table has been arranged around him. He has a warm smile and a large presence.

Bernie describes me to Andy as a famous country football writer. Andy is polite enough to express interest, but I can see in his face that he knows there is no such thing as a country football writer who has achieved any measure of fame. Before Bernie and I head off to Blackburn Park, I feel concerned that my host might have built me up a bit much for our night at the footy club.

It is dark when we enter the gates of the reserve at Blackburn Park, but I can see the outline of the totem poles that have achieved more fame than I could ever imagine. The poles commemorate an event of sadness: the exodus of farmers and their families from the Mallee, an exodus that has forced the extinction of several footy clubs. Even in the dark, however, I sense that the poles have a sense of fun about them, and a storytelling power. I enter the rooms ready to talk about the Kiamal twig and the totem poles of Ouyen United.

Map 2: Ouyen and District

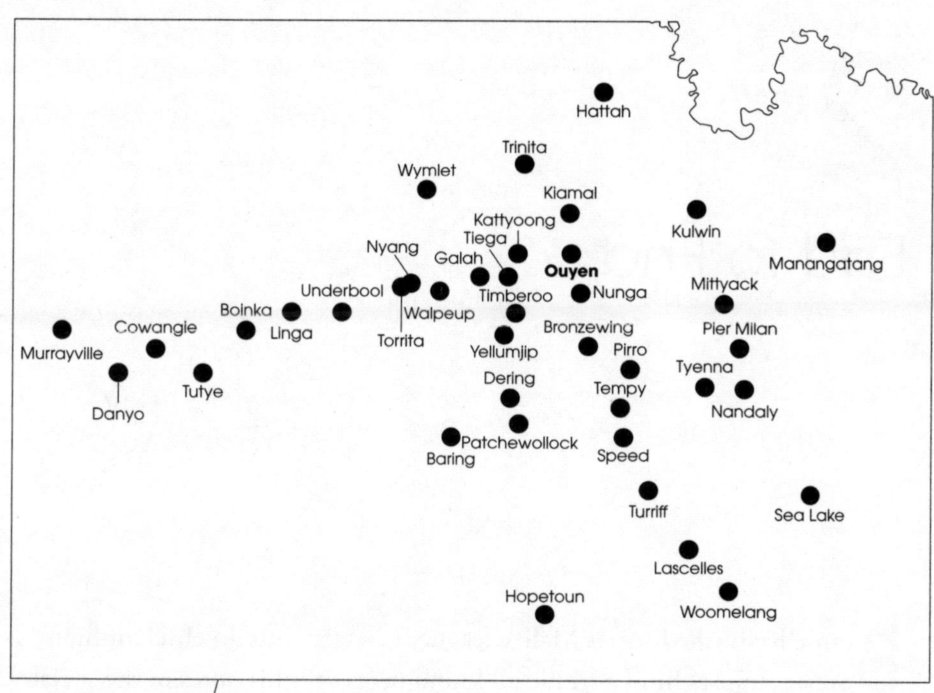

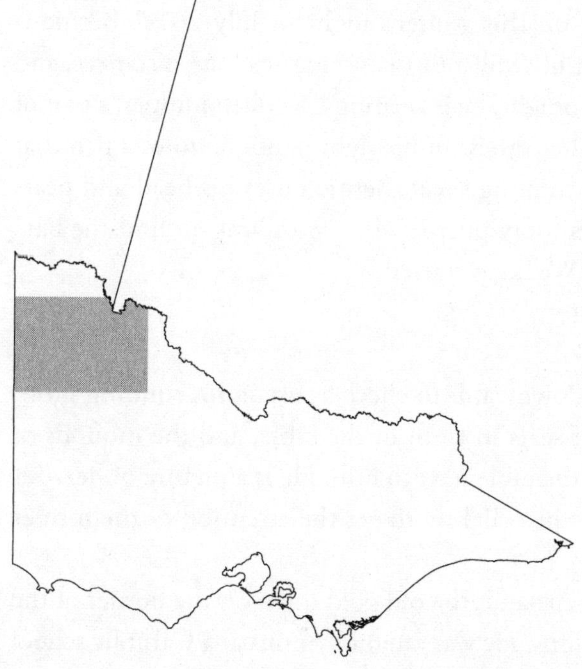

2

End to End

Bernie Kelly, the former Mallee league secretary, cuts an efficient figure as he stands behind a trestle table and peers over his notes in the social rooms at Blackburn Park on this winter's night in July 2017. Bernie is sixty-four years of age, but he's still a fit man. He runs long distances, and he's still a ball of muscle. Tonight, he is wearing a woollen jumper, a pair of fawn slacks and black leather shoes. In his right hand, he totes a pen that he uses to scribble on his running sheet. Bernie raises his head and peers at the twenty or so Ouyen footy people who are milling around the bar.

"All right," he says. "We'll get started."

There is little response.

"Ahoy, we'll get started."

Bernie casts his gaze downwards to check again on his running sheet. He looks over the rows of seats in front of the table, and the mounds of books that are nestled on the table next to him. He is a picture of nervous energy. He raises his voice just slightly to get the attention of the former footballers.

Bernie grew up in St Arnaud, the old gold town on the border of the Wimmera and Mallee regions. He was taught by nuns at a Catholic school whom, he says, were not interested in the few boys in the class. Bernie left school at sixteen years of age and settled into life in the public service. He was a clerk in the railway department in Ballarat before transferring to Ouyen. At twenty-three years of age, he decided to finish school. He studied Year 12 at Ouyen High School alongside a bunch of teenagers.

Bernie was not much of a footballer, but he loved the game, and he wanted to contribute towards the town. In 1977, he was just twenty-four years of age when he took on the role of secretary of the Kiamal Football Club. The next year, in 1978, he became secretary of the Mallee Football League. As it happened, he was the final secretary of the Mallee league in this era. The clubs respected his work ethic, and his dedication towards the league and its people.

At the time, the Mallee was part of the country recruiting zone for the Richmond Football Club. Part of Bernie's role as the league secretary was to liaise with the Tigers officials about potential recruits. Occasionally he headed down to Melbourne with fellow country footy officials to meet Richmond officials and discuss the state of the footy nation. Bernie and his country colleagues were from the Mallee, North Central, Mid-Murray and Sunraysia leagues. When they were in Melbourne, the country officials stayed at the Victoria Hotel in Little Collins Street, the traditional place of rest for country Victorians who found themselves in the city. Bernie enjoyed his trips to Melbourne in the company of his fellow country officials, but he thought the Richmond men had little idea of footy in the Mallee.

During his tenure as a league official, Bernie trained with various clubs as a means of keeping fit and keeping in contact with club officials. During these sessions, he found that he won many of the running drills. A few teachers at the high school told him they were heading to Adelaide to run in the Adelaide marathon. Bernie joined them. The marathon nearly killed him, but it also sowed a seed.

Bernie returned to Ouyen and began running on the long roads that stretched out from the town. He ran in more marathons, and got his time down to two hours twenty minutes. He gave football administration away in order to dedicate himself to running. He travelled down to Melbourne to run in track meets and cross-country meets with the

Kew-Camberwell athletics club. Bernie was slightly more solid in build than his string-bean rivals, but he ran with the singular spirit of a man who trained in dirt and dust, with only paddocks of wheat and strips of tarmac in view. Before long he was selected in an Australian team. He ran in a marathon in Taiwan. He was invited to run in Chicago. But without regular competition he found it difficult to get his personal best much below 2:20. He envied those who had embarked on the sport at a young age. He came to believe that he had started too late. He ran his heart out before, eventually, he decided he had achieved as much as possible, and he retired from competitive running.

Bernie remained a clerk for the railways, but away from work he went back to football – not as an administrator, but as a footy writer for local newspapers. As with all aspects of his life, he gave it everything. He studied match reports in metropolitan newspapers. During my time in Ouyen for the footy club function, he showed me some of his reports that had been published in the *Sunraysia Daily*. They were clear and concise, with a descriptive flair. Bernie was eager for advice. He had enjoyed many fruitful chats with Angus Dearlove, the sports editor at the *Sunraysia Daily*. But I was reluctant to give much advice. I just hoped he would continue to write with the singularity of a man who had plenty of life behind him, rather than try to ape the efforts of younger men with lesser minds.

While Bernie Kelly looks like a townie with his slacks and his running sheet, most of those in the rooms at Blackburn Park look like they are straight off the land. Almost to a man, they wear loose jeans, the bottoms of which crumple over elastic-sided boots. Some wear bulky jumpers, but most brave the night air in just a checked shirt. The shirts have a slit across the top of the pocket for a pen, but Bernie is the only one in the room who carries a pen. The farmers just want to talk footy, even if they appear to disagree with everyone around them.

In most local footy clubs, there are one or two outsiders who stir the possum with an opinion beyond the consensus. These outsiders are considered harmless enough. Most footy clubs proceed in harmony because everyone falls in behind the leaders. By and large, the opinions of the president and the coach become the opinions throughout. When the president and the coach disagree, footy clubs have a problem. In those circumstances, one or the other generally moves on. Then the club assumes a position of harmony again.

In the social rooms at Blackburn Park in Ouyen, I find a pleasant air of disagreement. Basically, everyone in the room appears to think that everyone else in the room is a person of unsound opinion. The former players have backgrounds at such a large range of clubs that there is no hope of numb agreement. Not too long into the night, I hear a rejoinder that strikes me as highly particular to the region and the circumstances of our gathering.

"Yeah, well, what would *you* know?"

"You're from Tiega!"

At fifty-one years of age, I am the youngest man in the room. All the others are of an age where they played footy against each in the Mallee league in the 1970s. They played for Tiega, Kiamal, Ouyen, Walpeup and Tempy-Gorya-Patchewollock. One man, the former ruckman Laurie Kalms, played for Murrayville, but he also coached Kiamal. Now the old Mallee footballers are united under the banner of Ouyen United, the club that resulted from the most complex series of mergers in Victoria, the club that plays at the ground where drivers stop to check out the painted poles that depict the club's story.

No matter how many premierships or wooded spoons the old footballers won with their old clubs, they are all in the same mob now, and they gather under a banner of thrilling success. Ouyen United had provided the story of the season in Victorian country footy the previous year, in 2016. In what was their first season in the Sunraysia league, they stormed through the finals in a performance that was described on news services around the state, including, most notably, on ABC Television, before winning the premiership. Now, halfway through the club's second season in the Sunraysia league, the Kangaroos are on top of the ladder and looking at another flag. The old footballers, once rivals from small but proud clubs, are now part of a polyglot nation, and they're having a hoot together, even if do spend a lot of time needling each other about days of old.

Finally, Bernie Kelly gets everyone to pay attention. He thanks me for driving all the way to Ouyen to speak to a bunch of old Mallee footballers. I speak about the machinations of the Mallee restructure in the 1970s, but it is clear that I am not saying anything they do not already know, and have lived through many times. They are more interested when I mention the upheaval in Bendigo in 1980, when the VCFL forcibly wound up the Golden City league and dispatched its eight clubs to join the six clubs of the Bendigo league. The man who announced in 1980 that the fourteen clubs would join together to form a new competition was Allan Dunstan, who was the head of the VCFL at the time.

Dunstan, a man from Donald, in the country to the south of Ouyen, was well known in the Mallee. Many at our gathering in Ouyen remember the dust-up he presided over in Bendigo. In the clubrooms in Ouyen, they find it reasonably interesting to hear about the pandemonium outside the Red Cross Centre in View Street, Bendigo during Dunstan's announcement; how rocks were thrown on to the roof of the building during the meeting; and how Graham Arthur, the highly respected field officer of the VCFL, was jostled by protesters as he left the building to return to his car near the Rifle Brigade Hotel.

Arthur had begun his career at Sandhurst. In 1961, he was the first premiership captain of Hawthorn. He later returned to country footy to coach Echuca, whom he led to a premiership in the Bendigo league. It seems a bit rough to the men in Ouyen that Arthur was given such a hard time after the VCFL meeting in Bendigo, although it is also understandable. The composition of country football leagues is an emotional issue. When I finish my talk, the old Mallee footballers shuffle forward to pick up the book they have agreed to buy on instruction from Bernie Kelly. Then they get on with the business of having a beer and a skite.

Gerald Leach is a former Walpeup player and official who is known to Mallee football people as Gerry. After the old Mallee players have made their way towards the bar, he comes forward to the trestle table to introduce himself. Gerry has twinkling eyes, a strong moustache, and a full head of hair. He was my other contact, besides Bernie Kelly, when I was writing about the Mallee restructure for the book on the history of the

VCFL. In 1978, when the VCFL's Mallee restructure was in motion, Gerry was a Walpeup veteran, playing mainly in the back pocket or on a wing, as well as the Walpeup delegate on the board of officials and the league vice-president. The 1978 season was a very eventful one in the Mallee league; it was the final season for the Ouyen Football Club before it moved to the Sunraysia league. Gerry played in the Walpeup team that defeated Ouyen in the 1978 Grand Final by three points. After that match, he sat in the rooms at Blackburn Park for several minutes after everyone else had left, soaking up the club's achievement. Then he ventured out to the club's ground on the Walpeup Ridge to join in the celebrations.

Gerry's family arrived in the Mallee from Sandford, in the Western District, in 1924. They selected land about fifteen kilometres north of the town of Walpeup, not far from the border of what was considered arable land. The next property north, which was owned by the Corbett famlly, was the final property on the land that was made available for settlement. Beyond there, the sandhills began their rolling march to the Millewa line farther north.

Gerry's father Leo was the oldest of five brothers who played footy in the Mallee. The other boys in the family, Bernie, Dermot, Brian and Grattan, completed a very Irish quintet. Leo Leach was a fast and clever rover. In 1928, at the age of twenty-four, he went down to Melbourne and had a run with Richmond, only to return home to the farm. Long after his retirement, many described him as the best footballer in the Mallee around the time of the Depression, and behind only the Tempy champion Ginger Robertson in the broad sweep of Mallee football.

Leo Leach was also a handy tennis player. He won two titles for the best player in north-west Victoria. On his attempt to win his third title, he was beaten by his youngest brother, Grattan, who was emerging as a brilliant sportsman, only for tragedy to strike.

Throughout the history of Mallee football, players have had to play on rock-hard grounds, especially early in the season. In 1934, Grattan Leach cut himself during a match on a hard ground. The wound seemed innocuous enough, but the dye from the trousers that he wore in shearing sheds during the week leaked into his wound and entered his blood stream. Grattan Leach was only twenty-one years of age when he died at home of blood poisoning a few days after the footy match.

After Leo Leach's retirement as a footballer, he moved north to Red Cliffs, on the southern outskirts of Mildura, where he hoped to find some fruit-picking work before moving on to Queensland. In Red Cliffs, he found work picking grapes, and he also met his wife. He married Mary Gould from Kinnabulla, near Birchip, and they raised their nine children in Red Cliffs.

Gerry was the middle child of the nine, which included five boys and four girls. He went to school at St Joseph's College in Mildura and played junior footy for Red Cliffs. At seventeen years of age, he left Red Cliffs to join his two uncles, Bern and Derm, on the family farm at Walpeup. Gerry settled into playing footy for the local club. He was the height of a rover, like his father, but he had not inherited the pace of his father. He made up for his slow legs with his fast brain, endeavouring to read the play ahead of his rivals. Gerry played in every position except ruck and full-back during a career with Walpeup that lasted 200 senior games. The club's premiership in 1978 was the clear highlight of his career.

Gerry Leach likes talking footy as much as everyone else in the room at Blackburn Park, but he has a lovely light touch, which he exhibits to great effect with a story that contradicts the notion that everyone in the Mallee is mad about the game.

When Gerry was a young man, he went to North East Victoria to visit friends. Over the course of the weekend he met Louise Fitzpatrick, the woman who would become his wife. Louise was from the Central Coast of New South Wales, which is a long way from footy territory; in that part of Australia, you can live an entire life without seeing or hearing any reference whatsoever to what is considered the southern game. Louise had no idea of footy when she moved to Victoria to teach at Upper Sandy Creek while she studied for her diploma of education through a Victorian institution. And she remained oblivious to the game after marrying Gerry and moving to the Mallee. Even after years of exposure to the game in her adopted home, she had picked up nothing through observation, nor anything by osmosis. She preferred to concentrate on her family and her role at the local kindergarten, at which she was very conscientious. In 2014, Louise won the state government's award for the early childhood teacher of the year.

As Dom, the son of Gerry and Louise, matured into an adult, he took up a role alongside his father on the farm and he became a good footballer for Ouyen United. For many years, Gerry has taken great joy from watching his son play. Every Saturday, he combines his filial interest in footy with his duties as the club timekeeper.

In footy terms, Dom inherited his father's lack of pace and penchant for thinking through a game. In 2010, Dom missed Ouyen United's season through injury. In 2011, he returned to the senior team and settled into a role as a small forward who took advantage of the lack of attention from opposition players. While panicked defenders were swamping his outrageously talented teammate Robert "Sonny" Lindsey, who played at full-forward, Dom Leach chimed in with a steady stream of goals from the pocket. He ended up with forty-two goals for the home and away rounds, Sonny Lindsay kicked ninety-eight, and they both kicked more goals in the finals as Ouyen United won the flag.

During the 2011 season, as Gerry describes it to me, he alerted Louise that their son was in flying form and she really should consider a trip to Blackburn Park to see him play. Louise duly went to a game. During the first quarter, she saw that her son was playing at the southern end and sat herself close to the action, on the fence behind the forward pocket. The next quarter she remained on the fence behind the pocket. Gerry, meanwhile, was in the timekeepers' box doing his job as a timekeeper. At half-time, he headed into the rooms for afternoon tea. He expected his wife would join him. When she failed to appear, he rang her.

"Where are you," he said.

Louise said she had gone to the kindergarten to do some work.

"Why?", asked Gerry, stressing the good form of their son in this golden season.

Louise explained that she had watched the first quarter. "Then he went up to the other end."

3

All for One

Over the course of the evening at Blackburn Park, I meet several former players who break away from needling each other for long enough to describe the life and times of the Mallee league. It is a competition they all miss greatly. Through their support for Ouyen United, they have found a focus for their shared backgrounds on diverse ovals in the district around Ouyen.

Bill Morrish, the former Tiega player and Underbool premiership coach, stands at ease as the banter flies around him. His jumper hangs loosely from his lean frame. Bill is from a family that has been in the Mallee since the earliest days of settlement. His grandfather, William Thomas Morrish, selected land at Tiega in 1909. The Tiega Football Club was formed the next year, in 1910, and it was one of the four founding clubs in the Ouyen and District Football Association. There was a member of the Morrish family in almost every Tiega team from the outset until the club merged with Kiamal seventy years later. The Scott and Gibbins families settled in Tiega around the same time as the Morrish family, and also played a large part in the early decades of the footy club.

During the period between the two world wars, the Tiega players would choose the captain before they ran out for the first match, and the role was often rotated around. In 1933, Ray Morrish was chosen as captain. In 1934, it was Stan Scott. On the eve of the 1935 season, Tiega announced that they would not appoint their captain until half-time of the first match, and Stan Scott would carry on as skipper until then. Ken Gillespie, having just returned from a stint of training with Essendon, was duly voted in as captain for the 1935 season, with Harry Howard his vice-captain.

Harry Howard had made his debut for Tiega in 1919, in the first season after the resumption following World War 1, and played for the club until the next world war broke out more than twenty years later. Bill Morrish says the Howard family was prominent alongside the Morrish, Scott and Gibbins families in the club's early decades.

As Bill tells it, his grandfather William Morrish had two sons, Ray and Alec, both of whom became prominent leaders of the club as players and officials. Alec started out as a rangy wingman before moving to other parts of the ground. He had four sons, starting with Lindsay and Bill himself. Fourteen years after Bill was born, twin boys Jack and Ray Junior were born.

Lindsay, Alec's oldest son, was a strongly built defender, and the only player to play in Tiega's fourteen consecutive grand finals from 1961 to 1974, which included six premierships. Bill played in almost all of the grand finals during the famous stretch. In 1974, he played in his fifth premiership team with Tiega. After the season, he accepted the playing-coach's job at Underbool, the club that had finished last that season.

During the build-up to the 1975 season, Underbool's star product Max Crow decided he would rather return home than stay in Melbourne and play with Essendon. Bill was hoping that Max would be able to play in Underbool's opening match of the 1975 season, against the reigning premiers, Tempy-Gorya-Patchewollock, at Patche. When Crow's clearance did not come through, Max agreed to be the runner. Bill resigned himself to hoping that his team would finish within five goals of the premiers. Instead, they won by five goals. With Max Crow in the team from Round 2, Underbool sailed through the season. Bill Morrish played himself in the forward line and in the centre. Underbool careened through the finals series to take out the flag – their only flag during their two decades in the Mallee league.

The next year, in 1976, Underbool lost half their premiership team and sank back to the bottom on the ladder. Bill says that, when he was a boy, his mother used to tell him off for failing to put things back where he had found them. It amused him after 1976 to think that he had taken Underbool to their ultimate achievement. Then he put them back exactly where he had found them.

Brian "Barney" O'Callaghan looks almost forlorn as he makes his way to the table to pick up his book. Barney is a former Tiega rover, some say the best rover to have played in the Mallee, but he looks to be in pain as he describes doing his knee on the eve of the 1971 Grand Final – a famous match in Mallee football.

Barney and his three brothers and two sisters grew up on the family farm to the east of Ouyen. Their mother, who was Kath Monaghan before she was married, was part of a Kiamal family, and the children barracked for Collingwood because the Magpies in Melbourne wore black and white stripes like the Magpies in Ouyen. The children, however, went to St Joseph's Primary School in Ouyen, where most of the children were from Tiega families. Their cousins from the Carroll and Shaddock families were prominent at Tiega. The O'Callaghan boys, Kevin, Denis, Brian and Garry, followed their cousins there.

While Kevin O'Callaghan was a rover, Denis's marking ability enabled him to be a focal point in attack. Despite being only 178 centimetres, he played at centre half-forward in two Tiega premiership teams while he was still a teenager, in 1964 and 1967. He then established himself in the senior team at Collingwood, and his story is worth recounting here for the innocence it portrays as much as the grandeur.

The story begins with the 1966 Mallee league Grand Final between Tiega and Tempy-Gorya. A Carlton scout was at the game to run his eye over the teenager Gordon Casey, whose father, Gordon Senior, had been a champion with Gorya. Young Casey's performance in the 1966 Grand Final duly earned him an invitation to join the Blues at Princes Park, but the scout was also impressed with Denis O'Callaghan, the seventeen-year-old forward from Tiega, and he made sure the Blues invited him down to Carlton as well. Denis O'Callaghan played in two practice matches with Carlton before the 1967 season.

At the time, Joe Pengelly was a Tiega player and official. When Pengelly was living in Melbourne, he had met former Collingwood players through mutual friends. Later, Pengelly moved back to Ouyen, where he worked in Stan Healy's Ford dealership.

A former Collingwood player, Terry Waites, did scouting work for the Magpies while he was travelling around country Victoria for work. Early in 1967, Waites was in Ouyen when he stopped in at Stan Healy's Ford dealership to attend to a car matter. Joe Pengelly emerged at the counter to chide Waites about the Magpies' apparent lack of interest in Denis O'Callaghan. Pengelly was acutely aware that Collingwood would be mortified by the thought of losing to Carlton in the race for a talented young player. "You blokes are missing out," he said.

Terry Waites put Collingwood officials on to the trail of young Denis. Graeme Fellowes, the former Collingwood ruckman, had a role in recruiting for the Magpies. Fellowes visited Denis O'Callaghan at the accommodation in Brunswick that Carlton had lined up for him and another country recruit, Bill Bennett. Fellowes knew O'Callaghan had just played in two practice matches with Carlton. He asked Denis whether he would now like to try out with the Magpies.

Denis O'Callaghan played in two practice matches with Collingwood in the next fortnight. He signed with the Magpies, and played in two reserves matches in 1967, but he played out the rest of the season with Tiega. In the 1967 Mallee league Grand Final, he was among the best players as Tiega defeated Murrayville to win the premiership.

In 1968, Denis returned to Collingwood on a six-match permit. He played the opening two games in the reserves then made his senior VFL debut against St Kilda in Round 3 of the 1968 season, before 29,500 fans at Victoria Park. He then played the next three games in the senior team as well. At the end of his six-match permit, he had to decide whether to return to the Mallee, where he would help his father Jim on the farm, or seek a clearance from Tiega to play with Collingwood. According to

Denis, his father told him: "It hasn't rained up here; you might as well stay in Melbourne."

Denis O'Callaghan played out the 1968 season with Collingwood.

Before the 1969 season, the mother of the six O'Callaghan children, Kath O'Callaghan, was sick, and Jim O'Callaghan was busy seeking medical help for his wife. Denis went along with his father's wishes to return home from Melbourne and help to run the farm. But when Denis sought a clearance from Collingwood to return to Tiega, the Magpies blocked his application. Denis even rang Jack Hamilton, the VFL general manager, to ask what would happen if he played for Tiega without a clearance. Hamilton informed him of the registration rules and advised him that he would be banned from playing in the VFL for several years if he played elsewhere without a clearance. Finally, Collingwood relented, and Denis resumed playing with Tiega.

On the farm, he pulled his weight during the sowing season. By the time the crop was in, his mother's health had improved, and he had come around to the idea of resuming at Collingwood. Two Magpie officials, including the general manager Peter Lucas, visited Ouyen to sign their man. The Magpie officials visited Frank Healy, the Tiega president, to gain the signature that was necessary from the club. Then they ventured out to the O'Callaghan family's farm to the east of Ouyen to gain the signature of the young footballer. After playing with the North Central Football League in an interleague match in the Victorian country championships, Denis played out the 1969 season with Collingwood.

The next year, in 1970, Denis O'Callaghan played in the backline for Collingwood during the Magpies' loss to Carlton in the Grand Final at the MCG. The attendance at that game, 121,696, remains the largest in Australian football history. Denis never played for Tiega again.

While Denis O'Callaghan was embarking on his career with Collingwood, his brother Brian was establishing himself at the top of the tree in Mallee football. Barney made his senior debut with Tiega in 1966, at fifteen years of age. The next year, he played in the premiership team alongside Denis. By 1968, at just seventeen years of age, Barney was considered Tiega's best player, and he was invited down to Richmond.

He headed down to Punt Road before the 1969 season to play in a few practice matches with the under-nineteen team.

He was named as rover in the first practice match. Neil Balme, a sixteen-year-old recruit from Perth, was named to play in the ruck. Before the first bounce, Balme asked his rover whether he had a nickname. Brian O'Callaghan said his friends called him Barney. Balme then tapped the ball to Barney during three ruck contests in the forward line and Barney kicked three goals.

After the match, Barney was asked whether he was interested in talking about his future. He headed up to the boardroom, where he was struck by the quality of the company around the table, and by the sprawling tiger skin on the boardroom table. Tom Hafey, Slug Jordon, Graeme Richmond, Ian Wilson and Alan Schwab were among the Richmond officials who listened while he explained that his father Jim had given him permission to play in the practice matches but he was not keen on him moving away. With the departure of Denis to Collingwood, Jim O'Callaghan had already lost one boy to football in the city, and he needed all available hands to help out with the new farm he had bought near Ouyen. The Richmond officials listened to Barney's story and wished him well.

In 1969 and 1970, Barney was considered the best player on the ground as Tiega won both grand finals. In this period, he formed an unstoppable partnership with the veteran ruckman Brian "Bricker" Weir. "At boundary throw-ins, he pushed the ball down my throat," Barney told me.

In 1971, Tiega were undefeated during the home and away rounds. In the Second Semi-final, Barney kicked five goals and his brother Kevin kicked three as Tiega defeated Kiamal by nine goals to earn their way into the Grand Final. On the first night of training in Grand Final week, Barney was taking part in a drill late in the session when he snapped a medial ligament in his knee. The coach, Harry Shaddock, and the entire club were aghast. On the day before he was due to play in the Mallee league Grand Final, Barney had a knee reconstruction in Ballarat. His father Jim went down to Melbourne to see Denis play for Collingwood against Richmond in the 1971 First Semi-final at the MCG. Other members of the family remained in Ouyen to see Kevin play in the Grand Final for Tiega. It would be a decision they came to regret.

Kiamal went on to win a famous flag, their only one during the three decades in which they played in the Mallee league. After a year of recovery from his knee injury, Barney returned to the field. He played in Tiega's premiership team in 1973. In all, he ended up with five premierships and several best and fairest awards. Kevin also played in five premiership teams, while Denis played in two Tiega premiership teams. In later years, Barney O'Callaghan became a coach and then president. His son Ryan became a champion footballer and coach. The O'Callaghan family, like representatives of several families in the room at Blackburn Park, has made a large contribution to Mallee football.

All these years later, however, Barney still looks incredulous when he talks about his decision against trying his luck with Richmond; instead, he agreed to his father's wishes, and returned to the farm in the Mallee. He places the cash for his book in to Bernie Kelly's ice-cream container, and strolls off to talk about the old days in Mallee football.

4

Magic Number

There are two ruckmen in the social rooms at Blackburn Park on this starry Wednesday evening in July 2017.

Laurie Kalms is large in stature and personality. Laurie's home club was Murrayville, the club towards the South Australian border. Laurie played in a Mallee league premiership with Murrayville in 1962, but with no ties to a plot of land, he was free to roam. In 1964, he was appointed as playing-coach at Kiamal because, in the words of the Kiamal president Lou McDougall, the Magpies had always fielded short teams and it was about time they had a decent big man. Laurie coached Kiamal for two seasons. A decade later, he coached the Magpies for another season. He also coached Walpeup in the Mallee league and Ngallo, a club near the South Australian border, in the Lameroo league. He played in three premierships with South Mildura in the Sunraysia league. He ran pubs throughout north-west Victoria, including the pubs in Murrayville, Underbool, Patchewollock, Ouyen and Yaapeet. Now he runs the pub in Lyndhurst, near Lake Eyre in the outback, but he often returns to his home country to look over his two pubs in Mildura. It's not unusual for him to turn up in Ouyen or Underbool or wherever for a footy function.

Wherever Laurie Kalms goes, there is the sense of an event. He just seems to make the occasion larger. A measure of his personality is that he has no problem with the constant references to his brother Richie, who was the player of his generation in the Mallee league. Richie Kalms was a centre half-forward with an extraordinary pair of hands and, apparently, the ability to kick drop-kicks from the wing that sailed through the goals. Everyone in the Mallee knows the story about Richie Kalms taking up an invitation to try out at Essendon. Or, as I would find out, everyone knows a version of the story of about Richie Kalms going to Essendon. It is true that, before the 1963 season, Richie caught the train from Murrayville to Ouyen. Then he caught the train from Ouyen to Melbourne, where he met an Essendon official at Spencer Street Station. Richie played brilliantly in two practice matches under the eye of Essendon's coach at the time, who was John Coleman. Then, unimpressed with city life, he caught the train back to Murrayville and resumed playing with his home club.

Richie Kalms won three league medals in the Mallee league, in 1964, 1969 and 1970, and he created awe through his performances at inter-league level. Later, he twice kicked 100 goals in a season for Dimboola before finishing his career at Swan Hill. He kicked nine goals in his final game, which was Swan Hill's victory in the Mid-Murray league's 1978 Grand Final.

Laurie Kalms is proud of his own feats. He played a season at West Adelaide. He played in premiership teams in the Mallee and Sunraysia leagues. He notes that he finished his career as a full-forward and won three league goalkicking awards. But he is also proud of the feats of his brother. It gives him more to talk about.

Donald McGregor, the other ruckman in the room on this night at Blackburn Park, grew up on a farm at Galah, just east of Ouyen, which is Tiega country. Donald's father, Jack McGregor, played in a premiership with Tiega in 1945. As a schoolboy, Donald and other students who went to school in Ouyen would get dropped off at a bus stop in Galah. While they were waiting at the bus stop for their parents to pick them up, one of the parents, Lou McDougall, would teach the boys to do drop-kicks. Lou was a long-time official at Kiamal. The boys from the bus stop all followed him to the Magpies.

Having finished school, Donald McGregor left Ouyen to live in Geelong for two years. He studied wool-classing at the Gordon Institute, where his fellow students included Geelong players Andy Preston and Murray Whitcombe. Donald returned to Ouyen for the 1979 season and played in the ruck for Kiamal. When I ask about the atmosphere at the club in the years leading up to the merger with Tiega, he gives a surprising answer. After the 1979 season, the Kiamal and Tiega players went on a joint footy trip to Broken Hill. Never before or since have I heard of two rival clubs sharing a footy trip.

Don injured his knee in 1980 and retired. Since then, he has been mindful of maintaining the history of footy in a region of constant change. His work as an agronomist puts him in touch with people throughout the Mallee. He believes the health of the Ouyen United Football Club is vital to the health of the region.

While Lou McDougall succeeded in enticing a bunch of Tiega boys to play at Kiamal, his daughter Lorraine went the other way. Lorraine McDougall was an accomplished netballer with Kiamal. When she married Harry Shaddock, the Tiega centre half-back, she switched her allegiance to Tiega, where she would be a top goal shooter for many years. Lorraine loved the netball, but she also loved the footy. On this night in Ouyen, she is the only woman in the rooms at Blackburn Park.

Lorraine approaches the trestle table with goods to share. She shows me some of her prized items of footy memorabilia, including the record from the country championships semi-final between the North Central league and the Hampden league at St Arnaud in June 1970. The record is in perfect nick. I hold it lightly, worried that I might smear it with my dirty hands or drop it in Bernie's Kelly's ice-cream container full of cash. When I tell Lorraine that it would fetch quite a few dollars on the memorabilia market, she casts her eyes downwards, trying to hide her distaste. The notion of giving away something that is a part of her is unthinkable. "I've got three trunks of old stuff," she says.

I love looking at team lists from that golden era of interleague football. I like to trace the links that stretch across the state and through the generations. In Lorraine's record from the country championships clash at St Arnaud in 1970, I note that the Hampden league team includes

Stewart Lord, Geelong's 1963 Brownlow medallist, who is the captain-coach of Camperdown. It also includes Peter Lyon, the former Hawthorn player who is playing for Mortlake. Peter Lyon would later lead Kyabram to the 1975 premiership in the Goulburn Valley league. His son Garry Lyon would become the captain of Melbourne.

The North Central team is led by the former South Melbourne player Bill McGrath, who is the captain-coach at Watchem-Corack. There are several Mallee league names in the North Central team, including Garry Sporn, Des Sporn and Richie Kalms, all from Murrayville. Barry Gniel is from Walpeup. Alan Robertson is listed as a player from Tempy when it should say Tempy-Gorya. Brian O'Callaghan is from Tiega. At nineteen years of age, he is the youngest player in the team.

The record includes the ladders for the North Central and Hampden leagues to the halfway point of the 1970 season. In the context of history, the ladders have an unlikely look about them. Port Fairy are on top in the Hampden league, ahead of Mortlake, while Donald and Wycheproof-Narraport are the top two teams in the North Central league. The North Central ladder is not unusual; the two leading clubs have long histories of success. But I know that both of them failed to win the premiership that season. Having written about Wedderburn in the past, I know that the Burners won the flag in 1970. I am fascinated to see in Lorraine's record that, at the halfway point of the 1970 season, Wedderburn are sixth of the eight teams in their competition.

Lorraine Shaddock is one of the great footy fans of Ouyen. She tells me she has been going to the footy in the Mallee every week for as long as she can remember. She gets to the ground in time for the thirds match. Then she stays for the seconds and the firsts. "I love watching the young ones come through," she says.

Towards the end of the evening, a voice emerges from the edge of the room. It belongs to Michael "Boozer" Robertson, who is a member of the family widely considered to be the most talented footy family in the Mallee and far beyond. Boozer's father Ginger Robertson played more than 500 senior games for Tempy and was still among the best players in the district well into his forties. Boozer is the youngest of Ginger's five prodigiously talented sons who played mostly for the club based near their farm in Tempy. Boozer himself has two sons who anchored a premiership team for Ouyen United.

On this night, Boozer is excited by the opportunity to talk footy with old friends, and by the opportunity to stir up Bernie Kelly. Bernie's openness and sense of decency make him a ripe target for gentle ribbing. While Bernie tries to maintain a sense of order for the evening, Boozer interjects to tell a story about Bernie's career in the Kiamal reserves team. Before Kiamal reserves games, so the story goes, Bernie Kelly was often so eager to get on to the ground to begin his warm-up that he would muscle past the captain, Alf Stone, and begin striding out on the patchy turf. Alf Stone became tired of Bernie's lack of respect for football's natural order. Before one match, he let Bernie edge past him. Then he stopped and put out his arm to curb the rest of the team from following Bernie on to the ground.

Bernie Kelly began striding out, as proud as a peacock, when he noticed that he was unaccompanied. He looked left. He looked right. Finally, he looked towards the boundary line, where he found Alf Stone and the rest of his teammates enjoying a chuckle while watching his performance.

In the social rooms in Ouyen, Bernie smiles at Boozer's tale, having heard it all before. Besides, he did win a Kiamal reserves' best and fairest award in that era.

Bernie Kelly proceeds to wind up the evening. Before he signs off, however, Boozer interjects once more, this time with a serious point to make. He says the totem poles at Blackburn Park tell only part of the story. The Ouyen United Football Club is the result of forty-three clubs merging into one over many years. He offers to take me on a tour of the old footy grounds of the Mallee, the same tour that his father Ginger once took him on.

Forty-three clubs! I sense immediately that the story of Ouyen United encapsulates in one club the story of country footy in rural areas across Australia: the story of the battle to maintain footy clubs while families continue to leave the land. After taking three years to write about the history of the VCFL, I have promised myself and my family that I will stop writing at length about country footy. But as I stand in the rooms in Blackburn Park I know that I am in danger of breaking my promise. On the other side of the oval, the totem poles stand in the dark like soldiers in a row. They have a bit of magic about them.

The following day, I head south along the Sunraysia Highway to make my appointment at the Donald footy club. My host is the club president, Danny Forrest, who is the principal at the local primary school, and a man of great energy. Many years earlier, I wrote in several instances about the Donald Farm, which was a farm run by supporters of the footy club to raise funds for the club. Now, Danny tells me the club has taken over the running of the local caravan park. They're certainly an enterprising mob at Donald.

The Donald footy club has an enviable culture in which everyone pitches in. But on the night that I speak to a dozen or so members in the expansive social rooms, there is something missing. There is not the banter of the Ouyen United rooms the night before.

In 1950, two clubs from outside Donald – Cope Cope and Laen-Litchfield – merged to form one club that might compete with their larger neighbours. Four years later, in 1954, Donald absorbed the merged outfit from out of town, and in doing so it became a club with several stories. But that was a long time ago. In 2017, when I'm in the social rooms at Donald, the footy club has a single narrative, which has existed without challenge for decades. Which makes it very different to Ouyen United.

I enjoy meeting Murray Gilmour, who played at centre half-back in the North Central league team that won the final of the 1974 country championships. Murray was invited down to Geelong on the strength of his performance during those championships, and he played a handful of senior games with the Cats before returning to his home town. After my function the previous night in Ouyen, however, the Donald Football Club seems so, well, singular. Clearly, my experience at Blackburn Park has got under my skin. I suspect I might take up Boozer Robertson on his offer to tour the old grounds.

5

The Dumosa Line

There is something about the word "Mallee" which goes far beyond its primary purpose as the name for a region. The most powerful regional names in Australia have nothing to do with direction; they are single words that conjure strong images. "The Pilbara" describes a land that is harsh yet majestic; bare plains sweep from the desert through gorge country to the ocean. "The Riverina" describes a land of long rivers and woolly sheep that grow fat under the sun. "The Mallee" conjures up images of farmers with their hats pulled low and their sleeves rolled up. It is a tough place, demanding sweat and toil. As the name for a region, "the Mallee" is among the most descriptive in Australia.

The boundaries of the Mallee region in Victoria are hard to define. According to John Pickard, an academic at Macquarie University in Sydney, the Victorian Parliament passed an Act in 1883 in which it declared the Mallee to be "all unalienated crown land in the north-western district of Victoria wholly or partially covered with the Mallee plant". It drew a line from a point on the Murray River near Swan Hill that took several jagged steps south until it reached the 36th parallel near the current site of Birchip. Then a line was essentially drawn along the 36th parallel until it reached the South Australian border. All land north of the line to the Murray River was declared Mallee land.

The botanical title of the "Mallee plant", as mentioned above, is "Eucalyptus dumosa". According to the writer Hugh Carroll, who wrote a superb history of Ouyen for the town's centenary in 2009, explorers and early settlers believed that Aborigines used the word "mallee" to describe the eucalyptus trees that thrived in the region's sandy soil. Carroll notes that it's difficult to verify the accuracy of words with origins in Aboriginal languages. It is unarguable, however, that the word "mallee" entered the national lexicon after being taken up as the descriptor for the region in north-west Victoria.

The eucalyptus trees in the Mallee region had deep roots and spindly leaves that were perfectly adapted to surviving dry spells. The trees were difficult to uproot because of the "root balls" that fought their way deep into the sandy soil in search of water. Hugh Carroll says that some root balls were so large that, in the years after settlement in the Mallee, one man would take hours, or even days, to dig a root ball out of the ground. Root balls became commonly known as Mallee stumps. To this day, the Mallee stump is a symbol of hardy resistance.

My family's path to the Mallee can be traced back almost a century. My great-grandfather, John Thomas O'Shannessy, known as Jack, was a share farmer with his brother Ernie near Bridgewater, just north-west of Bendigo, when he married Madalena (nee Baptiste) in 1908. Madalena gave birth to a daughter, Winifred, the next year, in 1909, but the young mother died of pneumonia eleven months after the birth. Jack O'Shannessy and baby Win moved in with family and stayed in Bridgewater for several years. Jack, however, remained stricken by grief, and left to start a new life in Western Australia. During this period, he left his daughter in the care of relatives. After a few years of "wandering around the West", as it was later described to me, Jack returned to Victoria. In 1922, he again decided to start a new life; this time he bought land at Ultima, to the west of Swan Hill, in the Mallee. Win, now aged fifteen, agreed to join her father and take care of domestic duties on the farm.

Ultima at the time was a busy railways centre on the Robinvale line. In 1936, a man called Joe Farrell was aged twenty-six when he moved to Ultima through his job on the railways. Joe had moved about ten times during his eleven years on the railways, but this would be his final transfer. He met and married Win O'Shannessy and moved on to the farm with Win and her father. Joe Farrell continued to work on the railways until his father-in-law, Jack O'Shannessy, died in a tractor accident in 1946. Joe, at thirty-six years of age, gave up the railways and dedicated himself to running the farm.

Joe and Win Farrell were my grandparents, and they lived long and full lives in a region they loved. Early in their married lives, they had four children, Marie, John, Joan and Judith. Marie, the oldest, is my mother. Mum went to boarding school in Swan Hill and Bendigo before going to teachers' college in Bendigo. John, my uncle, returned from school in Bendigo to join his father on the farm. Throughout the 1960s and '70s, John played 282 senior games for Ultima, all of them in the ruck. He won six club best and fairest awards, but he was never part of a premiership team. Ultima, although they went close, failed to win a flag during their thirty years in the Tyrrell league.

These days, whenever my mother returns to the country around Ultima, she finds the heat so overwhelming that she can barely stand up, but she still regards herself as a Mallee girl. Her email address is built around her description of herself as a Mallee girl. After almost sixty years in Melbourne, she still regards the Mallee as a large part of her identity.

My father, Terry Daffey, grew up the oldest of five children in Bendigo. His father, Jim Daffey, ran a used car yard just off High Street. After Dad had left school, he worked as a clerk at Hanro's knitting mills. On weekends, he played footy for Sandhurst in the Bendigo league. Tall and skinny, he made his senior debut just after he had turned nineteen. Mum was at the teachers' college in Bendigo. They met as late teenagers, and went to dances and balls with their many friends in the town.

After the failure of my grandfather's car yard in Bendigo, he moved to Melbourne for work. His family later followed. My father was twenty years of age when his parents shifted him and his four siblings to Essendon, the suburb that was chosen because it was just off the Calder Highway. Mum later moved to Melbourne to take up a teaching post. Mum and Dad married, and were living in Essendon when I was born. Within a few months of my birth, the young couple and their baby son moved just past Essendon, to a new suburb called East Keilor. I grew up the oldest of four boys in the north-west suburbs. We returned to Bendigo and Ultima throughout my childhood.

When I was a boy, my grandfather in Ultima, Joe Farrell, was a great man for newspapers. Every day he drove into town to pick up a daily newspaper from Melbourne and sometimes the *Bendigo Advertiser*. Three times a week he picked up the *Swan Hill Guardian*, and once a week he bought a copy of the paper known as the farmers' bible, the *Weekly Times*. I'm sure the sight of Pa reading his phalanx of newspapers had an influence on my later decision to become a journalist.

Pa was a man of few words, but strong opinions. At some stage of his journey, he developed a set against Bendigo. Often he would be reading a newspaper in his loungeroom, with the sun streaming through the curtains, when he would put down his paper and, for a reason that was never apparent to me, bark out his view that Bendigo was "a clapped-out mining town". I thought Bendigo was a fine town. I loved spending time there with family and friends. Pa's attitude intrigued me.

One day, Pa was again reading the *Bendigo Advertiser* and giving the old mining town a drubbing when I stopped him to ask why Bendigo was no good. He mumbled an answer that made no sense. When I asked him to name some towns that were good towns, he mentioned something indecipherable and continued reading his newspaper. When I asked him to name his favourite country town, he put down his newspaper and thought for a moment.

"Wagga Wagga," he said.

Pa went on to describe the main street of Wagga, the town in the Riverina that stretches from the train station at one end to the town hall at the other. Pa was born in Balldale, in the southern Riverina, and I suspect this had something to do with his fondness for the biggest town in the region. In his memory, the shops along the main street of Wagga were all bursting with items to sell to the prosperous local farmers. Pa had not been to Wagga for many years, even decades, when I asked him to name his favourite town, but in his mind Wagga was an Australian version of

El Dorado. He gave his newspaper a little ruffle and a snap, and set his eyes on the market report.

On another day, Pa was reading the *Bendigo Advertiser* when I asked a question that I had long suspected was important. There was always much talk in the Farrell house about the Mallee. I asked Pa where the Mallee started.

Pa down his newspaper. He cleared his throat and described various points on the map before thundering what he knew was certainly *not* the case.

"Wycheproof is *not* in the Mallee," he said. "It's just too far south!"

I was struck by the emphatic nature of Pa's non-statement. I felt it was up to me to make a decision. If the southern border of the Mallee was not Wycheproof, I decided it must be Dumosa, which is a railway siding just to the north of the town. We always drove past Dumosa on the way up to Ultima. I quite liked the name (although admittedly not as much as Teddywaddy, a railway siding just south of Wycheproof). In my mind, the Mallee would start at Dumosa.

Now that I find out that the real name for Mallee scrub is "Eucalyptus dumosa", it all seems to fit. The southern point of the Mallee, at least in my mind, is Dumosa. The southern border of Victoria's Mallee region extends from Dumosa across to South Australia, where they have their own Mallee region. As you enter Birchip along this southern border, you pass a sign that welcomes you to the Mallee. It's like a welcome to another land.

When I was a boy we occasionally headed up to Ultima on winter weekends. On those trips, I loved going to the footy at the Ultima Recreation Reserve, which was across the road from my grandparents' house. The Royal Blues seemed to beat every club except Nullawil, who always won the premiership. I remember the sensation of discovering saveloys, which were thin sausages cooked in a drum of pink water; I remember thinking they were exotic. When I was a young man, I became more aware of the sunsets that blazed across the Mallee sky. I am yet to see a finer sunset than those I have seen fill the sky over the footy ground in Ultima.

In late 1989, I had just turned twenty-four years of age when I moved to Bendigo to become a cadet journalist at the *Bendigo Advertiser*.

It was a move I embraced, largely because of my family's history with the town, but also because the members of my family were such avid readers of the town's newspaper. I played footy for Golden Square completely without distinction, and I got to know the clubs and towns in the region. After almost three years in Bendigo, I moved back to Melbourne for a short time, then on to London and Ireland before finally settling back in Melbourne. I was working as a freelance journalist in Melbourne, doing shifts as a sub-editor on the sports desk at *The Age*, when the sports editor took up my suggestion for some stories about local footy. I have been writing about local footy ever since. In writing about country footy, I tapped into my knowledge of the game around Bendigo, Swan Hill and Wangaratta, where another branch of the family was based, and I came to know the state of the game around the rest of Victoria to varying degrees.

I knew only a little about footy in the country north of Ultima until I began my research into the Mallee league during the writing of the VCFL book. When Boozer Robertson extended his invitation to me in the clubrooms at Ouyen to check out the unused Mallee grounds, it struck me as a brilliant way to learn more about footy in the heart of the Mallee. It also struck me as an effective way to describe the wider story of country football in rural areas, by depicting the exodus of families from the land.

At the time, I was reluctant to set out on another large country footy project. Because of the decline in newspapers, I was struggling to find work as a journalist. I had embarked on work as a tour guide, and I was quite enjoying it. But Boozer's invitation to tour the old Mallee grounds gnawed at me for several months. I knew I was in real trouble when I found myself checking Ouyen United's fixture for the 2018 season while I was on a tram.

Early in the 2018 season, Tracey Boyce, the secretary of the Redan footy club, invites me to attend a function before the club's first match under lights at its home ground, the historic City Oval in Ballarat. The evening is going well until the lights go out early in the last quarter. The players from both teams gather in the gloom before embarking on a few laps to stay warm while officials bluster about trying to turn the lights on. It might sound unfeeling towards those officials, who are turning the air blue with their curses towards the local council, but the night the lights go out at the City Oval is hilarious. Sport is unscripted drama, and this is drama of a most unexpected kind. The two teams are still jogging laps in the dark when I leave the ground.

A few weeks later, my oldest son and I divert away from a family trip to Wilsons Prom to sneak up to a footy match at Stony Creek. During the last quarter, the umpire is about to bounce the ball to resume play after a stoppage when a dog wanders on to the ground and begins trotting in circles around the ruckmen. The umpire decides to hold up play until the dog is removed from the oval. The dog, however, resists all attempts at capture. It scampers towards the centre square, and sets about baulking and weaving with great skill and poise while player after player tries to catch it. After a few minutes, players stop trying to chase the dog because they are worried about looking foolish. One player turns his back on the dog in an attempt to stir intrigue.

The umpire is standing with ball and whistle in hand, unsure of what to do, when finally the Stony Creek centre half-back, Andrew Logan, lunges at the dog and collars it. He celebrates by raising the dog above his head and toting it to the crowd. Andrew Logan turns around in a half-circle, revealing the No.33 on the back of his guernsey, while holding the dog aloft. Then he walks from the field, deposits the dog over the boundary line, and gives the crowd a smile and a wave. Under a steely sky in South Gippsland, it is a moment that brings immense sunshine. It makes me want to get back on the road and resume writing about country footy.

The clincher for my resumption of travels in country footy is the way the men at the Riddell Football Club treat my father when I take him back to his old club for a match early in 2018. Dad has been in failing health. Under the guiding hand of the club president, Gerrard Nolan, the men of Riddell make Dad feel special during his return to a place he regarded with such fondness. Dad played at Riddell, which is just north of Melbourne, for four seasons, from 1966 to 1969, and they were among the best times of his life. His coach during that period, Ron Howard, makes sure he is at the club to see Dad on his return, and I feel profoundly touched to see the way the two men respect each other. During our trip back to Melbourne that evening, I hear several stories from Mum and Dad that I have never heard before.

Footy at any level is fun. But it also brings connection and meaning. Boozer Robertson is offering the chance to look into a story that has large elements of fun, as well as large slabs of connection and meaning, in a region with a certain cachet and charisma. I'm also itching to resume further travels around country Victoria.

I ring Boozer to see if his invitation still stands.

How are you, I ask.

"Sensational," he says.

And we're off, planning our trip along the same route that he completed with his father, the great Ginger Robertson, fifteen years earlier.

Before I write about our tour, however, I feel I must describe the story of footy in the region. In trying to piece together the puzzle of just how many clubs played around Ouyen, I discover a history that reflects the nature of footy around the state, but with quirks that are particular to the Mallee. Before we visit the grounds, it might be worth knowing about some of the events that unfurled on these distant fields of dreams.

Part 2

From Stump to Stump

6

Otto's Empire

The story of footy in the heart of the Mallee begins later than the story of footy in every other part of the state for the good reason that the Mallee was the last region in Victoria to be settled, in part because it was so far from Melbourne, but also because it was so dry and dusty, and the land was so difficult to clear. The Mallee had a forbidding reputation from the time that Major Thomas Mitchell passed scathing comment about the harshness of the land during his explorations in 1836. It took another eighty years for the Victorian government to survey the land around Ouyen and make it available for settlement.

The heart of the Mallee came into view as a possible region for small land-holders after the railway line from Ballarat was extended through to Mildura in 1903. Three years later, in 1906, surveyors completed setting out farm blocks for settlement in the area around the railway siding at Ouyen. According to Hugh Carroll in his history of Ouyen, the surveyors carefully divided the parishes of Ouyen and Boorongie, to the east of Ouyen, into first-class and second-class holdings of 640 acres, or one square mile. They pegged out the holdings with numbered stakes. When a prospective selector was granted land, it was up to him to set out on horseback and find the stakes that marked out his land.

Amid the sandy soil that ran through the Mallee, the surveyors found a band of good soil that stretched out west from Ouyen. In 1908, the railways department began to build a railway line through the good land west of Ouyen to the South Australian border. It would be one of the few railways lines in Victoria to be built before the settlement of the land it would service.

The town of Ouyen took root next to the Ouyen railway siding on the line to Mildura. A merchant called Ben Oke, who had moved from Warracknabeal, bought a site on the western side of the railway line in 1909. Oke built a shop on the site and, over time, made such a large contribution to Ouyen that the main street in the town was named after him. It was also in 1909 that Constable Davie became the first policeman in Ouyen when he took up residence in a tent in the camp for railway workers. And in 1909 a former Carlton footballer called John "Otto" Buck moved to Ouyen to run a fruit, vegetable and confectionary store. Otto Buck had played three games for Carlton in 1897, the VFL's inaugural season. In 1909, Buck was thirty-three ears of age. He took up the lease on a billiard saloon in Ouyen, and he was the captain of the first football team to represent the town. Under Buck, the Ouyen football team caught the train south to Woomelang and played a challenge match against a team from there.

In 1909, selectors took up holdings on land at Boulka, Timberoo and Tiega, which were districts just to the west of Ouyen. According to Hugh Carroll, Tiega was one of the few locations in the area where there appears to have been a reliable water hole. The word "Tiega" is said to mean "surface water". Aborigines gathered at the water hole during trading trips to the Murray River. In 1909, the Scott and Morrish families were among the first families to select land in Tiega. The next year, in 1910, these two families were among those who established the Tiega Football Club.

The Ouyen District Football Association was formed in 1910 with four teams: Ouyen, Tiega, Box Tank and Walpeup. Box Tank were based in the Boorongie parish to the east of Ouyen. Walpeup was a district to the west of Tiega, based on what was reputed to be the best soil in the region. The events of the inaugural season in the Ouyen football competition are unknown, but according to the writings of A.S. Kenyon, the best-known early chronicler of the region, the bumper wheat crop of 1910 prompted a rush for land in the heart of the Mallee.

In 1911, the same four clubs competed in the second season of the Ouyen football competition, with Ouyen being crowned the premier team after finishing on top of the ladder. The population in the town of Ouyen in 1911, the year of the first Census in Australia, was 766. The first newspaper in the region, the *Ouyen Mail*, began publication in 1911.

The Box Tank Football Club folded after the 1911 season, never to be seen again. In the years to come, many clubs would arise throughout the region. With all farm blocks pegged at one square mile, properties were relatively close to each other. Farmers often had large families, and they often employed farm-hands to help out with the tough work of clearing land and planting crops, so there were many available footballers. The game was strong in the Mallee from the outset.

After four years of works on the railway line that ran west from Ouyen to the South Australian border, the line was completed in 1912. Before the official opening, the Ouyen Football Club travelled by train to Pinnaroo, the town just over the South Australian border, to play a challenge match. After the game, the Ouyen footballers attended a dance at the institute hall in Pinnaroo.

In 1912, according to the *Ouyen Mail*, the delegates from the three clubs in the Ouyen District Football Association – Ouyen, Ticga and Walpeup – resolved to play all matches under VFL rules, which was the common practice at the time. The delegates agreed that each club should draw its players from within a ten-mile radius of its ground. Matches were scheduled to start at 2.45pm,with a grace period of half an hour. The grace period was necessary because of the difficulty of travel on tracks that were pot-holed in dry conditions and muddy in the wet. Walpeup won their first premiership pennant.

The next year, in 1913, a team called East Rovers replaced Ouyen in the Ouyen football competition, and wore the red and black colours that Ouyen had worn. According to Geoff van Wyngaarden, a schoolteacher who has done extensive research on football in the Ouyen district, East

Rovers were likely to have been a splinter group from the Ouyen Football Club. The club would have been based to the east of the railway line in the town. East Rovers forfeited the final six games of their first season and were never seen again. The Ouyen Football Club resumed its place in the competition under its original name.

Another club, Nunga, based in a farming district to the south of Ouyen, joined the Ouyen competition in 1913. Timberoo, from the district south-west of Ouyen, joined the next year, in 1914. The five clubs in the Ouyen association began the 1915 season as planned, but they abandoned the fixture halfway through the season because of the privations arising from World War 1. Tiega officials were disappointed because their team was on top of the ladder and the club stood a strong chance of winning its first premiership.

Selectors arrived in the region in numbers after the completion of the railway line west to Pinnaroo, and in 1913 sportsmen formed football associations based in Underbool, the town about halfway along the line to South Australia, and in Murrayville, which was just on the Victorian side of the border. The inaugural five clubs in the Underbool competition were Boinka, Linga, Nyang, Tutye and Underbool. Halfway through the 1913 season, the Tutye footy club held a euchre and dance evening in the town's public hall on the Friday might before a match.

According to legend that has been passed down over generations, controversy surrounded the completion of the Underbool association's inaugural season after the Underbool publican played a merry hand in rallying business for himself. During the 1913 season, a teenager called Jack Helyer was in the habit of joining his parents during their journeys by horse and gig from their block at Boinka into Underbool on Saturday mornings to pick up provisions for the week. While he was in town for the day, young Helyer agreed to play football for Underbool.

After Underbool had defeated Boinka in the inaugural final of the Underbool and District Football Association, the Underbool players and officials enjoyed a night of celebrations in the Underbool Hotel. Afterwards, the publican advised Boinka officials that their rivals had fielded one player, young Jack Helyer, who lived outside Underbool's recruiting radius. In fact, he lived just inside Boinka's radius. Boinka lodged a protest. Their protest was upheld. Boinka players and officials celebrated their premiership with a night of celebrations in the Underbool Hotel.

The publican, whose name is unknown, then advised Underbool officials that it might be worth appealing against the decision to strip the club of the premiership. After all, young Helyer lived almost on the border of the recruiting radius for both clubs. Underbool did appeal. Their appeal was upheld. Underbool players and officials celebrated their premiership with a night of celebrations in the Underbool Hotel. The publican pocketed the money from the third night of speeches and toasts arising from one football match.

After World War 1, country football competitions resumed around Victoria. In the Mallee, four of the five clubs that had started playing in the Ouyen competition's abandoned season four years earlier re-formed. Timberoo, having played only one full season, in 1914, was the club that failed to re-emerge.

The two matches of the first round of the Ouyen competition in 1919 were played in mid-June. Spectators were charged an admission fee of sixpence; half of the proceeds went towards the funds that were being set aside for a hospital in Ouyen. In early September, Walpeup defeated Nunga in the Grand Final. A few days later, a combined team from the Ouyen association played a team from the North Western Football Association. The North Western association consisted of clubs from Tempy, Gorya, Woomelang and Lascelles, all of which were based along the train line south of Ouyen. Proceeds from this match also went towards the Ouyen hospital.

The decade of the 1920s was a decade of growth in the district surrounding Ouyen. When soldiers had returned home from the fighting of World War 1, many took up soldier settlement blocks in the Mallee. Farm labourers continued to pour in to the region, looking for work in shearing sheds and in the paddock. Many workers poured in for government jobs on the railways or the State Rivers and Water Supply Commission.

In the early 1920s, most people got around on foot, or on horseback or pushbike. The railways continued to run trains to the fruit blocks in

Mildura and the wheat fields near the South Australian border, but one of the clear markers of prosperity during this decade was the rise in car ownership. In 1924, a businessman called Edward Holden secured a contract with the American car firm General Motors to build car bodies for vehicles that were shipped to Australia. Cars became cheaper. With the establishment of car dealerships throughout the country, cars became more readily available as well. In 1925, according to the figures of the Royal Automobile Club of Victoria, there were 70,000 motor vehicles in Victoria. By 1930, the figure was 180,000.

In these times of optimism, there were regular theatre shows and plays throughout country Victoria. In 1925, the Wirth's circus tent was full during its performances in Ouyen. In the same year, more than 6000 people attended the eighth annual agricultural show at the Ouyen showgrounds, and the town held its first annual Easter tennis tournament. Jim Nulty, a prominent football official around Ouyen, ran a business called Nulty's Pictures.

The building of schools in this decade was an indicator of the rising population in the farming districts around Ouyen. According to Hugh Carroll, schools were opened in Gypsum (1922), Bronzewing (1923), Galah North (1924), Wagant (1924), Wymlet (1927), Rownack (1927), Kulwin (1929) and Trinita (1930). These schools offered education to the Merit level, which was equivalent to Year 8. Ouyen's Higher Elementary School, an early version of the high school, was opened in 1929, as was the Ouyen hospital. Sporting opportunities were also increased in Ouyen in 1929, with the formation of the cycling and athletics clubs.

In 1920, the Ouyen District Football Association was strengthened by the addition of a new club, Kiamal, bringing the tally of clubs to five. Before the next season, however, in 1921, the competition suffered a blow when the Ouyen and Walpeup clubs left to join three clubs on the train line to the west in a new competition, called the North West Mallee District Football Association. All clubs in the new competition were based along the train line from Ouyen to the South Australian border. The newspaper called it the "down the line" competition, and it marked a new high point in the quality of football in the Mallee.

In this era, the Ouyen Football Club would charter a train to take players, officials and supporters to the towns of their rivals along the railway line. In 1922, the club chartered a train for a match at Walpeup. The newspaper report made much of "the large number of Ouyen barrackers" who arrived by train as well as the many others from throughout the district who arrived by motor vehicle. "The numerous motor cars arrayed around the picturesque ground in its setting of native pines made for a pretty sight "

The Walpeup ground, with its abundance of Murray pines and belah trees, was a popular venue. Football supporters from Ouyen caught a special train to Walpeup for a semi-final in the North West Mallee District association in 1922 even though the Ouyen team had failed to make the finals. A record crowd of 500 paid £28 admission to see Walpeup host Cowangie. Walpeup won by seven points. Murrayville later won the premiership by defeating Walpeup in the final match, which was played at Cowangie.

The next season, in 1923, special trains from Ouyen and Murrayville converged from east and west and stopped at Walpeup on the day of the final match. A record crowd of 800 saw Ouyen defeat Cowangie in the final by sixteen points. The prominent Ouyen supporter Hugh Ingwersen, who was the owner of Ingwersen's Café, hosted a smoke night at the Ouyen Club to celebrate the football club's premiership. The Ouyen president, E.H. Arnold, was there to congratulate the players, but the captain, Reverend R.G. Reid, was an apology.

On a smaller scale to the down-the-line competition, the Boinka and District Football Association was formed in 1921 for the clubs from farming districts between Murrayville and Underbool, while the Ouyen District Football Association was re-formed in 1921 with three clubs, Kiamal, Nunga and Tiega, as well as a new club called Ouyen Wanderers. In the hierarchy of the time, the Boinka and Ouyen associations were known as junior competitions. The description had nothing to do with age; it meant they were second-tier competitions, ranking behind the competitions that were based along railway lines.

In 1922, Kiamal won the Ouyen District association's premiership just two years after the club had been formed. The Kiamal team included the Jardine brothers, Jim and Jack, who were new to the district, the Vallance brothers, Norm, Hec and Sam, and the Williams brothers, Bill and Joe, as well as Dan Carvill, Bill Hinks and Jack Carrolan. The school at Boorongie North was more suitable for functions than the Kiamal school so the celebrations were held there.

Ouyen Wanderers lasted only two seasons in the Ouyen association before folding after the 1922 season. Before the next season, however, three new clubs were formed, raising the number of clubs in the Ouyen association to six. The Ouyen Rovers Football Club was formed in the town and the Ouyen North West club was formed in a farming district about six miles north-west of the town. The Woornack Football Club was formed in a farming district to the south-east of Ouyen. The Ouyen Football Club itself continued to play in the down-the-line competition, the North West Mallee District association.

Before the 1925 season, the Ouyen District Football Association was reduced to five clubs when Tiega left to join the down-the-line competition. Of the remaining five clubs in the Ouyen competition, Kiamal had the highest tally of registered players, with thirty-nine. The number of registered players for the other four clubs was similar: Ouyen North West (37), Woornack, (36), Nunga (34), Ouyen Rovers (33). Jack Jardine was the Kiamal captain.

Before the 1925 season, the Ouyen Rovers president, Jim Blackburn, and vice-president, Hugh Ingwersen, led their club's annual meeting at Ingwersen's Cafe. The first item on the agenda for the annual meeting of any club or competition in this era was to hold a vote on whether to re-form. After Ouyen Rovers had voted to re-form, the committee decided to retain the Rovers' red and black colours, which were the same colours worn by the Ouyen Football Club in the North West Mallee competition, and buy six more jumpers. The Rovers' membership fee was set at five shillings; each membership was to include a ladies' ticket. One hundred memberships tickets and one-hundred ladies' ticket were printed by the new newspaper in town, the *Ouyen and North West Express*.

At the annual meeting of the Ouyen District Football Association on the eve of the 1925 season, delegates agreed to overturn the rule that imposed a particular recruiting radius for each club. Instead, a radius of twenty-three miles around Ouyen was imposed for every club. Early in the season, at the instigation of Jim Blackburn, the competition's delegates moved a motion that would attempt to improve the fortunes of football in the town as a whole. The idea was to allow the Ouyen Football Club to select players for its team in the North West Mallee competition from the team that had the bye in the Ouyen District competition. The motion was carried with only one dissenter, the Ouyen competition's president, W.G. McRae. It was a decision that would come to pose problems. With greater vigilance on who was playing where, clubs in the Ouyen District competition realised that rival teams were fielding players who had not gained a clearance from their original club. Meanwhile, clubs in the North West Mallee competition became resentful over the capacity of the Ouyen Football Club to fortify its ranks with players from the town's junior competition.

Halfway through the 1925 season, Ouyen Rovers became the first club in the district to hire a big-name coach, in this case Tom O'Halloran, who had played at centre-half forward in South Melbourne's VFL premiership team in 1918. O'Halloran was thirty-three years of age when he moved to Ouyen in 1925, and the Rovers were keen to tap into the knowledge he had accrued as well as his ability as a player. The Rovers booked the fire brigade hall in Ouyen for one night a week to give O'Halloran a venue in which to teach players and supporters the theory of the game, and to enable the players to train indoors. The Rovers defeated Kiamal by four goals in O'Halloran's first game at the helm.

Around that time, the delegates of the North West Mallee District Football Association held a meeting in Underbool in which they considered the Tutye Football Club's protest against Ouyen for fielding players who were registered with the Ouyen District association. After what was described in the newspaper as an animated discussion, Tutye's protest was dismissed. However, a North West Mallee official noted: "Permission will have to be obtained before such players can take the field in future."

The next week, Ouyen forfeited their match against Murrayville in the North West Mallee competition when only nine players showed up to catch the train to the South Australian border. Another Ouyen player, Reverend Reid, the captain, was left stranded on the platform at Walpeup, where he had been scheduled to join his teammates on the train for the journey west.

For Ouyen's next match, against Tutye, the Ouyen team included eight players from the Kiamal team that was having a bye in the Ouyen District association. Tutye still managed to win. At the end of the home and away rounds, Tutye finished third of the eight teams on the ladder while Ouyen finished seventh, ahead of only the winless Boinka.

In the Ouyen District association, the 1925 season became known for its intractable finals series. At the end of the home and away rounds, Nunga finished on top of the ladder. In early September, Woornack (second) played Ouyen North West (fourth) in a final at the Ouyen showgrounds. Ouyen North West surprised their higher-ranked opponents and sent Woornack tumbling out of the finals. After the match, Woornack protested about the eligibility of a footballer called Bradley who had played for Ouyen Rovers in a match in which the Rovers had defeated Woornack. The Woornack officials showed that player Bradley had played a match for Woomelang, in the North Western Football Association, early in the season and then joined Ouyen Rovers without a clearance. Woornack's protest was upheld. After they were awarded the victory for the match against the Rovers, the ladder was backdated to show that Woornack had finished the season on top. As minor premiers, they should have the right to challenge for the premiership. The finals series would have to start again.

Nunga countered that they, too, should be awarded the points for victory for a match against Ouyen Rovers in which Bradley had played. Therfore, they – Nunga – should finish on top of the ladder, as originally declared. Competition officials ruled that Nunga and Woornack would play against each other in a match on a Wednesday afternoon to decide the premiership. Nunga won by seven points, but Woornack remained unhappy. Association officials threw up their hands and referred the matter to Melbourne. The Ouyen District association was affiliated with the VFL, but VFL officials wanted no part in deciding the fate of a finals series in the far north-west of the state.

Finally, association officials decided to allow Nunga and Woornack to play against each other in yet another match to decide the premiership. The Grand Final was scheduled for Wednesday 21 October 1925, fully six weeks after the finals series had begun, with the cricket season under way and Melbourne's spring racing carnival in full swing. Nunga won by forty-nine points. In doing so, they became possibly the only club in Victoria to win a premiership in the same week as the running of the Caulfield Cup.

7

Old Blacky

In Jim Blackburn, the town of Ouyen had an official who kept the wider welfare of football in mind. Blackburn always had the welfare of the district in mind. He had a large impact throughout the Mallee during several years of tireless work that brought great gain to the region.

According to the research of Merle Pole, who is the president of the Ouyen District History and Genealogy Centre, Blackburn was born in Ararat in 1875 and moved to the north of the state in 1891, aged sixteen, to work for the State Rivers and Water Supply Commission. He became a structural engineer, based in Merbein, but he spent much time at the commission's camp in Ouyen before he and his family moved to the town permanently in 1926. His daughter Sheila attended Ouyen Primary School.

Known as "Old Blacky", Blackburn was a clever engineer with a brisk manner. He supervised the building of the vast gravitational channel system that drew water from the Grampians region to the Mallee. The system was one of the largest channel systems in the world, and Blackburn had many problems trying to keep the extensive channels free of the sand that was thrown about by dust storms. During hard times, he did his best to provide work for the men of the region who were struggling on the land. With his band of workers, he maintained the town's water supply in a difficult climate.

In 1932, Blackburn was the founding president of the Ouyen Bowls Club, which was based in the north-west corner of the town's recreation reserve. In such a dry region, his success in maintaining the rinks at the bowls club was considered a large achievement. The success of his channel system can be gauged by the fact that it remained the Mallee's source of water for more than seventy years.

In 1926, having just moved to Ouyen, Blackburn became a prominent football administrator. Before the season, the Ouyen Football Club withdrew from the North West Mallee association because it was struggling to field a team against its rivals along the railway line to the west. Instead, it threw its lot in with the North Western Football Association, which was based along the railway line to the south. Tempy and Gorya, a club formed some time earlier by the mergers of Speed and Turriff, would be Ouyen's nearest rivals on the line to the south.

Jim Blackburn followed up on Ouyen's decision to change competitions by suggesting that football in the town would be stronger if there were one team. The Ouyen and Ouyen Rovers football clubs were duly merged, and the merged club was called simply the Ouyen Football Club. But with a surfeit of players, the club decided to form a seconds team called Ouyen Juniors to play in the Ouyen District Football Association. The senior team had access to the junior team's players. Jim Blackburn, as well as being secretary of the Ouyen Football Club, was chosen as a selector to regulate the passage of players between the two teams. Halfway through the 1926 season, Blackburn sent the club a letter of resignation as secretary and selector because a couple of players in the senior team had refused to play in a match against Lascelles unless a particular player of their choice was selected. The committee voted unanimously for Blackburn to carry on as secretary, but he did step down from his role as selector.

Before the next season, in 1927, Ouyen Rovers re-formed and returned to the Ouyen District association, but the association ruled that the club's players would not be available for selection in the Ouyen senior team, which would again play against the clubs on the railway line to the south. Ouyen Juniors were disbanded. Jim Blackburn became the secretary of the Ouyen District association as well as the Ouyen Football Club, which battled through its second season in the North Western association. Once again, the Ouyen Football Club struggled to persuade players of the merits of travelling to play. The problem was highlighted at the end of the 1927 season when they went into a semi-final two players short.

The instability surrounding football in the town of Ouyen was replicated throughout the region. Before the 1926 season, Underbool paid the £10 fee to affiliate with the North West Mallee District Football Association, but at the club's meeting on the eve of the season, a large majority of the fifty members in attendance voted that their club should leave the competition and start its own. The other five clubs in the North West Mallee District association, stunned by Underbool's decision within a week of the opening round, ruled that Underbool must forego their affiliation fee. But the five clubs must have been stunned again when Underbool and their neighbours decided to give their new competition a title that was remarkably similar to the competition they had left. Underbool had left the North West Mallee District Football Association to create a competition called the North West Mallee Football League. Thus, the North West Mallee association consisted of five clubs stretching from Walpeup and Tiega in the east to Murrayville in the west, while the North West Mallee league consisted of four clubs based in and around Underbool, including the newly formed Tyalla.

The four clubs affiliated with the North West Mallee league in its inaugural season, in 1926, were: Boinka (blue and white), Linga (green and gold), Tyalla (maroon and gold) and Underbool (black and white). The four clubs agreed on an affiliation fee of £1 1s, or one pound and one shilling. The clubs agreed to stay in the competition for four years. On the question of a radius, it was decided that if a boundary ran through a man's block, he was in neutral territory so he could please himself which club he joined.

The people of Boulka formed a football club before the 1926 season, but no competition would accept the club in its ranks, so the club folded without playing a match. Nearby, the whispers about the probable demise of the Nunga footy club prompted the people of Bronzewing to form their own club, which they hoped would benefit from an influx of former Nunga players. As it happened, Nunga did re-form on the eve of the 1926 season, but Bronzewing continued with their plans to form a club. They joined the Ouyen District Football Association, bringing the number of clubs in the association to six.

Bronzewing, still waiting their shipment of maroon and gold guernseys on the eve of the 1926 season, played their first match in an all-white uniform. They defeated Woornack in their opening game, and went on to win the premiership in their inaugural season. Woornack folded soon afterwards.

After the machinations before the 1926 season, the merry go-round in Mallee football kicked fully into gear in 1927. While the North West Mallee District Football Association had been the glamorous harbinger of a new era when it was formed for clubs along the western railway line in 1921, it was wound up only six years later, on the eve of the 1927 season, and its five clubs were left to find new homes. Murrayville and Cowangie headed west to join a South Australian competition, Tutye joined the upstart competition based in Underbool, and Walpeup and Tiega turned their sights to the east.

On the eve of the 1927 season, the Yellumjip Football Club was formed during a meeting attended by thirty people in the Timberoo South public hall. O.L. Hahnel was elected as the first Yellumjip president. Yellumjip and Walpeup tried to join the Ouyen District Football Association but were rejected on the grounds of excess travel. The Ouyen District competition accepted Tiega into its ranks, but on one condition: Tiega had to clear three of their best players to the Ouyen Football Club, in order to strengthen Ouyen for their battles against rivals along the train line to the south, and to ensure that Tiega would not be too strong for the smaller clubs in Ouyen's junior competition.

Tiega rejected the condition and backed away from their plans to play in the Ouyen District competition. They joined forces with Walpeup and the newly formed Yellumjip in trying to create a new competition. Tempy, having left the North Western Football Association, met representatives from the three clubs in the Victoria Hotel in Ouyen, where they agreed to form a competition with four clubs: Tempy: (black and white), Tiega (red and white), Walpeup (royal blue) and Yellumjip (yellow and black). The delegates' choice of title for the new competition, the Western Mallee Football Association, was unfortunate. The region around Ouyen now was home to the North West Mallee Football League, the North Western Football Association and the Western Mallee Football Association.

Tempy won the first premiership in the Western Mallee association, in 1927. But Yellumjip struggled against their larger rivals. Before the next season, in 1928, Yellumjip joined forces with three newly formed clubs, Kattyoong, Torrita and Wymlet, to form the Walpeup and District Football Association. Given the title of the competition, it was unusual that the Walpeup Football Club was not a part of it; instead, Walpeup remained an affiliate of the Western Mallee association. The nascent Walpeup and District association also made an unusual choice with its first president. H.F. Richardson was not a club delegate who was elected to head the board of delegates; instead, he was an independent delegate. Torrita defeated Yellumjip in the match to decide the first premiership. The competition would last only two seasons.

While Yellumjip left the Western Mallee association before the 1928 season, Ouyen and Lascelles joined the competition, bringing the number of clubs to five. At the end of the season, Lascelles and Tiega earned the right to play in the final. By now, the railways department had become so concerned by the vandalism on chartered trains for football trips that they resolved to inspect each train before its journey and on arrival. Clubs were required to pay what was described as "a guarantee" to insure against damage. If the railway inspectors found damage to the extent that its repair was not covered by the guarantee, they would send a bill for the balance to the club secretary. The train that was chartered for the journey from Lascelles to Ouyen for the final match in the Western Mallee association's season in 1928 was so poorly patronised that the fares scarcely covered the guarantee. Lascelles won the match. It would be the last match played in the Western Mallee competition.

The 1929 season marked the apex of movement and growth in Mallee football. The first of many dominoes to fall on the eve of the season was the break-up of the Western Mallee association after Tiega and Walpeup left to join the Walpeup and District association and Lascelles left to join clubs like Woomelang and the powerful Hopetoun in the original competition to brandish the word "Mallee" in its title, the Mallee Football Association, which had been founded in 1903.

The departures of Walpeup, Tiega and Lascelles from the Western Mallee association before the 1929 season left their rivals from the previous season, Tempy, Gorya and Ouyen, without a competition. Tempy and Gorya sounded out the Ouyen District association about their prospects of joining that competition, but were dissuaded against taking the matter further. The two clubs tried to join the newly formed Patchewollock and District association but were rebuffed. The response of Gorya officials was to split their club into its original components, the clubs from Speed and Turriff, and invite Tempy to join them in trying to form a new competition. The formation of a club at nearby Pirro brought the number of clubs in the area to four, which was enough to form the intended competition. In its determination to use the word "Mallee" in the competition's title, the board of delegates called it the Central Mallee Football League. W.C. Pianta was elected to be the first president.

That left the Ouyen Football Club, the biggest club in the region, as the only club without a home on the eve of the 1929 season. The six clubs of the Ouyen District Football Association rejected Ouyen's overtures for several weeks, fearing that the town's original club would be too strong. Finally, on the night before the opening round, the clubs relented and the Ouyen Football Club was admitted into the competition that took the town's name. As Ouyen Rovers now wore Ouyen's original colours of red and black, the Ouyen Football Club took on the colours of yellow and black. Pressmen called them the Mustard and Tars.

With the Ouyen Football Club finding a home, the composition of all leagues and associations in the heart of the Mallee was settled for the opening of the season. The district around Ouyen hosted the following competitions in 1929: the Central Mallee Football League, the North

West Mallee Football League, the Ouyen District Football Association, the Patchewollock and District Football Association and the Walpeup and District Football Association.

In 1929, the Mallee was stricken by drought. Grounds were hard. During the course of the season, Hattah dropped out of the Ouyen District competition and Tyalla dropped out of the North West Mallee league. Torrita failed to turn up for a match against Wymlet late in the season in the Walpeup and District association. The Walpeup competition held its 1929 Grand Final at Walpeup. Play commenced after thirty points (eight millimetres) of rain had soaked the ground. Tiega defeated Walpeup by fourteen points.

In the Central Mallee league, a precocious playmaker called Henry "Ginger" Robertson began to make his mark with Tempy at the age of fourteen. Ginger would go on to forge one of the most remarkable careers in country football in the entire state, let alone the Mallee. Speed won the only grand final that the Central Mallee league would hold. The competition folded after one season.

In the Ouyen District association, the 1929 Grand Final was held under a shroud of darkness that proved an apposite portent of gloom. Ouyen had won through to the Grand Final after finishing the home and away rounds two games clear on top of the ladder. The second team, Bronzewing, had finished two games clear of their nearest rival. It surprised no one when Ouyen and Bronzewing were the two clubs that proceeded through to the Grand Final.

According to the *Ouyen and North West Express*, a blinding dust storm raged across the Mallee on the morning of the match. The Ouyen Football Club tried to have the match postponed, but Bronzewing were adamant that play should go ahead. A small crowd braved the elements at the Ouyen ground, but the spectators were unable to see the players through the dust. In the second half, driving rain created further discomfort. Spectators shivered in the cold, but the conditions for football improved. Bronzewing stacked the backline in the third quarter. By putting almost the entre team in defence, the Pigeons were able to restrict the favourites to three behinds. But Ouyen rallied against the wind in the last quarter and went on to win by sixteen points, 3.7 (25) to 1.3 (9). George Morrish and Frank Dunkley were outstanding for the victors.

About six weeks later, on 24 October 1929, the financial crash on Wall Street heralded the beginning of the Depression that would affect every country in the world. A month after the crash, about 100 unemployed men, most of them from the railways, held a meeting in Ouyen. It was the first meeting of unemployed men in the town. The Depression would go on to have a devastating effect on the Mallee, but the appetite for football remained strong. For some people, the weekly match at the local oval was one of the few things they could look forward to.

8

Life and Death

During the Depression, a growing number of farmers left the land. The 640-acre blocks that had been laid out in the early years of the century were no longer large enough to sustain many families. Farmers seeking larger blocks began to buy out their neighbours. With improvements in farm machinery, farm labourers were less in demand, forcing many of them to seek jobs in the cities and towns. The school at Trinita, having been opened in 1930, was closed three years later, and others schools would be closed in the years ahead.

The decline in population affected football. When the farming district of Wymlet failed, the Wymlet Football Club could no longer continue. One of Wymlet's favourite sons, the talented footballer Hugh Carroll, carved out a life as a successful sheep farmer in the area, but his story was uncommon. Some of the farmers and their families who closed the gate behind them in Wymlet and elsewhere moved into Ouyen, raising the town's population to 1169 in 1933, according to Census figures, while others moved farther afield, to Bendigo and Ballarat, to Melbourne and Mildura. In a world of improving communications, Mallee people took note of the goings-on in the large centres. Some moved to the cities and towns. Others returned. The greater mobility of the automobile age increased the comings and goings of Mallee people.

In 1933, the Mallee region received a boost when the state government established the Mallee Research Station in Walpeup. According to the centenary history of Ouyen, some wags believed that Walpeup was the wrong place to base a centre for agricultural research in the Mallee – because the soil was too good! The prices for primary produce began to grow around this time and life in the Mallee began to look up. In 1934, the Ouyen District Tennis Club was formed with six clubs from farming districts – Gypsum, Bronzewing, Kiamal, Wymlet, Trinita and Boorongie – and two from Ouyen, which were Ramblers and Railways. The next year, in 1935, the Ouyen brass band became active again and resumed raising money for the hospital. The band included George Morrish, a star footballer with Ouyen, and Jim Nulty, who had spent several years as the president of the Walpeup footy club.

In this era, the Victorian Country Football League established itself as the statewide administrative body for the game outside its metropolitan base. The Victorian Football League had formed the country body in response to a campaign led by a Frankston man, Herb McCulloch. Effectively, the VCFL was a sub-committee of the VFL. After its formation in 1927, the VCFL was led by a board consisting of sixteen delegates: eight from VFL clubs and the same number from the eight VCFL districts. The representatives from the country districts were called district councillors.

In 1929, the VCFL made its first change to district boundaries when it excised a wedge from the Wimmera and Bendigo districts to form the ninth district, the North Central District, which stretched from Bealiba in the south to Mildura in the north. The first North Central District councillor, F.E.D. Rankin, was from Birchip. His successor, Ted Chessells, was from Donald. Most North Central District meetings were held in Donald until Chris Brown, the president of the Underbool footy club and the president of the North West Mallee league, requested in 1932 that some meetings should be held in Ouyen.

On the eve of the following season, in 1933, the VCFL's North Central District Council held its first annual meeting in Ouyen. Chris Brown (president) and H.H. Walton (secretary) represented the North West Mallee league. The next year, in 1934, the North Central District was comprised by twelve leagues or associations, consisting of a total of seventy-five clubs. The North Central Football League was the district's designated major league. The eleven minor leagues affiliated with the VCFL through their North Central District included the Millewa league, the Mildura District league, the Yungera District league and the Nyah-Piangil association. In this era, the link with the VFL through the VCFL, and the emphasis on the word "league" on the titles of those two bodies, accelerated the trend for competitions to change their own titles to include the word "league". The Ouyen District Football Association changed its title to the Ouyen District Football League in 1935.

The composition of the competitions in the district around Ouyen remained volatile throughout the 1930s, especially in the early part of the decade. Before the 1931 season, the seven clubs of the North West Mallee league had a long discussion during their meeting at Linga over whether to include Murrayville. The main issue was travel, with Murrayville being almost forty miles (sixty kilometres) from Underbool. When the clubs voted to admit Murrayville, one of the officials commented on the competition's strong resemblance to the North West Mallee competition of a decade earlier: "It resembles the Ouyen-Murrayville line competition of older days."

To the south-west of Ouyen, the Patchewollock and District competition was wound up before the 1931 season. The four clubs that were in that competition merged to form one club, called Patchewollock, which would play in the Mallee association.

To the south-east of Ouyen, five clubs banded together to form the Pier Milan and District Football Association in 1931. The competition was based around the town of Pier Milan, which apparently was named after the Frenchman who had surveyed the region before settlement. Pier Milan defeated Mittyack before a large crowd at Nandaly in the first Grand Final. The competition would go on to produce several star players over the next decade.

In the Ouyen District competition, club delegates voted before the 1931 season to include a third club that had been formed in the town of Ouyen; the new club was called Ouyen Imperials. The Imperials bought a set of blue guernseys from Hartley's store in town. It would play home matches on the ground inside the trotting track. The five Williams brothers, Joey, Harry, Norm, Oliver and Mick, left Kiamal to join Imperials. Jack Trimble, Joe Walsh and Cec Davies left the Rovers for the Imps. Joey Williams was appointed captain and Jack Trimble vice-captain.

On the day of their first match, the Imps players met at Ingwersen's Café in Ouyen. Their truck left at 2 o'clock for the journey to Bronzewing, which was nine miles (fifteen kilometres) down the road. The Imps defeated the Pigeons by seven points. At the end of the home and away rounds, Tempy finished way clear of their rivals in the Ouyen District competition. Bronzewing, Kiamal and Ouyen Imperials were the teams that missed out on making the final four.

A controversy erupted on the eve of the finals in 1931 when the Ouyen District competition's delegates voted to overturn a previous decision that all finals would be played in Ouyen. With Tempy on top of the ladder, the delegates voted that the semi-final between Tempy and Ouyen Rovers would be played at the country team's ground. After consultation with the VCFL, however, the ruling body advised that the decision to play the match in Tempy should not have been made without all clubs taking the opportunity to refer the matter to their clubs for discussion. The delegates heeded the ruling and voted to return the semi-final to Ouyen.

Before the Tempy players jogged on to the Ouyen ground for the semi-final in 1931, they warned competition officials that they would refuse to play in protest against the decision to appoint umpire Peacock for the match in clear contravention of an earlier decision to appoint an umpire from outside the region. Umpire Peacock bounced the ball, and the Tempy players stood and watched as player Earnshaw, the Rovers captain, kicked a goal. The Tempy players walked off. An angry Earnshaw said the public deserved a match, so he organised his team to play a practice game. Later, the competition officials decided there would be a rematch of the semi-final the following week under the direction of an outside umpire. No admission fee would be charged.

Umpire McIntosh from Birchip was appointed for the rematch in Ouyen a week later. Tempy defeated the Rovers. In his report on the match in the newspaper, the writer said of the umpire: "He gave a good display, particularly in the first quarter before the rain spoilt the match. His interpretation of the holding the ball/holding the man rule was the essence of consistency."

In 1931, the Ouyen District competition adopted the finals format that had been adopted by the VFL, with a preliminary final and a grand final to conclude the season. In the Preliminary Final of the Ouyen competition, Ouyen Rovers defeated Tiega to earn a rematch against Tempy in the Grand Final.

On the day of the Grand Final, the match was due to start at 2 o'clock only to be delayed because three of the Rovers' best players, including Clarrie "Dido" Morelli, had failed to arrive from Hattah because their car had broken down. Finally, the trio completed their journey, and the match began in the shadow of 4 o'clock.

Dido Morelli was well known, having played seven senior games for Collingwood before moving around the state through his work on the railways. In 1930 he coached Weir United to victory in the Grand Final of the Ovens and Murray league. In 1931, he moved to Ouyen and joined the Rovers. Dido was tall, wiry, fast and talented. After play finally got under way in the 1931 Grand Final in Ouyen, the Tempy captain, Rupert Metherall, received what was described in the newspaper as a nasty cut on the chin. After the incident, the umpire asked Dido Morelli to remove a ring from one of his fingers. The Rovers went on to win a pulsating match by two points. The Rovers' Jack Dooley was considered best on ground, while Ginger Robertson, the sixteen-year-old from Tempy, was described as a dynamo for his team.

During the days after the match, tempers at Tempy were inflamed when Rupert Metherall was laid low because of an infection that arose from the cut on his chin. Tempy officials lodged a protest in which they claimed that the Rovers' George Caldow had not been cleared from his previous club and that two other players, including Dido Morelli, had played with another club, namely Trinita, during the season.

During a heated meeting, club delegates agreed that Tempy had grounds for complaint over the clearance of George Caldow from Bronzewing to the Rovers, but they decided that if the rules were applied to the letter of the law, five of the other seven clubs would have been punished over clearance technicalities during the course of the season. Trinita were unaligned with a competition. The delegates noted that the club had no officers and played only in what were described as Sunday social matches. The delegates ruled that Dido Morelli and player Cresp had no case to answer in turning out for Trinita. They dismissed Tempy's protests, and applied to the Rovers the only punishment that was allowable under their rules. They fined the club £5 for the late start to the match.

Metherall's infection from the cut on his chin was a harbinger of two tragedies that would befall Mallee football in the coming years. In 1934, Grattan Leach was a twenty-one-year-old star with Torrita when he died of blood poisoning after cutting his leg on a hard ground. Syd Cocking, meanwhile, was a respected player with Walpeup. In 1934, he won the club's best and fairest award. Late in the 1935 season, Cocking cut his hand and was forced to miss a match. The next week, he was again sidelined, and he went to Tempy to watch his team play. Walpeup duly scored a thrilling victory over the home team.

After the match, Cocking was waiting on the platform at Tempy train station when he collapsed and died. The local newspaper said he died of a poisoned hand, but presumably it was septicemia, or blood poisoning as a result of infection. Cocking was described as a single man, aged thirty-two, who had lived with the Gniel family at Kattyoong for sixteen years. About 150 mourners attended his funeral at the St Paul's Church of England in Walpeup.

Just before the 1932 season, the Ouyen Football Club revealed that it would disband because of a lack of players and a financial shortfall. Then the club announced that it would merge with Ouyen Rovers. To decide the merged club's name, two members, Bill Harrington of Rovers and Bill Bentley of Ouyen, were assigned to toss a coin. Bentley called heads, but tails won. The club was called Ouyen Rovers on the toss of a coin. It would wear Ouyen's traditional colours of red and black.

Patchewollock left the Mallee Football Association after just one season to join the Ouyen District competition in 1932. Patchewollock's entry into the Ouyen competition raised the number of clubs to eight, which lent the competition the kudos of hosting four matches each weekend. Patchewollock benefited when the highly rated Bryans brothers, Alf and Reg, were cleared from Bronzewing to join them. Before the opening match of the 1932 season, Patchewollock struck a deal with two local men that they would drive the players in their truck to eight games for £15. The deal would include the seven away games and one semi-final. The club's confidence that it would make the finals was well founded.

According to the *North West Express*, the Patchewollock truck accompanied ten or eleven car loads of Patche supporters to Tempy for the club's first game in the Ouyen competition. Patche won their opening game, and embarked on a winning streak. The club remained undefeated until they lost to Kiamal, the bottom team, by one point in the final home and away round. In the same round, Ouyen Imperials won their first game of the season when they defeated Bronzewing.

Ouyen Rovers, the club formed by the merger of two clubs in Ouyen, defeated Patchewollock, the club formed by the union of four clubs from the old Patchewollock association, in the 1932 Second Semi-final. Patchewollock were due to play Tempy in the Preliminary Final in Ouyen the following week. Interest was high in the clash between the two country clubs. A chartered train carried 170 supporters from Tempy to Ouyen for the match. Reg Bryans was superb in defence for Patche, while the Tempy teenager Ginger Robertson was the best player for his team. The Patchewollock full-forward, Percy Powell, having fallen off a motorbike during the week, played with bandages on his wrists. Powell kicked seven goals as Patche won their way through to the Grand Final.

According to a report in the *Weekly Times*, a crowd of 1000 – the largest to attend a football match in Ouyen – descended on the recreation reserve for the 1932 Grand Final. Patchewollock's Gil Robertson was staunch at centre half-back, while young ruckman and forward Hugh

Torney was unbeatable in the air. Patchewollock defeated Ouyen Rovers to win the premiership in their first season in the Ouyen competition.

In the North West Mallee league, Kattyoong appeared well-placed to challenge for the premiership in 1932 until their high-flying forward Stan Binns was kicked by a horse. Binns took the field for his club's final against Underbool, which was played at Underbool, but he had to retire at half-time. His teammate Ernie Woodall, one of the three Woodall brothers playing with Kattyoong, was also sidelined after tearing a cartilage in his knee during the match.

The 1932 North West Mallee league Grand Final, between Cowangie and Underbool, was played at Linga, a ground that had been widened during the previous finals series to accommodate better football. Cowangie won a high-scoring match by thirty-four points, 19.12 (126) to 14.8 (92). Old-timers noted the growing capacity of teams to kick large scores.

In the VFL, the Geelong full-forward George Moloney kicked 109 goals during the home and away rounds in 1932, while Carlton's Soapy Vallance, the brother of J.J. Vallance who had played for Tempy, kicked ninety-seven. Australia was still in the grip of the Depression, and the clouds over the country were yet to part, but the rising number of goals in football was a portent of the rising fortunes ahead.

9

The Big League

With growing confidence in their skills and the increasing mobility of the times, Mallee footballers began travelling down to Melbourne in greater numbers to try out with VFL teams.

The first player to gain attention in the *North West Express* after leaving the Mallee for Melbourne was Ernie Nunn from Tiega. Nunn was a policeman who played senior football at Footscray for three seasons, from 1929 to 1931, a period when he was also captain-coach of the Police team that competed in Melbourne's Wednesday league, which was a competition based on workplace teams. In 1932 Nunn played a handful of games in the ruck for Collingwood. According to a report in *The Herald*, he was a solid player "who put plenty of ginger into his work", but he was cut from the Magpies' senior list at the end of the season.

Stan Binns and Hugh Carroll played in a premiership team with Kattyoong in the North West Mallee league in 1931; Binns was a strapping forward, while Carroll was a rugged centreman. Before the 1932 season, they both tried out with South Melbourne. According to a report in *The Argus* in Melbourne, Binns was understandably not at his best in his practice match because he had travelled overnight from the north-west of the state and arrived at the ground only a few hours before the game.

The reporter noted that Binns had all the essentials to make the grade except experience. "His performance was full of promise."

Binns returned to Kattyoong, where he suffered misfortune during the 1932 finals series when a horse kicked him and curbed his high-flying ways. Stan's brother Bill Binns became the captain-coach at Walpeup. Stan Binns later gained a clearance to Jeparit. He made the final list at Melbourne in 1938, but he fell short of a senior game.

After failing to make the cut at South Melbourne before the 1932 season, Hugh Carroll headed north of the city and tried out at North Melbourne. He made the final list there, and played nine senior games in his one season at Arden Street. Unable to find suitable work in the city, however, he returned to the Mallee and joined his brother Jack Carroll at Ouyen Imperials. The two brothers led the Imps from the bottom of the ladder to the top, and in 1933 the club won its only premiership.

Before the next season, in 1934, the Carroll brothers were the fulcrum in a practice match between Imperials and Wymlet, the club from their home district, which had been in recess for five years. The match was more or less a social outing. *The North West Express* said the Carroll brothers were "always in the limelight". The Wymlet Football Club did re-form, and it applied for entry into the Ouyen District competition for the 1934 season, but it was rejected.

In 1934, the Carroll brothers again played for Ouyen Imperials. Late in the season, an outbreak of flu swept through the Mallee, and Imperials took the field for a final against Tiega with only thirteen players. The Carroll brothers battled gamely, according to the newspaper report, but the Imps lost and were eliminated. On the same day, Pier Milan forfeited a final against Mittyack in the Pier Milan and District competition because twelve of their players had been confined to bed by the flu.

After Patchewollock had won the premiership in their first season in the Ouyen District competition, in 1932, three of their players, Bub Jamieson, Reg Bryans and Hugh Torney, went to South Melbourne to play in a practice match before the 1933 season. The Bloods played Jamieson as a rover, Torney at half-forward and Bryans in the ruck. When the trio were informed they would not make the final list, Bryans returned to the

Mallee, while Jamieson tried out with Hawthorn and Torney took up an invitation to go to Essendon. Jamieson's venture stoked his ambition. He later tried out with Richmond and Geelong before gaining a clearance from Patchewollock to Stawell.

Hugh Torney's acceptance of Essendon's invitation turned out in his favour. He made the final list for the 1933 season, and made his senior debut with the Dons in Round 4 of that season, in a loss to Carlton at Windy Hill. At six-foot-three (191 centimetres), Torney was a big man for his era, and, being from rugged country, he had a strong work ethic, as well as a strong pair of hands. He would give Essendon wonderful service over many years.

Wally Kelly, a follower from Tutye in the North West Mallee league, played twenty-two senior games over six seasons for Footscray, mainly in defence. Bill Blair, from Ouyen Rovers, tried out with St Kilda in 1932 and Hawthorn in 1933 before playing two seniors games at half-back for Geelong in 1935. Before the 1937 season, he played in a practice match with Melbourne on one weekend and in another practice match with Hawthorn the next. He was also a professional runner. Blair finished third in the Tower Hill Gift in Koroit in 1938, but he played no more senior football in the VFL.

The most dynamic star to emerge from the Mallee in this era was Sandy McPherson, a centreman from Pier Milan who made a huge impression when he played with the Ouyen footy club in 1928. During the following off-season, he joined the Ouyen cricketers in Melbourne for Country Cricket Week. He then stayed in Melbourne to try out with the St Kilda Football Club during the practice matches in 1929. On the eve of the season, he signed with Bendigo league club Sandhurst. St Kilda tried to lure him back to the city, but McPherson stayed with Sandhurst and became an important player during the club's glorious era under the coaching of Bob McCaskill. After four years with Sandhurst, McPherson was still being sought by Geelong, but he remained in Bendigo.

Through the link with Sandy McPherson, Sandhurst coach Bob McCaskill was known to swing through the Mallee in his quest for talented players. Sandhurst signed a few players from Pier Milan, including the Rohde brothers, Lorrie and Carl. Lorrie Rohde played in Sandhurst's premiership team in 1930, alongside Sandy McPherson and another player who hailed from north of Bendigo, Mickey Crisp from Wedderburn. Before the new season, in 1931, Lorrie Rohde and Mickey Crisp took up an invitation to try out at Carlton. They both made the Blues' senior list.

Back in Pier Milan before the 1931 season, Carl Rohde was forced to put his plans to join Sandhurst on hold after an accident. Carl was cranking the engine of a truck when the engine backfired. In the resultant jolt, the footballer's arm was fractured. The arm was in a splint for several weeks before Carl returned to Bendigo, where he enjoyed premiership success with Sandhurst.

Lorrie Rohde returned from Carlton to the farm in the Mallee without playing a senior VFL game. Mickey Crisp, however, became a Carlton legend, playing almost 200 games over the course of a decade. Lorrie Rohde played out the decade with his home club, Pier Milan. In 1934 he lost the count for the best and fairest award in the Pier Milan and District competition by one vote to Myall's Rupert Metherall, the former Tempy player, but he won two league awards in subsequent seasons, and led his club through a period of success.

Frank Dunkley gained enormous respect through his performances as a wingman for Ouyen and Ouyen Rovers before he left for Melbourne, where he played with the Post and Telegraph team in the Wednesday league. He tried out with Hawthorn in 1933.

Four years later, in its eagerness to report on the journeys of Mallee footballers to the bright lights in the south, the *North West Express* reported that Dunkley was among the best players for Mornington in the club's victory over Frankston in a violent grand final in the Mornington Peninsula competition. Six Frankston players were reported. Two years later, in 1939, the newspaper revealed that Dunkley was now the secretary of the Mornington footy club.

In 1935, there was a development in Mallee football when two struggling clubs from adjacent farming districts voted to merge rather than fold. The Linga Football Club was tired of taking the field with fourteen or fifteen players. The club merged with Boinka to form the

Central Football Club, which would become known as Centrals. With the merger of two clubs into one, the North West Mallee league was reduced to five clubs.

To the east, the Ouyen District competition changed its title from "association" to "league" in 1935 and it entered its new era with a new club, Gorya, who had been playing in the Mallee Football Association. Gorya had won the final premiership in the Mallee association, in 1934, after which the competition was disbanded. Gorya were admitted into the Ouyen District competition in 1935 on the stipulation that they play homes matches at Speed, which was closer to Ouyen than their other ground, at Turriff. Gorya effectively replaced Bronzewing, who folded after much anguish over the departure of their players to neighbouring clubs. With the arrival of Gorya and the departure of Bronzewing, the number of clubs in the Ouyen competition remained at eight.

Gorya won the premiership in their first season in the Ouyen District competition, defeating Tempy in the 1935 Grand Final, and in doing so, they dashed the hopes of their neighbouring club of sending off a club great, Arthur McLean, on a winning note. Tempy later made a presentation to McLean that recognised his contribution to the club. The next year, in 1936, Gorya thrashed Ouyen Rovers in the Grand Final to win their second premiership from two attempts in their adopted competition. In the North West Mallee league, Underbool won their fourth premiership in a row with their victory in the 1936 Grand Final.

The 1936 season was significant in the Ouyen District league for the introduction for a best and fairest award as voted by the umpires, like the Brownlow Medal in the VFL. Harry Walker had been secretary of the Ouyen District competition for eight years before he stepped aside. His final contribution was to donate a cup for the season's best and fairest player, to be called the Walker Cup. After every match, the field umpire was asked to cast a vote for one player, whom he considered the best and fairest player on the ground. Alf Bryans, the Patchewollock full-back, won the inaugural Walker Cup after finishing ahead of two fellow champions, Tempy's Ginger Robertson and Hugh Carroll of Ouyen Imperials, in the 1936 vote count.

On the eve of the 1937 season, officials from the two clubs in Ouyen – Ouyen Rovers and Ouyen Imperials – decided they would have to make a change if they were to challenge the country clubs that had dominated in recent seasons. Joe Walsh, the owner of a drapery store in the main street in Ouyen, chaired the meeting at which the two clubs voted to merge and form a club called the Ouyen Football Club. The delegates from rival clubs debated Ouyen's request to join the competition for two hours before accepting it, and stipulating a recruiting radius for the club of twenty-five miles. The merged club would wear Ouyen's traditional colours of red and black. The demise of Ouyen Imperials prompted Hugh Carroll to go to Tiega, where he would play for many years.

The decision to form a single club in Ouyen was a forerunner to further change before the 1937 season. While club delegates voted to accept the entry of Lascelles into the Ouyen District league, the southern clubs – Tempy and Gorya – strongly resisted Walpeup's application to rejoin. After being readmitted, Walpeup moved a motion that the league, and not the clubs, should be responsible for chartering the special trains for matches. The motion was passed on the casting vote of the league president, W.C. Pianta.

On the application of Woomelang to join the Ouyen competition, only two clubs, Walpeup and Lascelles, were in favour. The remaining six clubs voted against it because they considered Woomelang to be too far south.

The final development in Ouyen on the eve of the 1937 season was the Ouyen Football Club's keenness to form a junior competition that would provide the opportunity for local footballers to play at a lesser level. Significantly, matches would be restricted to sixteen players for each team. Kiamal, having been in recession for one season, re-formed to play in the junior competition, while Bronzewing re-formed after two seasons in abeyance and Wymlet re-formed after almost a decade out of regular competition. Ouyen re-formed Ouyen Juniors, which would function as the club's reserves team.

Ouyen Juniors played in the same red and black colours as the senior club. Joe Williams was appointed as honorary coach of Ouyen Juniors, while Lou Mills was appointed as the gatekeeper and Tom Steward, a recruit from Werrimul, was named the football steward. Jim Fox was appointed boundary umpire on a stipend of five shillings a match. Jim Nulty was elected as president of the Ouyen Junior competition.

Ouyen Juniors defeated Kiamal in the junior competition's inaugural Grand Final, in 1937. Kiamal turned the tables the next year, defeating Ouyen Juniors in the Grand Final with a team that included three Munro brothers as well as members of the Jardine and Hickmott families. Although it was a junior premiership, Kiamal people were still proud to add it to their previous triumph, which had been earned in the Ouyen District competition sixteen years earlier.

The development of the junior competition did serve to fuel Ouyen's chances of success in the senior competition. In 1937, Ouyen and Gorya drew in the Grand Final in the Ouyen District league, 5.12 (42) each, but Ouyen went on to win the rematch. Ouyen then won further premierships in 1938 and 1940.

Ouyen's stars in this era included Jim Bolger, the brother of the Richmond premiership defender Martin Bolger. Jim had played in the Richmond reserves team for three seasons before moving to Ouyen in 1937 to work in the town's locomotive sheds. The main stars for Ouyen in the Grand Final rematch against Gorya in 1937 were rover Cyril Smith and ruckman Brownie Vallance, who both accepted invitations to try out with VFL clubs.

Smith tried out with Essendon. After failing to make the cut, he went to Sandringham, a club in the Victorian Football Association. He then rejected overtures from the Bendigo league clubs Sandhurst and Golden Square and returned to the Mallee. On his return he said he had not relished being in Melbourne with nothing to do. He would go down again only if he had a job to go to.

Brownie Vallance tried out with St Kilda before signing with the VFA club Brighton. Tiega's Ray Eldridge tried out with Essendon before returning home. George Archibald, who had played with Tempy and Gorya, tried out with St Kilda. He would eventually play senior football for Melbourne.

The North West Mallee league also expanded in this era of improved transport and financial upturn. Before the 1937 season, while the clubs around Ouyen were making decisions on their upheavals, the North West Mallee league delegates sprung a surprise when they accepted Murrayville and Danyo back into their competition, bringing the number of clubs to seven. The league's radius now extended from six miles west of Murrayville to six miles east of Torrita. Six clubs were given an exclusive two-mile radius around their towns. For Centrals, the radius was one mile around the grounds at Linga and Boinka. The league ruled that Murrayville could keep their maroon and gold colours, the same as Torrita, because their design included a wide vertical stripe down the middle of the guernsey, in the fashion of the panels worn by St Kilda and several clubs in the Bendigo league. Danyo would wear green and gold. Cowangie defeated Torrita in the first grand final in the competition's expanded format.

In the Ouyen District league, Tempy interrupted Ouyen's dominance when they defeated the Red and Blacks in the 1939 Grand Final. The triumph capped an extraordinary period for Tempy's champion player Ginger Robertson. After finishing second in the inaugural count for the Walker Cup in 1936, Robertson had won the past three cups for the best and fairest player in the competition, from 1937 to 1939. According to the *North West Express*, Robertson was fast and clever, and he had superlative judgement and marking ability.

Tempy celebrated its 1939 triumph with a premiership ball that was described in detail in the *North West Express.* Eric Burke hosted the event in his garage, while Jack Burke supplied the electric lighting. Two long tables were said to he laid most tastefully, with large poppies adding colour to the occasion. The feature piece of the evening was the premiership cake that was placed on the footballers' table. The icing on the cake, which was decorated by Gran McLean, featured a miniature ground replete with goalposts and a footballer wearing Tempy's colours of green and gold. Supper was described as excellent. "Judging from the disappearance of six turkeys, one ham and two sponges, one concludes that the partakers enjoyed themselves."

During the 1939 season, the people of Kiamal pooled their money to buy the Wagant hall, which was not being used. According to the club history notes of Ginger "Francis" Hickmott in the *North West Express*, Kiamal footballers Duncan Coleman and Dinny Wright were given the job of dismantling the hall and rebuilding it at a site that had been cleared of scrub and stumps by local people. According to Ginger Hickmott, Ken Blake laid fresh gravel and clay in the grounds of the hall. The hall itself was opened in April 1940 on a night on which the heavens opened. The revellers did not mind finding their cars bogged in the gravel and clay because the rain was overdue and a good season was now assured.

Tempy were strong again in 1941, but the tone of football in the region was more subdued. It was a difficult season for the Ouyen District league, with the people of the town and the farms divided on whether football should be played at all when so many of the nation's best young sportsmen were in Europe and the Middle East, fighting in the Second World War. In July 1941, a pall was cast over the competition when it was announced that three former Ouyen players, Jack Kenna, Brownie Vallance and Sandy McPherson, had paid the supreme sacrifice. Ouyen finished second last on the ladder. Kiamal, now back in the senior competition, finished below them. In a cheeky suggestion, Kiamal officials invited Ouyen members to join them at their wooden-spoon ball, which they were to hold in their revamped hall.

In 1941, Patchewollock rose into the top four for the first time since their premiership season of 1932, but their rise failed to ignite the cavalcade of excitement that had accompanied their campaign of a decade earlier. Tempy defeated Walpeup in the Ouyen District league Grand Final, with Ginger Robertson again the match-winner.

In the Pier Milan and District competition, Kulwin, in the finals for the first time in more than a decade, defeated Nandaly in their Grand Final at Nandaly. All competitions in the Mallee were then abandoned because of the war. Footballers played only the odd challenge match in what was described as a patriotic league.

The star of Kulwin's victory in 1941 was young follower Kevin Curran, who would go on to play senior football with Richmond. Hugh

Torney, meanwhile, would proceed into the ranks of Essendon greats after a decade of outstanding performances. In 1940, Torney won Essendon's best and fairest award and finished second in the count for the Brownlow Medal. In 1942, he was a member of the Dons' premiership team. He played for Victoria in three seasons. To this day, he remains the most decorated footballer to emerge from the Mallee.

10

Rubber Men

In May 1944, the Second World War was still being fought in Europe, North Africa and the Pacific, but the Allies were gaining confidence in their chances of victory, and Australia was beginning to see through the clouds of conflict. When it was announced that enough rubber had been released in Australia to provide for a restricted supply of bladders, the footballers of the Mallee were keen to buy new footballs and resume competition. The Ouyen District Football League was re-formed in May 1944 with four clubs: Kiamal, Tiega, Walpeup and Ouyen.

Alan Eldridge was busy at Ouyen in the first season back in competition. Eldridge served as the club's president and captain. In the 1944 Grand Final, he played at centre half-forward and was among the best players as Ouyen defeated Tiega on a day in late September that was described as more suited to cricket than football. The *North West Express* said Tiega were well served by thirty-six-year-old Hugh Carroll, "still playing brainy football after twenty years in the game", and the captain, Jack Healy, who played hard, vigorous football. Tiega turned the tables the following year, in 1945, and defeated Ouyen in the Grand Final to win their first premiership since their triumph sixteen years earlier, in the Walpeup and District competition's Grand Final in 1929.

South of Ouyen, four clubs – Gorya, Lascelles, Patchewollock and Tempy – comprised the Gorya and District Football League in 1945. The Ouyen District league hosted the Gorya and District league in an interleague match late in the season. The Gorya league was too strong, and won by twelve goals. Ginger Robertson and A.J. Allen each kicked four goals for the victors.

After the war had finished with victory to the Allies in late 1945, Australia as a nation took a little while to find its feet, but then enjoyed a surge in confidence and expansion that continued into the next decade. In Melbourne, General Motors Holden heralded a period of rapid growth in industry when, in 1948, the company made the first all-Australian motor vehicle, the Holden FX. The price set for each vehicle was high; at $733, it was the equivalent of almost two years of wages for the average worker. But demand was so strong that GMH could barely keep up with demand. In rural Australia, commodity prices were strong. According to the Australian Bureau of statistics, the price for wool rose by a factor of ten during the five years after the war, reaching its zenith in 1950 and 1951, when demand was at its peak because of the American need for wool during the Korean War. In this period, the price for wool was 144 pence for pound, which is more than ten times the price of wool in today's currency. This era was short-lived, and prices resumed more reasonable levels during the course of the decade, but some sheep farmers made a handsome living in this period. The price of wheat also rose, although not as extravagantly as the price of wool.

In the years after the war, the use of tractors surged. With improved machinery, farmers continued to buy out their neighbours, and families continued to move off the land and into the city to work in accountancy firms, construction firms and factories.

In the second Census, in 1921, Victoria's population was segmented into metropolitan, provincial and rural populations, with the provincial population defined as those in towns with a population of more than 1000. In 1921, Victoria's population was 1,531,280. In percentage terms, the breakdown was: metropolitan (50), provincial (12) and rural (38). By the time of Australia's fourth Census, in 1947, Victoria's population had risen by half a million, to 2,055,252, but almost the entire rise in population could be attributed to the surge towards the city. In percentage terms, the breakdown of Victoria's population in 1947 was: metropolitan (60), provincial (11) and rural (29). Essentially, Melbourne's proportion of the state's population had risen by 10 per cent in the previous twenty-six years, while the rural population had declined by 10 per cent. That trend would only gather pace.

Although small, there was a rise in overall population in country Victoria in the years after the war, and everyone benefited from the healthy commodity prices. In country footy, clubs and competitions jostled around for a few years before settling into a pattern of relative stability, at least when compared to the volatility of the era between the two world wars. In the district south of Ouyen, footy settled into three competitions, the Southern Mallee league, the Tyrrell league and the Nandaly-Bolton league. Around Ouyen itself, there were two competitions, the North West Mallee league and the Ouyen District league.

In 1946, the first year after the war had ended, both the North West Mallee league and the Ouyen District league picked up from the era before the war and entered the season with seven clubs. The Ouyen Football Club defeated Gorya in the 1946 Grand Final in Ouyen, while Underbool defeated Danyo in their competition's decider in Tutye. Bernie Brown, the son of the leading Underbool official Chris Brown, played well in the ruck for Underbool.

In this era, with so many more people now owning cars, competitions developed a taste for testing themselves against neighboring competitions in interleague games. The Ouyen District league struggled to defeat the Southern Mallee league in this era, with the Southern Mallee league winning their matches in successive seasons in 1947 and 1948, but the Ouyen District league fared better against the North Central league.

According to the structure of the VCFL, there could be only one major league in each district. The North Central league was nominally the major league in the North Central District. By definition, the Ouyen District league was a minor league. Yet the Ouyen District league won three of its four matches against the North Central league in the four seasons from 1946 to 1949. While the North Central league played in green and red guernseys, the Ouyen District league played in the red and black guernseys of the Ouyen Football Club. Henry "Ginger" Robertson, the Tempy champion, was the captain of the Ouyen District team in all four games. After the North Central league had won their match at St Arnaud in 1948, the Ouyen District league hosted the Northern Central league in Ouyen the following year.

In 1949, the Ouyen District league defeated their fancied visitors by twenty points in a match the *North West Express* described as one of the best seen on the Ouyen ground for many years. Ginger Robertson, who was now thirty-four years of age, kicked seven goals and received the umpire's nomination for best on ground. Cyril Smith, the Ouyen star, was unbeatable in the centre. The Patchewollock ruckman Merv Young, the son of former Patchewollock player Neil Young, was outstanding in the ruck.

Among the North Central players, Laen-Litchfield's Allan Dunstan played in defence. In his memoirs, Dunstan would later recall the impact that the match in Ouyen had on his opinion of Mallee football. Dunstan would go on to become the president of the North Central league, the North Central District councillor on the VCFL board and the president of the VCFL itself. After first catching a glimpse of Merv Young in this match, he would go on to become firm friends with Young during the Patchewollock man's time as a football administrator in the Mallee. The connection between Allan Dunstan and Merv Young, which began with the 1949 interleague match in Ouyen, would have a major impact on Mallee football.

At the end of the 1949 season, Ginger Robertson was captain of the Tempy team that defeated Patchewollock in the Ouyen District league Grand Final. Patchewollock's Les Auslebrook won the Fayrefield hat that was donated by Joe Walsh, the Ouyen stalwart, after being adjudged the most efficient player on the ground. Auslebrook was a leading player for several years. Before the 1951 season, he was appointed to be the captain-coach at Patchewollock on £4 a week.

It was in this era that the Ouyen Recreation Reserve was renamed. On the King's Birthday long weekend in June 1948, immediately after the running of the Ouyen Gift, the federal member for the Mallee electorate, Winton Turnbull, declared that the reserve would now be called Blackburn Park, in honour of the memory of the late Jim Blackburn, the state rivers engineer "whose energy and vision did much to make the park what it is today".

It was also in 1948 that the Ouyen District Football League revived the award for the best and fairest player in the competition. After accepting an offer from the Williamson brothers of £5 to be put towards an annual trophy, Ouyen District league officials agreed to run the award along the lines of the Brownlow Medal in the VFL, with field umpires awarding 3-2-1 votes to three players after every game.

The Patchewollock wingman Don Lynch won the inaugural vote count to decide the best and fairest player in the competition, ahead of Ian Johnston of Ouyen. Lou Goudie, the Ouyen District league president, presented the Williamson brothers' trophy to Lynch at half-time in the 1948 Grand Final.

Two players won the award twice each over the next four years, with the Gorya captain-coach Jim Jones winning in 1949 and 1951 and Kiamal's prodigious talent Frank Nicol winning in 1950 and 1952..

Jones, who had returned to Gorya from Carlton, defeated the Tempy pair Ginger Robertson and Phil Burns in the 1949 vote count despite missing the opening few rounds of the season. The *North West Express* described Jones as "cool and clever, whether forward or back, and always scrupulously fair".

According to the 1985 newspaper notes on the Kiamal footy club's history, Frank "Nicko" Nicol and his friend Laurie "Flipper" Donald joined the Magpies before the 1950 season, having left the city to try their hand at country life. The pair bought a truck in which they carted wheat during harvest time and transported stumps to the train line the rest of the year. They set up camp in an abandoned house. Nicko later married a local girl. By the time he returned to the city after six seasons with Kiamal, he had won five club best and fairest awards, two league awards and one goalkicking award, which he picked up after booting more than thirty goals in a match against Mittyack.

Kiamal's appointment of coaches in this era lends an idea of the background of many coaches in and around Ouyen. In 1948, Kiamal appointed Jack Moylan, a former Ballarat league player, as the captain-coach on an unspecified stipend. Some players left the club because they did not believe that any player should be paid. Moylan, according to Francis "Ginger" Hickmott in his notes on the club in the *North West Express*, kicked 14.1 in one match and 1.14 in another. In the interleague game against the North Central league, Moylan thrilled the crowd by taking a mark near the centre and kicking a goal. In 1949, Rube Matthews was appointed coach after moving to the area to work for his uncle, Percy Beaumont. In 1950, the ruckman Jumbo Mills, a dual premiership player with Ouyen, was appointed coach in recognition of his playing credentials. In 1951, Merv Kenny was appointed for two years after moving to Ouyen to be the assistant shire engineer. Merv Candy (1953) was appointed after being transferred to Ouyen through his job as a train examiner for the railways department. Jim Jones (1955), the former Carlton player who was originally from Gorya, came out of retirement to play for Kiamal, and marked everything at full-back.

A star emerged in the competition when the rangy nineteen-year-old Ron McDonald moved to Ouyen in 1952 through his work in a bank. McDonald had played in a premiership the previous season at Willaura, which is out of Ararat. In his first season with the Ouyen Football Club, he was described in the newspaper as a stripling full-forward. He kicked eleven goals in a match against Walpeup and a reported tally of 2.13 in a match against Kiamal. The next season, in 1953, McDonald played in the ruck and finished second in the league best and fairest award, behind Gordon Casey of Gorya. According to a later article in the *North West Express*, McDonald would have won the award had he not been forced to miss two matches because of military training.

McDonald played the next season with Harrow in the Western District, and six games on permit with Coleraine, before heading down to Richmond in 1955. He made his senior VFL debut in the second round of his first season, and went on to play at centre half-forward and centre half-back for several years. He was front-page news in the *North West Express* when he made the Victorian team in 1958.

The newspaper heralded the coming of another young star during the finals series in the Ouyen District league in 1954. After reporting that Ginger Robertson had passed the ball to his son Keith, who kicked a goal, the reporter mused on how long it had been since there had been a father and son in the same team in a semi-final in the Mallee. During that finals series, Ginger Robertson was thirty-nine years of age, while Keith was fifteen. The Robertson dynasty was under way.

At the conclusion of the following season, in 1955, Keith Robertson was adjudged best on ground in the Grand Final at Blackburn Park. He thought little of it when Collingwood invited him down to try out. At the end of the 1956 season, Keith was still only seventeen years of age when he won Tempy's club best and fairest award and he finished second in the count for the league best and fairest award, behind Ken McLean of Gorya. Keith Robertson finished school at the end of that year.

Early the next year, in 1957, the speedster headed down to Melbourne to study teaching. After moving into a hostel for country students, Keith joined a friend from the hostel who was going to Arden Street to train with North Melbourne. While Keith was watching the session, a North Melbourne official asked whether he could play. Keith was invited to join in training. Then he was invited to have a run in the practice matches. After just one month at his new footy home, Keith Robertson made his senior VFL debut in the opening round of the 1957 season.

Keith Robertson showed promise during his handful of senior games in his first season, but early in the 1958 season he was tired of the city and he wanted to play at home. For almost two seasons, in 1958 and 1959, he travelled back to Tempy every weekend to play alongside his father and his brothers Terry and Allan. Terry was a defender, while Allan, like his father, had pace and craft and the ability to balance the ball in his fingertips.

After going back to North Melbourne in 1960, Keith Robertson created an impression with his sizzling pace and sure hands. In 1962, he played two games for Victoria. At the end of the season, he finished second in the club's best and fairest count and was awarded a frypan. He played at Arden Street for one more year, in 1963, after which he left the city, aged twenty-four, to return to the Mallee. He took up a teaching post at Hopetoun, where he played for the Hopetoun footy club and won a best and fairest medal in the Southern Mallee league. After two years in Hopetoun, Keith and his family moved to Mildura, where he retired as a footballer and concentrated on calling games on local radio. He and his family later moved to Wangaratta after Keith accepted a job at Wangaratta High. The family settled in Victoria's North East. In 2018, Keith revealed the perambulations of his career during an interview with the writer Kevin Hill as part of Kevin's renowned series on sportsmen in Wangaratta.

11

The Good Times

After the Second World War, there was a period of relative calm in the Ouyen District league, and officials began to cast a wider gaze. Before the 1951 season, they introduced what they described as a second-eighteen competition. Reserves matches would be played as a curtain-raiser to senior matches. Any player who played six games in the seniors was ineligible to play in reserves finals.

In the same season, Tiega took the large step of moving the club's home base from its ground in a paddock just off the Mallee Highway, to the west of Ouyen, into Blackburn Park in Ouyen itself. Under the ground-sharing arrangement with the Ouyen footy club, the clubs would train on alternate nights, with Tiega training on Monday and Wednesday nights and Ouyen on Tuesday and Thursday nights. Tiega officials said they made the move in an attempt to increase membership and to enable a more social atmosphere.

The next season, in 1952, Tiega changed their jumpers from the old South Melbourne strip of white with a red sash to red jumpers with a white "V". They changed from predominantly white jumpers to predominantly red jumpers because, according to the club's history, the darker jumpers would be easier to clean under Mallee conditions. Significantly, St Joseph's Catholic Primary School was opened in 1952. The school would prove a fulcrum for many Tiega families.

Before the 1953 season, there was a realignment of clubs and competitions south of Ouyen when the Nandaly-Bolton competition folded. While most clubs moved into the newly formed Manangatang Football League, the Nandaly footy club headed farther south, into the Tyrrell league, while Mittyack headed north to join the Ouyen District league. The addition of Mittyack to the Ouyen competition brought the number of clubs to eight, eliminating the need for a bye, but the even fixture was short-lived. Mittyack folded after just two years in the Ouyen competition. Within a few years, three of their rivals from the early part of the decade, Annuello, Kooloonong and Kulwin, would also fold, as well as the Manangatang league itself, as the population continued to drain from the Mallee and force resultant challenges on country footy. The Kiamal Football Club benefited greatly when the Pohlner brothers, Don and Ray, joined the Magpies after Kulwin had folded. Don Pohlner would become one of the greats of the competition.

Officials from the Ouyen District league again revealed their widening vision when they renamed their competition the Mallee Football League in 1955. The decision was a shame for Ouyen stalwarts, because the name of their town would never again feature as the hub of a competition, but it acknowledged the reality of the broader fields in country footy, and it lent the opportunity to feature one of the nation's strongest regional identities in the title.

Before the 1955 season, the first season of the renamed competition, the Ouyen Football Club appointed the former Sandhurst leader Noel Evans as coach on £12 a week, the highest figure paid to a coach in the league's history. Before the 1955 Grand Final, the competition's long-serving official Lou Goudie presented the competition's two major awards, the awards for the best and fairest player and the leading goalkicker, to their recipients before the match. To the Ouyen centreman Ron Gregg, he presented a barometer that had been donated by the Williamson brothers for the best and fairest player. To Ginger Robertson, he presented a silver tray that had been donated by Joe Walsh, and "suitably inscribed" by the draper himself, for being the leading goalkicker.

After the match, the umpire adjudged Ginger Robertson's son Keith as the best player on the ground despite the fact that he had played in the losing team. Ouyen defeated Tempy by eight points in the 1955 Grand Final. Patchewollock won the next two premierships, in 1956 and 1957, during their run of ten grand finals in eleven seasons.

In the North West Mallee league, Underbool won the 1955 Grand Final in the final match before the competition began to fall apart. Torrita and Centrals folded in successive seasons. Murrayville applied for entry into the Lameroo and District league before the 1956 season, only to be rejected by the South Australian clubs because they believed Murrayville was too far away. When Murrayville again tried in vain to move into the Lameroo league before the 1957 season, Underbool took their cue to try to leave the North West Mallee competition. They applied for entry into the Mallee league, and were accepted. The North West Mallee league was down to four clubs, while the Mallee league was back up to eight clubs.

The four clubs left in the North West Mallee league – Murrayville, Danyo, Imperials and Veterans, a team for players older than thirty-five years of age – played on for another two seasons, in 1957 and 1958, before folding. With no football competition in the Murrayville region in 1959, some players joined clubs over the border in Pinnaroo while others joined Underbool. In 1960, the former clubs around Murrayville banded together to form one club, the United Football Club. The new club, based in Murrayville, entered the Mallee league under the coaching of Joe Morrison, a farmer from Boinka, whose brothers Don and Lance also joined. The catchment of the Mallee league now stretched from Murrayville in the west to Ouyen in the east, just like the old "down the line" competition forty years earlier.

In 1960, Jack "Curly" Burns, a farmer from Tempy who trained racehorses in the paddock behind his home, entered his sixth season as the president of the Mallee league. Norm D'Arcy, the league secretary, was assisted by Peter Williams. In the playing ranks, Kevin Cramp from

Gorya won the medal for the best and fairest player in the competition, ahead of Alan Robertson, the teenager from Tempy.

While several players returned from the Pinnaroo area to play for United, the club based in Murrayville, in 1960, the Bulldogs won only one game, the opening game of the season, against Tempy. In 1960, Walpeup emerged to win their first premiership in thirty-nine years, since their victory in the inaugural Grand Final in the down-the-line competition in 1921. The Walpeup team in 1960 included Les Latta, aged forty, at half-back, Ken McSwain in the ruck and members of the Woodall family whose forebears had played with distinction in the region a generation earlier. Ron Gregg played in the centre in Walpeup's breakthrough team. The next year, in 1961, Gregg headed back to the Ouyen Football Club, where he won another league medal and led the Red and Blacks to another premiership.

In 1961, Ouyen defeated Tiega in the Grand Final in a match that proved to be the final gasp for the old order. Ouyen would struggle to contend in coming years, as would Tempy, Gorya and Patchewollock, while the clubs from Murrayville and Tiega emerged to replace them at the top of the ladder.

In 1961, half a dozen players from the Murrayville region returned from Underbool to play for United, the club based in Murrayville, and the Bulldogs made the finals. United went on to win the next two premierships, in 1962 and 1963, with a team that featured an array of talented players, but none quite so talented as a teenaged star called Richard Kalms. In 1962, Kalms, known to all as Richie, was sixteen years of age when he played the season at centre half-back. At three-quarter time in the Grand Final against Tiega, he was moved to centre half-forward. Kalms kicked a couple of goals in the final quarter, and he remained at centre half-forward for the rest of his career with his home club.

Before the 1963 season, Kalms was seventeen years of age when he accepted an invitation to try out with Essendon. The club bought him a train ticket and gave him instructions to look out for a man in grey at the information booth at the Spencer Street Station. Kalms had never been to Melbourne, and had no family there. He boarded the train from Murrayville to Ouyen at 8 o'clock in the evening. At 11 o'clock, he boarded the train from Ouyen to Melbourne. Just after 7 o'clock the next morning, he made his way to the information booth at Spencer Street, where the man in grey introduced himself and drove him to a pub owned by the Essendon coach, John Coleman. Kalms was one of four or five country recruits who stayed in Coleman's pub while they trained and played and tried to make their way on to the club's senior list.

Kalms played at centre half-back in two practice matches and burned. But after a fortnight alone in the city, he decided it was not for him. He returned home to Murrayville and resumed working on farms and playing for his home club. After United's victory in the Mallee league Grand Final in 1963, Kalms again accepted an invitation from Essendon to try out. In early 1964, he played in another two practice matches with the Bombers, and once again he showcased his strength and talent with blistering performances at centre half-back. At six-foot-two, or 188 centimetres on the metric sale, with the ability to take high marks and kick the ball a country mile, the young Kalms appeared to have the tools to make the grade in the VFL, but he did not like his accommodation with a grieving widow in Essendon, nor life in the city in general, so again he returned home to work on the land and play with his home club. In 1964, Kalms was only eighteen years of age when he won his first medal for the best and fairest player in the Mallee league.

In 1961, Tiega began their extraordinary sequence of playing in fourteen grand finals in succession, establishing the greatest dynasty in Mallee football. Most Tiega players were from the families who had settled around Tiega and Galah, just to the west of Ouyen, but since the club had shifted into town in 1951 it had started to attract bank workers and schoolteachers. Significantly, the best Tiega players were from large families. There were members of the Morrish, Shaddock, Gibbins, Sleep and O'Callaghan families in every grand final team.

After losing three grand finals in succession, to Ouyen once and the club from Murrayville twice, Tiega broke through in 1964 when they defeated Kiamal in the Grand Final by twenty-three points. The best players for Tiega included Barry Phelan, who was the coach, defenders

Harry Shaddock and Joe Pengelly, and fifteen-year-old Denis O'Callaghan. Andy Bennett kicked three goals, including two in the last quarter that sealed the match. Vern Morrish, the son of Ray Morrish, was cool in attack and also kicked three goals. Ray Morrish had played in the club's premiership team in the Walpeup and District competition thirty-five years earlier, in 1929. Vern's cousin Lindsay Morrish was best on ground in the 1964 Grand Final. Lindsay Morrish, a rugged defender, would go on to play in every one of Tiega's fourteen grand finals in a row – the only player to do so.

This era was also significant because there was a distinct changing of the guard. It heralded the emergence of Richie Kalms just as his predecessor as the best player in the Mallee, Henry "Ginger" Robertson, was winding down his own career. Ginger was in his late forties when he retired in 1963 or 1964, having played more than three decades of senior football. It is unknown just how many games Ginger played, but over the course of more than thirty football seasons, each featuring an average of fifteen games plus finals, it seems reasonable to say that Ginger played in 500 senior matches – all with one club, Tempy. It is highly likely that his tally is the state record for senior games.

Unfortunately, the club, like Ginger, could no longer go on. A few days after the 1964 Mallee league Grand Final, fifty-eight members of the Tempy and Gorya football clubs met in the Tempy hall to vote on a proposed merger. Gavin Burns, a star player with Tempy, missed the meeting because of a car accident. Noel Phipps was in Geelong because his father had died. According to the *North West Express*, those present voted unanimously to form the first merged club in the district since Ouyen Rovers and Ouyen Imperials had combined forces almost thirty years earlier. The new club, to be called Tempy-Gorya, would wear St Kilda's red, black and white panels. It would play four games a year at Tempy and three at Speed. L.V. Shean was announced as the first president.

The Saints entered their first season as a merged club under the coaching of Trevor Cox, who had been an outstanding player with Woomelang-Lascelles. Kevin Pickering from Mildura coached Ouyen in 1965, while Rex Kent, a policeman, was in charge of the club at

Murrayville. The other coaches in the Mallee league that season were Barry Phelan (Tiega), Laurie Kalms (Kiamal), Peter Donovan (Walpeup), Arthur Huggard (Underbool) and Ray Lanyon (Patchewollock). Patche was the only club to enter the 1965 season without a seconds team. Ginger Robertson accepted a role as a selector for the interleague match against the Lameroo and District league.

At the end of the 1965 home and away rounds, Don Pohlner, the tough and resolute centreman from Kiamal, won the league medal on countback from Ken Parker from Murrayville. Richie Kalms, also from Murrayville, finished just behind them.

Tempy-Gorya, the newly merged club, won the Grand Final in 1965, then won again the following season. In 1966, the umpire adjudged Alan Robertson, the third son of Ginger Robertson, to be best on ground in the Grand Final after another tantalising performance in the centre. Gordon Casey Junior, the son of the Gorya legend Gordon Casey, kicked seven goals for the victors. Casey was only sixteen years of age. The best player for Tiega, half-forward Denis O'Callaghan, was seventeen years of age. A scout from Carlton who had gone to the match in Ouyen to cast his eye over Casey came away impressed by both Casey and O'Callaghan. Both were invited down to Princes Park. Casey would sign with the Blues, but O'Callaghan would sign with Collingwood.

In 1966, the Mallee league introduced a junior competition for under-sixteen players. A new generation of stars was coming through.

12

Young and Keen

As a footballer, Merv Young was a Patchewollock ruckman who gained the respect of teammates and opponents throughout the Mallee. He was tall and strong, and he was always fair. He led the club for many years as captain. He was a large part of the reason that Patchewollock played in ten grand finals in the eleven seasons from 1949 to 1959.

After retirement, Young served Patchewollock as club president. But it was in his later role as president of the Mallee Football League that he truly became a giant of Mallee football. Part of his legacy was the leading role he played in his competition's interleague success.

Early in 1968, Young was in his first year as the president of the Mallee league when he and the league secretary, Ken Robson, headed down to Melbourne to attend what would be one of the most controversial meetings in the history of the state's ruling body of country football, the Victorian Country Football League. Since the VCFL's inception in 1927 as a sub-committee of the major body, the VFL, the country body had been largely compliant to the wishes of the senior body. But that threatened to change in 1968 when the country leagues declared they were tired of VFL clubs acting according to one set of rules while country leagues and clubs were being expected to act according to another. Many country leagues were angry over being forced to accept the VFL's country zoning laws against their wishes. For Merv Young, a source of disquiet was the VFL's decision to grant Fitzroy a permit to allow Russell Crow to play for the club at Brunswick Street despite the fact that Crow's country club, Warracknabeal, had not cleared him. Crow had family links at Linga, just out of Underbool, and was well known throughout the Mallee. The tug of war over Crow did not sit well with football officials in the Wimmera or the Mallee.

A total of seventy-five delegates represented their country competitions at the meeting in Melbourne in 1968. The delegates voted 44-31 to break away from the parent body, the VFL. But as it happened, the country body did not go through with the wishes of the majority of its members. It remained affiliated with the VFL, and would fight to overturn country zoning until it became apparent that most country leagues had come to like the direct links with VFL clubs at Punt Road, Windy Hill and Victoria Park.

In this atmosphere of questioning the old order, Merv Young and his fellow president from the North Central Football League, Allan Dunstan, hatched a plan that would subvert the order within the ranks of country football, and bring country footy to the notice of fans throughout the wider footy world.

The VCFL's major vehicle for promotion in this era was the country football championships, which effectively was a rolling carnival of inter-league matches to decide the strongest country football competition.

When the VCFL was created in 1927, it adopted a structure of eight districts. The delegate for each district was called a district councillor. Two years later, in 1929, it created its ninth district, which was the North Central District. Other districts would be formed in coming years, including the Riverina and Central Gippsland districts.

The VCFL held its first country football championship over one weekend in Ballarat in 1954. Ovens and Murray were the inaugural winners. For the next five years, country football's ruling body tried several formats for its championships, none of which worked as well as hoped. It also continued to create new districts. By the end of the decade, the

VCFL consisted of fifteen districts including the Sunraysia and Northern districts. The Northern District was based around clubs from Gunbower to Cohuna and Kerang.

In 1961, the VCFL revamped its country championships to go over two seasons. In the first season, held in odd years, each district would compete in a knockout series of matches in an attempt to win their zone. In the second season, held in even years, the winners of the four zones would be paired off into semi-finals. The winners of the two semi-finals would meet in the final.

Each district consisted of one major league plus several minor leagues. Each district was entitled to select players from throughout its district, but it was unknown for any district to look beyond its major league when selecting its interleague team. Every district competed under the name of its major league.

The Wimmera and Bendigo leagues met in the first final under the revamped system, at the Horsham City Oval in 1962. At the time, Horsham was a town with a population of 9500. With excitement bubbling throughout country Victoria over the match to determine the strongest league, a crowd of 13,200 – almost 4000 more than the population of Horsham – saw the Bendigo league win the match and come away with the title. The South West District league, based along the south-west railway line in the Riverina, won the title in 1964, and the Hampden league won in 1966. Crowds flocked to ovals throughout the country to see their district's finest players pit themselves against exotic opposition at venues where, in many places, you could still nose your car up against the fence.

The North Central league fared poorly in the country championships during this period. In 1967, the situation became dire for the competition based around Donald, Birchip and Charlton when the Sunraysia league defeated the North Central league by thirteen goals in their first-round match at St Arnaud. The next year, in 1968, the Northern District league inflicted a heavy defeat on the North Central league during an interleague challenge match at Cohuna. In the final of the country championships in 1968, the Ovens and Murray league defeated the Wimmera league before a crowd of 10,000 at the Horsham City Oval. Allan Dunstan, as the president of the North Central league, decided to do something about his competition's poor performances in interleague matches.

Dunstan and Merv Young, the Mallee league president, had known of each other's deeds since they were on opposing teams in the interleague match between the Ouyen District league and the North Central league in Ouyen in 1949. Young was the ruckman in the Ouyen District team that had given Dunstan such a strong opinion of Mallee football. In 1968, after the North Central league's loss to the Northern District league in Cohuna, Dunstan approached Merv Young about the prospect of North Central selectors being able to choose from the pool of talent in the Mallee. In a canny offer, Dunstan offered the Mallee league 50 per cent of gate-takings and 50 per cent of prizemoney no matter how many Mallee league players were selected. Young accepted with enthusiasm.

The North Central coach in 1969 was Bill McGrath, the former South Melbourne player who had retuned to the Wimmera. When McGrath and his selectors chose five Mallee players in their team for the opening round of the 1969 country championships, the *North West Express* described it as a great honour for the Mallee players and their region.

The match – the Northern District league versus the North Central league – was to be held in Cohuna, on the oval where the representative teams from the two competitions had met the previous season, with the result going in the Northern District league's favour. In 1969, the North Central league selectors augmented their team to play the Northern District league with two players from the club now known officially as Murrayville, Garry Sporn and Richie Kalms, as well as Walpeup key forward Barry Gniel and the O'Callghan brothers from Tiega, Denis and Barney.

Sporn was a tall and skinny ruckman with long arms and the ability to take a mark. According to reports, he gave the opposition ruckmen a lesson in tap work. Kalms kicked the ball out of sight on the vast expanses of Cohuna, which was the largest oval in Victoria, while Barry Gniel was switched to full-forward and kicked seven goals. Barney O'Callaghan did not get a run, but the addition of the Mallee players proved a winning move. The Northern Central league defeated the host league by twenty-three points, 16.16 (112) to 13.11 (89). The five Mallee league players returned to their clubs as heroes.

Interest among Mallee people was so high before the second-round match, against the Mid-Murray league, that Mallee league officials postponed their scheduled round of matches so that supporters could head down to St Arnaud for the interleague game. The North Central league selectors were unable to choose Denis O'Callaghan, who had returned to Collingwood. In his place, they chose Milo Dalla Santa, a ruck-rover who had moved from Red Cliffs to Murrayville before the season to work on a farm. In total, there were three Murrayville players in the North Central team, and five players from the Mallee.

The match was held at Lord Nelson Park in St Arnaud, on the ground inside the trotting track. According to the *North West Express*, Sporn's palming of the ball was magnificent, while Richie Kalms unloaded a drop-kick that "must have travelled eighty yards". Gniel and Dalla Santa did "many useful things", while Barney O'Callaghan won many kicks when he came on to the ground. The North Central league defeated the Mid-Murray league by more than five goals. For the first time, the North Central league was through to the semi-finals to be played the following season.

A month later, in the lead-up to the final round of the 1969 season in the Mallee league, Tiega's Mick McKay was leading the goalkicking table ahead of Murrayville centre half-forward Richie Kalms. Murrayville were to play Patchewollock, who had not won a game for the season. At three-quarter time of the last game, Kalms had nine goals to his credit. In the last quarter, his teammates peppered him with passes. Kalms kicked ten goals in the final quarter to bring his tally to nineteen for the match and ninety-two for the season. Mick McKay, as it happened, kicked seven goals in the final game to finish on eighty-nine for the season. Kalms had pipped him for the goalkicking award, and he won his second medal for the best and fairest player in the competition.

In the Second Semi-final in 1969, Richie Kalms kicked eight goals to lead his team to victory over Tiega by thirteen goals. In the Grand Final, Richie kicked another six goals, bringing his tally to 106 for the season. His team, however, stumbled. In one of the great turnarounds,

Tiega clawed their way to victory over Murrayville in the 1969 Grand Final by five points. Barney O'Callaghan, his confidence sky high after his interleague selection, kicked five goals for Tiega and was best on ground.

On the sidelines, Mallee league supporters were abuzz with talk of entering a team from the region in a major league. The Mallee players were doing so well in interleague games that it made sense to explore a higher level of weekly footy. For some, it made sense to enter the Ouyen Football Club, the Mallee's central club, in the closest major league, which was the Sunraysia league.

Amid the hubbub over interleague success, the population of footballers in the Mallee continued to decline. The closure of the school at Linga, outside Underbool, was one indication of the departure of families from farming districts, but the starkest indication in football terms was Patchewollock's announcement in 1970 that the club was unable to field seniors and reserves teams. Instead, it could field only an under-sixteen team. Under the leadership of a Patchewollock man, Merv Young, the Mallee league's season got under way in 1970 with eight teams in the senior division, rather than nine, for the first time in a decade.

In the semi-finals of the country championships in 1970, the North Central league was pitted against the Hampden league at St Arnaud. Four Mallee players made the final team: Garry Sporn and Richie Kalms from Murrayville, Barney O'Callaghan from Tiega and Ron Smith from Kiamal. Walpeup champion Barry Gniel was selected, but injured himself at training on the Thursday night before the match. Alan Robertson, the artful Tempy-Gorya star, was an emergency.

According to the *North West Express*, Ron Smith scouted cleverly, while Sporn won his duel in the ruck. O'Callaghan came into the match in the second half, but it was Richie Kalms who shone the brightest. Kalms was best on ground. The North Central league, however, lost to the Hampden league by two points, 13.12 (90) to 12.16 (88). A few weeks later, the Hampden league outpointed the Ovens and Murray league in the 1970 final of the country championships at Warrnambool.

At the end of the 1970 season, Richie Kalms won his third Mallee league medal but again his team suffered defeat in the Grand Final. Tiega defeated Murrayville by almost eight goals. Barney O'Callaghan, with four goals, was again best on ground. Bill Morrish kicked five. Once more, there was talk on the sidelines about entering a Mallee club in the Sunraysia league. On the eve of the next season, in 1971, the Mallee league secretary, Ken Robson, used his newspaper column to hose down talk of a Sunraysia venture.

Before the 1971 season, the Murrayville ruckman Garry Sporn was lost to Mallee football. After resisting invitations to try out in the VFL, he was twenty-six years of age when he accepted North Adelaide's invitation to play in the South Australian National Football League. Sporn made the South Australian state squad in his first season, and he went on to play in three premierships in his first three seasons with the Roosters.

Back in the Mallee, a newly merged club entered the Mallee league in 1971, a club that would become known throughout Victoria because of the length and lyrical quality of its name. The merger of Tempy-Gorya and Patchewollock to form Tempy-Gorya-Patchewollock took shape under the coaching of John White, a former Ouyen defender, who midway through the 1971 season was included in defence in the North Central interleague team, along with his TGP teammate Alan Robertson, as well as the Underbool ruckman Chris Brown and the Tiega pair Barney O'Callaghan and Harry Shaddock.

In 1971, the bubble burst for the North Central league when they lost their opening-round match in the country championships to the Sunraysia league in Mildura. Not wanting to wait until the next championships in two years' time for their next match, North Central agreed to play against the Wimmera league at Warracknabeal in a challenge match halfway through the 1972 season. Alan Robertson played at half-forward and starred. In the newspaper report, it was said that Robertson dazzled spectators and opponents alike with his uncanny ball control and perfect disposal. Frank Tuck, the North Central coach, said Robertson's goal to seal the match in the last quarter was the best goal he had seen.

John White, the coach of Tempy-Gorya-Patchewollock, was rarely beaten at half-back. Walpeup's Bob Latta, the son of Les Latta, played well in the centre, while Chris Brown was a tower of strength, and took several strong marks. The North Central league defeated the Wimmera league by seven points. A few weeks later, the Bendigo league became the country champions of 1972 when they defeated the Murray league in the final at Cobram.

In 1973, officials in north-west Victoria agreed to create an inter-league bonanza on the day of their opening round of the country championships. The North Central league was to host the Mid-Murray league at Donald. To add spice to an already tasty encounter, the Mallee and Tyrrell leagues agreed to play against each other in a curtain-raiser.

In the curtain-raiser, Greg Robertson, the fourth son of Ginger Robertson, dominated in the centre for the Mallee league, while the Tiega big man Kevin Sleep was strong in the ruck. Don Pohlner, the Kiamal leader and the Mallee league captain, ploughed through packs, while his Kiamal teammate Frank O'Callaghan was in everything. Tiega's Des Healy bustled about when moved on to the ball. The Mallee league defeated the Tyrrell league by ten points.

In the main game, Bob Latta was best on ground while the rangy Underbool teenager Max Crow was named among the best players after the North Central league defeated the Mid-Murray league by five goals. Crow, a seventeen-year-old with the height of a ruckman and the stride of a wingman, looked an enticing prospect for VFL scouts. Essendon began working on him to leave the Mallee for Windy Hill under the country zoning laws.

Officials from the north-west of Victoria organised another interleague bonanza for the day of the second round of the championships. The Sunraysia league was to host the North Central league at the No.1 Oval at the Mildura showgrounds. The appeal for the hosts was the enormous contingent of supporters that was in the habit of accompanying the North Central league team to their games. In the newspapers, it was estimated that the North Central league had the most supporters of any team in the country championships. Certainly, they had the most fervent. Friendships were forged among fans from the East Wimmera and Mallee regions as they watched their team from the state's least populous area corner take on larger competitions.

Mallee officials agreed to field a team for a curtain-raiser in Mildura. Effectively, a second eighteen from the Sunraysia league would play a team from the Mallee league that would be without the competition's top five players. The day before the two showdowns, an article was published in a Melbourne newspaper which suggested that the second Sunraysia team was about to take on a bunch of hicks. Suitably incensed, the Mallee league players began their match against their Sunraysia opponents in the curtain-raiser with frightening force. Des Healy, the Tiega ruck-rover, bowled over a series of rivals in his pursuit of the ball, leaving Sunraysia players lying on the ground. Greg Robertson and Don Pohlner were again stars in the middle. Kevin Sleep won in the ruck, while the Morrish brothers, Lindsay and Bill, did their bit after coming off the bench. The Mallee players got over their rivals from citrus country to win by eight points.

The next morning, players and officials from the Mallee team that defeated the Sunraysia league gathered at Merv Young's farm house near Patchewollock for a team photo. A few players failed to turn up, having been unable to rise from their night of celebrations, while Walter "Spot Munro", the Kiamal defender, was unavailable because he had to play golf in Ouyen.

In the main game at the Mildura showgrounds, the five Mallee players made strong contributions for the North Central league. Bob Latta was a driving force in the centre, while Alan Robertson was creative in the first half. John White was tireless at half-back, while Max Crow again showed his marking ability in attack. Barry Gniel from Walpeup livened up the forward line in the last quarter. The North Central team got up by eight points in a tight match to win their zone. They were drawn to play the Ovens and Murray league in their semi-final the following year.

Before the 1974 season, however, North Central officials received stunning news when the Ovens and Murray league was disaffiliated from the VCFL. The Lavington Football Club had become powerful in minor leagues on the northern banks of the Murray River since the Lavington sports club had been opened. Under the law in New South Wales, the sports club could operate poker machines for the benefit of club members. The Lavington footy club operated under the umbrella of the sports club. The ten clubs of the Ovens and Murray league were dead against Lavington's attempts to enter their competition because they feared the club would use the bounty from the pokies to recruit an unseemly array of star players. When the VCFL ordered the Ovens and Murray league to admit Lavington to its ranks and the league refused, the ruling body took the only option to it and disaffiliated the competition. The Ovens and Murray league had been the most consistent league in the country championships, winning the inaugural carnival and reaching the semi-finals in almost every cycle since the revamp in 1961. But after the Ovens and Murray league's disaffiliation from the VCFL before the 1974 season, the league's representative team was unable to take its place in the semi-final of the championships that were run by the VCFL. The North Central league team went through to the 1974 final without taking the field in the semi-final.

The other semi-final of the 1974 country championships went ahead as scheduled, and the Hampden league thrashed the Latrobe Valley league at the Central Reserve in Colac. The final was scheduled for the Reid Oval in Warrnambool. It was a choice of venue that sent a shiver of dread through football people from the wheat fields in the country to the north.

In the newspapers in Ouyen, Donald and St Arnaud, the previewers of the final were appalled by the prospect of wet weather in Warrnambool. In Ouyen, the preview made much of Warrnambool's average annual rainfall of thirty inches – almost three times the average rainfall of their town. And Warrnambool had received one-sixth of its annual average in the weeks leading up to the final! The writers from the northern newspapers left the distinct impression that farmers from around Warrnambool spent their entire lives wearing rubber boots.

The North Central league's coach, Frank Tuck, was renowned as a former Collingwood captain, albeit an unlucky one. In 1953 he was a young defender when he missed out on Collingwood's victory in the Grand Final through suspension. In 1958, he was the Magpies' captain when he missed out on the club's most famous premiership because he had been ruled out of the Grand Final with injury. Tuck did play in three grand finals for Collingwood, in 1952, 1955 and 1956, but the Magpies lost all of them. As coach of the North Central league team, he was eager for success.

Tuck and his selectors chose five players from the Mallee league in the final team of twenty to represent the North Central District in the 1974 final. The five included Bob Latta and Barry Gniel from Walpeup, John White from Ouyen, and Chris Brown, the former Underbool ruckman who was now the captain-coach at Kiamal. While Alan Robertson had starred for the North Central league in recent years, his brother Greg Robertson now replaced him. Hampden league players must have been scratching their heads when they saw the home club of the fifth member of the Mallee Five; Tempy-Gorya-Patchewollock was possibly the most obscure club to have been represented in a final of the country championships.

The North Central league's party of players and supporters – the largest group of supporters in country footy – was in high spirits when it left the red earth of the north for the green fields of the coast on the Friday morning before the final, but sure enough, just as they were approaching their destination, the skies opened and the rain came down. The North Central league's team bus entered the outskirts of Warrnambool through a downpour. The first thing the players did when they arrived in town, however, was head to the Reid Oval to check out the ground. According to the report in the *Donald-Birchip Times*, the North Central league's captain, Maurie Wood, took one look at the black, waterlogged mulch in the centre-wicket area and said: "Chaps, I think I'll bowl."

Rain continued to beat down overnight, but when the North Central players took the field for the final on the Saturday they were surprised at how well the ground had held up. Their confidence grew as the match proceeded. According to the *Donald-Birchip Times*, supporters in the bar at Jack Hart's Wycheproof hotel had their ears pinned to the radio as the North Central league edged clear in the second quarter. Maurie Wood, a former wingman with North Melbourne, showed the way at half-forward. Jim Jess, a young teammate of Wood's at St Arnaud, dominated after being switched from attack into the ruck. Greg Robertson caught the eye with his ability to emerge from the gluepot in the middle and find a teammate in attack. Barry Gniel, now twenty-six years of age, who had kicked seven goals in the Mallee players' opening foray for the North Central team five years previously, was dangerous up forward. John White was unyielding in defence. In a verdant corner of Victoria, Frank Tuck finally enjoyed the rub of the green. North Central overcame the sodden conditions and their rivals from a famously strong competition to score a memorable victory by three goals.

At the end of the 1974 season, the major sponsor of the country championships, Caltex, sought to change the fixture of the rolling carnival to a one-year format. The VCFL was reluctant to agree. Caltex ended the sponsorship deal, and the championships went into recess. Even at the time, country football people knew that whatever happened in the years ahead, nothing was likely to challenge the North Central league's achievement of winning the country championships final in 1974. It was a triumph for a sparsely populated district in the north of the state over the teeming districts of the south. Mallee people saw the success of their players in the North Central team as a clear indication of the talent and pride in their region. The Mallee Five are still treated as heroes throughout the Mallee to this day.

13

Colour and Race

While the interleague campaigns of the early 1970s generated great excitement throughout the Mallee, the decade began amid difficulties at club level. Patchewollock were forced to sit out the season at senior level in 1970, but their merger with Tempy-Gorya the following season was a solution that worked better than imagined. The prodigious young talent at the triplicate club, Tempy-Gorya-Patchewollock, set up the Saints for an extended period of success. Early in 1971, the Underbool Football Club had a crisis meeting at which members resolved to continue.

According to the 1971 Census, the population of Victoria was just over 3,500,000. Of that figure, a whopping 72 per cent of the population of the state now lived in Melbourne, up from 50 per cent in 1921 and 60 per cent in 1947, during the period of rapid industry growth just after the war. The population of Ouyen, like most towns with a population of more than 1000, had risen since the war, from 1141 (in 1947) to 1564 (in 1971). The population of the next layer of towns in the district, Murrayville and Underbool, was stagnant, if slightly in decline. In this period, the bureau of statistics stopped taking figures for villages of less than 200, but the occasional closure of schools and clubs suggested that the villages were in decline. During this period, it was recognised that many farmers lived in Ouyen and drove out to their farms in outlying districts. It was a trend that was more evident in the north-west of Victoria than anywhere else in the state. The spectre of uncertainty would hang over Mallee football throughout the decade.

Tiega were undoubtedly the most powerful club in this era. Tiega teams played with spirit and purpose. On Sundays, the players gathered at 11 o'clock for what was described as "holy hour", which was usually held at the Weir family's farm. Brian Weir was a wonderful ruckman, and he took his turn as coach. Tiega had an outstanding array of talented locals, but they also developed a record of recruiting schoolteachers. Russell Parsons, a rover, moved to Ouyen to take up a teaching role at the high school and played in five premierships with Tiega. Joe Chant took up a teaching role at the Walpeup Primary School, and coached Tiega for three years.

Tiega, having won the grand finals in 1969 and 1970, appeared set to win their third consecutive premiership when they entered the finals series in 1971. Tiega maintained their undefeated status when they scored an easy victory, by seven goals, over Kiamal in the Second Semi-final. But luck turned against them in Grand Final week when Barney O'Callaghan, the star of the two previous grand finals and clearly the best rover in the competition, did his knee at training. On the day before the Grand Final, a surgeon in Ballarat reconstructed O'Callaghan's knee. Kiamal, having not won a senior premiership since 1922, almost fifty years previously, sniffed the prospect of triumph.

For all of Tiega's strength and talent, Kiamal had one of the most formidable leaders in the history of Mallee football. Don Pohlner, a wheat farmer from just north of Ouyen, was famously tough. Any attempt to stop him in his tracks, or even slow him down a little, would almost invariably come to nothing. Throughout Pohlner's long career, there was only one incident which interrupted his relentless pursuit of the ball, if only momentarily. It involved another famously hard-headed footballer, the Tempy-Gorya-Patchewollock centreman Peter "Doughie" Robins. The incident occurred during a final at Blackburn Park. Pohlner and Robins crashed into each other at full pace. Spectators were stunned to see the two old bulls unable to rise from the turf. Finally, the pair did get to their feet, and they resumed their pursuit of the ball. In Mallee folklore, there have been few more bruising encounters than the clash between Don Pohlner and Doughie Robins.

Pohlner had enjoyed premiership success when he was the captain-coach of the Walpeup team that won the Mallee league Grand Final in 1968. Three years later, in 1971, he was determined to lead Kiamal to a flag.

The 1971 Grand Final began in a blaze of controversy when Kevin O'Callaghan, the Tiega rover who was to start this match in a forward pocket, was decked by a sharp jolt from a rival defender before the opening bounce. The Tiega players were rattled by the sight of their teammate lying on the ground near a behind post. O'Callaghan was taken to hospital, and would play no part in the game. Kiamal got the jump from the opening bounce and pushed hard to maintain their edge. The Magpies kicked six goals in the opening quarter, with Don Pohlner kicking three, while Tiega kicked three goals themselves. The Magpies kicked four goals in the second quarter while Tiega kicked one. The Magpies led at half-time by thirty-three points, 10.4 (64) to 4.7 (31).

Tiega fought back in the third quarter, but Kiamal held their ground. Don Pohlner entered packs without fear. His brother, Ray Pohlner, was part of a backline that played with fanatic resolve. Walter "Spot" Munro, Philip Munro, Robert Perry and the veteran back pocket Ralph Hickmott, who was also the club president, played the games of their lives in defence. Leo O'Callaghan and Peter Kay were avenues to goal in attack. For Tiega, the Shaddock brothers, Harry and Eddie, and the Healy brothers, Rob and Des, tried hard to rally the favourites, but it was not enough. Tiega suffered their first loss for the season. Kiamal won by twenty-nine points, 14.9 (93) to 8.16 (64).

The *North West Express* was coy in its description of early events. "Tiega were unfortunate to be without their star rover Brian O'Callaghan, who was injured during the week; and Kevin O'Callaghan, who had to leave the field during the first quarter." But it was right to laud Kiamal's moment of triumph. The Magpies players lit a small fire on a roadside to the north of Ouyen and kept it alive for the next six weeks.

In this era, Tempy-Gorya-Patchewollock players enjoyed the occasional twig in a paddock after training at Patchewollock. The Saints, under the coaching of the interleague defender John White, built a strong spirit to add to their bank of talented young players. In the 1972 Grand Final, the Saints made the Grand Final against Tiega. It was a curious coupling given that Tempy-Gorya-Patchewollock's acronym, TGP, was almost as long as the full length of the name of their rivals, Tiega.

TGP led the Grand Final by seven goals only for Tiega to fight back and hit the front. The Tiega defender Tony Monaghan took a mark on the last line of defence in the dying moments to save the game. After the disappointment of the previous Grand Final, Tiega won in 1972 by six points. Stan Sleep, the Tiega captain-coach, was a strong leader in the ruck. Alan Robertson kicked eight goals for the Saints.

Tiega also defeated TGP in the next Grand Final, in 1973, with the veteran Barry Phelan kicking seven goals. In a letter to the editor, one Tiega supporter made sure that Tiega's Randy Bollig received due praise for his part in the team's success. Bollig was a schoolteacher who had come out from the United States on exchange. In his first year in Australia, in 1972, he taught at Ouyen High School and on weekends he took to watching Mallee league matches with rising interest. The next year, having never played Australian football, he joined Tiega and by the end of the 1973 season he was a valued member of the senior team. In the Preliminary Final, he kicked three goals, including one from the boundary line. The next week, he was part of Tiega's premiership team.

In 1974, Tempy-Gorya-Patchewollock suffered from the departure of Alan Robertson, who moved his burgeoning young family on to a grape block in Red Cliffs and began playing footy for Bambill in the Millewa league. Alan became a legend in the Millewa league before retiring at the age of forty.

TGP, however, benefited in 1974 from the emergence of the fifth and final son of Ginger Robertson, Michael. Better known as "Boozer", Michael Robertson was just as talented as his brothers. At sixteen years of age, he played on a wing in the team that turned the tables on Tiega to win the premiership, the club's first as a triple entity. Peter "Doughie" Robins, the fearless centreman, was the Saints' captain-coach. The team included Greg Robertson, who was Boozer's brother. It included Pat Burns and Gary Burns, who were cousins, and as well as Terry Monaghan and Derry Monaghan, who were also cousins. John Collins, a bullocking centreman who had shed a tear after the narrow loss to Tiega two years earlier, in 1972, received due reward for his years of toil. Lionel "Slim" Torney, a full-back who played in long sleeves, made amends for two grubbed kick-outs in the 1972 Grand Final with a solid game in the 1974 Grand Final. Slim's drop-kicks sailed towards the centre as the Saints scored a victory by eight points.

To the south of Ouyen, Nandaly became the big news of north-west Victoria in 1974 when they broke the premiership run of Nullawil in the Tyrrell league. Nullawil had played in the previous five grand finals; after losing the first two, they had won the next three. In 1974, the Maroons looked set to win their fourth consecutive premiership when they led Nandaly by eight points in time-on of the Grand Final, only for Nandaly to mount a charge. The Bombers kicked two late goals to win by two points. It was Nandaly's first premiership since their victory in the Pier Milan and District competition's Grand Final on the Nandaly oval in 1940, thirty-four years previously.

The 1974 season was also significant because a footballer from the Mallee, specifically Underbool, began to make his mark in League footy in Melbourne. Before the season, Max Crow had responded to Essendon's courting by agreeing to play for the Bombers' reserves team on permit. Under this system, a footballer from one club gained a permit to play six matches with another club. It was usually the means for a footballer to play at a higher level for a specified period before deciding whether to stay with his original club or apply for a clearance to the club which played at the higher level. Max Crow played the opening six matches of the season in 1974 for the Essendon reserves, after which his permit expired and he had to decide whether to apply for a clearance to Essendon or return to Underbool. Essendon enticed him to stay at Windy Hill by selecting him in their senior team to play against Richmond in Round 7 of the 1974 season.

The population of Underbool at the time was about 290. According to local estimates, more than half of the town headed to Melbourne to see their young star make his senior debut in the city. Many of the Underbool fans had never been to a VFL game; some had never been to Melbourne. On the morning of the match, Max Crow wandered down from his digs at the Royal Hotel, near the Essendon train station, to the motel in which the Underbool people were staying, the Alexander Motel, on Mt Alexander Road. Lance Morrison, a farmer whose property at Boinka was next to the Crow family's property, asked Max if it might be an idea to drive his car up to the ground to get it in the queue before the match.

Max was eighteen years of age, tall, bandy and athletic, when he jogged out on to the Windy Hill oval alongside another former country footballer, Ron Andrews, to play his first senior game. Max lined up in a forward pocket on another teenager, David Cloke, who was playing in only his sixth senior game for Richmond. Spectators brayed at the players from underneath the windsock and from the art-deco delights of the Showers Stand. Max joined an illustrious club when he kicked a goal with his first kick in League football. At half-time, he began walking towards the race when he was distracted by a commotion in his path. The infamous Windy Hill Brawl was under way. Players and officials from both teams were laying into each other during a duel that would ignite one of the greatest controversies in the history of the game. Max Crow had no idea what to think or do. He walked off the ground and up the race. Ron Andrews later sat down next to him, with blood pouring from a cut on his face.

The match resumed in the third quarter amid simmering tension. Richmond won by ten points, 16.19 (115) to 15.15 (105). Max Crow ended up with four of Essendon's fifteen goals. His debut was notable for his tally of goals, but also the ugliness of the occasion. After the match, Richmond ruckman Brian Roberts was revealed to have a broken nose, while Essendon fitness adviser Jim Bradley had a broken jaw. Ron Andrews was suspended for six matches for striking Roberts, while Bradley was suspended for six matches for striking the Richmond forward Mal Brown. The Essendon runner, Laurie Ashley was suspended for six matches for striking Brown. Brown himself was suspended for one match, while his teammate Stephen Parson, aged only seventeen, was rubbed out for four matches and later had assault charges dismissed in the Magistrates Court. The furore would play out over several weeks while Richmond fought penalties assigned by the VFL. The Tigers would go on to win the flag.

Max Crow went on to play ten senior games in his first season with Essendon, in 1974. Before the next season, however, he informed the club that he did not like Melbourne and he would be staying at home to play with Underbool.

The lead-up to the 1975 Mallee league season was exciting for all Mallee supporters for reasons to do with another sport. Jack "Curly" Burns, the Tempy farmer who was the president of the Mallee league for more than a decade, trained racehorses on a dusty track in a paddock on his farm. To the amusement of many, Curly used a stopwatch to note the sectional times of his horses while they galloped between certain trees.

Curly Burns's great mate, Ginger Robertson, had the farm next to him in Tempy, and Ginger often ventured along the path through their adjacent properties to discuss racing ventures. One day, Curly Burns and Ginger Robertson headed down to Boort because Ginger was interested in buying a horse. The pair did not even get out of the car. Ginger ran his eye over the horse while it stood in the paddock, and said he would take it. He paid $500. Ginger put the gelding in Curly's care. The horse, called Tudor Peak, would go on to win twenty-seven races, including the major cups in Bendigo and Broken Hill, as well as races in Melbourne and Adelaide.

In March 1975, Curly Burns entered Tudor Peak in the Australian Cup, a Group 1 race at Flemington. After the gelding was listed on the betting market at juicy odds, many Mallee footy followers backed him each-way. There were big collects all over the district when Tudor Peak finished second, beaten by a head by the champion mare Leilani. Curly and Ginger collected thousands.

For the Underbool footy club, the news of Max Crow's return was the most exciting of several developments that had emerged since their winless season in 1974. During the pre-season in 1975, the ruckman Chris Brown returned to his home club after one year at Kiamal. His brother, Kevin Brown, having tied for the best and fairest award the previous year in the First Eighteen at St Pat's College, Ballarat, completed a pre-season with Essendon before failing to make the cut and returning home to Underbool. Peter McDermott, a tough half-back, joined the club after moving into town to work on the rebuilding of the railway line to Murrayville. Wayne Aldous, a skilful half-forward who had played many reserves games at St Kilda, joined the club after moving into town through his role as a bank manager. Two seventeen-year-olds, Gary Crow, the brother of Max, and John Morrison, were emerging as proficient key defenders. On top of all that, Bill Morrish, the forward from the renowned Tiega family, agreed to leave his home club to become the captain-coach at Underbool.

On the eve of the 1975 season, Underbool did receive a setback when Essendon refused to clear Max Crow back to his original club. Max agreed to be the runner for Underbool's opening match, which was against the reigning premiers, Tempy-Gorya-Patchewollock, at Patchewollock. At 194 centimetres, Max Crow was possibly the tallest and most athletic man to have acted as a runner in Mallee football. Bill Morrish went into the opening game believing it would be a major achievement for his team to get within five goals of the premiers. Instead, they won by five goals. Essendon cleared Max Crow to Underbool the following week, and he played at centre half-forward for his home club in Round 2. At the end of the home and away rounds, Underbool finished second on the ladder and Max Crow lost the league medal on countback to the Walpeup champion Bob Latta. Tiega, having played in the previous fourteen grand finals, failed to make the final four in 1975.

The Second Semi-final was between TGP and Underbool at Blackburn Park. Max Crow kicked fifteen goals to propel his team to victory. A fortnight later, the Grand Final was again played at Blackburn Park. Underbool withstood a spirited comeback from TGP before winning a high-scoring match by ten points, 22.20 (152) to 21.16 (142). It would be the club's only premiership in the Mallee league. According to the *North*

West Express, Max Crow kicked 9.9 in the Grand Final, bringing his tally of goals in two finals to twenty-four – from centre half-forward!

Underbool's premiership team included four members of the Brown family and four members of the Stone family, as well as the Aikman brothers, Doug and Phil. Chris Brown and his cousins Mick and Dan Brown were all named among the best players for Underbool in the Grand Final. The Stone brothers, Kevin, Phil and Stan, were also named among the best, as were half-forward Geoff Hayter and the two recruits whose jobs had brought them to town, Peter McDermott and Wayne Aldous.

The next season, Underbool lost several premiership players including Max Crow, who resumed his VFL career at Essendon. Normal service resumed in the Mallee league, with Underbool returning to the bottom of the ladder and Tiega returning to the top. Barney O'Callaghan, in his first year as Tiega's playing-coach, led his club to the minor premiership with a team that still included a handful of multiple premiership heroes, such as Mick McKay, Russ Parsons and Jock Gibbins. The Gniel brothers, Geoff and Denis, who roared into Blackburn Park on their Kawasaki 1000cc motorbikes, were in the talented middle band of players, while half a dozen youngsters served to revitalise the team. The most talented of the teenagers was Wayne Carmichael, a sixteen year-old wingman who was still at St Pat's College in Ballarat.

Tiega came up against their keenest rivals of recent seasons, TGP, in the Grand Final. According to Colin Wallace in the *North West Express*, Tiega's vigour in the first quarter shocked the Saints. In the crowd, the Underbool ruckman Chris Brown found himself watching with a handful of TGP supporters. Brown was among those who thought the TGP team just needed a couple of big-bodied veterans to give the young talent a chance to shine.

Tiega went on to win the 1976 Grand Final by twenty-two points, with defender Ian John best on ground. According to the newspaper, Tiega coach Barney O'Callaghan was an inspiration to his team. The writer said it was typical of the spirit at Tiega that the club had defeated a team that looked superior on paper.

TGP followed through on conversations in the crowd during the Grand Final and approached Chris Brown to become the captain-coach for the 1977 season. Under Brown, the Saints again rallied towards the top of the ladder. The Ouyen Football Club, much improved after the addition of Rodney "Bushy" Vallance and others, led TGP by three goals at the final change in the Second Semi-final, only to slow up in the last quarter and eventually win by seven points.

In the lead-up to the Grand Final, TGP coach Chris Brown put one of his key players, Leo "Chugger" Burns, through a searching fitness test on his ankle on the final night at training. The coach ruled out his player, but the next day Burns insisted on another test. On a farm outside Underbool, Brown made Chugger Burns jump over fences and in and out of items of farming equipment. Burns then had to run up and down a horse trail. Finally, Chris Brown ruled that the courageous Burns could take his place in the team after all.

Ouyen led TGP by two points at three-quarter time of the Grand Final, but, as in the Second Semi-final, TGP rallied late in the match. Boozer Robertson kicked three goals in the final quarter as the Saints clawed to victory by six points. Ruck-rover Simon Grigg headed the list of best players for the Saints. After the siren, Chugger Burns was unable to undo his bootlaces. The trainer had to cut open the boots with his scissors.

On the first night of training the next season, Chris Brown instructed his players to go for a run on a prescribed route around the town of Patchewollock. The coach and players were surprised, and not a little proud, when dozens of locals gathered in front of the shops and the pub to applaud them as they jogged along the main street on their way back to the footy ground.

14

Out of Their League

The rise of the Ouyen Football Club into premiership calculations in 1977 added spice to a debate that had bubbled along for several years, causing much division throughout the region. Two decades earlier, in 1956, Sunraysia league officials had met officials from Ouyen to talk about the possibility of the Ouyen footy club leaving the Mallee league to join their competition. The debate gained renewed momentum during the North Central league's sally in the country championships in 1969. Some Ouyen supporters began to wonder about the prospects of a super-club from the region entering the closest major league, which was the Sunraysia league. Sunraysia league officials encouraged the idea. With the injection of Mallee players into their interleague team, the Sunraysia league might well make a charge towards its first country championships title.

Allan Dunstan, the VCFL's North Central District councillor, and Merv Young, the president of the North Central District as well as the president of the Mallee league, considered the idea of Ouyen's prospective transfer to the Sunraysia league with grave concern. Both knew that the low population in the Mallee made the region susceptible to change. In the late 1920s, the Patchewollock district had boasted its own competition, with four clubs. Merv Young himself had played with great pride for the Patchewollock Football Club during a period when the Tigers earned success in the Mallee league. But early in his tenure as Mallee league president, Young was involved in talks as the Patchewollock district proved unable to field even one club. Patchewollock's merger with Tempy-Gorya in 1971 was effectively the saviour of football across the swathe of undulating plains between Ouyen and Hopetoun. If one more club were lost to the Mallee, or several talented players made an abrupt decision to leave the region to play elsewhere, Allan Dunstan and Merv Young knew that it might upset the local ecosystem to the extent that the Mallee league could fall apart.

Dunstan and Young managed to dissuade any notion of a super-club for a short while before the Ouyen Football Club took matters into its own hands. Ouyen officials approached the Tiega and Kiamal footy clubs about pooling their resources to form one club to compete in the Sunraysia league. Tiega and Kiamal officials were horrified. Their main concern was preserving their own clubs and, by extension, the Mallee league.

It is difficult to overstate the prestige that major leagues enjoyed in country footy in this era. The VCFL's edict that each district was to feature only one major league, as well as several minor leagues, served to fuel the prestige. While Mallee league people acknowledged the appeal of entering a team in a major league, they found several aspects of a day at the footy in a major league to be unappealing. In the Mallee league, every Saturday featured an under-sixteen match followed by a reserves match and a senior match. A game for under-thirteen players, called the minis, was held during half-time of the senior match. In Mildura, the Sunraysia league held no netball games on Saturdays, nor did the smallest juniors get to play. All junior matches in Mildura were played on Sundays. Mallee league people considered a day at the footy in the Sunraysia league to be less appealing for families than a day at the footy in the Mallee league.

Without the support of their rivals in the Mallee league, the Ouyen footy club's bid to join the Sunraysia league was not compelling. The club had not won a premiership in the Mallee league since 1961, which was more than a decade previously. In 1974, Ouyen made the Preliminary Final. When the club then applied to join the Sunraysia league, the

VCFL felt its responsibility was to maintain the Mallee league rather than encourage Ouyen's ambition.

The next year, in 1975, Ouyen lost their appeal to join the Sunraysia league, but the club's persistence in trying to move to the higher competition put more noses out of joint. When Murrayville officials revealed that their club also wanted to leave the Mallee league, in their case to play in the Lameroo and District league, the issue became hugely unsettling for supporters in the Mallee league. If Ouyen left, their league could continue with six clubs, but if Murrayville left as well, the competition would be down to five clubs, and unlikely to survive.

The VCFL launched an investigation into the structure of football in the Mallee. The investigators' purview was to look into three competitions: the Mallee league, which had seven clubs, and the two fellow minor leagues to the south of Ouyen, the Southern Mallee league, which also had seven clubs, and the Tyrrell league, which had six. The Mallee league and the Southern Mallee league were open to change, or at least they were open to accepting new clubs to bolster their ranks. Tyrrell league officials, however, knew the most likely scenario was that their competition would be split up and their clubs dispatched to the other two competitions. They were implacably opposed to change – despite growing queries over the health of their competition.

The Tyrrell league competition had begun after the Second World War. It took its name from Lake Tyrrell, the salt lake to the north of the town of Sea Lake, and the Tyrrell Creek, which meandered through the region in rainy periods. The league was stable for many years with eight clubs. But in 1971, the year that the Tempy-Gorya-Patchewollock footy club was formed by a merger of two clubs, two clubs in the Tyrrell league, Chinkapook and Manangatang, merged to form a club that was described with affection as Chinky-Manang. In time, the club would drop the Chinky component and become known simply as Manang.

In 1975, four years after the Chinky-Manang merger, two other clubs in the Tyrrell league, Berriwillock and Culgoa, merged to form the club known as Berri-Culgoa. When the VCFL investigators looked into Mallee football in 1977, the Tyrell league's base of six clubs was looking shaky.

After the 1977 season, the VCFL investigators spoke to the presidents of the three leagues: Herb Hand (Tyrrell), Leo McFarlane (Southern Mallee) and Bernie Brown, the former Underbool ruckman and president who was now the president of the Mallee league. They also spoke to the league secretaries Leo Casey (Tyrrell), Russell Gravestocks (Southern Mallee) and Bernie Kelly (Mallee). Russell Gravestocks said the seven clubs in the Southern Mallee league had become stale after playing in the same configuration for several years. The Ouyen and Murrayville football clubs, meanwhile, again applied for clearances to other competitions, much to the chagrin of their rivals in the Mallee league.

On the recommendation of its investigators, the VCFL granted Murrayville's request to leave the Mallee league and join the Lameroo and District league in 1978. And it granted Ouyen's request to join the Sunraysia league, but not immediately. Ouyen officials were asked to show during the 1978 season that they could run their club to a satisfactory level for major league football, with regard to financial stability and public support. Then the Red and Blacks could join the Sunraysia league in 1979.

On the subject of the Mallee restructure, the VCFL supported two possibilities: a Mallee super-league, in which the three leagues were combined into one competition, or the formation of two leagues consisting of the following clubs:

> League A: Kiamal, Manangatang, Nandaly, Sea Lake, Tempy-Gorya-Patchewollock, Tiega, Ultima, Underbool, Walpeup

> League B: Beulah, Berri-Culgoa, Brim, Hopetoun, Nullawil, Rainbow, Woomelang-Lascelles, Yaapeet

Halfway through the 1978 season, Allan Dunstan chaired a meeting in Lascelles, a central town in the Mallee, for representatives from each league and club. According to the *North West Express*, the Tyrrell league president, Herb Hand, expressed concern over the distance that Ultima would have to travel in any of the suggested configurations. He said the clubs in his league realised that something must be done, but they were reluctant to be split up. He personally favoured one big league that covered the Mallee. The delegates from most Tyrrell league clubs said they wanted the Tyrrell league to remain intact, with the addition of two or three clubs from the neighbouring competitions.

Russell Gravestocks, the Southern Mallee league's secretary, said the club delegates from his competition unanimously accepted the proposal for the two leagues, but they would listen to alternatives. Bernie Brown said the Mallee league had not resolved anything after taking the matter to a vote. "The feeling of the meeting was a little divided. Some were very much in favour of leagues A and B; others favoured the setting up of one league from three. My personal opinion is that the A and B idea is the best. One big league would be 'too big, too quickly'."

The delegate for the Mallee league club Walpeup, Gerry Leach, said he supported in principle the two-league structure; he said one league would require just too much travel. Most Mallee league delegates at the meeting agreed with him, although the TGP delegate, John Collins, said his club strongly favoured one league, and the Tiega delegate, Bob Saunders, said his club had voted narrowly in favour of one league. When asked about the suggestion of a merger between Tiega and Kiamal, Saunders said a merger might become necessary if the Ouyen Football Club were allowed to go into the Sunraysia league as planned. The Kiamal delegate, Ron Vine, said it was difficult for his club to state its position without knowing the fate of Ouyen.

A fortnight after the meeting of league and club officials in Lascelles, in early July 1978, the Ouyen footy club suffered its first loss of the season in the Mallee league when Walpeup defeated the home team by three goals in wet and wintry conditions at Blackburn Park. Walpeup's champion centreman Bob Latta was best on ground. A week later, Latta was prominent for the Mallee league in what was shaping up to be the competition's final interleague match.

The Mallee league hosted the Southern Mallee league at Blackburn Park in mid-July 1978. The Mallee league wore red and black, the colours of Ouyen, while the Southern Mallee wore red and white. The TGP pair Chris Brown and Michael Robertson kicked eight goals and five goals respectively, but in yet another high-scoring match, it was not enough. The Southern Mallee league won by seven points, 22.17 (149) to 22.10 (142). Ron Payne, the tenacious rover who was the captain-coach at Underbool, was the Mallee league's best player.

According to VCFL minutes, the Ouyen Football Club held a public meeting late in the 1978 season at which sixty-three members attended. The Ouyen president, John Archibald, said all those at the meeting were unanimous that the club should go though with its plan to enter the Sunraysia league.

The Mallee league president, Bernie Brown, later told VCFL officials it was not surprising that Ouyen club members had voted to go with the club's wishes, but he stressed that the wider township of Ouyen, as well as Mallee league supporters from throughout the region, were overwhelmingly against the proposal for the Ouyen Football Club to leave them. Brown said the Mallee league had held a public meeting a week after Ouyen's meeting. He said 390 had attended. About 370 voted in favour of advising the VCFL to reject Ouyen's application for a clearance.

Ouyen maintained their position at or near the top of the Mallee league ladder late in the 1978 season. Their main challengers were Tempy-Gorya-Patchewollock, who were perennial finalists, and Walpeup, who had rarely made the finals since they had won the premiership a decade earlier. In the Preliminary Final, TGP led Walpeup by ten goals, 10.2 (62) to 0.2 (2), at quarter-time. Early in the second quarter, Walpeup's star forward Neil Blandthorn kicked a goal – and the Blues were away. They whittled back TGP's lead until they finally hit the front late in the game. Walpeup then moved clear in the time-on period to win by nineteen points, 18.20 (128) to 16.13 (109). Neil Blandthorn ended up with eleven goals.

On the Tuesday night of Grand Final week in 1978, Allan Dunstan hosted a meeting for league and club delegates from the three Mallee competitions in Woomelang. According to the *North West Express*, Dunstan handed down the VCFL's recommendations for the Mallee restructure, with the main point being that the three competitions would be dissolved and two competitions would be formed in their place. Ultima, whose players mainly lived in Swan Hill, would be permitted to transfer to the Kerang and District league instead of joining a Mallee competition. Dunstan reiterated that the Ouyen Football Club had already been granted permission to join the Sunraysia league. He said Sea Lake had applied to transfer to the Mid-Murray league, but they were unsuccessful. Berri-Culgoa and Nullawil had considered the possibility of merging and applying to join the North Central league but nothing had come of it.

Dunstan read out two letters that the VCFL had received about the restructure. The first, from Tempy-Gorya-Patchewollock, reiterated the club's strong support for a single competition in the Mallee. If two leagues were formed, the letter said, TGP would prefer to play in League B, which was the proposed southern league. At the meeting in Lascelles, the TGP delegate, John Collins, said travel would not be an insurmountable problem if the one-league option were adopted. He said that if the restructure resulted in the formation of two leagues, his club would prefer to join the southern league because it was likely to be more stable.

The second letter, from the Southern Mallee league, supported the formation of two leagues and the recommendation to clear Ultima to the Kerang and District league. Elaborating on his letter, the Southern Mallee secretary, Russell Gravestocks, told the meeting in Lascelles that the formation of two leagues would be "a goer" if clubs were prepared to ensure the success of the new arrangement. The Southern Mallee league's six delegates at the meeting were unanimous in their support for two leagues.

The Tyrrell league delegates were equivocal. The Manangatang delegate, Tom Ryan, said his club had voted narrowly to support the formation of two leagues, although the members felt that the number of clubs in the proposed northern league would dwindle through the decisions of clubs to merge or fold. When the Sea Lake delegate, Bill Briscoe, said his club would like a year's grace to stay in the Tyrrell league. Allan Dunstan told him that this option was "not on". The issue of the restructure would be resolved at this meeting.

The Berri-Culgoa delegate, Bryant Barry, told the meeting that the members of his club had voted 31-11 to merge with Nullawil if one league were formed, but the club's eventual decision was to support the formation of two leagues. Tom Barker from Nullawil said his club had not pursued an option to merge and join the North Central league because it wanted to wait for clarification on the Mallee restructure. Ultimately, his club supported the formation of two leagues.

The Mallee league delegates were also divided. The Tiega delegate, Russell Parsons, was animated by the possibility that Ouyen would not take their place in the Sunraysia league. When Allan Dunstan asked whether there was any evidence that Ouyen were having second thoughts about going into the Sunraysia league, Parsons admitted there was no evidence. It was just a view he had formed after talking to Ouyen players and noting an element of dissension. When Parsons asked what the VCFL would do if the Ouyen members were to change their minds, Dunstan replied that if that were to be the case, the club should make its position clear at once. "Everyone in this room is getting sick and tired of coming to these meetings."

Parsons said that, at the most recent meeting at Tiega, members had again voted in favour of one league – by the narrowest of margins. He said if there were to be eight clubs in League A, which was the proposed northern league, the club could well change its mind and support the formation of two leagues.

The Kiamal delegate, Ron Vine, said it bugged him that the people of the town of Ouyen had voted overwhelmingly for the Ouyen Football Club to stay in the Mallee but their wishes had been rejected. Allan Dunstan noted that no members of the Ouyen Football Club's committee had been at the public meeting that Mallee league officials had called to discuss Ouyen's future.

Gerry Leach from Walpeup said he wished his fellow delegates would stop talking about a single league; he also wished they would stop talking about the potential for instability in a northern league. The two league structure was sound, and offered the prospect of stability. Leach added that if Ouyen were to go into the Sunraysia league and later on seek to return to Mallee football, his club would welcome them.

The three league presidents said they had not changed their minds since the meeting in Lascelles two months earlier. Bernie Brown (Mallee league) and Leo McFarlane (Southern Mallee league) were convinced that two leagues would be the best outcome, while Herb Hand (Tyrrell league) believed one league would be the best option in the long term.

A motion was moved to adopt the VCFL's recommendation to form two Mallee leagues of eight clubs, and allow Ultima to join the Kerang and District league. The motion was carried by ten votes to six. With the final ratification of the VCFL board, the newly configured Mallee competitions for the 1979 season were thus:

Northern Mallee Football League	**Southern Mallee Football League**
Manangatang	Berriwillock-Culgoa
Kiamal	Beulah
Nandaly	Brim
Sea Lake	Hopetoun
Tempy-Gorya-Patchewollock	Nullawil
Tiega	Rainbow
Underbool	Woomelang-Lascelles
Walpeup	Yaapeet

After the meeting in Woomelang, there was much emotion throughout Ouyen and its surrounding district in the lead-up to what was now ratified as the last grand final in the Mallee Football League. Feelings ran high against the Ouyen Football Club, which was being painted as the villain for its repeated attempts to leave the competition, attempts that many believed were the catalyst for the demise of the Mallee league. Before the game, Bernie Brown, the Mallee league president, asked Gerry Leach, the Walpeup veteran and one of the league's two vice-presidents, whether the Blues would do a lap of honour after the Grand Final even if they lost. It would be a way of acknowledging the final match in their beloved competition. Gerry told Bernie Brown that, even in the circumstances, the disappointment of the losing players would be too great for them to consider running a lap.

Typically for this era, the game featured a cavalcade of goals. Walpeup kicked eleven in the second quarter but still managed to lead by only two goals at half-time, 13.7 (85) to 11.7 (73). Ouyen, under captain John White, struck back in the third quarter to lead by three goals at the final change. Walpeup pushed their noses in front during the last quarter and were three points ahead, 23.11 (149) to 22.14 (146), when the final siren rang. Neil Blandthorn, despite playing with a broken cheekbone, kicked eight goals for Walpeup, bringing his tally to nineteen in two finals, while Bob Latta and Peter "Bones" Greenham kicked four goal each. The high-flying Robert Dixon, a teacher at Ouyen High School, kicked ten for the losing team.

In the Walpeup rooms, Gerry Leach enjoyed a moment of reflection after everyone else had left. It was a bittersweet moment. He was ecstatic after playing his heart out in a winning grand-final team with his home club, but he was regretful about the demise of the competition. Ultimately, he was grateful that the 1978 Grand Final would be regarded as one of the greatest matches in the history of the Mallee league. The competition was wound up on a high note.

Tempy Football Club, 1929 – Back: Sturt Fraser, Arthur McLean, Bob Pianta, Jack Collins, Eric Burke, Rod Rowney, Jack McLean, Alan Parker, Mick McLean, Charlie Pianta, Doug Hill; Middle: Eddy Barbary, Henry "Ginger" Robertson, Ted White, Rupert Metherall, Arthur Hornsby, Gordon Dalton; Front: Eric Nichols, Jim Lacy, Bob Boschert [Mary Collins]

The **1902 Northern Combined** team, comprised by players from Buckrabanyule, Charlton, Nine Mile Reef and Woosang. The photo was taken at the Upper Reserve in Bendigo after the country team had defeated South Bendigo in a challenge match. Back (all officials): R. Jones, T. Morley, G. O'Connor, W. Stuart, H. McGurk Senior, R. Kelly, W. Cossar Senior, D. Ross; Third row: W. Sinclair (trainer), A. Long, J. O'Neil, F. Hindson, D. Walton, P. Arundell, W. Kelly, G. Pell (trainer); Second row: S. Smith (trainer) W. Gillett (vice-captain), F. Cossar, J. McGurk (captain), W. Barrett, P. O'Neil, R. McFarlane; Front: R. Dowsett, J. Fanning, M. Hindson, F. Kierce, S. Hall, T. Sharp [Debbie Feeny]

Tempy Football Club, premiers, 1934 – Back: George Toivonen, Ken Griffiths, Bob Pianta, Tom Morrish, Bill O'Shannessy, Doug Hill, Henry "Ginger' Robertson, Rupert Metherall, Jack McLean, Dad Robertson, Bill Allen, Les Satchell; Middle: Bob Boschert, Art Hornsby, Eric Burke; Front: Lester Dalton, Harry Parkinson, Bill Baldock (umpire), Big Jack McLean, Ted White; Absent: Ed Barbary [Mary Collins]

Woosang Football Club, premiers, 1928 – Back: Frank Donaldson, Jim Glasheen, Jim Cossar, Jack Glasheen, Keith Cossar, Ted Glasheen; Middle: Wally Round, Charlie Jackson, Hughie McGurk, Bill Cossar Junior, Henry Round, Jack Cossar, Billy Stewart, Spider Hayes; Front: Billy Hindson, Sydney Cossar, Joe Muntz (secretary), Joe Gould (captain, holding mascot Allan Cossar, Syd's son), Sam Giblett (president, with the Pappos brothers' trophy), Alec Black, Foster White [Debbie Feeny]

Centrals ruckman Tom Crow with his daughter Christine at the Tutye ground in 1954 [Chris Brown]

Underbool ruckman Bernie Brown in 1955, a premiership year for the Magpies [Chris Brown]

Torrita Football Club, runners-up, 1954 – Back: Les Corbett, Jack Hahnel, Des Clement, Eric Pryse, Ron Elliott, Brannie Smith, Tom Smith: Middle: Alex Elliott, Alan Kruss, Herb Munro, Neil Kruss, Allan Pryse, Lance Cheeseman, Rex Munro Front: Tony Lester (trainer), Norm Stone, Eric Stone, Charlie Stone, Ray Foley, Les Stone, Alan Munro, Ken Earhardt, Tom Foley (president) [Chris Brown]

Walpeup Football Club, premiers, 1960 – Back: Dermot Leach (president, goal umpire), Dennis Bell, Les Latta, Gary Raeck, Ron Gregg, Dennis Zanker, Harold Woodall, Neil Kruss, Ken McSwain, Arthur Wakefield, Roy Woodall, Ray Schubert, Paul Hannig (timekeeper); Front: Arch Gniel (trainer), Norm Latta, Tom Blandthorn, Alan Munro (secretary), Arthur Mann (vice-captain), Basil Sheahan (captain-coach), Barlow Woodall (assistant secretary), Charlie Tuohey, Norm Stone, Ken Logan, Eddie Gniel (trainer) [Chris Brown]

Tiega Football Club, premiers, 1967 – Back: Lindsay Morrish, Mick Gibbins, Eddie Shaddock, Ron Drendel, Tony Monaghan, Bill Scott; Middle: Barney Cavanagh (trainer), Denis O'Callaghan, Joe Pengelly, Brian Weir, Kuni Karparvicius, Barry McIntyre, Jock Gibbins, Russell Parsons, Brian Freeman (trainer), Tom McBain (trainer); Front: Barry Phelan, Harry Shaddock (vice-captain), Michael McKay (coach), Frank Healy (president), Kevin Shaddock, Brian O'Callaghan, Andy Bennett; Mascots: Michael Kelly, Garry O'Callaghan; Absent: Bill Morrish [Peter Healy]

North Central Football League, semi-finalists, 1970 – Back: Tom Sullivan (trainer), Ron Smith, Clive Gordon, Allan Taylor, Terry Stockton, Jeff Connelly, Alan Taylor (trainer); Third row: Alan Stewart (trainer), Barry Gniel, Ike Ilsley, Tom Speedie, Murray Gilmour, George Capuano, Darryl Campbell, Garry Sporn, Richard Kalms, Merv Young (Mallee league president), Eddie Gniel (trainer), Vic Jonasson (trainer); Second row: Allan Dunstan (North Central league president), Brian O'Callaghan, John Burt, Bill McGrath (captain-coach), Ross Jackson, Bob Steel, John Giblett, Des Darcy (selector); Front row: Les Cameron, Ian Fithall [Peter Healy]

CALTEX

V.C.F.L. CHAMPIONSHIP

SPONSORED BY THE CALTEX OIL CO.

Semi-Final

NORTH-CENTRAL

V.

HAMPDEN

CURTAIN RAISER:

ST. ARNAUD UNDER SIXTEENS

V.

DONALD UNDER SIXTEENS.

Saturday, June 6, 1970

Lord Nelson Park, St. Arnaud

MAIN GAME TO COMMENCE 2.15 P.M.

SOUVENIR PROGRAMME

PRICE 10c.

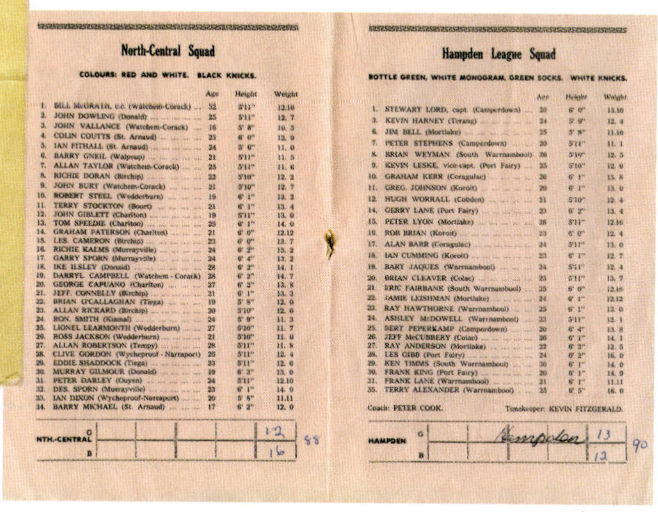

North-Central Squad

COLOURS: RED AND WHITE. BLACK KNICKS.

		Age	Height	Weight
1.	BILL McGRATH, c.c. (Watchem-Corack)	32	5'11"	12.10
2.	JOHN DOWLING (Donald)	25	5'11"	12. 7
3.	JOHN VALLANCE (Watchem-Corack)	16	5' 8"	10. 3
4.	COLIN COUTTS (St. Arnaud)	23	6' 0"	12. 9
5.	IAN FITHALL (St. Arnaud)	24	5' 6"	11. 0
6.	BARRY GNEIL (Walpeup)	21	5'11"	11. 5
7.	ALLAN TAYLOR (Watchem-Corack)	25	5'11"	11. 6
8.	RICHIE DORAN (Birchip)	22	5'10"	12. 2
9.	JOHN BURT (Watchem-Corack)	21	5'10"	12. 7
10.	ROBERT STEEL (Wedderburn)	19	6' 1"	13. 2
11.	TERRY STOCKTON (Boort)	21	6' 1"	13. 4
12.	JOHN GIBLETT (Charlton)	19	5'11"	13. 0
13.	TOM SPEEDIE (Charlton)	25	6' 1"	14. 0
14.	GRAHAM PATERSON (Charlton)	21	6' 0"	12.12
15.	LES. CAMERON (Birchip)	23	6' 0"	13. 7
16.	RICHIE KALMS (Murrayville)	24	6' 2"	13. 2
17.	GARRY SPORN (Murrayville)	24	6' 4"	13. 2
18.	IKE ILSLEY (Donald)	28	6' 2"	14. 1
19.	DARRYL CAMPBELL (Watchem - Corack)	28	6' 2"	14. 7
20.	GEORGE CAPUANO (Charlton)	27	6' 2"	13. 8
21.	JEFF. CONNELLY (Birchip)	21	6' 1"	13. 3
22.	BRIAN O'CALLAGHAN (Tiega)	19	5' 8"	12. 0
23.	ALLAN RICKARD (Birchip)	20	5'10"	12. 6
24.	RON. SMITH (Kiamal)	24	5' 9"	11. 3
25.	LIONEL LEARMONTH (Wedderburn)	27	5'10"	11. 7
26.	ROSS JACKSON (Wedderburn)	21	5'10"	11. 0
27.	ALLAN ROBERTSON (Tempy)	28	5'11"	11. 8
28.	CLIVE GORDON (Wycheproof - Narraport)	25	5'11"	12. 4
29.	EDDIE SHADDOCK (Tiega)	23	5'11"	12. 6
30.	MURRAY GILMOUR (Donald)	19	6' 3"	13. 0
31.	PETER DARLEY (Ouyen)	24	5'11"	12.10
32.	DES. SPORN (Murrayville)	23	6' 1"	14. 0
33.	IAN DIXON (Wycheproof-Narraport)	20	5' 8"	11.11
34.	BARRY MICHAEL (St. Arnaud)	17	6' 2"	12. 0

NTH.-CENTRAL							
	G					12	88
	B					16	

Hampden League Squad

BOTTLE GREEN, WHITE MONOGRAM, GREEN SOCKS. WHITE KNICKS.

		Age	Height	Weight
1.	STEWART LORD, capt. (Camperdown)	28	6' 0"	13.10
3.	KEVIN HARNEY (Terang)	24	5' 9"	12. 4
6.	JIM BELL (Mortlake)	25	5' 9"	11.10
7.	PETER STEPHENS (Camperdown)	20	5'11"	11. 1
8.	BRIAN WEYMAN (South Warrnambool)	26	5'10"	12. 5
9.	KEVIN LESKE, vice-capt. (Port Fairy)	25	5'10"	12. 9
10.	GRAHAM KERR (Coragulac)	26	6' 1"	13. 8
11.	GREG. JOHNSON (Koroit)	20	6' 1"	13. 0
12.	HUGH WORRALL (Cobden)	21	5'10"	12. 4
14.	GERRY LANE (Port Fairy)	23	6' 2"	13. 4
15.	PETER LYON (Mortlake)	28	5'11"	12.10
16.	ROB BRIAN (Koroit)	23	6' 0"	12. 4
17.	ALAN BARR (Coragulac)	24	5'11"	13. 0
18.	IAN CUMMING (Koroit)	23	6' 1"	12. 7
19.	BARY JAQUES (Warrnambool)	24	5'11"	12. 4
20.	BRIAN CLEAVER (Colac)	25	5'11"	13. 7
21.	ERIC FAIRBANK (South Warrnambool)	25	6' 0"	12.10
22.	JAMIE LEISHMAN (Mortlake)	24	6' 1"	12.12
23.	RAY HAWTHORNE (Warrnambool)	25	6' 1"	13. 0
24.	ASHLEY McDOWELL (Warrnambool)	23	5'11"	13. 1
25.	BERT PEPERKAMP (Camperdown)	20	6' 4"	13. 8
26.	JEFF McCUBBERY (Colac)	26	6' 1"	14. 1
27.	RAY ANDERSON (Mortlake)	22	6' 3"	13. 5
28.	LES GIBB (Port Fairy)	24	6' 2"	16. 0
29.	KEN TIMMS (South Warrnambool)	30	6' 1"	14. 0
30.	FRANK KING (Port Fairy)	20	6' 1"	14. 9
31.	FRANK LANE (Warrnambool)	21	6' 1"	11.11
35.	TERRY ALEXANDER (Warrnambool)	25	6' 5"	16. 0

Coach: PETER COOK. Timekeeper: KEVIN FITZGERALD.

HAMPDEN							
	G		Hampden			13	90
	B					12	

The front cover of the record and the team lists for a semi-final of the 1970 Victorian country championships. Hampden won by two points. Ovens and Murray defeated Bendigo in the other semi-final [Lorraine Shaddock]

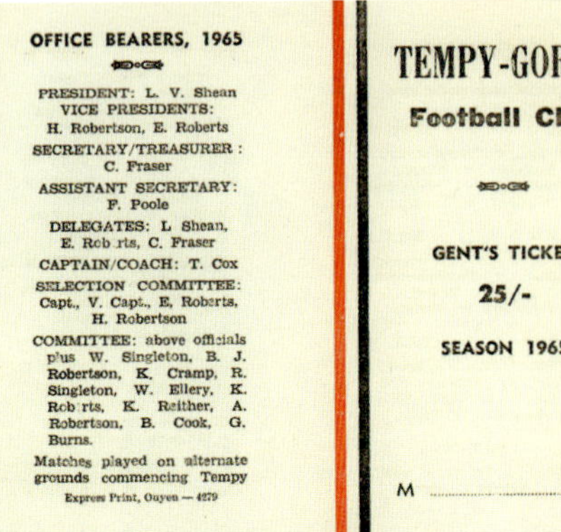

OFFICE BEARERS, 1965

PRESIDENT: L. V. Shean
VICE PRESIDENTS:
H. Robertson, E. Roberts
SECRETARY/TREASURER:
C. Fraser
ASSISTANT SECRETARY:
F. Poole
DELEGATES: L Shean,
E. Rob rts, C. Fraser
CAPTAIN/COACH: T. Cox
SELECTION COMMITTEE:
Capt., V. Capt., E. Roberts,
H. Robertson
COMMITTEE: above officials plus W. Singleton, B. J. Robertson, K. Cramp, R. Singleton, W. Ellery, K. Rob rts, K. Reither, A. Robertson, B. Cook, G. Burns.
Matches played on alternate grounds commencing Tempy
Express Print, Ouyen — 4279

TEMPY-GORYA
Football Club

GENT'S TICKET
25/-
SEASON 1965

M ....

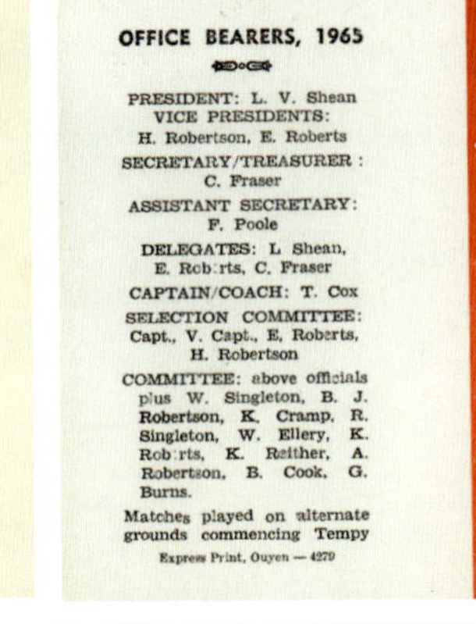

OFFICE BEARERS, 1965

PRESIDENT: L. V. Shean
VICE PRESIDENTS:
H. Robertson, E. Roberts
SECRETARY/TREASURER:
C. Fraser
ASSISTANT SECRETARY:
F. Poole
DELEGATES: L Shean,
E. Rob rts, C. Fraser
CAPTAIN/COACH: T. Cox
SELECTION COMMITTEE:
Capt., V. Capt., E. Roberts,
H. Robertson
COMMITTEE: above officials plus W. Singleton, B. J. Robertson, K. Cramp, R. Singleton, W. Ellery, K. Rob rts, K. Reither, A. Robertson, B. Cook, G. Burns.
Matches played on alternate grounds commencing Tempy
Express Print, Ouyen — 4279

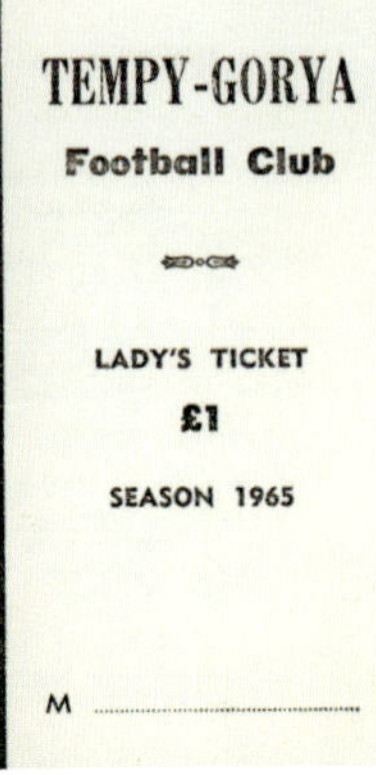

TEMPY-GORYA
Football Club

LADY'S TICKET
£1
SEASON 1965

M ....

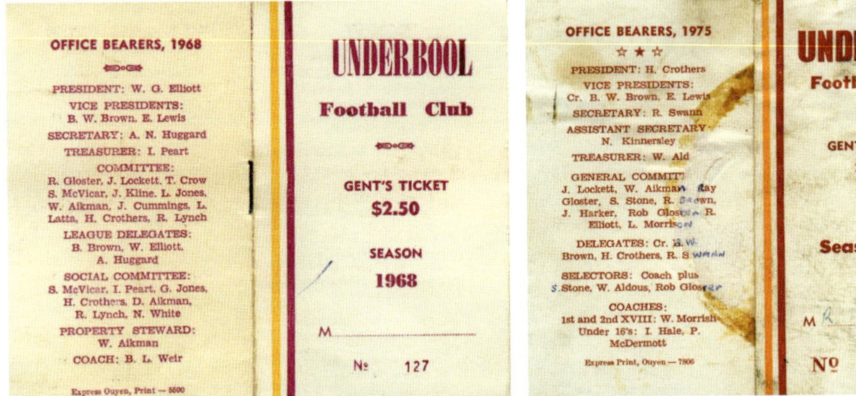

OFFICE BEARERS, 1968

PRESIDENT: W. G. Elliott
VICE PRESIDENTS:
B. W. Brown, E. Lewis
SECRETARY: A. N. Huggard
TREASURER: I. Peart
COMMITTEE:
R. Gloster, J. Lockett, T. Crow
S. McVicar, J. Kline, L. Jones,
W. Aikman, J. Cummings, L. Latta, H. Crothers, R. Lynch
LEAGUE DELEGATES:
B. Brown, W. Elliott,
A. Huggard
SOCIAL COMMITTEE:
S. McVicar, I. Peart, G. Jones,
H. Crothers, D. Aikman,
R. Lynch, N. White
PROPERTY STEWARD:
W. Aikman
COACH: B. L. Weir
Express Ouyen, Print — 5600

UNDERBOOL
Football Club

GENT'S TICKET
$2.50
SEASON
1968

M..
№ 127

OFFICE BEARERS, 1975
☆ ★ ☆
PRESIDENT: H. Crothers
VICE PRESIDENTS:
Cr. B. W. Brown, E. Lewis
SECRETARY: R. Swann
ASSISTANT SECRETARY:
N. Kinnersley
TREASURER: W. Ald
GENERAL COMMITT
J. Lockett, W. Aikman, Ray Gloster, S. Stone, R. Brown, J. Harker, Rob Gloster, R. Elliott, L. Morrison
DELEGATES: Cr. B. W. Brown, H. Crothers, R. Swann
SELECTORS: Coach plus S. Stone, W. Aldous, Rob Gloster
COACHES:
1st and 2nd XVIII: W. Morrish
Under 16's: I. Hale, P. McDermott
Express Print, Ouyen — 7806

UNDERBOOL
Football Club
☆ ★ ☆
GENT'S TICKET
$4.00
☆ ★ ☆
Season 1975

M R. K. BROWN
№ 22

Members' tickets from Tempy-Goyra's first season as a merged club; the Saints won the premiership. Underbool finished down the ladder in 1968, but won the flag in 1975 [Mary Collins, Chris Brown]

Mallee Football League, 1973 – Back: Geoff John (Tiega), Des Healy (Tiega), Greg Hosking (Kiamal), Joe Chant (Tiega), Greg Robertson (Tempy-Gorya-Patchewollock), Bill Morrish (Tiega), Frank O'Callaghan (Kiamal); Middle: Billy Doyle (trainer), Lindsay Morrish (Tiega), Eddie Shaddock (Tiega), Kevin Sleep (Tiega), Stuart Thompson (Kiamal), Phillip Short (Ouyen), Eddie Gniel (trainer); Front: John Archibald (selector), Alan Peters (TGP), Ron Wareham (secretary), Don Pohlner (captain-coach), Merv Young (president), Neil Blandthorn (Walpeup), Brian O'Callaghan (Tiega), Ralph Hickmott (selector) [Michael Robertson]

Tempy-Gorya Football Club, premiers, 1965 – Back: Alan Robertson, Ken McGough, Kevin Reither, Lindsay Anderson, Terry Robertson, Frank Poole; Third row: Colin Fraser (secretary), Josie Trotman (trainer), Noel Phipps, Gavin Burns, Lenny Finch, Ivan Clark, Michael Burns, Bill Singleton (trainer), Len Shean (president); Second row: Gordon Casey Junior, John Collins, Trevor Cox (captain-coach), Kevin Cramp, Graham Archibald; Front: Geoff Torpey, Stuart Edgar, Des Robertson, Leo Sampson [Des Robertson]

Underbool Football Club, premiers, 1975 – Back: Russell Swann (runner), Robert Gloster, Peter McDermott, Dan Brown, Kevin Brown, Michael Brown, Chris Brown (vice-captain), Max Crow, John Morrison, Stan Stone, Phil Stone, Ross Elliott, Ernie Harvey (trainer); Middle: Ron Lockett (trainer), Howard Crothers (trainer), Russell Stone, Doug Aikman, Rob Cummings, Bill Morrish (captain-coach), Wayne Aldous, Geoff Hayter; Front: Kevin Stone, Gary Crow, Phil Aikman [Chris Brown}

Tempy-Gorya-Patchewollock Football Club, premiers, 1974 – Back: Roy Jones (president), Patrick Burns, Phil Vallance, Clive Young, Ray Roberts, Robin Yetman, Graham Jolly, Greg Jackson, Ray Kerr (trainer), Gordon Jolly (secretary); Middle: Andrew Picone, Peter Young, Lionel Torney, Peter Robins (captain-coach), Gary Burns, Rodney Fuller, Greg Robertson, John Collins; Front: Michael Robertson, Kelvin Jolly, Derry Monaghan, Terry Monaghan, Daryl Decker [Des Robertson]

MALLEE FOOTBALL LEAGUE
FINALS
Record

GRAND FINAL
at OUYEN
SATURDAY, SEPTEMBER 7, 1974

SENIORS, at 2.30 p.m.
Tiega v Tempy/Gorya/Patche
UMPIRE: WALLACE

SECONDS, at 12.30 p.m.
Mur'ville v Tempy/Gorya/Patche
UMPIRE: TERRY EBBELS

UNDER 16's, at 10.45 a.m.
Underbool v Tempy/Gorya/Patche
UMPIRE: JOHN FOLEY

Admission to Grounds, 70c.
Children Under 16 Free

PRICE, 10c
MERV. YOUNG, President   RON WAREHAM, Secretary

Save Save Save — at Underbool
For a Quote on All Your Requirements, Contact
GREG BROWN, Phone 24

The front cover of the record and the team lists for the 1974 Grand Final of the Mallee Football League [Chris Brown]

For All Your Bulk Fuel and Oil Requirements
Contact... I. L. & B. M. GREGG
BP AGENTS . . . Ouyen

SENIORS

TIEGA

White Knicks   Red and White

1.	J. Chant c.c.	18.	M. Robson
2.	B. Pickering	20.	B. O'Callaghan v.c.
3.	L. Morrish	21.	J. Gniel
5.	N. McDonald	22.	R. Healy
6.	J. Gibbins	23.	R. Moss
8.	M. McKay	24.	E. Shaddock
9.	D. Gniel	29.	D. Healy
11.	B. Phelan	31.	W. Morrish
12.	R. Bollig	32.	I. Hastings
10.	I. John	33.	P. Shaddock
14.	K. Maginness	62.	M. Gibbins
15.	K. O'Callaghan	81.	N. O'Callaghan
17.	G. Barnes		

1st quarter	2nd quarter	3rd quarter	4th quarter	TOTAL

OUYEN SHOE STORE   FOR THE BEST IN QUALITY FOOTWEAR
▸ MELBOURNE PRICES GUARANTEED ◂
A. H. & B. O. HARMER
Box 33   Travel Goods, etc.   Phone 92
6

Contact—
DALGETY MERCHANDISE
For All Your Farming Needs
▸ DALGETY, Ouyen, and Agents

SENIORS

TEMPY/GORYA/PATCHE

Red, Black and White   Black Knicks

1.	Peter Robins c.c.	14.	John Collins
3.	Terry Monaghan	19.	Greg Robertson
4.	Ray Roberts	20.	Neil Roberts
5.	Derry Monaghan	21.	Robin Yetman
6.	Peter Young	23.	Pat Burns
7.	Lionel Torney v.c.	26.	Roger Young
8.	Gary Burns	30.	Kelvin Jolly
9.	Michael Robertson	31.	Clive Young
10.	Andy Picone	39.	Phillip Vallance
11.	Greg Jackson	40.	Daryl Decker
13.	Alan Peters	54.	Graeme Jolly
		92.	Chris Blythman

1st quarter	2nd quarter	3rd quarter	4th quarter	TOTAL

A. E. LOVERIDGE & SONS Pty. Ltd.
Timber and Hardware
IRON . . . STEEL . . . WIRE and PRODUCE
HAY-MAKING EQUIPMENT . . . BALERS . . . RAKES
(AGENT for MOBILCO CHAIN SAWS)
Ample Supplies of Calf Milk & Veterinary Requirements
OUYEN. PHONE 4; After Hours, 169
7

15

Storms to the North

On the eve of the 1979 season, there was much anticipation for the new era in football in the district around Ouyen, with the Ouyen Football Club entering the Sunraysia league and the Northern Mallee getting under way with eight clubs. Further south, the VCFL announced that Allan Dunstan, the North Central District councillor, had risen to the role of the ruling body's president, making him the most powerful country football official in the state. Merv Young was reinstalled as the president of the North Central District. The interchange rule, having been introduced in the VFL the previous season, in 1978, was now compulsory at all levels of country football.

The Ouyen Football Club entered its first season in the Sunraysia league with Graham Gation as coach and John White, the champion centre half-back, as captain. The club's opening weeks in the major league were a harbinger of the ups and downs that would follow. In the first round, the newcomers lost to the Mildura Football Club by 116 points, 25.16 (166) to 8.2 (50), while their seconds and thirds teams lost by 180 points and 237 points respectively. Bushy Vallance, the wonderfully skilled centreman, won the Clarke's Drapery award for his standout performance in Ouyen's senior team, but the club looked dreadfully undermanned as it embarked on its new venture.

In an epic turnaround, however, Ouyen won their second match when they defeated Merbein by fifty-five points at Merbein. The writer for the *North West Express* made special mention of Bushy Vallance, John White and Phillip Short, who had turned down large offers to stay with Ouyen during their inaugural season in the major league. The paper also noted that the winning team included nine footballers who had played on permit from their Northern Mallee league clubs, including Don Hahnel, Tony Goode, Cocky McDonald and the Healy brothers, Rob and Des.

The next week, in the third round of the season, Ouyen lost four players – the Morrish twins John and Ray, as well as Billy White and Des Healy – from their selected team before their match against Wentworth. The club from over the Murray River defeated the club from the heart of the Mallee by ten goals. The issue of player availability would underpin Ouyen's rollercoaster ride. There was more than enough talent in the district for a club from Ouyen to challenge the larger clubs from Mildura, but most players around Ouyen wanted to stay with their home clubs and play in the newly configured Northern Mallee league.

Before the inaugural season in the Northern Mallee league, officials announced they would distribute 150 copies of the Football Record to their eight clubs every Saturday. Each copy of the record would cost twenty cents. Bernie Brown, Bill Briscoe, Frank Healy and Bob Marks were announced as the selectors for the competition's first interleague team.

At Tiega, Bill Drendel was elected to head a new committee, while Dale Ryan was announced as the coach, with Peter Young his assistant. The coaches of other clubs included Laurie Carter (Kiamal), Pat Curran (Manangatang), Ian Busse (Sea Lake), Don Hahnel (Walpeup), Chris Brown (TGP) and Gary "Rolla" Burns, the former TGP dynamo who was now in his fourth season as coach of Nandaly. Another TGP dynamo, Michael "Boozer" Robertson, left his home club to take on the coaching role at Woomelang-Lascelles, who were to play in the newly configured Southern Mallee league.

Even in his absence, however, Boozer Robertson distinguished his home club with shining performances at interleague level. In this period, Boozer matched the honour that had been bestowed on two of his older brothers when he, too, represented the North Central league with flair and distinction. Boozer, like his brothers, sparked a sense of wonder with his skill and ball-handling. In 1979, he was best on ground as the North Central league defeated the Northern District league by one point.

In 1980, Boozer was still the playing-coach at Woomelang-Lascelles, but all fans in the north-west of the state knew of his background at Tempy-Gorya-Patchewollock as he embarked on a season that has rarely been matched by a footballer from an isolated region in Victoria. In the first round of the country championships in 1980, Boozer played on a wing for the North Central league against the Latrobe Valley league in the slosh at Morwell. While the conditions deterred his many of his teammates, Robertson showcased his trademark ball-handling despite the greasy conditions. Marcus "Louie" Burns, a former teammate from TGP, also played for the North Central league in this game. Unusually for a member of the sprawling Burns family, Louie Burns was a rover.

A month after the match in Morwell, Boozer Robertson was chosen in the VCFL's first representative team, which was due to play the Canberra Australian Football League at Manuka Oval in Canberra. Boozer's teammates in the Victorian country team included the legendary Bendigo pair Ron Best and Tony Southcombe, as well as the Leongatha dairy farmer Ian Salmon, who had played 100 games for Footscray, and Ross Weightman, who was a rover with South Mildura. Boozer was the only player in the VCFL team who played in a minor league. When he joined his teammates for the flight from Melbourne to Canberra, it was the first time he had boarded a plane.

The match in Canberra was televised throughout country Victoria. The team from the national capital overwhelmed their country rivals in the second half. Kevin "Cowboy" Neale, the former St Kilda hard man, kicked ten goals from full-forward to spearhead the Canberra team to a comfortable victory.

Boozer's home club, Tempy-Gorya-Patchewollock, was forced to swap from St Kilda geurnseys before the 1979 season because Manangatang had been given the all-clear to stick with the Saints guernseys, which they had worn in the Tyrrell league. TGP swapped to Richmond guernseys, replete with garish yellow shorts, because the Patchewollock footy club had worn the yellow and black colours until their last game in the Mallee league a decade earlier.

TGP's captain-coach, Chris Brown, was named captain-coach of the inaugural team to represent the Northern Mallee league, in a match against the Southern Mallee at Blackburn Park midway through the 1979 season. The match was closely contested, but the Southern Mallee league gained the edge and won by nine points. The Northern Mallee league's trophies went to Wayne Carmichael, Tiega's talented wingman; Jack Pryse, the promising ruckman from Walpeup; Kevin Brown, the reliable key defender from Underbool; and Marcus "Louie" Burns, the rover from TGP. In its report, the *North West Express* warned that the Northern Mallee league must consider suspending players who made themselves unavailable for interleague selection without substantial reason.

Supporters of the old Mallee league had reason to feel chastened after the home and away rounds in the first season of the Northern Mallee league when the three former Tyrrell league clubs – Manangatang, Nandaly and Sea Lake – filled three places in the top four. TGP, who finished third, was the club that split them. Walpeup's performance was especially disappointing. Just one season after their dramatic victory in the last Mallee league grand final, the Roos suffered badly from the loss of key players, and failed to win a game in their first season in the new competition.

Nandaly defeated Manangatang by four goals in the inaugural Northern Mallee league Grand Final. Rolla Burns, the former TGP player who was now the Nandaly coach, was best on ground. The bittersweet news for Mallee supporters was the performance of John White, the Ouyen captain, who finished equal on top of the leaders' board after the count for the best and fairest player in the Sunraysia league, despite playing in a team that had won only one game. Geoff Lucas (Mildura), Garry

Robinson (Red Cliffs) and White all polled nineteen votes, but Lucas was awarded the McLeod Medal on countback.

In 1980, Tempy-Gorya-Patchewollock embarked on a period of dominance that swept them though the first half of the decade, despite the apparent instability brought on by an annual turnover of coaches. From 1980 to 1984, the Tigers had five coaches in five years but never missed a beat, in large part because of the club's talented playing group.

In 1980, under full-forward Murray Dyer, the Tigers went through the season undefeated before beating Manangatang by more than ten goals in the Grand Final, with Dyer kicking eight. The next year, in 1981, TGP were led by Pat "Patto" Burns, a full-back, who was yet another member of the Burns family from Tempy. The Tigers marched in step with Manangatang towards the finals while, in the background, events were unfolding that would justify the fears of those who believed a competition in the northern Mallee would suffer from instability.

Jock Gibbins, the president of the Tiega footy club, was steeped as deeply in the history of his club as it was possible to be. In 1910, Billy Gibbins, Jock's grandfather, was a foundation member of the Tiega Football Club during the inaugural season of the Ouyen District Football Association. Billy Gibbins had selected land at Galah, just west of Ouyen, and his family would remain central to the region and its football club for the duration of its history. Joe Gibbins, Jock's father, played in premiership teams with Tiega in 1927 and 1929. Jock himself embarked on a career in 1962 that would be difficult to match in terms of success. He was sixteen years of age when he played in the Tiega team that played in the reserves Grand Final that season. The next year, in 1963, he played in the reserves Grand Final again. In 1964, at eighteen years of age, he became a regular member of the Tiega senior team just as it was entering its period of sustained glory.

Tall and slender, he settled into a pattern of starting matches at full-forward and swapping with Brian "Bricker" Weir in the ruck. Tiega played in every grand final from 1964 to 1974, and Jock played in all of them. The club's golden run ended in 1975, when they finished just short of the finals, but Tiega won the premiership again in 1976, with Jock

Gibbins in the team. All up, he played in twelve senior grand finals for seven premierships. A few years later, he was the club president as Tiega grappled with a growing shortage of senior players.

Bob Marks was a shearing contractor who played in the ruck and in the backline for Kiamal for many years. In 1981, he was the Kiamal president at a time when a shortage of senior players was forcing his club to consider its future as well.

Throughout the 1970s, the Tiega players drank in the pub, the Victoria Hotel, while the Kiamal players drank in the club, which was officially the Ouyen and District Community Club. However, the players and supporters of both clubs had plenty in common. In a town the size of Ouyen, they could hardly avoid each other. After the 1979 season, the players from the two clubs went on a joint footy trip to Broken Hill.

Jock Gibbins and Bob Marks were close friends. In 1981, they were presidents of their respective footy clubs when Gibbins hired Marks to assign a team of shearers to visit his farm at Galah, just west of Ouyen. While Gibbins and Marks moved among the lambs and the ewes, they chatted about their footy clubs. Both clubs had decent numbers of juniors, but increasingly thin ranks at senior level. When the players finished school, they tended to leave town. The outcome of those chats in a shed in Galah would change the course of football in Ouyen.

At the end of the home and away rounds in 1981, Kiamal finished fifth, but three games outside the top four, while Tiega finished in last place with one win. The under-sixteen teams from the two clubs played off in the junior Grand Final, with Tiega winning by three goals, but the members of both clubs were ready to accept their fates. Six weeks after the season, in early November 1981, eighty members of the Tiega and Kiamal football clubs gathered in the VRI Hall in Ouyen to vote on a proposal to merge the clubs.

Len Shean, the former Tempy-Gorya president, chaired the meeting, which proceeded without fuss. The Tiega and Kiamal footy clubs voted to merge and form a club called Ouyen Rovers. The new club would bear no relation to the club by the same name that had existed fifty years previously. The new Ouyen Rovers would wear Melbourne's colours, which at the time were royal blue with a red yoke, and they would play home games at Blackburn Park. The inaugural members of the executive committee were divided between the two contributing clubs. Bob Marks was elected president, while Jock Gibbins agreed to become vice-president. Kevin Crook, the secretary, was from Tiega, while Barry Dean, the treasurer, was from Kiamal. The other eleven members of the inaugural committee included long-time footballers and officials from both clubs. The Rovers scheduled their first social function for three weeks hence, a cabaret evening featuring the Mildura band Kaine.

A few weeks after the merger of Tiega and Kiamal to form Ouyen Rovers, eighty members of the Walpeup and Underbool football clubs met in the Torrita hall to vote on a proposed merger of their clubs. Tony Lester, a former Torrita player and official, chaired the meeting. After a unanimous decision to merge the clubs, the presidents of the two arms of the club, Robert Gloster of Underbool and J.H. "Brannie" Smith of Walpeup, tossed a coin under the lamp-post in Torrita to decide the club's name. Brannie Smith won the toss; the club was club called Walpeup-Underbool.

As with Ouyen Rovers, the executive positions were split between the two arms of the club. Robert Gloster was installed as president, while Brannie Smith was named senior vice-president and Howard Crothers was named junior vice-president. David Blandthorn, who had played alongside his brother Neil in Walpeup's premiership team in 1978, was named secretary, with Chris Brown, the full-forward in Underbool's premiership team in 1975, who had returned home from TGP, as his assistant. The treasurer was the champion Walpeup centreman Bob Latta. The committee included names from both clubs, all of which were familiar to most people in Mallee football.

Throughout their twenty-five years in the Mallee league, Underbool had worn maroon jumpers with a gold "V" and called themselves the Kangaroos, although it was a nickname that was rarely used. Walpeup had worn royal blue jumpers with a white sash until 1977, when they changed to North Melbourne's royal blue and white vertical stripes. They were called the Blues, although they called themselves "Walpy" far more than they called themselves the Blues. For the merged club, the committee wanted the jumper of a VFL club for the sake of convenience. They considered Essendon, Hawthorn and Footscray jumpers before deciding on the Footscray option. Despite an argument to take the Kangaroos nickname, they went along with the jumper's provenance and called themselves the Bulldogs.

During the 1981 finals series in the Northern Mallee league, TGP lost the Second Semi-final to Manangatang by five points before avenging that loss with a crushing victory over Nandaly in the Preliminary Final – by 130 points, 33.21 (219) to 13.11 (89), with Barry Jolly kicking ten goals and the seventeen-year-old wingman Trevor Poole kicking six. The Tigers then accounted for Manangatang in the Grand Final by almost four goals, with ruck-rover Simon Grigg being named best on ground, a regular occurrence in the club's big matches in this period. TGP's best players also included Rolla Burns, back at the club after five years with Nandaly, as well as Adrian Burns, Leo Burns and Boozer Robertson, who was also back at his home club. Rolla Burns won the Tigers' best and fairest award that season. Defender Chris Monaghan won the most consistent award, while wingman Lindsay Yetman won the most improved award.

The following season, in 1982, the Sunraysia league held its opening round a week before the Northern Mallee league was due to start its season. Three premierships stars from Tempy-Gorya-Patchewollock, Rolla Burns, Boozer Robertson and Simon Grigg, took the opportunity to play for Ouyen on permit. The trio played significant roles as Ouyen blitzed Robinvale to win by 106 points, 29.16 (196) to 14.6 (90). The other key players for Ouyen were John White, still dominating at centre half-back, and Barney O'Callaghan, who had returned from another long-term knee injury to play good football.

Boozer Robertson received glowing praise from the writer in the *North West Express* for his performance in this match for Ouyen. "After seeing many VFL games, including nearly all the grand finals since 1968, I can say without doubt that Boozer is the best ball handler I have seen. He is a complete wizard with the ball, and he seems to excel in these games. There is not much of him, but he can mix it with the best of them

As a North Central official once said: 'He may have legs like a shell parrot, but don't let that fool you. You would not find a more skilful player.' "

Once again, the injection of talent from the TGP stars lent an indication of Ouyen's potential if the best players in the region were prepared to play for the town's club. But the TGP trio returned to their home club the next week and Ouyen battled through another season, with a victory over Irymple being the highlight.

After the merger of four clubs into two during the off-season, the Northern Mallee league began the 1982 season with six clubs. The two newly merged clubs, Ouyen Rovers and Walpeup-Underbool, played each against each other in the opening round before a large crowd at Blackburn Park. The Rovers won by six goals, with Steve Manley, Craig Carmichael and Greg Hosking among the Rovers' best players. The two clubs took a little while to find their feet. Somè in the Rovers camp were distracted by the political intrigue that continued to linger after Ouyen's departure for the Sunraysia league. The Rovers finished the season in third place while Walpeup-Underbool finished fifth, ahead of only the winless Nandaly. Sea Lake defeated TGP by twenty-one points in yet another high-scoring Grand Final, 21.24 (150) to 20.9 (129). The league president, Kevin Robinson, was also the Sea Lake club president. There was much muttering in the crowd when he presented the premiership cup to himself.

After the 1982 season, the Mallee's favourite horse trainer, Curly Burns, brought much excitement to the region when he entered Dry Wine in the 1982 Melbourne Cup. According to an article in *The Age*, Burns held little hope for his horse, but he was rapt to simply have a runner in the race. After finishing tenth in the Werribee Cup having started at odds of 100/1, Dry Wine was listed at 330/1 in the betting market on the morning of the Melbourne Cup at Flemington. He ran accordingly.

16
Ruckus and Rovers

During the lead-up to the 1983 season, the players from the Ouyen and the Ouyen Rovers football clubs called a meeting to which club officials were not allowed to attend. According to the *North West Express*, Bill Opie chaired the meeting of sixty-seven players, who, according to a spokesman, declared they were "fed up with the bitterness and unnatural animosity dividing the clubs and the town".

The players voted overwhelmingly, 62-5, to support an amalgamation of the two clubs to form one club, which would play in the Northern Mallee league. The players elected a delegation to approach the committees of the two clubs to see if a compromise could be reached. The four delegates were Mick Mellington, who was the Rovers coach, Des Healy and Peter Taylor, who played for the Rovers, and Brian O'Callaghan, the former Tiega champion who played for Ouyen and coached the club's junior team.

A fortnight later, Mick Mellington addressed a meeting of 120 members of the Ouyen Rovers footy club. Mellington said the players were sick of two clubs in a divided town and wanted one united club. Jock Gibbins, the Rovers president, said a merger would be impractical for several reasons:

- at the Rovers' annual general meeting, no mention had been made by players or members about a merger or disbandment
- the Rovers' set-up had been put in place by eighty members only twelve months previously
- too many players would miss out on a game if the clubs were combined
- as it was now mid-March, it was too close to the season to consider upending the arrangements that were in place
- if the number of clubs in the Northern Mallee league was too low, the league might be disbanded and the town would be forced to field a team or teams in the Sunraysia league.

After Gibbins had spoken, the president of the Northern Mallee league, Kevin Robinson, advised the meeting that the Ouyen Football Club had been accepted into the competition that afternoon. A member of the Ouyen Rovers club put forward a motion for a vote of confidence in the Rovers' committee. The motion was passed with an overwhelming majority.

The Ouyen Football Club was embattled after four years of largely heavy defeats in the Sunraysia league. The club entered the Northern Mallee league in 1983 with Kevin Manley as president and John White as coach. The Red and Blacks struggled to six victories, which earned them fifth place. TGP finished on top of the ladder despite the loss of a handful of star players including Simon Grigg, who was the playing-coach at Walpeup-Underbool. Grigg found the going hard at the Bulldogs. Whereas it was a regular occurrence for forty players to attend TGP training at Tempy or Patchewollock, only fifteen or twenty players would attend training at Walpeup or Underbool. The Bulldogs finished last with one win.

On the eve of the 1983 finals, the TGP coach, Roger Stannard, expressed his concern to the defender Kelvin "Buster" Jolly about the number of goals that rival forwards were kicking against them. Buster Jolly told his coach not to worry. He said the Tigers players had not been serious to that stage of the season.

TGP duly sailed through the finals with strong victories over Ouyen Rovers in the Second Semi-final and Manangatang in the Grand Final.

In an uncanny reprisal of Max Crow's output for Underbool in the finals series in the Mallee league eight years earlier, in 1975, the TGP full-forward Andrew Picone kicked fifteen goals in the Second Semi and nine goals in the Grand Final.

The next year, in 1984, Simon Grigg returned to TGP to coach his home club while John White left Ouyen to coach Walpeup-Underbool. TGP finished second on the ladder, two games behind Sea Lake, but again enjoyed a strong finals series. Before the Grand Final, the VFL influence on country footy was evident when the TGP and Sea Lake teams both ran through banners as the players jogged on to the ground. Andrew Picone kicked nine goals in the Grand Final, bringing his tally for the season to 105, while Boozer Robertson kicked six, including five after half-time, to get the Tigers home by five points, 19.12 (126) to 18.13 (121). It was TGP's fourth premiership in five years.

Ouyen, despite defeating Ouyen Rovers in the First Semi-final in 1984, approached their co-tenants at Blackburn Park about a merger in the lead-up to the 1985 season, but were rejected. On the eve of the season, the Ouyen Football Club went into recess. The Rovers, under president John Donaghy, agreed to absorb elements of the Ouyen Football Club but, he said, the Rovers committee would conduct all operations and the club would continue to play as Ouyen Rovers. Barney O'Callaghan was so disgusted by what he described as the poor attitude of some Rovers people towards the remnants of the Ouyen Football Club that he quit all involvement in club football.

With so many junior players at the Rovers, the club agreed to farm out a portion of their young players to Nandaly, who were struggling to field an under-sixteen team. Harry Shaddock, the former Tiega centre-half back, took on the coaching job with the Nandaly juniors. Some Ouyen people felt so unwelcome at the Rovers that they transferred their allegiance to Nandaly. Peter "Sparks" Darley was a prominent former Ouyen player whose loyalties came to lie with Nandaly during this period.

Just before the 1985 season, members of Victoria's railway historical society travelled from Melbourne to Patchewollock on the last passenger train to enter the Mallee town. When they arrived in Patchewollock, the travellers enjoyed a breakfast of bacon and eggs, which awaited them at the silos next to the railway siding.

In the opening round of the 1985 season, Ouyen Rovers signalled a changing of the guard when they defeated Tempy-Gorya-Patchewollock, the reigning premiers, by 113 points, 27.18 (180) to 10.7 (67). The Rovers' best in that match included the Morrish brothers, Stephen and Paul, and rugged half-back Mick Donaghy, who wore Boozer Robertson like a glove. The most significant addition to the Rovers team was the ruckman Glen Petrie, a recruit from North Darwin via Jeparit, who was 195 centimetres and 110 kilograms of muscle and aggression. With Petrie in the ruck, his Rovers teammates walked tall.

In the final game of the home and away rounds in 1985, the Rovers defeated Walpeup-Underbool by 169 points, 36.14 (230) to 9.7 (61), with Dean Cross kicking nine goals and Craig Carmichael kicking eight. In the Second Semi-final, the Rovers defeated Sea Lake by eighty-nine points, with David Whitelegg kicking seven goals and Craig Carmichael kicking five. Sea Lake fought back in the Grand Final but the Rovers still managed to see them off by thirty-eight points. The Rovers' pint-sized rover Martin Floyd was best on ground. The on-ball player Andrew Lorincz, who had won the league best and fairest award the previous two seasons, enjoyed the ultimate team success in his third year at the club.

Ouyen Rovers again achieved the ultimate success the following two years, but in far more dramatic circumstances. In 1986, the Rovers outlasted Manangatang in the Grand Final by five points; midfielder Stuey Locke was among the Rovers' best players. The next year, in 1987, the Rovers lost the Second Semi-final to TGP by nine points after TGP's prolific full-forward Andrew Picone had kicked eleven goals. The Rovers then defeated Manangatang in the Preliminary Final by one point after the tall and athletic forward Ricky Marks, the son of the late Rovers president Bob Marks, took a mark at centre half-forward and kicked a goal at the twenty-six minute mark of the final quarter. In the Grand Final, the Rovers snatched the lead at the twenty-four minute mark of the last quarter when the forward Kevin Maginness snapped accurately from an angle. Troy Cook, the ruckman, then kicked a goal from half-forward to give the Rovers victory by twelve points, and their third flag in a row.

Tempy-Gorya-Patchewollock kept pushing for a premiership. The Tigers finished on top of the ladder in 1988 and second in 1989, but were unable to get over the line. In 1988, TGP defeated Sea Lake by eleven goals in the Second Semi-final then led the Swans by three goals at half-time of the Grand Final, only for Sea Lake to kick eight unanswered goals in the second half and pull off a stunning premiership. Sea Lake's best players included Greg Daniels, who had returned to his home club after playing five senior games at Collingwood. TGP's best included a trio of familiar veterans, Buster Jolly, Rolla Burns and Simon Grigg.

The next year, in 1989, TGP lost the preliminary final to Walpeup-Underbool by one point after Ray Morrish, the former Ouyen player, snapped a goal for the Bulldogs in the dying minutes. Walpeup-Underbool's best players in a determined effort included John Mead, the Morrish twins John and Ray, and Rob and Dan Willsmore, who were brothers. Chris Brown, the former ruckman and forward, was the club president. John Cummings, the dedicated trainer, would later receive a life membership. Rolla Burns, the TGP coach, was magnanimous in defeat in his understated way. He told the newspaper: "They just finished that little bit keener."

Walpeup-Underbool went on to fall just short of their bid to win the flag from fourth place. Manangatang defeated the Bulldogs amid a series of brawls in the Grand Final by fifteen points, earning the Saints their first premiership since they had won the Tyrrell league flag in 1967, twenty-two years previously.

In this era, five TGP players became members of the Tigers' 200 games club: Kelvin Jolly (310 senior games), Chris Monaghan (264), Lindsay Yetman (257), Barry Jolly (238) and Derry Monaghan (217). However, the declining population around the villages of Speed, Turriff, Tempy and Patchewollock was beginning to take effect on the football club's fortunes.

The practice of running through banners before finals matches was far from the only perceivable recognition of VFL influences during this era. Early in the 1983 season, an ad appeared in the *North West Express* which confirmed the growing tendency of country football people to take an interest in footy amid the bright lights of Melbourne, even from the far north-west of the state. The ad was posted by the Mallee Collingwood Supporters Group, which was organising a bus trip to Melbourne to see Collingwood play a match against Hawthorn at Victoria Park. The bus was scheduled to leave Ouyen at 6 o'clock on the Saturday morning and arrive at Collingwood's ground at midday. The group would stay at a motel in Queens Road, South Melbourne before returning to Ouyen after breakfast on the Sunday. The cost for the weekend – $61 for members and $71 for non-members – included the bus fare, admittance to the ground, and a light meal in the Black and White Room before and after the match. The trip organisers were Mandy Sleep, from the well-known Tiega family, and Bernie Kelly, the former secretary of the Mallee league, who had now taken up marathon running.

The decade finished with an ad in the paper from Laurie Kalms, the Mallee footy identity whose entrepreneurial streak now extended to organising a trip to Melbourne for the 1989 VFL Grand Final at the MCG. For $195, patrons were promised coach travel, an undercover seat for the game, and two nights' accommodation. Get in touch with mine host at the Patchewollock Hotel.

By now the VFL had become a national competition, with the West Coast Eagles and the Brisbane Bears raising the number of clubs to fourteen. In the new decade, the focus of the competition would become truly nationwide. As the game grew larger at the professional level, it began to shrink further from view in regions like the Pilbara, the Riverina and the Mallee in Victoria's north-west.

17

National Concern

During the 1990s, the AFL's national competition captured the attention of almost every footy fan within reach of a television. Meanwhile, country football was drifting further away from farming districts and towards the provincial towns. In the district around Ouyen, this trend became evident through the struggles of Tempy-Gorya-Patchewollock during a period when Ouyen Rovers were able to hold their ground. As the decade progressed, clubs based in small communities became imperiled all around Victoria, resulting in a shake-up of competitions on a scale that had not been seen since the volatile years between the two world wars.

Ouyen Rovers began the decade with a premiership, but only after an interruption of a type that was all too common in this era. In the 1990 Grand Final in the Northern Mallee league, Manangatang were holding a handsome lead over Ouyen Rovers when a wild brawl erupted during the third quarter. Rovers forward Anthony "Pud" Manley was knocked out-cold and taken to hospital. His teammates, however, rallied and wrested control of the match in their favour. The Rovers kicked six unanswered goals in the last quarter to win by six points. The half-back John Plozza, a railway worker originally from the Wimmera town of Kaniva, was best on ground.

Before the 1993 season, Brian "Barney" O'Callaghan returned to club football after a decade on the sidelines when Steve Manley, the Ouyen Rovers centre half-back and coach, asked him to be a selector. The Rovers defeated Sea Lake by seven points in the 1993 Grand Final. The next year, in 1994, Barney O'Callaghan agreed to become club vice-president. Steve Manley won the medal for the best and fairest player in the competition.

Before the 1994 season, Nandaly conceded their long and valiant fight to remain a club in their own right and approached Sea Lake about a merger. The merged club, Sea Lake-Nandaly, struck success in their second season. In the three years from 1994 to 1996, Manangatang won two premierships, in 1994 and 1996, while Sea Lake-Nandaly won in 1995. The clubs around Ouyen were runners-up in those three grand finals, with Walpeup-Underbool losing twice and TGP losing once. It would prove to be TGP's last gasp.

In this era, the general manager of the VCFL, David Code, responded to growing alarm around the state by sending out a questionnaire to gauge the reasons behind the decisions of country footy clubs to go into recess. The replies mostly mentioned population decline and administrative demands. In 1994, while Sea Lake and Nandaly merged in the Mallee, Echuca South and Echuca East merged to form Echuca United, while Gunbower went into recess.

In the next three years, from 1995 to 1997, in just the Wimmera and Mallee regions alone, Minyip and Murtoa merged, Jeparit and Rainbow merged, and Kaniva and Leeor merged, as did Noradjuha and Quantong. Birchip and Watchem-Corack combined to form Birchip-Watchem, while, in the region where the Wimmera meets the Western District, Douglas-Harrow-Miga Lake and Balmoral combined to form Harrow-Balmoral.

In the Northern District, Leitchville and Gunbower merged, as did Koondrook and Barham, while the two Cohuna clubs, Cohuna and Union, merged to form Cohuna Kangas. In a twist that reflected the burgeoning influence of the national competition, Cohuna Kangas adopted a guernsey based on Fremantle's design, but with a kangaroo in place of the anchor that was the central feature of the Dockers' jumper. Kerang Rovers and Appin merged, later to be subsumed by the Kerang Football Club.

In the Northern District, officials from the Mid-Murray league and the Kerang and District league spoke about combining their clubs and forming a divisional structure. In 1996, however, the Mid-Murray league took in three clubs from the old Northern District league – Kerang, Koondrook-Barham and Cohuna Kangas – to form a competition of eleven clubs, which they renamed the Central Murray league. Leitchville-Gunbower joined the North Central league, but later moved to the Central Murray league to join the clubs that had been formed from the remnants of their old rivals. The Kerang and District league, under pressure from the VCFL to rebrand itself, agreed to become the Golden Rivers league but only if the competition received $3000 from the VCFL to cover any costs incurred through the name change.

The same pressures that were forcing the hands of country football officials around the state forced the hands of those in charge at Tempy-Gorya-Patchewollock, who had a serious problem with the lack of juniors coming through. From the year of the merger in 1971 until 1990, TGP fielded at least one team – seniors, reserves or under-sixteens – on grand final day, and every one of those teams was comprised almost entirely by local players. The rot, however, set in during the 1989 and 1990 seasons. While the TGP senior team was up towards the top of the ladder, the club's under-sixteen team failed to kick a single goal in either season. For the next three seasons, from 1991 to 1993, the TGP under-sixteens managed to kick the occasional goal, but they still failed to win a game. The decline in the population of young footballers around Tempy, Speed and Patchewollock in this period forced the club to recruit players from wherever they could find them. The Tigers even bought a car for the recruits who travelled from Mildura to play.

When Sea Lake and Nandaly merged before the 1994 season and decided to base the club's entire operations in Sea Lake, the coach of Nandaly's former junior team, Peter "Sparks" Darley, offered to bring a carload of juniors to TGP. Sparks lived in Ouyen, as did most of the teenagers who had played for the Nandaly junior team. Rather than travel to Sea Lake to train and play, it made just as much sense to travel to Tempy and Patchewollock. There were a handful of highly talented juniors at

TGP, including Ryan Monaghan and Dustin Burns, who promised to shine if only the club could muster enough players to form a team. The influx of former Nandaly players before the 1994 season provided the opportunity for TGP's talented core to shine.

In the opening round of the 1994 season, the TGP juniors won the club's first game at under-sixteen level for more than five years when they defeated the reigning premiers, Walpeup-Underbool. Under coach Derry Monaghan, TGP went on to finish the home and away rounds in second place. The Tigers then defeated Sea Lake-Nandaly by five points in the Preliminary Final and Walpeup-Underbool by nine points in the Grand Final to earn a premiership that gained notice around the state.

The Age in Melbourne described the TGP under-sixteen team's premiership in 1994, having not won a game during the previous five seasons, as an achievement that struck a similar sense of wonder as Steve Moneghetti's victory in the marathon in the Commonwealth Games in 1990 and Shane Warne's opening delivery to dismiss Mike Gatting during the Ashes series in 1993. Derry Monaghan, who had played in seniors and reserves premierships with TGP, said coaching the club's under-sixteen team to the premiership in 1994 was the highlight of his career.

The next year, in 1995, Michael "Boozer" Robertson stepped in to become the club's senior coach. As a man of persuasive enthusiasm, it was his job to entice local products to return to the Mallee each weekend in a bid to win one last premiership. Craige Mott and the Woollard brothers, Billy and Bernie, were among those who drove many miles to play for their home club in 1995. Boozer also gained a bump from the under-sixteen team's success. TGP made the Grand Final in 1995, but lost to Sea Lake-Nandaly. At the end of the season, Boozer stepped aside and was replaced by co-coaches Darren Smith and Scott Hulland, a member of the talented Hulland family from Patchewollock.

During the 1996 season, it became apparent to TGP's committee that the club would be unable to go on. While the club had some highly talented players, the numbers were thin. The club considered just drifting off into the Mallee sunset, their legacy ensured by their string of premierships in three-part harmony during the previous two decades. The alternative, a merger with Ouyen Rovers, was not a popular option because the Tigers had played in many fierce battles against the Rovers over the years, but during the course of the 1996 season, the TGP president, Simon Grigg, and Boozer Robertson thought better about their club fading into oblivion. They approached the Rovers about a merger.

Barney O'Callaghan, now the Ouyen Rovers president, called a meeting of his committee at the Ouyen tennis and golf club rooms to explain TGP's position. Barney, with the bitterness over the division between Ouyen and Ouyen Rovers a decade earlier still fresh in his mind, was a proponent of the merger, but at a subsequent meeting, the committee voted narrowly against the merger.

At a meeting in Patchewollock, the TGP committee addressed the players and members of both clubs about their hopes that a merged club would play a total of three games a season at TGP's two bases, Tempy and Patchewollock. The Rovers centreman Matt Mellington, the son of former Rovers coach Mick Mellington, got a laugh – and broke the considerable tension in the room – when he said he would be happy to play on the Patchewollock oval if the club filled in the rabbit burrows, but the players were broadly in favour of merging if it would benefit football in the district.

At the third meeting in the tennis and golf rooms in Ouyen, Barney O'Callaghan invited the TGP trio Simon Grigg, Boozer Robertson and Rolla Burns to address the Rovers' members. Jock Gibbins, the former Tiega champion and Ouyen Rovers president, was among several speakers who opposed the merger. Michael O'Callaghan, a cousin of Barney O'Callaghan, was a member of the saleyards committee and a respected figure in town. His sons David and Andrew O'Callaghan were Ouyen Rovers footballers. After listening to opinions from around the room, Michael O'Callaghan stood up and made an impassioned speech in favour of the merger. He belted his fist on the table, and asked the room: "Why *wouldn't* you amalgamate?"

He sat down. The motion to merge was passed.

The merged club agreed to play a total of three home games between Tempy and Patchewollock, with the balance of matches at Blackburn Park. The club would continue to wear the Melbourne jumper, which was now back to navy blue and red, but it would change its name from Ouyen Rovers to Ouyen United. Barney O'Callaghan was elected as Ouyen United's first president, with Boozer Robertson vice-president.

The decision to merge the two clubs into one left the Northern Mallee league with five clubs, a figure that was considered untenable. At a time when the VCFL was conducting several investigations around the state, the ruling body held another investigation into the structure of Mallee football.

In the Southern Mallee league, the merger of Jeparit and Rainbow before the 1996 season had left that competition with seven clubs. Under the VCFL's direction, it was agreed to pool the two Mallee competitions, the Southern Mallee league and the Northern Mallee league, and, in a reversion of history, give the new competition the obvious title: the Mallee Football League.

The original competition known solely by the "Mallee" appellation, the Mallee Football Association, existed from 1903 to 1934. The competition based around Ouyen that was known as the Mallee Football League existed from 1955 to 1978. The catchment area of the third competition to be known solely by its Mallee descriptor, the one that began in 1997, covered almost the entire region of those two previous competitions. Strictly speaking, with matches being played at Jeparit, the new version of the Mallee league stretched down into the Wimmera. The distance from Ouyen to Jeparit was 180 kilometres.

Jeparit-Rainbow won the inaugural premiership in the new Mallee league, after defeating Beulah in the 1997 Grand Final. After that season, Barney O'Callaghan stepped aside as Ouyen United president to become a selector and Boozer Robertson succeeded him as president. Ever social, Boozer worked hard to unite the two supporters groups in the merged club in 1998, introducing whacky ideas for social functions such as a bowling night using large melons as the bowling balls. In this season, the club organised a grain auger, with a shaft about fifteen metres long, as the structure from which to hang lights for training at Patchewollock. Late in the 1998 season, the club organised for two grain augers to be used as lighting frames.

Under the coaching of Cameron McKay, Ouyen United were among the top teams in 1998, but their prospects for the flag looked dim after Beulah thrashed the Demons in the final home and away round. Ouyen United won through to the Grand Final, but were clear underdogs before the match against Beulah. The match was to be played at the Woomelang Recreation Reserve. Ouyen United's team included half a dozen teenagers. In their favour, the warm conditions favoured young legs.

Beulah stunned the inexperienced Demons by kicking seven goals in the opening quarter. The Demons then hit back to kick ten goals in the second quarter. Ouyen United went on to cause a major upset. Simon Robertson, Boozer's son, kicked six goals and won the two medals for best on ground, the VCFL medal and the umpires' medal. Boozer's other son, Adam, played well at half-back. The team also included Hayden Bell, who was from a prominent family at the Ouyen Football Club. It included Jayde Shean, a grandson of the highly respected Tempy administrator Len Shean, as well as Travis White, the son of the legendary 1970s defender John White. Dustin Burns was the son of the legendary TGP centreman Rolla Burns, while Justin Kay was the son of former Kiamal key forward Geoff Kay. The Munro brothers, Dean, Jarrod and Grant, were members of Kiamal's famous Munro family.

Boozer later said the 1998 Grand Final provided his greatest moment in footy. Only one player was from outside the district: Steve Whitty, who was a policeman. Every other player was from a prominent Mallee football family. Boozer said the win was also important because it served to unite the two strands of the merged club, the strands from TGP and Ouyen Rovers.

The only other club that remained in existence in the Ouyen district, the Walpeup-Underbool Football Club, struggled in the early years of the new Mallee league. The club had to change from their Bulldogs guernseys to accommodate Jeparit-Rainbow. They choose North Melbourne's blue and white stripes because Walpeup had worn those colours in their final years in the old Mallee league, twenty years earlier. The club also adopted the Roos nickname.

In this era, Walpeup-Underbool celebrated the first batch of players to pass the milestone of 200 senior games since the amalgamation of the two constituent clubs, Walpeup and Underbool, in 1982. By the halfway mark of the 1998 season, six players – Neil Vallance, Col Lockett, John Mead, Daryl Elliott, Peter Jones and Andrew Willsmore – had all passed the 200-game milestone.

Walpeup-Underbool found further cause for celebration when, for the first time, it was listed as the home club of an AFL player. Kane Munro, drafted by West Coast as a midfielder, gave everyone at Walpeup and Underbool and throughout the district a thrill when he was named to play for the Eagles in their match against Fremantle at the Subiaco Oval in Round 21 of the 2000 season. The Dockers won by one point.

Before the 2001 season, Walpeup-Underbool re-elected Gary Crow, a member of Underbool's 1975 premiership team, as president and Greg Vallance as secretary. The committee in turn announced the appointment of Brad Montgomery as coach. Montgomery had joined the club after moving to Walpeup to work at the Mallee Research Station as an agronomist the previous year.

Scott Munro and Darren Latta, one of Bob Latta's three sons, were appointed as Montgomery's assistants. Before the 2001 season, the club received a huge boost through the returns of Danny O'Shannessy, Jeremy Brown, Jim Wakefield, Sam Ovenden and Scott Brown, as well as the recruitment of Luke Crow's friend, Ben Kelly. As in any country footy club, the return of half a dozen favourite sons can give the club's chances of success a sharp spike. At the end of home and away rounds in 2001, the Roos were third on the ladder, behind Beulah and Berri-Culgoa.

Berri-Culgoa, going for their fifth premiership in seven years, largely through the agency of half a dozen legendary veterans, defeated Walpeup-Underbool in the Qualifying Final by ten goals. The Roos fought back to defeat Sea Lake-Nandaly and Beulah in the next fortnight to earn another crack at Berri-Culgoa in the Grand Final. The match was held at Hopetoun. The day was so warm that many fans wore shorts and T-shirts.

The Walpeup-Underbool team included four sons of Michael Brown, who had played on a wing in Underbool's 1975 premiership team. Marcus, the oldest of the four, played in defence, while Todd was named on a wing and his twin, Jeremy, and Matt played up forward. Matt, the full-forward, kicked a goal in the opening quarter that made him the first player from Walpeup-Underbool to kick 100 goals in a season. Berri-Culgoa led by three goals at three-quarter time, but in such warm conditions, Walpeup-Underbool felt their younger legs would give them a chance. The Roos pressed home in the last quarter, kicking five goals to two, before Brad Montgomery, the coach, marked about fifty metres out from goal on the siren, with his team one point in arrears. Montgomery gave the ball a mighty roost. It sailed through for a behind. Scores were level, 15.10 (100) apiece. It was a drawn grand final.

After the match, key defender Travis Latta and his fiancée Narelle Stone were forced to move their wedding date to accommodate the rematch the following weekend. Brad Montgomery organised his uncle, Ken Montgomery, to drive up from Echuca to address his players about how to approach a grand final rematch. Ken Montgomery had played at half-back in the North Melbourne team that drew with Collingwood in the 1977 VFL Grand Final then defeated the Magpies in the rematch the following week. His presence in the rooms at Underbool in September 2001 gave the Roos players a shot in the arm before their rematch against their experienced rivals from down the highway.

The Mallee league's 2001 Grand Final Rematch was held the day after the Brisbane Lions had defeated Essendon in the AFL Grand Final. Walpeup-Underbool got the jump early and held off Berri-Culgoa's challenge to win by sixteen points, 13.10 (88) to 10.12 (72). The assistant coaches, Scott Munro and Darren Latta, shared the medals for best on ground, with Munro winning the VCFL medal and Latta the umpires' medal. Travis Latta, Jeremy Brown and Brad Montgomery were also among the best players, while Matt Brown kicked four goals. Chris Brown, the full-forward in Underbool's 1975 premiership team, was the Mallee league president. Chris was a proud man as he hung a premiership medal around the neck of his son Scott Brown. Walpeup-Underbool's first flag as a merged entity was due reward after a lot of hard work from two resilient communities.

18

On the Road

The formation of the Mallee Football League with twelve clubs in 1997 was meant to bring a measure of stability to football in the region, but it failed in this regard almost immediately. After just one season, Nullawil left the Mallee league to join their former Tyrrell league rivals Ultima in the newly formed Golden Rivers league, which was based around Kerang. Nullawil officials figured that, as many of their players were driving from Melbourne and Bendigo, they had to play in a competition that was based closer to those cities. Versions of the Nullawil decision would be repeated over and over while the Mallee league dwindled dangerously towards extinction in the coming years.

By the turn of the century, almost every club in the Mallee league recruited their coach from Mildura or Swan Hill. When recruiting a coach from a regional centre, the clubs expected that the coach would bring several players with him. An injection of half a dozen talented players from a larger town could not only boost a club's prospects, it could give the club ammunition to approach further players who would travel only if they had the chance to play in a successful team. Clubs in the Mallee cast their nets wider and wider in the new century. They had no choice if they were to survive.

In the new century, almost every school graduate in the Mallee left home to take up an apprenticeship or embark on university studies in a regional centre like Ballarat or Bendigo or, in many cases, in Melbourne or Adelaide. The gathering force of a withering drought, called the Millennial Drought, also provided an impetus for young footballers and netballers to leave the land and find opportunity in construction firms and insurance offices in the cities and towns.

Chris Brown, by now a life member at Walpeup-Underbool and the president of the Mallee league, put the task for Mallee football clubs in context when he cited the example of his own family to *The Sunday Age* in Melbourne in June 2003. In 1910, his grandfather, Chris Brown senior, was among the first to select land at Underbool. His block, like all surveyed blocks, was 1 square mile, or 640 acres – the equivalent of 260 hectares on the metric scale.

Almost a century later, Chris Brown and his brother Kevin, himself a life member of the football club, owned the equivalent of fourteen blocks, which amounted to 3600 hectares. On an expanse of land that once kept at least fourteen families, there were now two. And even those families were subject to inevitable fragmentation. Chris Brown's three oldest children were studying in different cities while his youngest, sixteen-year-old Dean, was about to start a building apprenticeship in Mildura. Chris Brown and his wife Christine encouraged their children to take their opportunities elsewhere despite their fears that the family might have to sell the land it had held for almost a century.

In the town of Underbool, the post office and the supermarket were subsumed into the operations of the general store, and the pub was largely deserted. The departure of government services and small businesses, as well as the exodus from the farms, made fielding three football teams at the local footy club each weekend a monumental task.

According to Census figures in 2001, during the previous twenty-five years the population of Mildura had doubled, from 14,000 to 28,000, while the population of Swan Hill had swelled from almost 8000 to almost 10,000. The increases in Melbourne, Ballarat and Bendigo were even more pronounced. Ouyen, however, had reached its high-water mark twenty-five years previously, with a population of just over 1600 in 1976. Since then, the town's population had dwindled to 1150, while the population of Underbool had decreased by about seventy people, from about 290 to 220. (No figures were available for towns of less than 200.)

These shifts in population were reflected in the changes to the Mallee league after its formation in 1997 with twelve clubs.

1997: Mallee Football League's inaugural season:
Berriwillock-Culgoa, Beulah, Brim, Hopetoun, Jeparit-Rainbow, Manangatang, Nullawil, Ouyen United, Sea Lake-Nandaly, Walpeup-Underbool, Woomelang-Lascelles, Yaapeet

1998: Nullawil leave to join the newly formed Golden Rivers league
Mallee league down to eleven clubs

2000: Yaapeet fold
Mallee league down to ten clubs

2001: Brim merge with Wimmera league club Warracknabeal to form Warrack Eagles
Merged club enters Wimmera league
Mallee league down to nine clubs

2003: Sea Lake-Nandaly and Berri-Culgoa merge to form Sea Lake-Nandaly Tigers
Merged club enters Mallee league
Mallee league down to eight clubs

2004: Manangatang merge with Central Murray league club Tooleybuc to form Tooleybuc-Manangatang
Merged club enters Central Murray league
Mallee league down to seven clubs.

While the Mallee league was in the process of diminishing, news of the merger and closure of country football clubs throughout Victoria was reaching the halls of Parliament House in Spring Street. Midway through the 2003 season, the Victorian government announced it would hold a parliamentary inquiry into country football. The seven Members of Parliament who comprised the Rural and Regional Services Development

Committee would add the topic of football in the regions to their investigations into telecommunications in the country and the issue of death and injuries on farms. The seven members of the committee consisted of four members of the ruling Labor Party, one each from the Liberal and National parties, and one independent.

Of those seven members of the committee, the National Party MP, Peter Walsh, had played football for North Central league club Boort, and he had served as club president for three years. The independent MP, Craig Ingram, had recently come out of retirement at thirty-eight years of age to play in a key forward post for Buchan in East Gippsland. In announcing the inquiry, the government said its impetus was the death of fifty Victorian country football clubs during the previous twenty years.

Of the fourteen public hearings that were held throughout the state, hearings were held in Horsham, Kerang, Robinvale and Sea Lake in March 2004, and in Bendigo in May 2004. Terry Kiley and Chris Brown, the president and immediate past president of the Mallee league, were among those who spoke at the hearing in Sea Lake, along with Beverley Cummings from the Mallee Netball Association.

A year after those hearings, midway through 2005, the findings of the inquiry were revealed. Among other things, the inquiry found that:

- football-netball clubs were, to a significant degree, "the glue" that held many rural communities together
- people in rural and regional communities were proud of their clubs irrespective of on-field performance
- football's strengthening link with netball had given football officials a growing awareness of the need to create an inclusive environment
- the scale of the economy at country football clubs placed a heavy burden on volunteers, some of whom were unaccustomed to dealing with large sums of money
- there was an urgent need to improve facilities, especially for netballers and umpires
- governments and peak football bodies should work towards reducing the workload of volunteers

- the viability of football in rural areas depended on its ability to adapt to population movement.

The main result of the report was a joint announcement from the Premier, Steve Bracks, and the AFL chief executive, Andrew Demetriou, in June 2005 that the state government and the national body had each pledged $2 million towards the improvement of facilities at football and netball clubs throughout country regions. The government then invested a further $6 million to be administered by Sport and Recreation Victoria, for a total pool of $10 million.

The district around Ouyen received little of this money directly because, of the 880 clubs around country Victoria, there were only two clubs left in or near Ouyen to receive it. The inquiry's point about population change was the most apposite. Ouyen United and Walpeup-Underbool were both well served by volunteers who were happy to roll up their sleeves. Both clubs were financial, largely through the local farmers' habit of donating a portion of their crop towards the footy club. But clubs in the Mallee remained desperately short of players, specifically in the vital age bracket of eighteen to twenty-five years of age. While administrative practices and facilities were improving, the problem of player shortages in isolated regions was growing only worse.

In 2006, Ouyen recruited a playing-coach from Mildura, Stephen Bell, who brought with him a few players, including one of the most talented footballers to take the field in country Victoria, Robert "Sonny" Lindsey. An explosive forward, Lindsey was on the radar of AFL clubs including Richmond and Port Adelaide until his poor discipline prompted those clubs to drop their plans for him. In 1999, Lindsey played half a season with Sunraysia league club Red Cliffs before he fell out with the coach. He then switched to Mildura Imperials, where he enjoyed a good relationship with the Imps' coach, Tony Hickey. In the 1999 Grand Final, Lindsey proved a match-winner. He kicked six goals as the Imps defeated Robinvale by two points. The next year, in 2000, Lindsay rejoined Red Cliffs. He kicked 124 goals during the home and away rounds and another ten in the finals to boot the Tigers to the premiership. The club then sacked him.

Lindsey played briefly for Wimmera league clubs Nhill and Horsham United before enjoying an outstanding season with his third Wimmera league club, Dimboola; in 2005, he kicked 117 goals for Dimboola during the home and away rounds. In 2006, he agreed to join Ouyen United. The coach, Stephen Bell, arranged to pick up Lindsey at home in Mildura and drive him to training sessions and matches. Lindsey rewarded his coach and the club with a season in which he kicked 105 goals in the home and away rounds before embarking on a memorable finals series. Some older fans believed that Sonny Lindsey's performances during this series rivalled the performances of Richie Kalms when the former Murrayville champ was at his best.

At about 190 centimetres, Sonny Lindsey was a good size for a country full-forward. He was strong and robust, but he also moved with great agility. His prodigious talent allowed him to mark and kick goals from anywhere, but he was also courageous, and not afraid to throw himself at the ball.

Ouyen United finished the 2006 season in fourth place in the seven-team competition and were not expected to proceed far during the finals. The First Semi-final was against Sea Lake-Nandaly Tigers at Woomelang. Sonny Lindsey was restricted by injury. Towards the end of the second quarter, he was reduced to limping around the forward line. Late in the match, however, he shook off the pain to chase down a defender. His tackle saved the match. The performance of the Demons' captain and defender, Jarrod "Jasper" Munro, on Dale Lewis, the former Sydney Swans player, whose brother Wes Lewis was the Tigers' coach, was another crucial element in the Demons' advance to the next round of the finals.

Ouyen United's Preliminary Final was against Beulah at Sea Lake. Sonny Lindsey played at full-forward with the wind and loose in the backline against the wind. He picked up a welter of kicks in defence, and propelled the Demons into the Grand Final. The deciding match was against Woomelang-Lascelles at Hopetoun. Sonny kicked nine goals from full-forward to lift the Demons to victory by eleven points. The Demons' team included the Robertson brothers Ben and Mark, the sons of the artful former Tempy-Gorya-Patchewollock star Greg Robertson, who for several years had run a law practice in Swan Hill. Of those listed among the best players for the Demons in the 2006 Grand Final, Marc Hahnel, Jasper Munro, Corey Gregg and Brenton Jardine had surnames that had featured on best-player lists in the district around Ouyen for almost a century.

Sonny Lindsey left Ouyen United for a few seasons before returning in 2010 when Ryan O'Callaghan, one of Barney O'Callaghan's three sons, was appointed playing-coach. Ryan O'Callaghan had played junior football with Ouyen Rovers before he was recruited to the Bendigo Pioneers, the north-western region's club in the AFL's elite under-eighteen competition, the TAC Cup. In 1996, Ryan O'Callaghan was the Pioneers' co-captain, along with Kristian Shevlin from Golden Square. After his Pioneers career was over, Ryan played with the St Kilda's reserves team, Bendigo's VFL team and West Adelaide in SANFL, before taking on the playing-coach's role at Sunraysia league club Mildura in 2003. He coached Mildura for seven seasons before taking the job in Ouyen in 2010, at thirty-one years of age. O'Callaghan continued to live in Mildura, where he was a schoolteacher with a young family, but he was eager to travel to Ouyen to play alongside his brothers Adam and Corey in his home town club before the end of his career.

O'Callaghan's book of contacts served him well when he enticed Brett Knowles, a former teammate at St Kilda, to drive across from Adelaide, a journey of four hours, to play with Ouyen United. Knowles was originally from Yinnar, in the lush dairy country of Mid-Gippsland, but he thrived on the red earth of the Mallee. O'Callaghan also enticed his former ruckman at the Mildura Football Club, Craig Deckert, a Sunraysia league best and fairest medallist, to play for Ouyen United.

With players converging from north and west, Ouyen United pressed towards another premiership. After losing the 2009 Grand Final to Sea Lake-Nandaly Tigers, Ouyen United again went close in Ryan O'Callaghan's first year at the helm; the Demons lost to Beulah in the 2010 Grand Final. The next year, in 2011, the Demons were on top of ladder and looking forward to the finals when the club received a blow: the highly respected captain, Jasper Munro, injured his ankle and was ruled out for the season. The Demons, however, surged through September, defeating Beulah by 103 points in the Second Semi-final and Sea Lake-Nandaly Tigers by eleven goals in the Grand Final. Sonny Lindsey, having kicked ninety-eight goals during the minor rounds, kicked thirteen goals in the finals to bring his season's total to 111 as the Demons earned their third premiership under the moniker of Ouyen United.

Walpeup-Underbool pioneered the path from Adelaide to the Mallee when they recruited a handful of players with West Adelaide connections in 2006. The initial conduit was a former Roos player, Nick Timmers, who had grown up in Torrita but was now living in Adelaide. Timmers provided introductions for Luke Nathan, who had played almost 100 senior games with the Bloods, and Josh Charles. A car-load of Walpeup-Underbool officials, with Matt Brown and Andrew Willsmore among them, drove to Adelaide to meet their prospective recruits. After the West Adelaide pair had signed, another two former Bloods players, Daniel Harris and Nick Malinowski, signed on with Walpeup-Underbool a few rounds into the 2006 season. The Roos missed the finals in 2006, but they laid a solid foundation for improvement.

Before the 2007 season, Walpeup-Underbool signed Chris Vorwerk as their playing-coach. Vorwerk was a policeman in Hopetoun. He had coached the Hopetoun footy club in the Mallee league, but he was keen to take the job at Walpeup-Underbool because he could see that the club was building something. The Roos signed Vaughan Noonan and Matt "Chicken" Palmer, who were living in Adelaide. Palmer had grown up in Swan Hill and played in premiership teams with Swan Hill and Ultima before moving to Adelaide and joining a suburban club. When the chance came to return to Mallee footy, he jumped at it. Both Luke Nathan and Matt Palmer would meet their wives during their years with Walpeup-Underbool. The Roos built their teams with local products who returned from Mildura and elsewhere, augmented by a car-load of serious talent from Adelaide.

Walpeup-Underbool received another enormous boost in this era when Kane Munro returned from Perth, having played eighteen AFL games with West Coast. Kane joined his brothers Scott and Kyle in Ouyen, from where they ran their farming operation. With such a talented line-up, Walpeup-Underbool won successive premierships in 2007 and 2008. After a fallow period, the club rose again in 2012 under the coaching of Jeremy Rowe, who was also recruited through Adelaide connections, and defeated Sea Lake-Nandaly Tigers by 109 points in the 2012 Grand Final. Having failed to win a premiership for almost two decades after the amalgamation, Walpeup-Underbool had now won four senior flags in twelve seasons.

Just months after the 2012 Grand Final, the club was dealt a tragic blow when two members of the premiership team, Scott Munro, 35, and Tim Vallance, 26, were killed in a light-plane crash near Ouyen. The pair were highly talented footballers. When, during the 2012 season, Walpeup-Underbool celebrated the thirtieth anniversary of the amalgamation, both players were named in the best team of those thirty years, with Munro named as rover and Vallance on the bench. Both were also hard workers around the club, eager to pitch in with any task, and their deaths rocked their community and the entire district around Ouyen. More than 1000 mourners turned up for the combined funeral at the Walpeup hall. Most mourners were forced to stand outside in the heat.

According to an article in *The Sunday Age*, the deaths of the popular duo left their grieving teammates in no mood to resume preparations for the 2013 season. However, the sight of the late Scott Munro's younger brothers, Kane and Kyle, throwing themselves into training was the impetus for their teammates to pick themselves up for their club. Walpeup-Underbool people had heavy hearts when they headed south to play Jeparit-Rainbow in the opening round of the 2013 season. After a slow start, the Kangaroos kicked clear to win by fifty points, with Kane Munro, the captain, among the best players in the midfield and Kyle Munro kicking five goals up forward. The club's latest star recruit from West Adelaide, Ben Fisher, was also among the Kangaroos' best.

Tears flowed the next weekend when the club hoisted its premiership flag before its match at Underbool against Hopetoun. The Kangaroos won that match, and finished third at the end of the season. Neither Walpeup-Underbool nor Ouyen United challenged for the flag during the finals in 2013 and 2014.

Before the 2015 season, the two clubs were disappointed if not surprised when three rival clubs made difficult decisions in an attempt to combat the problem of declining population. Jeparit-Rainbow transferred to the Horsham and District league, largely because they drew most of their players from Horsham, while Beulah and Hopetoun, two clubs that had been strong rivals since the inaugural season of the Mallee Football Association more than a century earlier, in 1903, elected to merge into one club.

Instead of taking a hyphenated name, the merged club employed the strong identity of their region, the Mallee. For their choice of guernseys and nickname, they went with the connection lent by their inaugural coach, Geoff Burdett, one of Hopetoun's favourite sons, who had maintained contact with the former Essendon coach Kevin Sheedy since their days together at Windy Hill. Sheedy was now an ambassador for the AFL expansion club Greater Western Sydney, whose nickname was the Giants. The newly merged club in the Mallee league took the name of the Southern Mallee Giants. Like the Giants in the AFL, the Southern Mallee Giants would wear guernseys of orange and charcoal.

With the departure of one club and the merger of two others before the 2015 season, the Mallee Football League was down to five clubs. The competition's lack of future was abundantly clear. Officials from the league and the remaining clubs had decisions to face.

19

Poles of Power

In its original form, a totem pole was a carved and painted log, constructed by indigenous tribes in North America. The carvings and decorations on a totem pole could symbolise a revered guardian or ancestral being. They could commemorate beliefs or legends. They could recognise clan lineages or notable events. Ultimately, they could embody any story of significance to the people who carved and installed the pole.

Geoff van Wyngaarden was a teacher from Williamstown with a qualification in history and mathematics when he and his family moved to Ouyen in 2000 so that Geoff could take up a position at the high school. After a few years, Geoff was placed in charge of the school's department that covered history and geography. Without a curriculum to follow, he devised one that covered local history, geography and football. He started reading old newspapers at the Ouyen District History and Genealogy Centre and the microfilms of old newspapers in the state library during visits to Melbourne. Geoff's students enjoyed the departure from regular content in his history classes. Geoff's articles in the *North West Express* in which he described footy history in the Mallee drew a keen readership.

In 2004, the Ouyen Secondary College gained a teacher who would go on to develop an entirely novel way to depict the history of footy in the Mallee. Nerida Fry had grown up in the south-east suburbs of Melbourne.

After studying education, she took a job teaching at Ulladulla, on the South Coast of New South Wales. However, her keen interest in showing horses forced her to consider a move. She needed to live on flatter land, where she could better manage her horses. When a job was offered at the school in Ouyen, she accepted it. Nerida had never been to Ouyen before she began work there. She agisted her horses on the farm of Noel Morrish, just outside town. In tending her horses, she met Noel's son Jason Morrish. The pair married. Nerida Morrish became ingrained in her town in the heart of the Mallee.

Being part of the Morrish family, Nerida was never far away from footy talk. Her brother-in-law Paul Morrish had played about thirty games at AFL level. One day, a member of Blackburn Park's management committee, Lyndal Munro, approached Nerida about painting a series of totem poles to depict the elaborate lineage of the clubs that had merged into one another to form Ouyen United. Talks began about what the poles should look like, and where they should go.

In 2009, Nerida informed the students in her Year 9 and 10 art class that they would paint totem poles to represent the various clubs that had folded into each other to create Ouyen United. Dean Munro, a half-back with Ouyen United and a local farmer, had a selection of old power poles that were gathered in a pile on his family's property outside Ouyen. Dean Munro and Jason Morrish, Nerida's husband, took the poles to the school, where Jason inserted them into the ground next to the school's ag area. He made sure he inserted them loosely so that it would be easier to transfer them to Blackburn Park later on.

The students learnt about the histories of the clubs. Then they used their findings to design their colour schemes for the poles. Ron Vine, a stalwart of the Kiamal and Ouyen Rovers clubs, described the exact shade of red for the Tiega pole and the precise shade of green for Tempy. The students decided that the Ouyen Rovers pole would be royal blue in keeping with the club's adoption of the Melbourne guernsey as it was during the club's first year in 1982.

The students began painting the poles during lessons. Before long, they became so keen that they painted the poles during their lunch breaks.

Jason Morrish, an earth mover and concreter, carefully pulled the poles out of the ground and, after much toil, placed them at intervals behind the forward pocket at the southern end of Blackburn Park. He set them in the ground with limestone and concrete. To protect the poles against the harsh climate, the students painted over the poles with Dulux Solar Shield. In all, there were nine poles, representing the clubs that had merged to form Ouyen United since the Second World War.

After the construction of the poles in 2009, it became a common sight for drivers to halt their journeys along the Calder Highway and check out the poles. Travellers were intrigued by the depiction of the many clubs that had folded into one. Photos of the poles popped up on social media sites. The town of Ouyen already had a novel claim to fame as the home of the best vanilla slice in Victoria. Now, the totem poles of Ouyen United provided another unlikely tourist attraction.

While Walpeup-Underbool had won premierships in the Mallee league, the club was never far away from speculation that it would become the final club to fold into the club in Ouyen. During this period, Walpeup-Underbool suffered a series of tragic blows that rocked everyone at the club and many throughout the Mallee. After the death of Scott Munro and Tim Vallance in a light-plane crash near Ouyen in early 2013, the club was left reeling during the 2013 season when Peter Phillips, a reserves team manager, was killed in a car crash and Daryl Elliott, a former club president, died as a result of a brain tumour. Elliott, who played 250 games for the club before serving as an official, was awarded a posthumous life membership.

Walpeup-Underbool received a boost after the 2013 season when local product Dallas Willsmore was taken by Hawthorn in the AFL rookie draft. Willsmore's family was a huge part of Walpeup-Underbool. His father, Andrew Willsmore, had played more than 300 games for the club, and had served as club president. His mother Tanya had won many netball best-and-fairest awards, and was still playing in the Roos' A-grade team. The boost from the AFL rookie draft, however, was short-lived. A month after the draft, a member of another prominent Walpeup-Underbool family, Danny Stone, died on Christmas Eve 2013 after injuring himself when he dived into a pool. Less than a year later, in November 2014, the club was assailed by yet more tragedy when Anthony Wisneske, a footballer and cricketer with Walpeup-Underbool, was killed at twenty-eight years of age when he was crushed by a grain silo. According to the *Weekly Times*, Wisneske was helping with a lupin harvest when the silo collapsed. His funeral was held in the clubrooms at Underbool.

At the beginning of the 2015 season, the ruling body of country football, now AFL Victoria Country, surprised no one when it recommended that the Mallee league should be dissolved and its five clubs should be assigned to varying futures. Under the recommendations, the Southern Mallee Giants were advised to transfer to the Horsham and District league, while Sea Lake-Nandaly Tigers and Woomelang-Lascelles were advised to merge and form a club that would enter the Central Murray league. Ouyen United and Walpeup-Underbool were advised to merge and form a club that would enter the Sunraysia league. The sparseness of the population in the Mallee was apparent in the recommendation that five clubs should be wound back to three, which would enter competitions based on the distant borders of the region, in Swan Hill, Horsham and Mildura.

While Ouyen United might have been able to continue as an entity in their own right, Walpeup-Underbool appeared to have no such luxury. For a decade, the club had followed a policy of fielding a senior team comprised of local products plus a car-load of blue-chip talent from Adelaide. In 2015, Walpeup-Underbool's Adelaide recruits included Shane Birss, who had played AFL football at the Western Bulldogs and St Kilda, as well as Ben Fisher, Ryan Anderson and Brad Dabrowski, who had played plenty of senior footy in the SANFL. Dabrowski, a 200-centimetre ruckman, had played a total of 150 senior games for West Adelaide and Woodville-West Torrens, and he had represented South Australia. It might have been possible to continue under this model; the club had the finances, through the hard work of club members, to continue to pay for recruits. But the club's tenuous future was also underpinned by the increasing difficulty of convincing fatigued local products to return every weekend from Adelaide, Melbourne, Bendigo and Ballarat to play for their home club.

Also among the considerations, Walpeup-Underbool officials were reeling after their series of tragic ordeals, with the president, Jamie Latta, among those most affected. Latta's roots in his club and community were as deep as it was possible to be in the unforgiving Mallee soil. He was a member of the Latta family that had sustained their local club for decades.

The Latta family moved on to a block at Kattyoong, north-west of Walpeup, soon after the land was opened up for selection. George Latta was from Buninyong, near Ballarat. After moving his family on to the block in the Mallee, he was on the first committee at the Kattyoong school when it was opened in 1917, with nineteen pupils in the first intake.

Les Latta, Jamie's grandfather, was born in 1920, the eleventh child in his family. Les began playing footy for Torrita, without the knowledge of his parents, at fourteen years of age. After his parents became aware of his football proclivities, Les transferred to Walpeup, where he played in defence without decoration for decades. In 1960, Les Latta was aged forty when he was a member of Walpeup's breakthrough premiership team. Twenty years later, he was still playing in the Walpeup reserves. *The Sun* in Melbourne ran a story on his retirement in which he estimated he had played in a combined tally of 800 seniors and reserves games. Les was never reported. He rarely ventured forward of the centre. He just loved playing footy. Les Latta still had a strength and bullishness about him when he died in 2014 at the age of ninety-four.

Unlike his father Les, Bob Latta became one of the most decorated footballers to play in the Mallee. Bob was a centreman who played in two premiership teams with Walpeup, in 1968 and 1978. He won three league best and fairest awards, in 1971, 1975 and 1976, as well as seven club best and fairest awards, and he was a star player in the North Central interleague teams that made their legendary run from 1969 to 1974, culminating with the victory over the Hampden league in the country championship final in Warrnambool.

Jamie Latta, who is the oldest of Bob Latta's three sons, said his father took a lot of hits during a career that ended with a king hit in 1984, when he was thirty-eight years of age. Jamie's only clear memory of watching his father play at Walpeup was one passage of play in which Bob took the ball from a centre bounce and ran forward before kicking long to the goalsquare, where full-forward Bob Lester shepherded the ball through for a goal.

Jamie himself played about seventy senior matches for Walpeup-Underbool and about 200 games in the juniors and reserves, but he knew early that his greater calling was in administration. He was named assistant secretary at eighteen years of age. Later, he served as treasurer, secretary and, eventually, president. "You find ways to contribute," he said in an interview for this book. "The footy club is the biggest institution in a country town."

Jamie's brothers Darren and Travis became legends on the field. Darren and Travis both played in four premiership teams with Walpeup-Underbool (2001, 2007-2008, and 2012), and both played more than 320 senior games for the club. Jamie, meanwhile, did a power of work in the background. Thirty years after taking his first role in administration, he was the club president when Walpeup-Underbool had to decide whether to seek a merger with Ouyen United.

Jamie Latta said his own family's farm set-up indicated the major reason there were so few footballers left at Mallee clubs. In 2015, Jamie and his two brothers and their families operated their farming business on 20,000 hectares of land, stretching over an area of seventy kilometres, from Trinita in the north to Patchewollock in the south. Under the early system of settlement, the land would have comprised about seventy-five blocks, meaning it would have supported at least seventy-five families. Now it was supporting three.

When Jamie was at Walpeup Primary School in the early 1980s, there were about fifty students. The number of students declined steadily until the school received a fatal blow in 2014 with the closure of the Mallee Research Station after eighty years of operations. The research station had employed a staff of thirty. When the Walpeup Primary School was closed a year later, in early 2015, the number of pupils at the school was down to six. The football club was always going to struggle if there were no juniors to come through.

The closure of the Walpeup school further convinced Jamie Latta that, for the good of his community, Walpeup-Underbool had to merge with their neighbours in Ouyen. A merger would ensure contact among farmers and their families through familiar rituals. "Farmers lead isolated lives," he said. "The weekly trip to the local footy is critical."

Jarrod "Jasper" Munro, the Ouyen United president in 2015, was also from a family with a long and distinguished pedigree in the district around Ouyen. The name "Munro" had featured on Kiamal team sheets from the time of the club's formation in 1920. Jasper's father, Walter Munro, better known as Spot, was a top defender for many years. Spot won four club best and fairest awards, and he played a key role in Kiamal's victory in the 1971 Mallee league Grand Final. In his notes on the history of the Kiamal Football Club that were published in the Ouyen newspaper in 1985, Ginger Hickmott said Spot Munro was his choice as the best footballer to have played for the Magpies. Jasper Munro described his father as "a short centre half-back", much like himself. Both father and son were 182 centimetres tall, or a whisker under six feet.

Jasper grew up in Ouyen. Not uncommonly, the family lived in town and travelled out to its farms on the fringe of town. In 1995, the Munro family bought the final block of land owned by Frank Healy, the former Tiega defender and president. As a way of keeping Frank connected with the land, Jasper picked him up once a year during the harvest to take him out to the paddock. Every year without fail, while Jasper was levering Frank up in to the cabin of the header, Frank would say, "Whoa, I haven't been this high since I was playing footy." For several years, it was part of the ritual of harvest time. Frank Healy died late in 2018 after a long and full life. He was ninety-one years of age.

Jasper Munro played his first senior game for Ouyen United at fifteen years of age. He played in the 1998 and 2006 premiership teams, and he was captain in 2011 when the Demons were sailing towards another flag, but he injured his ankle and was ruled out of the finals. The Demons won the flag without him. After his ankle was reconstructed, Jasper returned to the field halfway through the 2012 season while continuing his role as football operations manager. Halfway through the next season, in 2103, tragedy struck the Ouyen United footy club when the president, Tony Cua, died of a heart attack. Through his administrative role, Jasper had been close to Cua. The key defender had sought to concentrate on trying to get a kick, but after the death of his friend, he agreed to retire as a player and assume the presidency. Jasper Munro had played 270 senior games before hanging up his boots at thirty-seven years of age.

In early 2015, Jasper agreed when Jamie Latta sought a meeting to discuss the possibility of a merger between Ouyen United and Walpeup-Underbool. Four delegates from both clubs met on five occasions in the rooms of the Walpeup Tennis Club, which was about halfway between the towns of Ouyen and Underbool, and offered no prospect of participants being interrupted by curious onlookers. According to Jamie Latta, delegates from both clubs occasionally stood up and threatened to walk out. At meetings back at the two clubs, there was much dissent among members. However, with AFL Victoria's Wimmera Mallee commission making plain to the two clubs that a merger was in their best interests, the leaders pressed on with talks.

Finally, as the 2015 season entered the dead of winter, the merger of the two clubs was announced as a means of bringing new life to football in the district. The merged club would be called Ouyen United but it would take Walpeup-Underbool's North Melbourne jumper and nickname. In a twist, the fact that the Sunraysia league club Wentworth called themselves the Roos meant that Ouyen United would have to call themselves the Kangas. The merged club would play five home games in Ouyen and three in Underbool. Whereas the Ouyen Football Club's foray into the Sunraysia league in 1979 had failed because most Mallee league people were against the idea, Ouyen United's venture into the Sunraysia league in 2016 promised much because the district was overwhelmingly in favour of it. Despite the froth and bubble at the club meetings, the vast majority of footy people around Ouyen believed the merger and subsequent move into the Sunraysia league was the only choice for football in the district.

After the announcement, two stalwarts of Mallee footy, Boozer Robertson and Donald McGregor, were standing in a paddock on Boozer's farm outside Tempy, talking about footy and commodity prices, when they hit upon the idea of bringing together their old friends in the Mallee league before the end of club footy in the Mallee as they knew it. The pair organised a reunion for all footballers who played in the Mallee league between 1960, which was the year of Murrayville's entry, and 1978, the year that this particular version of the Mallee league was wound up. Netball people organised a reunion of the Mallee league team that won the night series in Mildura in 1975. The reunions were scheduled to be held at Blackburn Park on the day of the final match between Ouyen United and Walpeup-Underbool, late in the 2015 season. Boozer organised the publicity, writing his cheeky prose for the *North West Express* and persuading the *Herald Sun* to take a photo of club representatives in the many jumpers of the Mallee league in front of the silo at Torrita.

A grand final-sized crowd of 1500 swarmed on Blackburn Park on the day of the reunions. Eight premiership flags were hung from a cherry-picker. The ground was festooned with memorabilia from all clubs. The displays included blazers and ties, football records, premiership photos, interleague photos, netball attire, an array of club jumpers, and Kevin Healy's kitbag, replete with neatly packed boots, socks, jockstrap, shorts and jumper. Kevin, the twin brother of Frank Healy, had retired as a footballer with Tiega more than fifty years earlier. His gear was still in pristine condition.

About 200 former players formed a guard of honour for the senior teams as they ran on to the ground. Some of those who lined up had flown in from Darwin, Cairns and Perth. Their ranks included former Collingwood player Denis O'Callaghan, as well as Mallee league greats Richie Kalms and Des Sporn from Murrayville, Barry Gniel from Walpeup and John White from Ouyen. The netballers from the victorious 1975 team included Lyn Floyd, Lorraine Shaddock, Julie Monk, Rosalee Newey, Rhonda McLean, Kerryn Bursill and Val Munro. The Ouyen United president, Jarrod Munro, made sure his grandmother, Phyllis Munro, a Mallee football fan throughout her 100 years, was at the ground.

The two captains of the day acknowledged the former footballers before running through a banner together. A helicopter delivered a specially minted coin for the toss. Two of the greatest footy stalwarts of the region – Norm Vallance, a committeeman with Kiamal and Ouyen Rovers for fifty years, and Ray Gloster, a timekeeper with Underbool and

Walpeup-Underbool for sixty years – were given the honour of jointly tossing the coin.

In a season in which Ouyen United and Walpeup-Underbool filled the fourth and fifth places on the five-team ladder, Ouyen United won the match by three points. The Demons' list of best players included two with family names that had been familiar in the Mallee for decades, Todd Barker and Brad Vallance. The Roos' best included Brad Dabrowski, the big ruckman, and Travis Latta, as well as Luke Nathan, the midfielder who had married into an Underbool family after being recruited from West Adelaide a decade earlier.

After the match, supporters from throughout the Mallee squeezed into the social rooms at Blackburn Park. The coin that had been delivered by helicopter was auctioned off; Laurie Kalms, the former ruckman and current hotel magnate, bought it for $450. A ball signed by every player on the day and a copy of the photo that was taken in front of the Torrita silo were also put up for bid. Raylene Vine, who had married into the family of the former Kiamal player and official Vivian Vine, sang a song she had written for the occasion. Representatives from each of the nine clubs that had played in the Mallee league from 1960 to 1978 were allotted fifteen minutes to describe their club's time in the competition. The former players' stories filled the room with laughter. One of the most memorable stories was the admission of Peter "Doughie" Robins, the former Tempy-Gorya-Patchewollock centreman, that, forty years after his famous clash with Don Pohlner, he was still jolted awake at night by a vision of Pohlner flying through the air towards him while mounted on an anvil!

Rather than a day or mourning, it was a day of celebration. It set the tone for the venture into the Sunraysia league.

After the home and away rounds in 2015, Ouyen United finished fourth with five wins and eleven losses. In a five-team competition, fourth place was enough to make the finals. The Demons advanced through September, defeating Southern Mallee Giants and Woomelang-Lascelles to earn a berth in the 2015 Grand Final. In the lead-up to the big match, Geoff van Wyngaarden submitted an excellent history of Mallee football for the Grand Final edition of *The Final Siren,* which was the Mallee league's record. Ouyen United's opponents in the Grand Final were Sea Lake-Nandaly-Tigers, who were led by Scott Weekley, a league best and fairest winner, and Col Durie, a veteran who was among the most decorated footballers in country Victoria. The Tigers proved too strong, increasing their lead throughout the match to win by nine goals. Ouyen United's two best players were Henry Armour and Aron Morrish, who were young and keen. The future looked bright for the brave new world of Ouyen United.

20
On the Hop

Jarrod "Jasper" Munro was announced as president and Jamie Latta as vice-president of the Ouyen United Football Club before the Kangas made their debut in the Sunraysia league in 2016. Andy Jardine, a key defender with Ouyen United, and Kane Munro, the former West Coast midfielder who had returned to Walpeup-Underbool, were named as co-coaches. With the memories of the thrashings that the Ouyen Football Club received during its foray into the Sunraysia league from 1979 to 1982 still clear in the minds of many, the second club to venture into the Mildura competition under the Ouyen banner was determined to be competitive.

Brad Vallance had played in the midfield for Ouyen United during the club's final years in the Mallee league. During the off-season, he took the path of a growing number of Victorian country footballers and played with a club in the Northern Territory Football League, whose season was scheduled from October to March, during the Top End's Wet Season. Brad played at Southern Districts, a club based in the southern suburbs of Darwin. Before the 2016 season in Victoria, he was the conduit for talks between Southern Districts teammates and officials from Ouyen United. The Kangas signed five recruits from Southern Districts for the

2016 season. Henry Armour and Dean Staunton were known to Mallee football followers, having played with Ouyen United in the Mallee league. However, ruckman Lyndon Brandy and the Farrer brothers, Will and Josiah, were exciting new signatures. The Farrer brothers, especially, were renowned for their ability to sway matches to their will.

To play for Ouyen United, the Darwin contingent had to fly to Melbourne on Friday evening then catch a small plane to Mildura, where an Ouyen United representative would meet them at the airport. The club man would ferry the players to their digs in Ouyen or Mildura so they could rest before the following day's match. In all, the journey took about eight hours. The journey for Jo Farrer, however, was more arduous than even that of his fellow recruits. Jo lived in Katherine. He had to knock off work at lunchtime on Friday before driving three hours north to Darwin to meet his brother for the flight to Melbourne.

Ouyen United's first game in the Sunraysia league was against South Mildura at the No.3 Oval at the Mildura showgrounds. In the days leading up the match, Jamie Latta pulled off a final coup when he signed another former SANFL player, Lachie Medhurst, who had been a ruckman with Sturt. Medhurst walked into Ouyen United's rooms before the match against South Mildura without knowing a soul. During the course of the match, he was cleaned up and had his neck broken. Ben Mole, the ruckman, had his collarbone broken. Jason McGlynn had his arm broken. In a torrid introduction to the Sunraysia league, Ouyen United lost by six goals.

The next week, the Kangas hosted Irymple at Blackburn Park, and won by seven goals. By the time Ouyen United were due to host their first match at Underbool, in Round 5, the club was still finding its feet. The build-up to the match at Underbool was like another Mallee reunion. Old footballers converged on the Underbool Recreation Reserve for training on the Thursday night and continued on their course of conviviality for two days. All the old rivalries and ripostes were trotted out. The Kangas lost to Mildura Imperials, a traditional powerhouse in the Sunraysia league, by two goals, but they lost few friends in doing so. The good times rolled long into the night.

Halfway through the 2016 season, the Kangas found a measure of form. In the five matches from round 13 to 17, they lost only once, to Merbein. In the final match, in Round 18, they lost to the premiership favourites, Mildura, by five goals. The final four at the end of the home and away rounds in 2016 consisted of Mildura and Irymple on thirteen wins, ahead of Ouyen United and Merbein, both with nine wins. Will Farrer, the Kangas full-forward, won the goalkicking award with fifty-four goals.

Ouyen United swept through the early finals, scoring convincing victories over Merbein and Irymple to win a berth in the Grand Final against Mildura. During Grand Final week, ABC Television's flagship current affairs show, *7.30*, did a story on the Kangas' emergence from a sea of hardship to make a fairytale run towards a flag. The attention galvanised the Kangas. With so many players with experience in big matches in Darwin and elsewhere, they believed they stood a good chance against a club that was striving to win its first premiership in a decade.

The Kangas burst out of the blocks, kicking nine goals to three in the opening quarter. They were held goal-less in the second quarter, but maintained control in the second half and ran out winners by twenty-nine points, 16.10 (106) to 11.11 (77). Jo Farrer, the relentless and creative midfielder, won the medal for best on ground. His fellow Darwin recruit, Henry Armour, was also among the best players, but the other four players listed among the best – Brad Vallance, Aron Morrish, Marcus Healy and Marc Hahnel – were all from families with long and strong links to football around Ouyen.

On the boundary line, the club's leaders, Jasper Munro and Jamie Latta, embraced on the siren. After the final tumult of the Mallee league and the eventual merger, both struggled to believe what their club had just pulled off. Ouyen United's premiership in 2016 was one of the great stories in country football.

The Kangas unfurled their 2016 premiership flag before their match against Merbein in Round 3 of the 2017 season, and once again the good times rolled. They defeated the Magpies by 108 points. Halfway through the season, Will Farrer struck a golden patch. In five matches, he kicked a total of forty goals, including thirteen against Merbein and eight against

Robinvale-Euston, who were fellow finals contenders. When Ouyen United had a bye during that period, Farrer stayed in the Top End and attended a conference on indigenous affairs.

At the end of the 2017 home and away rounds, Will Farrer won the goalkicking award with ninety goals, and the Kangas finished second on the ladder, behind Mildura. While Ouyen United had careered through the finals in 2016, this time it was Irymple who made a dash for glory. Irymple defeated Robinvale-Euston and Mildura in the early finals to earn a shot at Ouyen United in the 2017 Grand Final. The match was even until Irymple kicked four unanswered goals in the second quarter. The Kangas pegged them back only to just fall short. The Swallows won by seven points, 9.15 (69) to 9.8 (62).

Mallee supporters of Ouyen United were disappointed, but philosophical. As farmers in Victoria's dry north-west, they knew the odds were against them having two perfect seasons in a row.

Part 3

The Grand Tour

21

Nandaly Natterings

Before I hit the road to Ouyen to embark on Boozer Robertson's grand tour of the old Mallee grounds, I decide to warm up by hearing the stories about an unused oval just to the south of Ouyen, in Nandaly. The Nandaly Football Club was a proud club that battled way beyond its capacity for many years before finally seeking a merger. When I rang the Nandaly stalwart Terry "Jacko" Kiley to see if he would meet me at the ground, he was happy to oblige.

As I pull into the grounds of the Nandaly Recreation Reserve, the Mallee sky begins to turn pink and orange in the gathering dusk. A metal rail fence forms a barrier around the oval. The oval itself features a patchwork of grass tufts on red soil. I get a footy out of my van, ostensibly to boot it towards the goalposts which stand in defiance at the western end, but I do not feel inspired to take a shot. It seems frivolous to try to send a banana kick or even a drop punt curling towards goal. It feels wrong to try anything of a curling nature. The boundary line at my feet bumps over the uneven surface as it traces its path around the oval.

The man I have arranged to meet, Jacko Kiley, is wearing work boots and shorts. So are his friends. I thought I was just meeting Jacko, but eight or nine others turn up as well. Most have no real idea why they're here.

Jacko just told them there's a bloke from Melbourne who's coming to town and he wants to talk footy. We're arranged in a circle on the parquetry floor of the old social rooms. Most of the former Nandaly footballers sit on chairs they've pulled in from the edge of the room. One is sitting on an Esky. He offers me a beer. Pictures of best-and-fairest winners, most holding a football at forty-five degrees, hang on the walls around us. Many of the players have awful, shapeless haircuts, straight out of the 1970s, which happens to be the decade that provided Nandaly with their moments of greatest glory. All the players in the photos look shy, but they beam with pride at having won the highest award at their local club.

The rooms are modest, but it's a testament to the people of Nandaly that the rooms are in any condition at all. Nandaly footballers have not played at their own ground since 1993. For twenty-five years, the ground has hosted Auskick sessions but very little else to do with footy. Unusually, it was the decision of the Nandaly footballers to forgo the opportunity to play on their own ground. When the club approached Sea Lake about a merger, Sea Lake offered to play a share of games at Nandaly, but the negotiators from Nandaly said no. They reasoned that Sea Lake had the best facilities in the Mallee. They would be mad not to play all their matches there.

During my family's trips to Ultima when I was a boy, I saw Ultima play the odd match in the Tyrrell league, but I never saw them play against Nandaly. I do, however, remember Nandaly's presence in the competition. In the Tyrrell league's record, the club notes appeared under the heading, "Nandaly Natterings". The Ultima notes ran under the heading, "Ultima Utterings". As a boy who was accustomed to the *Football Record*, the VFL's more sober match-day publication, I was intrigued by the Tyrrell league's penchant for alliteration.

Most of the players in the room on this Friday evening in Nandaly played in that era of alliteration. Jacko himself was a rover who made his senior debut in 1971, when he was still at boarding school at Sunbury, and he continued playing for another fifteen years. In his retirement, he poured his considerable energy into administration. Jacko has been club president or league president, or on a football board of some description, in every season since he hung up his boots. His willingness to work for the good of the game, while always maintaining a smile, is renowned throughout the Mallee.

Jacko was the best player on the ground in Nandaly's most famous match, the victory over Nullawil in the 1974 Tyrrell league Grand Final. Alan "Shifty" Larmour was a half-forward in that team. Shifty gained his nickname during a euchre night. After holding back his trumps, he was described by an opponent as a shifty bastard. Jacko chuckles when he says that Shifty is the most honest bloke in the world, but he's been stuck with his nickname since that fateful night of cards.

Shifty's work as a shearer, a job that required him to bend over all day while he separated the sheep from their fleece, meant that he struggled to bend down on the footy field by the mid-point of his career. Nor could he turn around without sending out a warning party. By the time of Nandaly's victory in the Northern Mallee league's inaugural Grand Final in 1979, Shifty was playing at half-back. Most shearers end up in the backline. Shifty sits next to me and emits the odd, understated comment, all of them honest as far as I can tell.

Greg Conlan played at centre half-forward in the 1979 Grand Final team at sixteen years of age. He later went down to Richmond, where he played six senior games during an era when the Tigers were still finals contenders. In one game, against Sydney at the Sydney Cricket Ground late in the 1983 season, he kicked two goals and was among the Tigers' best players. The next year, he played two games, against Essendon and Hawthorn, but that was the end of his League career. It seems a bit rough. Essendon and Hawthorn were clearly the best teams in that era. Greg might have been fine if he got to play against St Kilda.

Greg Conlan is not unusual in the room at Nandaly in that he is from a family of many boys but no girls. He himself grew up as one of six boys. Jacko Kiley was the third of nine boys. The Parkinson family had six boys, while the Peucker family had five boys. Nandaly did well to field football teams for as long as they did, but the netball teams must have had an even tougher struggle.

Of the others in the room, Terry Elliott played mainly in Nandaly's reserves team before contributing a great deal as an official. He was the

Sea Lake-Nandaly treasurer for a decade. Now, in 2018, his son Matt Elliott is the playing-coach at the club based at Sea Lake. Greg Martin, a bear of a bloke, played in the ruck in Sea Lake-Nandaly's 1995 premiership team. His grandfather, Gordon Martin, was a member of the Pier Milan teams that produced an array of champions while dominating their local competition between the two world wars.

The Pier Milan railway siding is nine kilometres north of Nandaly. The siding was built on the line to Kulwin, which is a little farther to the north again. Apparently, the Pier Milan district was named after the Frenchman who surveyed the area before settlement. I presume his name was Pierre, but when a post office was opened next to the railway siding in 1911, it was described as the post office in Pier-Millan. In 1940, the postal service dropped the hyphen. The post office that was next to the railway siding was closed in 1971. These days, according to Australia Post's directory of postcodes, Pier Milan is spelt with one "l".

When the Pier Milan and District Football Association was in swing during the 1930s, all grand finals were played at the Nandaly Recreation Reserve. According to reports in the *North West Express*, each grand final grew a larger crowd than the previous year. Excitement bubbled around the reserve, lending the atmosphere of a carnival. Pier Milan, under the leadership of the follower Lorrie Rohde, won five grand finals in a row. Nandaly won one premiership, in 1940. Kulwin, having not played in finals for more than a decade, won in 1941. The competition had five clubs when the privations of World War 2 forced it to go into recession.

After the resumption of football towards the end of the war, three clubs from the Pier Milan association – Kulwin, Myall and Pier Milan – failed to re-emerge. The Mittyack and Nandaly clubs were re-formed, and became founding members of the Nandaly-Bolton Football League. Nandaly transferred to the Tyrrell league in 1952. Mittyack transferred to the Ouyen District league the following year, in 1953. The club was thrashed almost every week. In 1954, opposition full-forwards kicked bags of twenty goals at Mittyack. Young supporters of visiting teams spent much of the afternoon fetching the ball out of the trees behind the goals. At the end of that season, Mittyack folded, leaving Nandaly as the only club from the old Pier Milan association to survive.

Nandaly played in three grand finals in the Tyrrell league in the next decade, but it could not quite nail a premiership. Gordon Martin was the club president when Nandaly lost another Grand Final, in 1967. John Morrison from Tyntynder was the Nandaly coach that season.

Sea Lake defeated Culgoa in the following year's Grand Final, in 1968, in what was the last year in which Nullawil would fail to feature in the grand final for the duration of the competition. Nullawil played in every grand final from 1969 until the Tyrrell league was wound up as part of the Mallee restructure. The Maroons lost two grand finals, both to Sea Lake, before winning three in a row, from 1971 to 1973. Nullawil were hot favourites to make it four in a row when they went in against Nandaly in the 1974 Grand Final.

Even now, forty-four years after the event, the old Nandaly footballers break into a series of self-conscious smiles at the mention of the 1974 season. It was the season in which Geoff McMillan announced himself as a star when, at fifteen years of age, he played with an athleticism that had rarely been seen in the district. On training nights, the teenager ran ten kilometres from the family farm into town before lacing up his boots and jogging on to the oval. On Saturdays, he played at centre half-forward and leapt on to the shoulders of leaden opponents to take mark after mark. His rise was among the reasons his Nandaly teammates drew belief that they could end Nullawil's run of success.

During the finals in 1974, Nullawil defeated Nandaly in the Second Semi-final but Nandaly earned another crack at the Maroons when they defeated Sea Lake in the Preliminary Final. The Grand Final was played at Sea Lake. According to a report in the *North West Express*, Nandaly suffered a blow in the third quarter when Keith Parkinson, the centre half-forward, twisted his ankle while taking a strong mark, and had to be carried from the ground.

Nandaly were eight points down during the time-on period of the last quarter, but they made a desperate rally. Graeme "Rooster" McMillan, the older brother of Geoff, kicked a goal with one minute to go to give his team victory by two points. While Jacko Kiley was best on ground, the others listed among the best players included the Peucker brothers Geoff and Noel, and Kevin "Boxer" Conlan. Robert "Chook" Hender and Dale Ryan were also among the best. The players from Nandaly's large families of boys became the men of their generation.

In the rooms in Nandaly on this Friday evening in 2018, the players from that team in 1974 clearly feel it might look a bit showy to express too much joy over the triumph they achieved so many years ago. Instead, they express their delight by moving slightly in their chairs. Some give a crooked smile. Others shake their heads and laugh, and take a thankful swig of beer. Jacko Kiley gives a trademark grin when he recalls Rooster McMillan's decisive moment. "Nullawil still reckon it was a point," he says.

The next season, in 1975, Geoff McMillan was only sixteen years of age when he was the victim of an unfortunate shortfall at the hands of the umpires. While Tyrrell league officials were counting the votes to decide the best and fairest player in the competition, they came across the cards for three matches in which the umpire had given the three votes for best on ground to "G. McMillan". These votes could have been meant for either Geoff McMillan or Graeme McMillan, so they were ruled invalid. At the end of the count, Geoff McMillan finished equal with Neil "Ninga" McLennan of Nullawil. All these years later, the old Nandaly players believe there was no way those nine votes would have been meant for Graeme. "They were not for Rooster," says Jacko. "They would have been for Geoff, don't worry."

Geoff McMillan went down to Richmond and played eleven senior games over two seasons, in 1978 and 1979, but he struggled to settle in Melbourne. In 1980, he was still only twenty-two years of age when he left Punt Road and headed over to Adelaide. He played one game with Norwood, in the opening round of the 1980 season, but then injured his knee and was sidelined for a year. He returned to the field, but was unable to fulfill his considerable promise. Although Geoff McMillan had played at Nandaly only as a teenager, everyone in the rooms on our evening in 2018 believes that he was clearly the best footballer to have played with the club. Their heads drop when Jacko adds that Geoff died from a brain tumour in 2001 at the age of forty-three.

Geoff's brother, Rooster McMillan, went on to play many fine games for Nandaly after the triumph of 1974. I come to believe that his old teammates were a bit rough on him in scoffing about the 1975 vote count when I learn that he won the final medal for the best and fairest in the Tyrrell league, in 1978; then he won the inaugural medal for the best and fairest in the Northern Mallee league, in 1979, making it two league medals in two years. During the 1979 season, Rooster McMillan played mostly at centre half-back. In the Grand Final, he played at full-back as Nandaly defeated Manangatang to win their second premiership in five years.

When later I ask Jacko Kiley whether he can list Nandaly's premiership teams from the backline, he reveals that Shifty Larmour had only recently remembered where he had found a copy of the 1979 team. It was written in black Texta on a door of the catching pen in the shearing shed on the Parkinson family's farm, a few kilometres west of town. Jacko finds a photo and sends it down to me. The team as listed omits the interchange players. Jacko shrugs and says two of his brothers, Mick and Phil, were on the bench that day. In keeping with the club's policy of looking outside for a coach, the leader of the 1979 team was the former Tempy-Gorya-Patchewollock centreman Gary "Rolla" Burns, who was best on ground in the Grand Final. Noel Peucker and Rooster McMillan were also among the best players in that match.

Nandaly remained in the Northern Mallee league after their 1979 triumph, but looked on with concern as the number of clubs in the competition dropped from eight during the inaugural season to six only three years later, in 1982, when four clubs merged into two. In one of those mergers, Tiega and Kiamal merged to form Ouyen Rovers. Jacko says the worst moment he can recall at the Nandaly ground occurred in 1985 during a match against Ouyen Rovers. Nandaly's playing-coach, Steve Manley, lived in Ouyen but he had strong connections to Nandaly because his wife was from there. During this particular match, Manley was knocked out during a brutal clash. After the incident, his brother, Anthony "Pud" Manley, who was playing for the opposition, walked from the field.

Jacko Kiley says the Mallee has not been the same since the big drought of 1982 prompted families to leave the region in greater numbers. Throughout the following decade, the Nandaly footy club battled manfully against the odds. The club was well run by enthusiastic officials, but it simply ran out of players. During the 1993 season, the Bombers approached Sea Lake, their neighbours to the south, about the possibility of a merger, and received a generous response.

For decades, Sea Lake had enjoyed the advantage of being based in a town with banks, government departments, a hospital and a high school. Opposition clubs grumbled whenever Sea Lake signed up a teacher who had just arrived in town. One of their famous recruits was Gerard Fitzgerald, whose career at Geelong had been cut short by a knee injury after three senior games. In 1981, Fitzgerald took a teaching job in Sea Lake and was appointed as Sea Lake's playing-coach. He won the Northern Mallee league's best and fairest medal in his first season. Before the next season, in 1982, the Swans received a huge boost when they moved to the high school's ground, which had been funded by the education department. The ground was part of what was known as "the complex". In footy terms, the complex provided the best facilities in the region. In 1982, Sea Lake won the premiership, breaking the dominance of Tempy-Gorya-Patchewollock. Fitzgerald's influence on Sea Lake was pronounced before he returned south and eventually made his name by coaching premiership teams at North Ballarat.

In 1985, a Sea Lake local, Greg Daniels, won the medal in the Northern Mallee league. In the opening round of the next season, in 1986, Daniels made his senior debut with Collingwood. He played five senior games with the Magpies before returning to the Mallee. His son Brent currently plays for the GWS Giants. Sea Lake always had a healthy number of talented footballers, and the facilities in which they could flourish. Their major problem was a paucity of officials. When Nandaly approached Sea Lake in 1993, their president, Bryan Hanns, was a senior player. Most Sea Lake officials were players. While Nandaly could offer few footballers to a merged entity, they could offer a wealth of experience in administration. As well as ceding any wish to play matches in Nandaly, the Nandaly officials agreed to wear the Sea Lake jumper, which was the old South Melbourne jumper: white with a red "V".

Sea Lake-Nandaly entered the Northern Mallee league as a merged club in 1994. The next year, in 1995, the Swans won the premiership with only four players from Nandaly – Zane Kiley, one of Jacko's two sons, as well as Greg Martin, Shaun McInerney and Peter Roberts – but an entire committee filled by Nandaly officials. The club was well run. It achieved success during the final years of the Northern Mallee league, which was wound up in 1996, and it was around the mark during the early the years of the Mallee league, which began in 1997 as an amalgam of the old Southern Mallee and Northern Mallee leagues.

In 2002, five years after the inaugural season of the latest incarnation of a competition called the Mallee league, Sea Lake-Nandaly's closest neighbours, Berri-Culgoa, approached them about a merger because they, too, had run out of players. Berri-Culgoa wore Richmond jumpers. They wanted to play a handful of games at both Berriwillock and Culgoa. During the merger talks, the two parties agreed to play the odd game at Berriwillock and Culgoa, and they agreed to wear the Richmond colours of yellow and black, but they would limit the number of place names in the new entity by calling it Sea Lake-Nandaly Tigers.

The super club based in Sea Lake won the Mallee league premiership in 2009 before winning the final two grand finals in the competition, in 2014 and 2015. Their rivals in the 2015 Grand Final, Ouyen United, were themselves a super club after announcing the merger of the Ouyen United club, as it then existed, with Walpeup-Underbool to form an expanded version of Ouyen United. While the new version of Ouyen United would enter the Sunraysia league in 2016, their fellow super club to the south, Sea Lake-Nandaly Tigers, applied for entry into the North Central league.

On this Friday evening in the rooms in Nandaly, Jacko Kiley and his circle scoff at the attitude of officials from Wycheproof and Charlton who believed the Tigers would be too hick to compete in their competition. Footballers from Nandaly have always competed against rivals from larger towns. In their first year in the North Central league, in 2016, the Tigers finished sixth of the eight teams. But in 2017 they finished third after losing the Preliminary Final to the eventual premiers, Wycheproof-Narraport. Now, halfway through the 2018 season, they are well placed for another tilt at the finals.

During the course of the footy chat, Jacko reveals that, just that afternoon, he has signed the documents for the town's pub to be reopened as a community hotel. The Nandaly boys are feeling pleased. They are just beginning to click into gear when I reveal that, to my great regret, I have to resume my trip. I feel extremely rude, given that I'm abandoning a party that has been thrown in my honour, but I have no choice if I'm to keep my next appointment, which is at Bernie Kelly's home in Ouyen. I'm already an hour late. I need to get back on the Calder Highway and speed through Pier Milan and beyond.

The Nandaly boys wave goodbye with an expression of slight bemusement, but they wish me well. Jacko Kiley sees me to the door and asks me to say hello to Boozer Robertson and other footy mates to the north. The air is still and mild. As I walk towards the van, I note the goalposts standing proudly, defiantly, in the darkness at the western end. They're a strong mob at Nandaly.

22

One in Seven

Twelve months after Boozer Robertson's invitation to undertake a grand tour of the unused ovals in the Mallee, I arrive in Ouyen to take him up on his offer.

On the first night I am staying at Bernie Kelly's home to the east of the railway line. By the time of my arrival, it is well past the appointed hour, but Bernie welcomes me warmly and sits me down at the kitchen bench for a lovely roast that has been prepared by his wife, Sue. Bernie, as always, has been busy. As well as writing footy match reports for the newspapers in Mildura, Hopetoun and Ouyen, he has been umpiring senior and junior matches in the Central Murray league, which requires regular trips to Swan Hill and beyond, as well as matches in the Mallee league in South Australia. At sixty-five years of age, he continues to enjoy running and staying fit. His most recent exploit involved running over Mallee sands on a jaunt organised by Boozer.

A fortnight before my arrival in Ouyen midway through the 2018 season, Boozer had hosted an event over the long weekend in June that he described as the Mad Dog Morgan Festival. It is well-known that Dan Morgan, better known as "Mad Dog" Morgan, was a bushranger who robbed and murdered in North East Victoria and the southern

Riverina during the latter years of the Gold Rush. Mad Dog gained his fruity nickname through his erratic behaviour. According to his profile in the *Australian Dictionary of Biography*, he was once described as "the most bloodthirsty ruffian that ever took to the bush in Australia". It is less well-known that, at one stage during his efforts to escape the police, Mad Dog took to the bush in the Mallee. Apparently, he spent a few weeks traipsing through the scrub in the region between Rainbow and Patchewollock. Eventually, in 1865, he was surrounded by police near Wangaratta and shot dead.

Over the long weekend in June 2018, almost eighty people gathered near Rainbow to retrace Mad Dog's desperate steps through the Mallee more than 150 years earlier. A total of forty-six walked the entire trail to Pine Plains, a distance of twenty-six kilometres, while another thirty walked part of the way. Two men ran the trail: Bernie Kelly, a sexagenarian postal worker, and Marcus Healy, a star forward with Ouyen United.

Marcus is the grandson of Stan Healy, who was a brilliant player with Tiega and the Ouyen District competition's interleague teams during the post-war years. In 1949, Stan Healy and his brothers Jim and Jack were named among the best players in the Ouyen District league's interleague team that so impressed Allan Dunstan when it defeated the North Central league at Blackburn Park.

In 2016, Marcus Healy kicked four goals and was among the best players in the Ouyen United team that won the Sunraysia league Grand Final in the club's first year in the competition. In 2017, Marcus was in the Ouyen United team that narrowly lost the Grand Final to Irymple. During the following summer, he was on a kick-boxing camp in Thailand when he badly injured his leg. His ambition to run the full length of the Mad Dog Morgan Trail was his way of testing his leg before he decided whether to return to footy. Bernie Kelly wanted to run the Mad Dog Morgan Trail for the challenge, but mostly because he wanted to back Boozer and his venture.

While sitting at his kitchen bench, Bernie sees no reason to make a fuss over his feat. He says the sandy soil was difficult to run through in patches, but he pulled up reasonably well.

Bernie has several items of memorabilia throughout his large and comfortable home, but only one footy item that I can see. It is a photo of Bernie and fellow country footy officials from throughout Victoria's north-west with their hosts from the Richmond Football Club at the Victoria Hotel in Little Collins Street in 1980. The officials were gathered for the annual seminar that Richmond officials put on to glean intelligence on players from what was then their country recruiting zone. Almost forty years later, Bernie is still of the view that the Tigers' leaders had no idea about footy in the Mallee, but in the photo he is smiling from ear to ear, his red hair ablaze next to the grey heads of his peers in the hotel's drab surrounds. Clearly, the trip to Melbourne to meet Richmond leaders like Ian Wilson and Alan Schwab in the company of country officials like Frank McGrath and Allan Dunstan was an adventure that Bernie relished.

Now, however, he is keen to show me the chicks he is raising to add to his collection of rare birds. His backyard features a panoply of enormous cages that houses exotic creatures with feathers in shades of pink and yellow and cobalt blue. Even in the darkness, I feel struck by an assault on the senses when I peer at the range of fantastical hues. Some birds have large, hooked beaks; others have big, black eyes. It's an unexpected scene on the eastern edge of Ouyen.

Bernie takes me over the road to see Lorraine Shaddock, whom I had also met in the rooms at Blackburn Park twelve months earlier, in July 2017. On that night, Lorraine had noted my interest in her football record from the North Central v Hampden interleague game at St Arnaud in June 1970. As much as the contents, I was struck by the perfect condition of the publication. Lorraine invited me then to check out her memorabilia when I returned to Ouyen. But when I walk in to her house on this night in June 2018, I am unprepared for the scale of the display. It is not quite an assault on the senses like Bernie's menagerie of birds over the road, but it is arresting in its range and colour nonetheless. Lorraine has arranged jumpers and scarves over the backs of couches and chairs. She has spread out football records and newspaper clippings over a table and a dresser. There are family footy photos propped up here and there, and more photos on the wall. I feel embarrassed that Lorraine has gone to so much trouble to show me her collection. Her husband, Harry Shaddock, the former Tiega defender and coach, leans back in his favourite chair, his hands clasped in his lap, while I cast my gaze over the evidence of a shared football life.

Before I had left Melbourne, I was told that Harry Shaddock was one of the few players with a reasonable record against the great Richie Kalms. Harry was short for a centre half-back, but he had the ability to jump over Kalms to spoil him. I mention Harry's performances against Richie Kalms to Lorraine, who bursts into paeans of praise – not for her husband, but for the great man from Murrayville. She describes the first trip that Richie Kalms made to Melbourne to try out with Essendon. The story is like a sacred stone for Mallee football people. I will hear variations of it several times over the course of the weekend.

Lorraine's variation on the Richie Kalms story is minor: she tells me that, after Richie had caught the train from Murrayville to Ouyen and down to Melbourne, he was instructed to seek out a man in white at Spencer Street Station. When I later ask Richie about his famous journey, he tells me that he was instructed to look for a man in grey. More than one of Richie's admirers over the weekend would tell me that he kicked six goals in a practice match with Essendon, whereas, in fact, he played at centre half-back. Someone told me that John Coleman met Richie at the station. Another said that Coleman promised to move Ken Fraser away from centre half-forward if Richie would sign. These twists and turns would add to the colour surrounding a country footy tale that is redolent of its time.

Among the many footy records that Lorraine has arranged in her loungeroom, I see the interleague record from the match in St Arnaud in 1970 as well as several records from Northern Mallee league finals series during the late 1980s. I tell her again, as I mentioned in the rooms at Blackburn Park a year earlier, that country footy collectors would pay good money for these records. But the notion of parting with anything from her collection unsettles Lorraine. She looks forward to seeing the Ouyen United thirds play in the early game at Underbool in the morning.

Every Saturday morning during footy season, Lorraine picks up a friend, Joyce Jardine, and the pair head off to the footy to watch every minute of the club's three games for the day: the thirds match, the reserves match and the senior game, from the opening bounce to the final siren. For sustenance, they pack a Thermos of soup, a Thermos of coffee, sandwiches and sweet biscuits. For matches in Mildura, they leave at 7am. Joyce is the mother-in-law of Denis O'Callaghan, the Tiega forward who left to play for Collingwood in 1968. In recent years, she has gained much pleasure from seeing her grandson, Andy Jardine, Ouyen United's playing-coach, lead the Kangas to success in the Sunraysia league. In 2018, Joyce is ninety years of age, but she still loves her days at the footy with Lorraine.

The next morning in Ouyen is still and frosty. I arise before dawn and join Bernie Kelly in his morning ritual of enjoying a coffee in front of the fire. He sits in silence and looks out the window while his exotic birds explore the early rays of light. I have lived most of my life in noisy houses. I am unaccustomed to sitting in silence, but I enjoy my half an hour of repose, looking over the breaking of the Mallee morning.

Our quiet entry to the day is later broken when Michael "Boozer" Robertson – farmer, footballer, entrepreneur – walks into the hallway of Bernie's home. Boozer has a large personality. When someone asks how he's going, he replies every time, without fail, "Sensational". Sometimes he might drag out the second syllable, or say the word with more or less enthusiasm than usual, but the answer is always, "Sensational". Today, when I ask Boozer how he's going, he gives his automatic response, but then he admits he might not be feeling entirely sensational. He's hobbling, although he's not sure why. When I ask whether it might be an old footy injury, he says it's more likely to be a cricket injury – the result of decades of bowling on concrete pitches on long, summer days.

Everyone I've asked about Boozer has mentioned his bald head, skinny legs and supreme skill with a football in his hand. The reason for mentioning his appearance is that he apparently never looked like a footballer. He had what many have described to me as "chicken legs". Lorraine Shaddock gave the best description when she said: "He looked like a rope with a bit of a knot in it."

While Boozer's legs were skinny, they were fast. And above his skinny legs, he was blessed with a broad pair of shoulders. He had far more strength than his appearance suggested. But it was his exquisite touch that most Mallee footy people remember. On several occasions, I was told that Boozer seemed to be able balance the ball on his fingertips. A pack could be descending on him and he was still able to control the ball without grabbing it. Opponents would be infuriated to see him race away while toting the ball like a jeweller holding up a ring.

Boozer is the youngest of the six children born to Henry "Ginger" Robertson and Alice McLean. The five boys were all blessed with outrageous football ability. Marree, the fifth of the six children, was a highly talented netballer. While Ginger, the patriarch, was considered the best footballer of his generation, and arguably the best footballer to have played in the Mallee, his boys did not get all their ability from him. The McLean family provided exceptional footballers for Tempy and Gorya over many years. Arthur McLean tried out at St Kilda, but returned to the Mallee. His twin brother Jack, who was known as "Dummy", was also a brilliant footballer. Their younger brother Mick played for Tempy before transferring to Gorya because his wife was from Speed. The McLean brothers were talented and fiery. Between the two world wars, the McLean family had a broader influence on footy in their district than even the Robertson clan.

The five sons of Ginger and Alice Robertson – Keith, Terry, Alan, Greg and Michael – all began playing senior football as mid-teenagers. Gerry Leach, the Walpeup stalwart, told me it was noticeable that the higher the level in which the Robertson brothers were chosen to play, the better they performed. Keith played for North Melbourne and Victoria as a young wingman but then returned to country football. While injury ruined Terry's career after he had played at centre half-back in two premiership teams with Tempy-Gorya, Alan, Greg and Boozer are all remembered for their exploits with the North Central league in the Victorian country championships as much as their performances at club level. The word "magical" was used to describe the brothers throughout their careers.

Bill Morrish, the former Tiega champ, told me the best story I heard to illustrate the Robertson family's outrageous wit and fortune. After Ginger Robertson had played about 500 senior matches, he continued to serve the game long after his retirement. He coached the under-sixteen teams of his home club for many years. And he always watched his sons play in the senior match. In one match, Alan, his third son, lined up for goal from beyond the half-forward line. Few players would have had the capacity to take a shot from so far out, let alone expect to kick the goal. Alan Robertson kicked high and handsome, with his usual grace and flair, only for the ball to veer off course and go through for a behind. Ginger Robertson let the occasion sit for a moment before calling out his sage advice: "You'll never win if you don't kick the easy ones."

Several members of the Robertson family members were also wonderful cricketers. Peter Healy told me a story that highlighted the way in which Boozer's appearance served to disarm unsuspecting opponents. They were playing for the Ouyen District Cricket Association in a Bendigo Country Cricket Week match at Cohuna. It was a cool morning. No cricketer in the Mallee owns a white cricket jumper because the weather over summer is never cool enough to warrant wearing a jumper. On this morning in Cohuna, however, Boozer did need a jumper. He threw on the only one he had brought. It was a bright green number, which looked rather curious over the top of his cricket whites. He also smothered his bald head with sunscreen, which added to the unusual nature of his appearance. Boozer stands about 175 centimetres, which is not a fearsome height for an opening bowler. As he stood at the top of his mark to bowl, he looked more like a ring-in than a representative paceman. The opening batsmen were smiling in anticipation of facing him.

Boozer always had a beautiful, rhythmic approach to the crease. He made it look effortless as he rolled his arm over in languid fashion to deliver the ball at lightning speed. On this morning in Cohuna, his green jumper and shiny pate clearly lent an underwhelming first impression. But the batsmen spent the innings hopping and ducking and failing to get bat on ball while Boozer Robertson, with his easy action, whipped the ball off the pitch and into the stumps.

I first came into contact with Boozer Robertson during the course of my history of the Victorian Country Football League. As part of my research, I contacted a handful of players who were in the first team to represent the VCFL, the team that played against the ACT competition's interleague team at the Manuka Oval in Canberra in 1980. To illustrate the backgrounds of country footballers at the time, I tried to determine the jobs of those who made the team. Ron Best, the legendary full-forward, ran a pub in on Eaglehawk Road in Bendigo, while Tony Southcombe was a stock and station agent, also in Bendigo. Ian Salmon, the Latrobe Valley league defender, was a dairy farmer outside Leongatha, while Kevin Adams, the Mid-Murray league defender, was a builder in Swan Hill. Of the two players from the South West District league in the Riverina, Victor Hugo was a truck driver in Narrandera while Greg Nichols was a bookmaker's clerk in Wagga. Boozer Robertson was unlike the rest. Besides being the only player to be chosen from a minor league, in his case the Southern Mallee league, he described himself to me as "a farmer and rabbit catcher".

Boozer explained that when he flew with the squad from Melbourne to Canberra, it was his first flight. He said he enjoyed playing in Canberra because, after a career of playing on dusty grounds at Tempy, Ouyen and Patchewollock, it was wonderful to get the opportunity to play on lush grass.

Boozer later explained to me how he got his nickname. He was only three years of age when the family threw a party for his oldest brother, Keith, on the occasion of his twenty-first birthday. After seeing the barman squirt beer from the keg into the glass, the infant Micheal grabbed the beer gun in the spirit of inquiry and tasted it. "Look at him," someone said. "Look at the little boozer." He's been called Boozer ever since. As a young man, he tried to rid himself of the nickname, but no one listened. So he just had to accept that everyone in the Mallee and beyond would call him by the nickname he was given as a child.

He's not called Boozer because of his capacity to drink beer. He rarely even drinks beer. But he does have strong social proclivities that give some the impression that he earned his nickname through a fierce intake. Ginger Robertson, his father, once told Boozer as a young man that, as a wheat farmer in the Mallee, you learn to expect one good season in seven. Young Michael decided that, if living on the land was going to be that hard, there was no point waiting around for the good times. He would create the good times. For many years now, Boozer Robertson has made people smile. Everyone who has ever passed through the Mallee has a story about him.

On the morning of our tour in Ouyen, Boozer it is not only feeling less than sensational because of his cricket injury, he is also feeling a bit furry after an evening in the Patchewollock Hotel. Before he starts the ignition of his Subaru Forrester, he informs me that he must have a bacon and egg sandwich from a café in town. We dawdle through Ouyen, along quiet streets with neat gutters and spindly eucalypts, before Boozer pulls up the car at an unprepossessing building at the T-intersection where Oke Street, the main shopping street in Ouyen, meets the Mallee Highway, the road which heads west to Murrayville and the South Australian border. It is an old-fashioned service station, replete with a kitchen that serves fried food for breakfast. Several customers enter through the aluminium door to pay for petrol or order food to soak up the night before. Boozer tends to know them all. When a compact man of advanced years shuffles to the counter in his overalls, Boozer says: "There's the great Ron Gregg!"

Ron Gregg is now eighty-five years of age, but he has long been considered one of the finest sportsman to have played in Ouyen. After beginning his footy and cricket careers as a fifteen-year-old in 1947, Ron won the region's highest honours in both sports. In footy, he won two league best-and-fairest medals while playing with Ouyen. And he played in the centre in the Walpeup team that won the premiership in 1960. As a cricketer, he only ever played for Ouyen. In one grand final, he made 221 not out to lead his team to victory over Kiamal. On many occasions, he threw away his wicket so his teammates could get a bat.

On this Saturday morning in the servo in Ouyen, Ron is holding out a single note, folded in two at the base, to give to the attendant behind the wooden counter when he hears the mention of his name. He turns his torso towards the voice.

"How are you, Boozer?" he says.

"Sensational," replies Boozer, before embarking on a riff about The Great Ron Gregg's performance for a Victorian country cricket eleven against a touring West Indies team in Mildura fifty years earlier, in late 1968.

Ron Gregg etched himself into folklore in that match when he faced the West Indies bowlers in Mildura without gloves.

"You made 36," says Boozer.

"No, I made 30 or 31," says Ron. "But I was not out."

When the West Indies paceman Lester King hit Gregg on the hands, the Ouyen batsman was forced to retire hurt and head to Mildura Base Hospital for x-rays. Boozer raises his eyebrows in approval at the tale before reiterating the absence of protection on the now octogenarian's hands.

Ron Gregg shrugs.

"No one wore gloves in those days," he says.

Ron's grandson Josh Gregg is now showing the skill and anticipation for which he himself was renowned. Young Josh lives in Adelaide, where he played senior football for West Adelaide, but he now drives home every weekend to play for Ouyen United. Halfway through the 2018 season, he is favoured to win the McLeod Medal for the best and fairest player in the Sunraysia league. As Ron Gregg hands over his note to pay for his petrol, he is unsure whether he'll pop out to Underbool to see his grandson play that afternoon. Boozer says goodbye to the great sportsman. Then he finishes off his bacon and egg roll and tosses the wrapper into the bin.

When we get in to the car, Boozer continues riffing on Ron Gregg. He tells me that the story about Ron's innings without gloves in Mildura reminds him of an incident at Tempy in his youth involving a man he describes as "one G.L. Casey". The man described by his initials is Gordon Casey Senior, who is well known as a footballer who was a champion with Gorya in the 1950s, and won the trophy for the best and fairest player in the Mallee league in 1953. Gordon Casey Senior was a schoolteacher who imposed on himself a certain standard of dress. One cricket season in the Mallee, Gordon was padding up to bat for Tempy. Boozer says that Casey was immaculately turned out in his creams (not whites), as always, when he slipped his hand into his glove and received a rude shock.

"There was a mice plague in the Mallee at the time," he says. "G.L. Casey put his hand in his glove … and a mouse bit him!"

Boozer grins, and effects what I now see as a regular trait: he raises his eyebrows just slightly. He likes the thought of a man who takes pride in his appearance being disabused of his vanity by a small rodent. Boozer drives about a kilometre, past the pub on the left and the pool on the right. He drives across the Calder Highway, and through the gates of Blackburn Park. He is still grinning when he stops the car near the playful figures of the totem poles.

23

The Tarpaulin of Tiega

Boozer Robertson has brought me to Blackburn Park to meet Donald McGregor and other Mallee football people, but I'm also keen to check out the totem poles in the day time rather than in darkness, as was the case during my previous visit.

The nine totem poles were built between the oval and the netball courts at the southern end of Blackburn Park in 2009. The first pole represents the Tempy Football Club, which existed as a club in its own right until 1964. The guernsey on the Tempy pole has been painted in a delectable shade of lime green, topped off with a yellow "V". The next pole represents Gorya, which was itself the product of a merger between Speed and Turriff. The Gorya Football Club was also in existence in its own right until 1964, when it merged with Tempy. The guernsey on the Gorya pole is royal blue with a red "GFC" monogram. The faces on the Tempy and Gorya poles both feature a hint of smile.

The face on the Tempy-Gorya-Patchewollock pole is more quizzical; a slight frown suggests concern over the unfolding of events. The TGP face also features a handlebar moustache, suggesting the changing mores of 1971, the year when the club came into being. The pole that represents the Ouyen Football Club features the club's red and black vertical stripes, which has always been one of my favourite traditional guernsey designs. Whenever I see the red and black stripes, I lament the choice of most of the clubs that played in that design to switch to Essendon's black jumper with a red sash. Ouyen's stripes look strong and bold in the weak morning sun.

The final two poles represent Kiamal and Tiega, the clubs that merged to create Ouyen Rovers in 1982. The Kiamal pole features the black and white stripes of Collingwood. The Tiega pole features a rich shade of red with a white "V", an inversion of the old South Melbourne guernsey of white with a red "V". In a practical decision, Tiega switched from mainly white to mainly red in 1952 because it was too difficult to keep white jumpers clean in the Mallee dust. The Tiega pole is so red that it is what paint charts would describe as vermilion. The exuberance of this shade creates a vibrant finish to the row of totem poles.

Twenty years ago, in 1998, I lived in Cork, on the south coast in Ireland, where I worked for a short time as a sub-editor for the *Cork Examiner* (known in local parlance as "*Da Paper*"). Just around the bay from Cork is a town call Cobh (pronounced *Cove*), which is the port from where many thousands of Irish emigrants left their home land to begin new lives in Australia, Canada, the United States and elsewhere. In Cork and Cobh, there are various plaques and monuments that recognise the grief of those who left Ireland to escape a life of poverty and pain. The monuments also depict the grief of those they left behind. In Cobh, there is a statue that depicts Annie Moore, the first Irish immigrant to the United States who passed through federal immigration inspection at Ellis Island in New York harbour. Moore and her brothers, Anthony and Philip, aged fifteen and twelve, left their native Cork for New York in 1892. The statue of the trio on the waterfront in Cobh depicts the excitement of their new adventure as well as the melancholy surrounding their decision to leave.

Ireland and the Mallee are very different. Ireland exists under a shroud of drizzle. The grass is so lush that there are said to be forty shades of green. In the Mallee, farmers are happy with one shade of green if it means there has been enough rain to encourage new shoots of life.

Yet, in terms of exodus, Ireland and the Mallee have similarities. Farmers of the Mallee might not have been subject to the utter devastation of the farmers in Ireland during the Great Famine of the mid-nineteenth century, but they, too, have chosen to leave in numbers because they have seen a better life elsewhere.

Ultimately, the totem poles of Ouyen United depict the exodus of farmers from the Mallee, an exodus that has forced the mergers of various football clubs into one. It is therefore undeniable that the totem poles depict an event of sadness. The glorious aspect of these totem poles, however, is that they depict a sad event in a way that is fun, and even celebratory. Perhaps it is because the poles feature such rich dollops of colour. Perhaps it is because they were created by teenagers who were blessed with the optimism of youth. While it is true that the population of the Mallee has declined and footy clubs have folded, footy in the region continues to survive because of the strength and resilience of those who have remained. That, to me, is the spirit of the totem poles of Ouyen United.

Like the region they represent, the totem poles have been forced to survive an extreme climatic event. When the poles were first constructed in 2009, their designer Nerida Morrish instructed her students to paint the poles with Dulux Solar Shield, but the protective paint was no match for the rain that wreaked havoc throughout Victoria in early 2011. Without some form of a cap over them, the poles had no protection against the water that seeped in to the wood. Six years later, in 2017, the poles were falling into disrepair when Nerida enlisted a group of Year 9 students to paint them again. While the pole's creators had been Year 9 and 10 art students who took much care with the design, the students who embarked on the job in 2017 gained much out of the exercise because many of them were footballers and netballers who might not otherwise have shown any interest in the juxtaposition of shapes and colours. Some of the students were from families with long histories on the sporting fields of the region. The clubs that had folded into the club for which they were playing were a source of intrigue. In order to protect the poles, Nerida instructed the students to apply three coats of primer and at least two top coats.

On the oval at Blackburn Park, Boozer and I meet some supporters who wish to present me with a map of the Mallee that includes the location of the many clubs that have fed into the current form of Ouyen United. The group is headed by Donald McGregor, an agronomist who, with Boozer, organised the reunion of the old Mallee Football League at Blackburn Park late in the 2015 season. Don and a few others have made quite an effort to find the map beneath a pile of detritus in the clubrooms. We are standing on the oval out the front of the social rooms when Don presents the laminated map to me rolled up as if it is a scroll from the Holy Land. The map is entitled "Mallee Football Ovals". It is apparent that it is the last one from the batch that was handed out when the Kangas entered the Sunraysia league. I feel quite humbled to have the final map, the last holy scroll. I know then that I will want to document the many strands of Ouyen United.

In 2003, Ginger Robertson was eighty-eight years of age when he took Boozer on a tour of the grounds on which he had played during his career, which had begun in the late 1920s and extended through until the early 1960s. Boozer filmed the tour for a Mallee legends night. Fifteen years later, midway through the 2018 season, he is giving me much the same tour that his father gave him, albeit with a few short cuts because we've got to get to the footy in Underbool that afternoon.

"We'll start with Kiamal, which is just to the north of town," he says.

Kiamal is a railway siding about eight kilometres north of Ouyen. In the years after World War 1, the siding at Kiamal was bustling with men who loaded wheat and wool on to the train for delivery to Melbourne and Geelong. Many of those who worked at the siding played footy for Kiamal after the formation of the club in 1920. Most players from the club were local farmers, but Kiamal also benefited from the arrival of men who worked for government agencies or banks or stock and station agencies in Ouyen.

Boozer Robertson noses the car off the Calder Highway just short of the siding at Kiamal and turns right into Dingo Tank Road. Our first destination is the ground to the west of Dingo Tank Reserve where Kiamal played after the Second World War. We arrive at the entrance to a small property that features metal images of two guitars on the front gate. The owner is an Elvis fan. The branches of a bushy tree reach down towards the necks of one of the guitars. In the back blocks of the Mallee, it's a most unlikely scene.

Boozer says that, while the owner likes Elvis, he does not care for visitors. However, we've come too far to turn back. Boozer noses the car around the side of the house, along a track that features a row of spindly eucalypts to our left and the corrugated-iron fence of the house to our right. Behind the house, a small orchard features a few orange trees – and a warning against trespassers.

Boozer starts to get nervous. He points to the north.

"That's where the ground was," he says.

I see no semblance of a football oval – just a few citrus trees and, beyond the orchard, a nondescript paddock with a clearing that looks barely big enough to have hosted two teams of eighteen men chasing a ball around. There are no goalposts, no fence, no scoreboard. I sense nothing except Boozer's jitters about the owner of the property.

"We'd better get out of here," he says.

We head a couple of kilometres farther east along Dingo Tank Road and pull off the road and stop next to another clearing. This is where Kiamal played in the years between the two world wars. There is nothing here except tufts of grass and stunted scrub, but the expanse of the clearing does look large enough to have hosted footy matches.

My main point of curiosity in Kiamal is the site of the twig after the 1971 Grand Final. Boozer is unsure of the location of the twig. During his many years with Tempy-Gorya-Patchewollock, it was a regular occurrence for the footballers to finish training at the oval at Patchewollock then head to the Patche pub for a few drinks. After closing time, they would convene for a twig at a crossroads just out of town. Almost every social function at the footy club ended with a twig just out of town. Twigs were much loved, but unremarkable. They were just part of the fabric of life in the Mallee. Boozer says the Kiamal twig is part of Mallee folklore because it went for so long, but he has never known of its location.

We head back south along the Calder Highway, past Ouyen's Victoria Hotel, which is an enormous building with elaborate iron lacework on the upper balcony, and draw level with the entrance to Blackburn Park, with its oval and totem poles inside the iron gates. Just opposite the entrance to Blackburn Park, we turn right and head past the café where we chatted to Ron Gregg about his gloveless innings against the West Indies. We head west along the Mallee Highway, towards the old Tiega ground.

According to the booklet that Tiega produced in 1981, the Tiega Football Club had five grounds after its formation in 1910. The first was in Tiega. The next two were in paddocks in Galah. In 1931, the club moved to the Tiega Recreation Reserve because its previous ground at Galah got too muddy. The Tiega reserve was fenced off, allowing the club to charge an entrance fee at the gate. The Lawler brothers were the gate attendants in this period. The club made its final shift when it moved into Blackburn Park in Ouyen in 1951.

About ten kilometres west of Ouyen, we turn left and drive a little south along Morrish Road before Boozer turns off the track. We ride the bumps in a rough old paddock before Boozer stops the car in another nondescript clearing. We are now on the site of the old Tiega Recreation Reserve. The highway is just to the north of us. The farm of Alec Morrish is next door. It is the farm where Alec and his wife Marion raised their four sons, Lindsay, Bill and the twins Jack and Ray, all of whom played with Tiega and other clubs with such distinction.

In the 1930s, opposition players and supporters would catch the train to the Tiega station, which is one and a half kilometres to the north. The players and supporters would walk across a heavy clay flat and over the highway to reach the reserve, which hosted two grounds. One of the grounds had a channel around it; the ball often found its way into the channel. Boozer says a tarpaulin was attached to a few Mallee trees to create makeshift change rooms.

I imagine the players getting changed behind the tarp. Footy had an earthy quality back then. I sometimes wonder whether the millions of dollars being spent on flash new facilities in the modern era is money well spent.

At the Mallee legends night at the Ouyen United footy club in 2003, the local schoolteacher and historian Geoff van Wyngaarden paid $220 for an original goalpost from the Tiega ground. Quite often, I find it difficult to tell whether money is well spent.

24

The Day of the Swoop

After leaving the Tiega ground, we head back into Ouyen and resume our journey along the Calder Highway. About eight kilometres south of the town, Boozer begins to look out for the Nunga silo. When he spots it by the railway siding to the west of the highway, he searches for a clearing in the scrub over the road. He slows down enough to find the clearing. He noses the car off the shoulder of the road and down a dip and until we pass through a small gap in the bushes. We emerge into a clearing. We are just a few metres off the Calder Highway but it feels like we could be miles from anywhere. Once again it's difficult to imagine footy being played on this scrubby old patch of dirt.

Nunga played in the Ouyen District Football Association from 1913 until 1929. Boozer drives to a spot just off the centre of the clearing. "There's a cricket pitch in here somewhere," he says.

Beneath the grass and scrub, Boozer finds a strip of concrete that had not been apparent to me. In touching the abandoned pitch, I feel satisfied to find a tangible link with sporting contests from the past. We leave the pitch and head back through the gap and up on to the highway.

About six kilometres farther south, we turn off at a sign that says "Bronzewing" and head westwards, towards the old Bronzewing railway siding, or least the site of the siding until it was recently bulldozed. Now, all that's left is a salt pan, a flat patch of tawny soil, where the oval used to be. Bronzewing played here from 1926 until 1940. The Fox brothers, Jack and Frank, flew across the oval until they broke the club's heart by seeking a clearance to Tempy. Their pursuit of a clearance effectively broke the club.

The salt pan extends from the railway line to a small rise that is dotted with salt bushes. It's an open area, so it's not hard to see how it could have hosted footy matches, but it's desolate. It looks too sick and salty to have hosted much life at all. Boozer, however, says evidence of footy at Bronzewing is not far away. The family of George Caldow, a Bronzewing footballer who later lived in Tempy, still has the 1934 medal that George won for the club's best and fairest award.

We turn away from the railway line. We are heading back towards the highway when Boozer stops the car near the concrete footings of the old Bronzewing school. A plaque notes the details of the school. Boozer's enthusiasm rises a notch when he says that this is the building in which Mollie Kalms was a young student. He raises his eyebrows slightly. I'm looking at the plaque and wondering about its importance in the context of our tour when Boozer launches into a dissertation on the Kalms family and the family members' contribution to Mallee football.

Mollie Kalms was called Mollie Dow when she was a girl. She grew up on a farm at Bronzewing and went to the local school. At eleven years of age, she went to boarding school at Clarendon College in Ballarat, and she later stayed in Ballarat to go to teachers' college. Her first teaching job was at Murrayville, where she met and married a man called Fred Kalms. The couple had four children: two boys, Laurie and Richie, and sisters Pauline and Wendy.

Mollie was an excellent tennis player while Fred Kalms played footy for Danyo, a club in a farming district near Murrayville. Fred was described as a player who made up for his lack of skill with plenty of determination. In 1947, he was a member of the Danyo team that knocked off the previously undefeated Murrayville in the Grand Final of the North West Mallee league.

Fred and Mollie's boys had plenty of skill as well as determination. Both of them were stars from a young age. I had met Laurie, the former ruckman and full-forward, in Ouyen the previous year. And I had heard plenty about Richie from people all over the Mallee – especially the stories about him playing in practice matches with Essendon, only to come home and never return to the city.

Boozer describes his version of the Richie Kalms and Essendon story. To his credit, he says he is unsure of the details. But he adds much detail about Richie's performances in the North Central interleague team, beginning with the match in which he blitzed against the Northern District league in Cohuna in 1969. Boozer says Richie Kalms was built like Gary Ablett Senior, with powerful thighs that enabled him to leap over packs or hold his position at ground level. He says Richie and Gary Ablett were similar players, but Richie was a better mark and a longer kick.

Boozer's enthusiasm drops when we leave Bronzewing and head south towards Tempy, which is his home town. Basically, he is reluctant to talk about Tempy because he is reluctant to talk about himself. He volunteers that the word "Tempy" is short for Temporary Railway Siding. Authorities called the town Tempy as a stopgap measure and never got around to renaming it. But when I ask about his own footy career, about memorable matches on the Tempy Recreation Reserve, he finds ways to dodge the questions that suggest his artfulness in dodging opponents on the field.

I do ascertain that Boozer made his senior debut with Tempy-Gorya-Patchewollock in 1973, when he was fifteen years of age. On the last day of the season, he played in the under-sixteen Grand Final then in the senior Grand Final. While the junior team won their match, the seniors lost to Tiega. The next year, in 1974, Boozer was sixteen years of age when he played in his first senior premiership team. Three years later, in 1977, he played in his second premiership team. By then, he was established as a star of the bush. But, the way he tells it, he just never managed to become a consistent footballer. He went to Richmond for five minutes before returning to the Mallee. Apart from his stint as the playing-coach at Woomelang-Lascelles, in 1979 and 1980, he just preferred to play at his home club.

I sense that Boozer's self-deprecation is genuine. He often wonders what all the fuss is about. He does offer that he never appreciated his early success. After playing in two premierships as a teenager, it all seemed so easy. Even interleague footy was a lark. His idea of pre-season training was to go for a jog with his teammates then head to the Patche pub. He just sought to enjoy himself. His teammates at his home club were the same.

In the early years of the Northern Mallee league, which began in 1979, Tempy-Gorya-Patchewollock won four out of the five premierships between 1980 and 1984. Boozer played in two of those premiership teams, in 1981 and 1984, for a total of four senior premierships overall. He played his last senior match in the 1995 Grand Final, which TGP lost to Sea Lake-Nandaly. His favourite footy memories include playing with mates and the people he met through the game.

The oval on which we are standing hosted football in Tempy for about eighty years. In 2000, the Ouyen United committee agreed that the club would play its final match at Tempy; from then on, all matches would be played in Ouyen. It is only in describing this final match at Tempy that Boozer achieves a level of excitement when talking about his home patch. Boozer organised the celebrations for Tempy's curtain call. In keeping with his penchant for spectacle, he organised a local pilot, Mark McCleary, to contribute an aerial stunt or two before the senior game.

While we stand on the oval at Tempy, I recall my own version of the events that day. I remember it clearly because of my own unusual circumstances. I was in the Northern Riverina, having driven from Melbourne to watch Chris Daniher play for the Daniher family's home club, Ungarie. On the Sunday morning, I joined Ungarie officials on their drive to the neighbouring town of Condobolin, where they were to attend a league meeting in the pub to decide on venues for the upcoming finals series.

While the delegates were in their meeting, I stood in the phone booth outside the pub and made the calls to gather material for my weekly column on local footy in *The Age*. I remember learning about the hoopla surrounding the last match at Tempy. Mallee people who had left the region returned from all over Australia for the send-off. The celebrations included an aeroplane that swooped over the ground before the senior game. I remember contemplating the distance between the celebrations in the Mallee and the phone booth in which I was standing in the Northern Riverina. The next day I would spend eight hours driving back to Melbourne. This was not the life I had imagined for myself. I wondered whether I was on the right path, although I sensed the path I was on was not all bad.

That afternoon, after our time in Condobolin, I greatly enjoyed our return journey to Ungarie. Lindsay Henley and Viv Koop, two long-time servants of the Ungarie footy club, took me on a diversion past the oval that was, until just a few years previously, the home of a club called the Four Corners Football Club. The club was so called because its oval was at the junction of four properties. There was no town; the oval was just a clearing in the bush.

Viv Koop, a wonderful man with a stoop and a smile, told me stories about "Jelly" Ray Preuss, the Four Corners full-back, who kicked out from the goalsquare with drop-kicks that sailed to the wing, and Dudley Ireland, who owned one of the four properties. Most of their teammates were farm labourers. I looked at the tufts of grass that emerged between divots of dirt. The sighing branches of an old gum tree hung over one forward pocket. The behind post leaned away from its neighbouring goalpost in the other forward pocket. All the posts consisted of boughs of trees that had been fashioned into slender poles, albeit with a series of knots in them.

My hosts beamed. They were so proud to show me the old Four Corners oval even though it was not their own ground. The Four Corners oval was a symbol of the earthiness, the rootedness, of footy in their region. Although the Four Corners club had folded only six years earlier, in 1994, it felt to me as if I were looking at a scene from sixty years earlier. I think now that my experience with my Ungarie hosts at Four Corners set in train my interest in abandoned ovals.

And yet it is not until I stand on the oval at Tempy with Boozer Robertson that I have any idea of the carnage that almost followed the aerial stunts before the final match at the ground in 2000. Boozer describes the events that preceded the game with much mirth.

The pilot on that day late in the 2000 season, Mark McCleary, is the grandson of Roby Manuel, who was an ace fighter pilot during World War 1. At the conclusion of the war, Roby Manuel was among the pilots who were chosen to swoop along The Strand in London as part of the Allies' victory celebrations. Roby, however, became over-stimulated by the pomp and pageantry of the occasion, and broke away from his fellow pilots to fly under the Tower Bridge. His antics delighted the crowd – but horrified the country's rulers. Roby Manuel escaped certain punishment by leaving for Australia the next day.

Mark McCleary had a penchant for flying an SE5 plane, which was a replica of the plane that his grandfather had flown during the war. Just before he was due to perform stunts before the match at Tempy, he had a work accident in which some foreign material was lodged in his eye. He hopped into his plane before the football celebrations wearing an eye patch. As he ascended into the sky, his eye began to irritate him. As he reached the zenith of his trajectory, the irritation grew. Mark McCleary intended that his plane would stall at its high point, then embark on a series of spirals during its descent to earth. The spirals, however, were higher in number than intended, and his promised swoop out of trouble as the plane neared the ground looked to be in jeopardy.

As Boozer describes it, reserves players stopped in their tracks while senior players emerged from the rooms to watch the unfurling drama. Officials and supporters looked on in disbelief as the plane plummeted. Children ran towards their parents, who looked on in in horror as the showpiece performance threatened to end in a tangle of flaming metal in the centre square.

Finally, the pilot managed to overcome the irritation to his eye and pull the plane out of its descent as it feathered the grass on the oval. The senior match began in a haze of shock and relief. Players barrelled about in pursuit of the ball, aware of the silliness of their task when their lives had just been imperilled by an errant plane. The match ended in favour of the hosts, with Ouyen United defeating Hopetoun.

25

Home Patch

We leave behind the rundown surrounds of Tempy and make a dash towards Speed, which is surely the most ironically named town in Victoria. The town consists of a few houses and the remains of the primary school. The school was housed in a weatherboard building that has retained an element of charm despite years of dereliction. Speed had its own footy club for a few intermittent years before and after World War 1, but it has not had its own club since the Speed footy club merged with Turriff, a club just to the south, for the last time in 1930. The merged club was called Gorya, which was the name of the local parish.

Gorya played at the grounds of both Speed and Turriff. When the club merged with Tempy to form Tempy-Gorya before the 1965 season, the merged club split most of its game between Tempy and Speed. When that club merged with Patchewollock to form Tempy-Gorya-Patchewollock before the 1971 season, the triplicate club alternated home matches between Tempy and Patchewollock. Speed was abandoned as a venue in the early days after the merger.

Since then, the site of the footy ground at Speed has been the site of the ninth hole of the local golf course. The course is now looking unloved. The nearby tennis courts look like they have been unloved for many years.

The nets hang low from rusting poles. Grass emerges through cracks on the baseline. Throughout isolated regions in Victoria, the demise of tennis clubs has proceeded in step with the demise of footy clubs. There is just no one left to send down the next serve.

After leaving Speed, we take a dirt road that stretches west and head towards Patchewollock. Boozer Robertson, my tour guide, glances towards a farmhouse that is set back slightly off the road. The house sits behind a row of Mallee pines. It looks neat and comfortable, if a little past its best. Boozer raises his eyebrows just a fraction. "That's Merv Young's house," he says.

If Richie Kalms is considered the best footballer of his generation in the Mallee league, Merv Young must be considered the competition's most respected figure. Merv was a wheat farmer who played in the ruck for Patchewollock. He was tall and strong, and he was always fair. He led the club during its most successful era. During the eleven seasons from 1949 to 1959, Patchewollock played in ten grand finals but won only three. In one of those three triumphant years, in 1956, the Tigers were undefeated. Merv Young's combination with the Patchewollock rover Lindsay Smale in this era was legendary. Smale won two Mallee league best and fairest awards.

In retirement, Merv Young led the Tigers for eight years as president. In 1968, he became the president of the Mallee league. A story from the early years of his tenure as the head of the league indicates his practical approach to administration. Before a match in which Tempy-Gorya were to host Walpeup, the Walpeup selector Albert Bell informed Young that the clearance papers were yet to come through for a player whom they were hoping to select. Young replied that the Blues should play their recruit. "We're in the business of putting players on the field; not keeping them off it," he said.

Merv Young's appointment as the Mallee league president marked the beginning of the Mallee players' influence on the fortunes of the North Central league's representative teams. From 1969, Merv Young joined the leaders of the North Central league, Darky Dunstan and Des Darcy, in their efforts to field the strongest possible combinations to represent the

North Central District. For almost a decade, Merv Young would drive the Mallee league's representatives to interleague training with their North Central teammates in Birchip.

As Boozer and I drive along the dirt road to Patchewollock, Boozer remembers being part of the Mallee crews that piled into Merv Young's car to go to interleague training. He says Merv was a selfless man who gave everything for the Mallee – its football and its people.

Merv Young achieved a measure of fame when Carlton & United Breweries filmed a commercial for Victoria Bitter in a shed in Patchewollock. Every Vic Bitter commercial in that period featured men who sweated through activities of great exertion before slaking their thirst with a swig from a stubbie. "A big thirst needs a big, cold beer," was the opening line of the slogan. "And the best cold beer is Vic …

"Victoria Bitter."

Merv Young was an inspired choice to appear in the Vic Bitter ads. It made Mallee people proud to see one of their leaders representing their region in such a manly manner, with the sweeping plains outside Patchewollock as the back drop.

Merv Young had three talented sons, Gary, Clive and Jack. The younger two, Clive and Jack, played in premiership teams with Tempy-Gorya-Patchewollock, and Clive was an interleague ruckman. Gary was also a superb athlete, considered a certainty to make the grade in League football, only to be blinded by sparrow shot during an accident when he was sixteen years of age. After the accident, Gary Young became a stock and station agent in Patchewollock. His office was about 150 metres from the Patchewollock Hotel. His blindness was the catalyst for him to develop an uncanny awareness of his surrounds. Gary became famous for his ability to pick up a lamb and correctly guess its weight. He became more famous for his ritual of walking from his office to the pub. Without breaking stride, he would open the door of the pub and seat himself at the bar.

Gary Young went to the football every week to watch Tempy-Gorya-Patchewollock. Often he sat with Des "Speedie" Robertson and John Collins, who both played and served as officials for many years. Speedie and John Collins would describe the events on the field for Gary Young. The fact that Gary was unable to see these events with his own eyes did not stop from making comment. In a voice that rang across the oval, he would often question the eyesight of the umpires and the breeding of opposition players. For many years, the booming voice of Gary Young was part of the fabric of Mallee football.

When we reach Patchewollock, Boozer stops at the footy ground, which is to the north of the road as you enter town. Ouyen United played their last match here in 1999. As in Tempy, the brick changing rooms are in a state of dilapidation, but unlike Tempy, the oval in Patchewollock has been marked off into three sections. Wire fences have been placed along the half-forward and half-back lines for use during sheepdog trials.

At the southern end of the ground, one behind post has been snapped off near the base, but the other posts look strong and enduring. A large silo looms into view in the paddock beyond the southern goals. Behind the goalposts at the northern end, a small section of the reserve has been set aside as a camping ground. The success of the Patchewollock Music Festival and other delights in the town has created the need for accommodation areas.

When Boozer's five older siblings decided that a life on the land was not for them, he was happy to take up a life on the land on the family farm. These days, he continues to grow crops, but he has also taken on sundry ventures, such as ensuring that the Patchewollock Hotel remains open for the benefit of Mallee people.

Boozer was among those who got the Patchewollock Music Festival off the ground. While Robin Yetman, an old TGP teammate, took care of the music, Boozer organised the sheep races that have proved a highlight of the festival's attractions outside the line-up of musical acts. According to Boozer, the fastest sheep from around Australia compete in the main sheep race, which he rather grandly calls the Patchewollock Gold Cup.

The Patchewollock Music Festival now attracts 2000 music fans for one weekend every October. In June 2018, the inaugural Mad Dog Morgan Festival showed potential. A few dozen gathered at the Patche pub on the first night to watch a screening of the 1976 film that traces the bushranger's wild days, called simply *Mad Dog Morgan.* The next day, dozens more gathered to begin their passage along the Mad Dog Morgan Trail. Boozer is the first to admit that he struggles to maintain concentration on any one idea, but the Mallee community is grateful that his zest for life brings so many people together to enjoy their region's charms.

In recent years, tourists have descended on Patchewollock because it's at the northern end of the Silo Art Trail, which is an unforeseen phenomenon in Australian tourism. The art trail features outsized portraits of farmers on silos in six locations stretching from Rupanyup in the Wimmera to Patchewollock in the Mallee. Its popularity has stunned farmers from the six towns along the trail almost as much as it has stunned tourism authorities.

The portrait on the silo in Patchewollock offers a point of difference. While the other portraits tend to celebrate ageing farmers who have earned respect for their deeds over many years, Fintan Magee, the artist who was commissioned for the portrait in Patchewollock, was very specific in that he wanted his subject to be a relatively young man who was tall and lean. By choosing a subject of lean proportions, Magee said he stood a better a chance of painting a portrait to his liking on a canvas that was unusually high and narrow. The length of the portrait on the Patchewollock silo, from top to toe, would be thirty-five metres.

After staying in the Patche pub and getting to know a range of local people, Fintan Magee met Nick "Noodle" Hulland, a Patchewollock farmer, and knew he had met his muse. Magee described Noodle as rugged and lanky, with a hard-working spirit that exemplified the people of the region. The artist's portrait is striking. Noodle gazes across the Mallee plains. He is wearing a blue flannelette shirt. In his hand, he holds a green shoot that signifies new life in the Mallee.

After tourists have taken in the portrait of Noodle, they often repair to the pub over the road. They enjoy a drink at the distinctive horseshoe bar before ordering a counter meal in the lounge. The walls in the lounge feature several Patchewollock footy photos, but few tourists would realise there's a footy ground just 150 metres away that now hosts sheepdog trials. Nor would they care. And to be fair, I detect no particular emotion in Boozer when he mentions the Patche oval. In observing him having a short yack with the publican, I detect that he's more excited by what is in prospect at the bar than he's downcast about what has been lost at the footy ground.

The publican, Bryce Harriman, takes a moment from his duties when he sees Boozer pull up outside the front door. Bryce is a man in his mid-forties who is wearing jeans, a fleecy top and an Essendon beanie. He looks weary, but his eyes and range of conversation suggest a mind in motion. He's originally from Kyneton, in the cold Macedon Ranges in the south of the state, but he's lived for long periods in various parts of Western Australia and in the mining country of Queensland. With his hair stretching down slightly over his collar, he does not look like the farmers who drink in his pub; he looks like a geologist who checks out rocks in craggy hills. Bryce pushes off the car door and turns to chop wood for the fire. He's expecting a few tourists at the pub that evening.

Boozer and I leave Patchewollock, promising to return to the pub later, and head north along the road towards Walpeup. The undulations of the golden paddocks surprise me. My short time in the region south of Ouyen has taught me that my concept of the Mallee is rooted in the country around Ultima, where the only slopes to be found are those on the rooftops of corrugated iron. The country to the south of Ouyen features vast plains that form a series of undulating waves. As later explained to me in the Patche pub, this part of the country was once an inland sea. The plains rise and fall like an ancient seabed. The rolling paddocks north of Patchewollock have a mesmeric effect, lulling me into a pleasant dreaminess.

As we approach the Mallee Highway and the town of Walpeup, Boozer warns me that the local footy ground has a large slope. The ground is certainly a long way from town. We drive over the railway line and turn on to a straight and narrow road that is flanked on both sides by a rich forest of Mallee pines. Eventually, the road enters a clearing that was the home of the recreation reserve. The reserve is on the Walpeup Ridge, which, at an elevation of more than 100 metres, is the highest point in the Mallee. The reserve is flanked on all sides by Murray pines and belah trees, which is notable. Wherever those trees were found, they were normally ripped out of the ground because they indicated the location of the best soil. The rich, natural vegetation that was left to flourish at the Walpeup Recreation Reserve makes it a somewhat exotic location in these parts.

The slope on the Walpeup footy ground is still evident. The surface is relatively flat from the western end to the centre, after which it falls away to the eastern end. Gerry Leach, the Walpeup stalwart, later tells me that the slope provided the home team with a distinct advantage. Walpeup were adroit at bottling the ball up in the south-eastern corner, whereas they scored most of their goals while kicking uphill. The last match played at the ground was the Mallee league's Qualifying Final between Beulah and Ouyen United in 1998. During the subsequent summer, the Walpeup Recreation Reserve's committee decided it was not viable to maintain the oval for four matches a year. From 1999 onwards, Walpeup-Underbool played all home games at Underbool.

We head another twenty kilometres west and reach the town of Underbool. The town's main establishment, the Underbool Hotel, is a grand, brick building that looks robust enough to have weathered dust storms, hailstorms and storms of any kind. Maurie Sheahan, the full-back in Richmond's premiership teams in 1932 and 1934, ran the pub while he coached Underbool in the old North West Mallee league. Despite the pub's appearance, however, it was not robust enough to withstand the problems that beset the Mallee and the rest of rural Victoria as the years progressed. In 2016, the pub was shut. Given the cost of refurbishment, it's unlikely that it will be reopened.

Boozer turns off at the pub and heads towards the Underbool Recreation Reserve, where we are due to see Ouyen United host Merbein. There are teeming signs of life from the moment we enter the gates.

26

Tipping Point

At many country footy grounds, if you look beyond the reserve you see paddocks and plains that stretch off into the distance, but that's certainly not the case at Underbool. The reserve at Underbool is surrounded by native Mallee scrub. Not the stately pines like those of Walpeup, but tough and gnarly trees, with branches that stay low to escape the sun. It is a wonder to see that the native scrub has been left untouched at such a popular gathering place.

As Boozer Robertson parks under the canopy of branches behind the goals, he describes big days at Underbool in the early days after the final merger to create Ouyen United. During the club's first year in the Sunraysia league, in 2016, the three matches at Underbool were like unofficial reunions, with former footballers arriving from throughout the Mallee and beyond to talk about old times. Drinks continued well into the night. Boozer says he's not up to such shenanigans these days, but he looks happy to be back in the fold as he heads off on the track towards the social rooms.

I hop over the fence near the behind post and walk across the oval towards the wing. The Ouyen United reserves team has enjoyed a comfortable win, by about six goals. I walk by the players as they shake each other's hands. A hum of voices emerges from a large tent has been erected near the fence. A guitarist strums a few chords. It is Ladies' Day. The tent is full of women, young and old, who have converged from near and far to share each other's company. I stand on the oval and glance around at the native scrub. I enjoy sensing the energy that emerges from the ladies' tent while the reserves players walk past me on their way from the ground. The Ouyen United reserves coach looks like a familiar figure, as well he should. It's Noodle Hulland, the man in the portrait on the silo at Patchewollock. Noodle looks less rangy in real life than he does on the silo, and he's wearing a weather-beaten jacket rather than just a shirt, but his face is open and expressive, just as it is on the curved panel of the silo.

While Noodle makes his way through the Ouyen United supporters, he seems to walk through a path that has been cleared for him, as if he has a charisma that sets him apart from his surrounds. Maybe I'm projecting my expectation after seeing an image of him stare across the paddocks from such a commanding height. Noodle goes inside to enjoy the aftermath of the win.

As the senior players jog out of the rooms and make their way through the huddles of supporters, I sense no particular anticipation about the match. It is clear that everyone expects Ouyen United to enjoy a clear victory despite the fact that half a dozen of their best players are not here to play. Most of the Darwin boys have taken a weekend off from arduous travel and stayed in the Top End. Their replacements include Travis Latta, the brother of vice-president Jamie and the former wingman and rover Darren. Travis Latta played in four premiership teams during his career of 300 senior games with Walpeup-Underbool. After playing in two reserves premiership teams with Ouyen United, in the 2016 and 2017 teams, he is today making his senior debut for the club – at the age of thirty-nine. At the other end of the spectrum, two teenagers, Liam Munro and Oscar Smith, are making their debuts in senior football. Liam, 16, is the son of Jasper Munro, the former premiership defender who was Ouyen United's president when they entered the Sunraysia league in 2016. Oscar Smith, 17, is the son of Darren "Disco" Smith, a former player from Patchewollock, who played at centre half-back in Ouyen United's 1998 premiership team.

Merbein have long battled to keep pace in the Sunraysia league. The Magpies enjoyed a moment of riotous success when they won premierships in 2002 and 2003 under the coaching of the former Essendon star Merv Neagle, but that success owed much to the club's bunch of highly talented recruits from Darwin. As soon as the Darwin boys went elsewhere, Merbein returned to the foot of the table, and even had to battle off the threat of extinction.

From the moment the ball is bounced in this match between Ouyen United and Merbein, it is clear that there will be little competition throughout the afternoon. Ouyen United take the ball away from just about every ball-up and throw-in with monotonous ease. The lack of tension is disappointing, but not shocking. While the town of Ouyen is smaller than the town of Merbein, Ouyen United play with the pride of a team that is representing an entire region. The Mallee provides a strong identity for every player who is wearing the royal blue and white stripes.

It is fascinating to note the make-up of the Kangas' team. The defender Mitch Taylor is from Darwin, but now lives in Ouyen. Mark Jamar, the former ruckman with Melbourne in the AFL, has driven up from Melbourne, where he is a ruck coach at Essendon. After playing with Southern Districts in Darwin, Jamar has joined Ouyen United through Darwin connections. Of the other players, Matt Palmer was recruited from Adelaide many years ago and now lives in Underbool, while David Gregory is a teacher at the school in Ouyen, and Keegan Keely is the son of a local policeman. The policeman, Tony Keely, has become so enmeshed in the fabric of Ouyen United that, before the 2018 season, he replaced Jasper Munro as the club president.

Every other player in the Ouyen United team has a family link at one of the old Mallee clubs that comprises the club's extraordinary family tree. These players are too young to have seen clubs like Kiamal, Walpeup, Tempy or Tiega play against each other, but they have heard about those clubs throughout their lives and they are highly aware of their family backgrounds. Ouyen United could well have been named Mallee United, given the backgrounds of the players who turn out for the club on the day that I see them.

Sixteen of the twenty-one players have backgrounds that stretch back three or even four or five generations in Mallee football. Tom and Alex "Scoop" Morrish, who are brothers, and their second cousin Aron Morrish are descendants of William Thomas Morrish, who helped to found the Tiega Football Club in 1910. Tim Gloster's family represented the Underbool footy club from the time of settlement, while Andy Jardine and Liam Munro have backgrounds at Kiamal that stretch back to the club's formation a century ago.

Ryan Monaghan's family underpinned teams out of Tempy long before the club was forced into mergers. Jake Cresp's forebears were part of the Ouyen teams that dominated the 1930s, while Marcus Healy's grandfather, Stan Healy, was one of the seven Healy brothers who provided the backbone of Tiega teams in the years after World War 2. Jacob Grigg's family were legends around Patchewollock; his father, Simon Grigg, played in many premierships with Tempy-Gorya-Patchewollock and was the club's last president before the merger with Ouyen United. The family of the Mead brothers, Sam and Joab, were legends at Torrita and Walpeup, while Josh Gregg's grandfather, the great Ron Gregg, played in premierships at Ouyen and Walpeup, and is considered one of the best sportsmen in the history of the district.

The most impressive player to my eye is Tom "Tiddles" Morrish, a twenty-year-old midfielder who is tough and elusive, and canny in attack. He kicks early goals, and looks to be on the way to a huge bag. Marcus Healy, having decided to return to football after running the Mad Dog Morgan Trail, plays at half-forward in his first game for the season, and he shows no sign of the groin injury that hampered him after his kick-boxing camp. Healy attacks the ball in the air and marks with clean hands before scooting clear of defenders. His fitness is clearly a strength.

Josh Gregg is an accomplished midfielder. I try to keep an eye on him because I have been told of his virtues, and because I met his grandfather while he was paying for petrol in Ouyen that morning. However, I lose interest in the match because of Ouyen United's dominance, so I fail to watch the younger Gregg as closely as I have planned.

During the second quarter, I take a wander on the red dirt that forms a trail around the oval. I chat to Greg Vallance, who is manning the scoreboard. The scoreboard is a solid construction of steel rails and panels, which holds its ground against the gnarled trees behind it. A selection of four-wheel drives has been backed up against the walkway of the scoreboard.

The scoreboard is not electrified, which is unusual in these times. Greg must choose from his array of tin numbers and manually change the figures after every score. He leans over a steel rail and speaks to me while keeping an eye on the game. The name Vallance is one of the major footy names in the Mallee. Greg himself was the Walpeup-Underbool president for a time. He says the merger has worked out better than anyone could have imagined. It is a sentiment I will hear all day. Greg changes the score to record another goal to the Kangas.

At half-time, I head to the rooms to catch up with Chris Brown, whom I have met previously through his role as a board member of the Victorian Country Football League during the VCFL's final years. I met Chris during a period when he was the sole voice on the VCFL board from an isolated region. He and his wife Christine were proud parents when their three sons all returned from work or study in Bendigo, Mildura and elsewhere to make contributions to their home club. Scott (2001), Andrew (2007-2008) and Dean (2007) all played in premiership teams with Walpeup-Underbool. Their daughter, Kyra, was captain of a netball state-league premiership team in Adelaide before she, too, returned home to play, and she enjoyed success on the netball court with her home club.

But Chris Brown was always aware that the Mallee would struggle to hold young footballers and netballers who were seeking to make their way in the world. And he saw it as his role to try to improve the lot of players and officials from clubs with fragile numbers.

Chris is from a line of officials who have served country football at every level. His grandfather, Chris Brown senior, was among the first settlers in Underbool; having moved from Gooroc, near St Arnaud, he selected a block of land out of Underbool in 1910. Besides setting to work to clear the land, Chris Brown Senior helped to establish the Underbool Football Club. He was president of the club for many years, as well as president of the North West Mallee league.

His son, Bernie Brown, played in defence and in the ruck for Underbool. He, too, became the president of the Underbool Football Club, and in 1976 he was elected as president of the Mallee league. The next year, in 1977, it was his job, as league president, to present the premiership cup to his son, Chris Brown, who was the captain-coach of Tempy-Gorya-Patchewollock when the Saints won the 1977 Grand Final. Bernie Brown said it was his proudest moment in football when he presented the cup to his son. He went on to become the inaugural president of the Northern Mallee league after the formation of that competition in 1979.

Chris Brown Junior, who is now sixty-eight years of age, and I enjoy a leisurely chat about Mallee footy while he rests a foot on a chair in the capacious social rooms at Underbool. Chris began playing in the Underbool seniors in 1965, aged only fourteen. For three years, he boarded at St Patrick's College in Ballarat and played with Underbool when he returned home during the school holidays. In 1968, having finished school, he returned home and settled into a life of farming and sport in the Mallee.

The Underbool footy club struggled through Chris Brown's early years. He himself had a knee reconstruction that kept him on the sidelines during the 1972 season. In 1974, he left for Kiamal to embark on his coaching career. He also continued to play representative football. Halfway through the 1974 season, he was one of the five Mallee footballers who were members of the North Central league team that defeated the Hampden league in the country championships final. More than forty years later, during our chat in the social rooms at Underbool, a passer-by interrupts us to make sure I know that Chris was a member of North Central's famous team in 1974. Chris was twentieth man for the final, and he was not brought on to the ground. But he was happy just to be part of the team, and I doubt he'll ever tire of references to that day of wine and roses in the sodden heart of Warrnambool.

The next season, in 1975, Chris Brown left Kiamal to return to Underbool. He played in the ruck and up forward, where he proved a burly foil to his brother-in-law, Max Crow, the teenager who ignited the Mallee league that season. Underbool won the premiership in 1975, the only one in their existence as a stand-alone club in the Mallee competition. Chris played another season with his home club before agreeing to become the captain-coach of Tempy-Gorya-Patchewollock. He had three seasons at the helm at TGP, after which he returned to his home club, Underbool, and was an instigator of the merger between Walpeup and Underbool before the 1982 season. He continued to play until he was thirty-five years of age, after which he settled into a life of administration.

While Chris was the coach of TGP, he continued to play cricket for Underbool and serve on the management committee for the Underbool Recreation Reserve. More than twenty years later, he was still on the Underbool reserve's management committee when he drove the push for new rooms. To raise the funds for the rooms, the management committee won a government contract to ferry wheat from silos around the district to the train line during harvest time. The federal government later contributed towards the construction of the rooms, but the Underbool reserve's management committee covered almost the entire bill with the proceeds of the wheat contract. By the time the rooms were opened in 2006, they had come at a cost of $380,000, and the management committee did not owe a cent. As we stand in the rooms at Underbool during the third quarter of the match against Merbein, Chris Brown says that playing his part in the construction of the rooms is among his proudest achievements in sport.

The genesis of the need to build new rooms at Underbool is a classic country footy story. It begins on an unknown date during the 1990s. Underbool's then publican, Billy McKellin, was idling in his car in the town's main street when Chris Brown leaned on the door rail to have a chat. When Chris noticed a load in the back of the publican's ute, he asked about the contents of the load. The publican said it was just stuff that had been gathering dust in the pub. He was now taking it out to the tip.

Chris's antenna was alerted. In those days, the rooms at the Underbool oval consisted of only a single room in which a partition separated the two teams while they prepared for the game. After senior matches, the club's supporters had to wait for the players to shower and dress before they could pull back the partition and use the room for their social gatherings. In this one room, it was impractical to house the club's memorabilia; flying footballs would create a threat to anything on the walls. Instead, the premierships photos and flags and all forms of memorabilia were kept at the Underbool Hotel.

When the publican mentioned his intended tip run, Chris politely inquired whether he could take a peek at the pile. To his alarm, he found trophies and artefacts from the Underbool Football Club's earliest days. The most precious discovery was a Mallee stump with a premiership pedigree.

The postmaster in Underbool in that era, Bert Johnson, was a woodturner. After Underbool had won the Mallee league's Grand Final in 1975, Johnson carved a Mallee stump into the shape of a football. On the ball, he mounted a plaque that listed every premiership player and every official who had contributed towards the triumph. The stump was highly valued for its novelty and sense of place. It was not every day that the region's most recognised form of sawn-off flora, the Mallee stump, was adorned with details of an Underbool premiership.

When Chris Brown asked whether he could take possessions of some of the footy items, the publican invited him to take the lot. Chris took the dusty bounty back to his shed, and kept it safe until a new home could be arranged. The near loss of the Mallee stump and sundry items was among the motivations for the decision to build new rooms at the Underbool Recreation Reserve.

27

Pocket of Interest

It is halfway through the third quarter of the match between Ouyen United and Merbein in Underbool. The match is continuing to fall in the home team's favour when Chris Brown leads me outside the social rooms to introduce me to two of the grand old men of foothall in Underbool, or football anywhere, Ray and Ken Gloster, who are ninety-one and eighty-nine years of age respectively.

When Ray and Ken were boys, their father, Joe Gloster, told them stories about the horses and buggies that were backed up along Underbool's main street. In 1927, just after General Motors Holden had embarked on a program to lease out dealerships around Australia, Joe Gloster established a dealership in Underbool, and the business remained in the family for ninety years.

Ray Gloster, the older brother, played only one match for Underbool. On every other Saturday in his early adult life, he worked in the car dealership. In 1955, however, he began to perform the role of timekeeper for the Underbool Football Club. He was the club's timekeeper for a short time during the Magpies' final years in the North West Mallee league. In 1957, when Underbool left to join the Mallee league (and changed their nickname to the Kangaroos), he retained the timekeeper's job, and he kept doing it for twenty-five years. When Underbool merged with Walpeup to form Walpeup-Underbool in 1982, he became the merged club's timekeeper, and he remained the Bulldogs' timekeeper for another thirty-three years. In all, Ray Gloster was a timekeeper for more than sixty seasons before he finally put down his clock after the final game of the Mallee league in 2015. He was eighty-eight years of age when he stepped aside.

In 1996, Ray Gloster received a coveted Medal of Recognition from the VCFL for his services to country football. I have not met anyone who has served country footy in one role for a longer period.

Ken Gloster, the younger brother, left Underbool to study at the Maryborough Tech on a manual arts studentship in 1946, when he was seventeen years of age. Ken played for Primrose in the Maryborough District league for two seasons, and he was a member of the club's premiership team in 1946. When he returned home to Underbool in 1948, his father wanted him to work in the car dealership rather than play footy. A deal was struck. Ken could play footy only if he used his footy contacts to bring business through the door.

Ken Gloster played his first game for Underbool in 1948, when he was nineteen years of age. He was a fiery and athletic ruckman. On the King's Birthday long weekend in June that year, he took a diversion from footy and finished second, behind K. J. Thomas of Pinnaroo, in the Ouyen Gift. The next year, in 1949, he again finished second in the Ouyen Gift. In 1952, by which time the organisers were advertising the prizemoney for the Ouyen Gift as the most for an unregistered gift in the southern hemisphere, Ken won the event. He tells me that his purse for winning the event was the equivalent to fifteen weeks' wages.

A few years after his victory in the Gift, in 1955, Ken Gloster revealed himself to be a truly versatile sportsman when he was the captain of the Underbool team that won the premiership in the North West Mallee Football League and he became the inaugural president of the Underbool bowls club. He continued to play footy and bowls for Underbool until 1970, when he moved to Bendigo. He then played footy for another four years, for Kennington-Strathdale in the Golden City league, before retiring from the game at the age of forty-four. He continued, however, to play bowls. Now, almost fifty years after moving to Bendigo, he is still playing and involved in administration at the Bendigo East bowls club and the local bowls association.

In 2018, as the Gloster brothers and I stand on the wing during Ouyen United's match against Merbein, it strikes me that that Ken Gloster first played on this ground seventy years previously, in 1948, which is a very long time ago. But even now, aged eighty-nine, he still has a glint in his eye when he talks about playing footy.

Although Ken Gloster had no part in the family car business after 1999, his brother Ray and Ray's sons and grandsons continued to run their car dealership, A.J. Gloster and Sons, until late December 2017, when General Motors Holden informed them that, in keeping with the company's decision to close small dealerships around Australia, it would no longer support the operation in Underbool. Ray Gloster told the *Sunraysia Daily* that he understood the decision, as Australians were no longer buying cars made at home, but he was shattered nonetheless.

Now, Ray Gloster's custom of going to the footy helps him to stay connected with friends from Underbool and throughout the Mallee. Ken Gloster, the younger of the brothers, comes up from Bendigo when he can.

On the field before us, Tom Morrish brings his tally of goals in this match to five while Aron Morrish kicks four. Travis Latta kicks two goals in his return to senior football, while Marcus Healy kicks two, and deserves to kick more. Josh Gregg is widely adjudged to be best on ground, with Jacob Grigg not far behind. Joab Mead and the coach, Andy Jardine, are also among the best players as Ouyen United career away to victory by seventy-nine points.

After the match, the old rooms are buzzing as supporters join the players for a natter under the low roof. There is no partition to pull back. It's just one big, happy family, comprised by members of several families from throughout the Mallee.

As it happens, the gathering with the largest presence in the Ouyen United rooms is that of a family that is not from these parts at all. Members of Mark Jamar's family have driven across from Adelaide to see

Mark play for his adopted club. Mark's parents and his brother and sister are all uncommonly tall. They make for an arresting sight as they discuss the match while Mark stands among them in his shorts and jumper, with his ankles still swathed in tape. Mark kicked two goals from strong marks, but he had only a minor impact on the game. I talk to him briefly. He's still finding match fitness, but he's enjoying playing for this unique club so far from Melbourne. He seems at home in country footy.

Officials gather at one end of the room to sort out their after-match affairs. I enjoy a brief chat with Gerald Leach, whom I had met in the rooms at Blackburn Park the previous year, in July 2017, when he told me the excellent story about his wife Louise's departure from Blackburn Park because their son had changed ends. Gerry is Ouyen United 's timekeeper. He held the position with the club before the merger in late 2015, and he has remained the club's timekeeper since its move into the Sunraysia league in 2016.

When we discuss today's victory over Merbein, Gerry makes comment on the Roos' score, 18.19 (127). He says a high tally of behinds on this ground never surprises him. He looks almost conspiratorial, peering over his glasses, when he informs me that very few footballers pick the bias of what he describes variously as the southern end, or the town end, or the railway end – "take your pick" – on the oval at Underbool. The forward pocket closest to the change rooms features a slope that creates a subtle imbalance in the stance of players when they are lining up for goal. The players, standing slightly off an upright axis, always curve the ball from left to right, resulting in the ball drifting just beyond the far goalpost or across the goals altogether. Gerry's detail is borne of astute observation. I sense that he could tell me stories about Mallee football for hours.

Gerry Leach makes a distinct impression on me when he mentions his son Dom, who, earlier in the day, had kicked two goals in the reserves match and was named among the Kangas' best players.

Dom works alongside Gerry on their farm at Walpeup, and on weekends he plays his heart out on the footy field. Father and son share keen interests in footy and farming, and the heritage aspects of both. Gerry is keenly aware that so many sons leave their family farm as young men and never return. He regards himself as a lucky man because his son has chosen to stay alongside him on the farm, and because his son is aware of the strength of the bonds created by a shared heritage. As a father myself, I feel moved when Gerry describes himself as a lucky man because his son has stayed beside him, and because his son lives out the values that have been impressed upon him. It's all that any father could wish for.

In the social rooms, the former players from clubs like Kiamal, Tiega and Underbool stand in small clumps near the bar. I speak briefly to Michael Brown, a member of Underbool's storied 1975 premiership team, who, in 2015, was the president of the Mallee league in its final year of competition. Michael, who is Chris Brown's cousin, is now on the board of the Sunraysia league, and is keenly aware of the importance of the links created by football. He says the success of the Ouyen United merger is a reflection on the hard work of the club's leaders.

The former players talk footy around the bar, while young parents sit along the trestle tables nearby and tend to the needs of their children. Outside, a couple of dozen youngsters aged from eight to twelve kick a footy or throw a netball at a hoop. The air is still and mild. The children look fresh and happy.

Bernie Kelly, fresh from interviewing players for his report for the *Sunraysia Daily*, introduces me to some of the players. Matt "Chicken" Palmer, the defender who stayed with the club after marrying a girl from Underbool, looks like a Mallee hipster, with his stubble and checked shirt and hair over his eyes. He has a winning smile, and a clear affection for Bernie Kelly, whom he goads gently about his footy reports. Chicken is a builder in the Mallee, but he looks like he could easily slide into a gathering at the Standard Hotel in Fitzroy.

Josh Gregg has known Bernie all his life, having grown up alongside Bernie's son Gerard. He, too, shows an affection for Bernie by answering his footy questions with modesty and humility, and waving off suggestions that he is on track to win the league medal. Josh tells me that he drives across from Adelaide every weekend because he enjoys playing for the club from his home town, alongside talented teammates. He does not say explicitly that he and his teammates take great pride in representing the Mallee in their clashes against clubs from the Sunraysia region, but that is the way that I read it.

I join Boozer in walking back across the oval towards his car. The volume of music emerging from the women's tent on the wing has gone up several notches over the course of the evening. Voices are raised as one, projecting their shared joy into the night air. There is no sense of sadness at the merger of so many clubs into one. They are singing for those who have stayed, for those who choose to live here, in a region they love. They're having a great time.

Boozer drives me back to Ouyen, where I pick up my car and make the journey out to Patchewollock to join him at the Patchewollock Hotel. The pub features a horseshoe bar. I like the bars of Melbourne – and these days the bars of Ballarat and Bendigo – with their clean lines in confined spaces, but the unusual nature of the bar in Patchewollock offers curious appeal. The horseshoe shape invites those at the bar to project their voices and lives towards a central space, which lends a shared sense of purpose to the evening's events. Behind me, Mallee stumps crackle in the fire, sending small sparks of warmth and connection towards the boots and trouser legs that are backed up against it.

In the next room, the walls of the lounge are hung with a series of photos of the town. Some photos feature thin posts and big smiles outside the shops along the main street. Of the footy photos, players from premiership teams fold their arms and look into the lens with an openness befitting the vast spaces behind them.

An item on the menu catches my eye: the Wyperfeld steak. Apparently, it is a large steak, sourced from the butcher in Ouyen, with an egg on top of it. Bryce the publican thought the word "Wyperfeld", borrowed from the Wyperfeld National Park down the road, might suggest something of the feel of the area.

I love the description. The use of the word "Wyperfeld" suggests an experience that is big and sprawling, with an earthy goodness that holds up against threats from harsh conditions and modern cuisine. I order one. It is magnificent. I hope the Wyperfeld steak becomes a legendary dish, a totem for the region, like the totem poles of Ouyen United.

Part 4
The Last Quarter

28

Fun in the Sun

Within a few days of returning from the Mallee, I am back on the road to continue my journey into footy's heartland in country Victoria. While conditions were mild in Underbool and Patchewollock, with weak sunlight that touched the skin, it now seems like I was immersed in a tropical firestorm compared to the conditions in which I find myself in the opposite end of the state.

During the 2018 season, I did a weekly country footy show on the Racing Sports Network, better known as RSN, in Melbourne. The station's head of content, Adam White, asked me to join him on air for a look at issues, results and the lighter side of footy outside the capital. To prepare for the show, it was my habit to check through the results around the state. As the season settled into a pattern, I noticed a weekly phenomenon in the Mid-Gippsland Football League, which was comprised by ten clubs based in the farming region outside the industrial works of the Latrobe Valley. In most rounds, one of the five matches was decided by a margin of a goal or less. In early June, the occurrence of close games went up a notch when, in Round 9, Mirboo North defeated Newborough by four points and Trafalgar defeated Yinnar by two points. The next week, in Round 10, there were two draws: Newborough and Yarragon drew 6.5 (41) apiece at

Newborough, while Yinnar scored 8.6 (54) to Mirboo North's 7.12 (54) at Yinnar. The close matches in the Mid-Gippsland league provided a welcome contrast with the propensity for blowouts in other competitions.

Around that time, my weekly observation of the Close One in the Mid-Gippsland league was drawing the notice of Paul Dodds, who was the president of the Boolarra Football Club. The Demons had not won a senior match for a season and a half, but their narrowing margins of defeat suggested a win was around the corner. Paul emailed me to confirm that the Demons were confident of impending victory. But whether or not they achieved their breakthrough in the near future, morale was high. On Thursday evenings, the club was serving about 100 meals after training. He described for me the menu of the week just gone:

> The fare? A small slice of quiche, a slice of vegie flan, a small noodle basket with eggs and the like – all served in a warm friendly atmosphere.
>
> For our club, the community is just as important as wins and losses (although a bloody win would be good).

Paul Dodds asks whether I would like to pop down for a meal in the beautiful foothills of the Strzelecki Ranges. I decide to take him up on his offer. And while I'm in the region, I'll check out reports that the league is fighting off suggestions of a shake-up to include clubs from other competitions.

It is a frigid evening when I drive through rain along the Monash Freeway, then turn south near Morwell to proceed along a curving road towards the southern range. I arrive at the Boolarra ground and step on to the wet tarmac. Training has just finished. The oval is empty in the damp night air.

Inside the commodious social rooms, a fire crackles in a coonarra. Diners of all ages are seated around large, round tables. Players and supporters gather in loose circles near the bar. Paul Dodds, the Boolarra president, is tall, with a goatee beard and a clear enthusiasm for his role at the club. He worked in a bank in Swan Hill before being transferred to

Morwell. Now he works as an agribusiness manager for Saputo, the dairy firm, in nearby Mirboo North.

Paul could not be more welcoming. He introduces me to his wife Cathleen. He introduces me to everyone in sight before whisking me towards the kitchen, where I meet those responsible for the weekly nosebag at Boolarra.

In 2014, Greg and Ann Carter were a semi-retired couple seeking a tree change when they moved from Melbourne to the beautiful hill country near Boolarra. In an effort to get to know some local people, they offered to help out in the kitchen at the football club. Greg also joined the local historical club, while Ann joined the wool club, where she could chat about life in the hill country while knitting jumpers and scarves to ward off the cold.

Early in 2015, in their second season at the football club, Greg and Ann posted in the window of the post office a general invitation for meals in the Boolarra clubrooms after training on Thursday nights. Their invitation attracted the interest of many who were not involved at the footy club. Pensioners, especially, were keen on the weekly fare. In 2015, the club began serving about thirty meals a night. At the jumper presentation on the eve of the 2017 season, it served 140 meals. The post-training nosh-up was a local phenomenon.

Every week during footy season, Ann Carter buys the ingredients for the meals in Morwell on Tuesday morning. The next day, she begins her preparations. This week, the menu features chicken schnitzel with chips and salad as well as a small pasta pie as a side serve. Meals costs $15 for a large serve or $12 for a small one. I order a large. It is delicious, and features flavours that I have not previously enjoyed at a footy club. When I ask Ann the contents of the salad, she tries to conceal her secrets, but after a bit of prodding, she says it consists of lettuce with toffee, sunflowers, almonds and pepitas, which are small pumpkin seeds.

When I ask Ann whether it's the first time that pepitas have been served at a country footy club, she is uncertain, but she assures me that local palates have become more adventurous over the course of the past three years. When she first put oranges in a salad, there was uproar.

Another club official, Lisa Holmes, describes the first time she put avocado in a post-training salad. Admittedly, she says, it was several years ago, before avocado was a regular component of Australian diets. The players frowned at their plates before one of them asked the pressing question.

"What's this green stuff?"

On this night in Boolarra in June 2018, the kitchen staff serves ninety-seven meals, which raises $1200 for the club coffers. After our meals, I stand in a circle with the kitchen workers and long-time supporters like John Cargill and his partner Elaine Smart. As the drizzles falls to the ground outside, John glances out the window. A smile spreads across his face. "Welcome to the sunny Strzeleckis," he says.

Lisa Holmes, the woman who served avocado before her time, is in the circle with her husband, Keith who, like his friend John Cargill, is smiling like the sun has just caressed his cheek. Clearly, they find the weather amusing. Lisa and Keith Holmes live on a farm just a few tumble punts south of the ground. Their son, James Holmes, is Boolarra's assistant coach. He lives in the Melbourne suburb of Hawthorn and trains on Tuesday nights with the Ormond Amateurs, but he returns home every Thursday evening to help out with Boolarra training and every Saturday to play for his home club. James Holmes has played almost 200 games in Boolarra's senior team. Keith smiles broadly when he reveals that James was a member of the team that won the 2011 senior premiership.

Keith himself was an average footballer. He played a few seasons in the juniors and a handful of games in the Boolarra reserves before hanging up his boots and going on to the committee. As a club official, he speaks with great pride about the rooms in which we're standing. To build the rooms, the club took out a loan of $40,000. In 1996, the Demons formed what they called the 500 Club, whose members agreed to donate $500 a season towards covering the loan. The club built the rooms using second-hand materials. The wooden panels on the walls were once the floorboards at the Traralgon RSL. Other materials were found in the machine room at the Morwell Tech. The door trimmings were procured from abandoned houses. The seven-year loan was paid off in six years.

Keith Holmes again smiles, this time especially broadly, when he informs me that the building was finished in 1996. "And we put two flags in it the next year."

Boolarra were a foundation club of the Mid-Gippsland league in 1935, along with Brown Coal Mine, Morwell Bridge, Morwell Seconds, Yallourn Imperials and Yinnar.

Boolarra won only two senior premierships in their first sixty years in the competition, in 1955 and 1958, so it was a big deal when the Demons won both the seniors and reserves flags in 1997. Keith Holmes guides my eye towards the two premiership flags that are draped from the ceiling nearby. His own eyes are twinkling, The coonarra continues to throw out heat in the corner.

Before the 2011 season, Boolarra signed a handful of players with strong connections to the club, including Rob and Steve Fox, whose grandfather Noel Fox was a club legend. Matt Dyer, who had left the town of Boolarra at the age of eight, returned from Geelong to play with his family's old club. Tony Giardina, a former coach at Mirboo North, agreed to become the Boolarra coach.

The Demons received a further boost just before clearances closed when Jock McFarlane, a midfield veteran from Morwell, signed on. McFarlane had lost his pace, but his deft hands set up Boolarra for a run of victories. James Holmes played in the midfield. John Cargill's son Jordan played at full-back. The Demons finished fifth on the ladder after the home and away rounds in 2011. They then stormed through the finals to win an unlikely flag. Even now, in the midst of a losing streak that has lasted a season and a half, I sense that the glow from the 2011 premiership remains undimmed.

When I ask supporters whether the Boolarra footy club has produced any AFL players, the answer pleases me greatly. A decade ago, a historian from Monash University's then campus at Churchill, just south of Morwell, sent me a book that was based on some redoubtable Gippsland characters. The book, *House of Trees* by Chester Eagle, has an unusual structure: it's a local history as told through a few profiles. It is, however, a powerful tale, and it remains one of my favourite non-fiction books.

Tonight I find out that the man who sent it to me, Patrick Morgan, lives just out of Boolarra. His son, Danny Morgan, played in a handful of senior games with Essendon. After Danny's footy career ended, I enjoyed listening to him when he was a journalist on ABC Radio.

Tonight is one of those modern Thursday nights in footy: there is an AFL game on the television, in this case between Sydney and Richmond. At half-time of the match in Sydney, the television's sound is turned down and Paul Dodds addresses the club about the importance of a victory in their game at home in two days' time. Their opponents, Yarragon, are only a few games off the bottom of the ladder themselves. "We need a win," the Boolarra president says.

The reserves coach, Mark Carnes, reads out his team in a style that is remarkable for its economy of words. He says nothing by way of introduction. He just reads out his team from the backline, revealing each player by nickname only: "Gus, Jell, Beamer … Oz, Steve, Cleaves … Smittie, Duano, Billy …"

He signs off by mentioning the time to meet at the ground.

"11.30 …

"Thanks, boys."

The senior coach, Tony Giardina, is short and genial, with clear, olive skin and a gift for communication. Tony's parents emigrated from Italy as children in the 1950s. When Tony was a boy, he and his brother Paul had to finish their work on the farm before they were able to go to footy training. Tony played senior football for his local club, Mirboo North. He coached Mirboo North for four years, from 2002 to 2005. Six years later, in 2011, he guided Boolarra to their unexpected premiership. Before the 2018 season, he returned to Boolarra because he wanted to prove to himself and others that the Demons' rally through the finals in 2011 was not a fluke.

Tony Giardina and his brother Paul grows potatoes and onions on their small farm (150 hectares) outside Mirboo North. In 2017, the *Weekly Times* published an article on the brothers' innovative approach to growing potatoes in the rich soil of one of Victoria's spud-growing hubs. They were the first to introduce to the region a washed red potato variety called Mozart Red.

Tony Giardina's son Jesse plays in his team at Boolarra. Tonight, in the rooms after training, the fifty-one-year-old coach says he is proud that every player in his team has a Boolarra connection.

We all stay to watch the second half of the AFL match and chat in the warmth of the Boolarra rooms. After the match has finished, I say my goodbyes and receive a stream of advice that I must get to the footy by half-time on Saturday so that I can enjoy the cakes and scones during the best afternoon tea at a footy club in Gippsland. Paul Dodds, the president, assures me that Mid-Gippsland officials ask the women of Boolarra to cater for their afternoon tea at the grand final.

I am about to head off towards my accommodation in Mirboo North when Keith Holmes jumps in my van; he says the roads out are confusing and he wants to make sure I get on the right one. Lisa drives along behind us. At a fork in the road on the western edge of town, Keith points me towards the right. As he gets out of the van, I ask what he has in store for the following day.

"Just fixing a trough," he says, laughing, as if fixing a trough is so disagreeable that it must somehow be funny.

Keith joins Lisa in the family car. They wave as they drive off, happy as larks on this gloomy night. They are sunny souls, the two of them.

Map 3: Mid-Gippsland

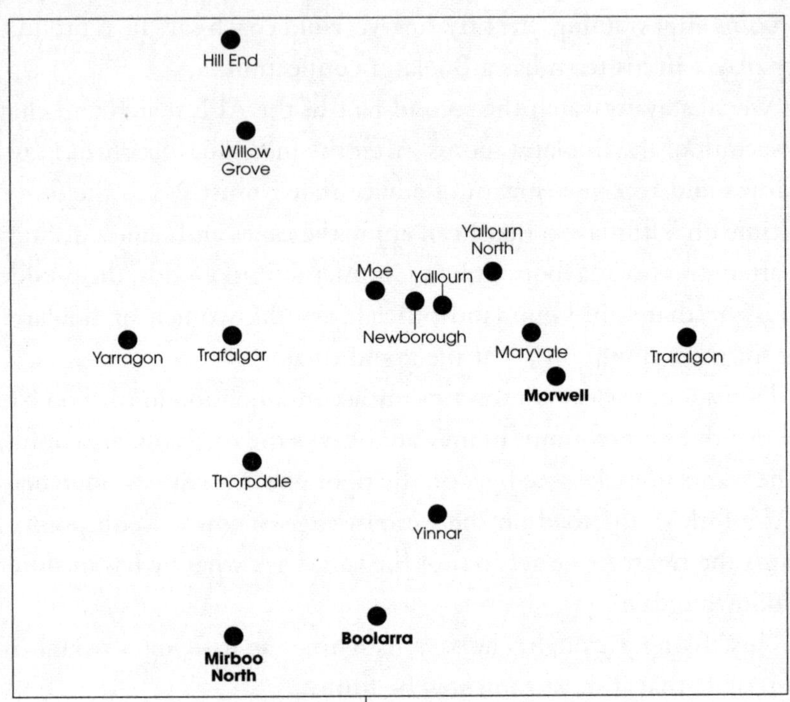

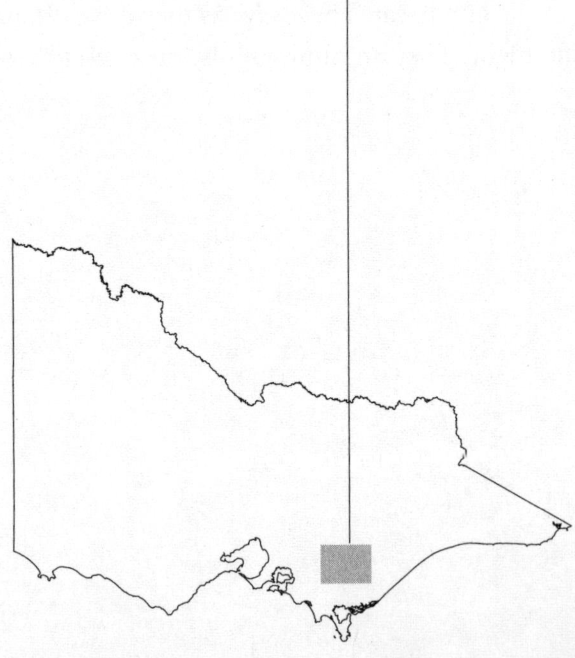

29

Spooky Times

The day after enjoying a fine feed in the rooms at the Boolarra footy club, I seek to explore the talk around changes to the Mid-Gippsland league. To do so, I drive to Morwell to attend the get-together that the Mid-Gippsland league officials enjoy every Friday at the home of the league treasurer, Charlie Cauchi.

Charlie is a boilermaker who played 300 games in the Mid-Gippsland league, mostly at Morwell East, but also at Boolarra. He was a playing-coach at both clubs. He played in two premiership teams with Morwell East, and he won the league best and fairest medal in 1978. For the past thirteen years, from 2005 to 2018, Charlie has been the treasurer of the Mid-Gippsland league.

In the kitchen of his home in a quiet street in suburban Morwell, Charlie Cauchi places a hot serve of party pies on the table while I meet his fellow officials. The men around the table include Stan Kerrigan, Rod Lucas, Laurie Williams and Peter Rennie. Like Charlie, these men are all life members of the Mid-Gippsland league. The other man at the table is Tony Giardina, the Boolarra coach, whom I had met the previous night in the Boolarra rooms.

Stan Kerrigan, the league vice-president, works in operations at the electricity plant. In 1974, when he was thirty-two years of age, Stan and his family emigrated from Northern Ireland because he felt there were more opportunities in Australia. More than forty years later, the edges have been knocked off his Ulster accent, but he still speaks in a way that is uncommon at Australian football clubs.

Stan played soccer on arrival in the Latrobe Valley, but he developed a taste for footy through watching his son David play at Churchill. He became involved at Boolarra, and served as the Demons' club president for four years. He's now been a Mid-Gippsland league official for more than a decade.

Rod Lucas is a carpenter who played a few reserves games at Morwell East before moving into administration. He was appointed as club secretary at Morwell East. He's now been league secretary for twenty-six years. His predecessor, Cliff Greenwood, was the league secretary for twenty-five years. As the men around the table reveal their roles, it becomes clear that stability has been a feature of the league's administration.

Peter Rennie is a groundsman at Kurnai College in Morwell, but he is better known as the eternal footballer of Gippsland. Peter is slim and wiry, like many footballers who enjoy long careers. Many years ago, I wrote a small profile on him for a book on country footy that I did with the photographer Ian Kenins. Having interviewed Peter by phone, it's good to meet him in person.

Peter Rennie tells me he has now played 766 games in the Mid-Gippsland league, including 280 senior games, mostly with his original club, Yinnar. After starting with Yinnar in 1966, he played for the Magpies for twenty years. He played for Boolarra for thirty years. He also played at Maryvale and Churchill for a season each, but he regards Boolarra as his home club. He is still on the Demons' committee. While he's not on the league committee, he is the Boolarra club delegate, and it would be a rare gathering of Mid-Gippsland officials without his presence. Peter Rennie has been part of the furniture for as long as anyone can remember. At seventy-one years of age, he still puts his footy boots in his bag every Saturday in case the reserves are short.

I am delighted to meet Laurie Williams, the league's long-time historian, because he is responsible for an anecdote that I enjoyed reading in his history of the competition. According to Laurie's book, the Haunted Hills Football Club joined the Mid-Gippsland league in 1936. Naturally enough, they were called the Ghosts. Their original home was the ground inside the Moe racecourse, where they got changed in an old shed.

Before a match in 1939, the players walked in to the shed and found a dead swaggie. Oddly enough, the Ghosts refused to play until the matter of the dead person was sorted out. It was 3.30pm before the police and medicos had cleared the corpse. According to Laurie's book, the players were not up to their best, as their minds kept falling back to the unfortunate swaggie, but they did manage to eke out a win over Yallourn Imperials by three points, which struck me as a clear example of the Ghosts rising above the occasion.

Laurie co-wrote the book, called *From the Ashes*, with Cliff Greenwood before the competition's fiftieth anniversary, in 1985. At the time, Laurie was an official at the Maryvale Football Club, whose players mostly worked at the paper mill to the north of Morwell. In 1987, Maryvale were unable to find a coach or officials, so the club folded. As we sit in Charlie Cauchi's kitchen in Morwell in 2018, it was the last change in the structure of the competition. The Mid-Gippsland league has had the same ten clubs for more than thirty years. The greatest distance between those clubs is sixty kilometres, which is the stretch from Willow Grove, the home base of the Hill End footy club, in the north of the competition's catchment area, to Mirboo North in the south. The journey between those two towns takes only fifty minutes. The Mid-Gippsland league has the distinct advantage of being one of the most closely settled competitions in country Victoria.

As the Mid-Gippsland officials dip their party pies into the sauce, they become animated over suggestions of change. While other competitions in Gippsland might well be in turmoil, they see no reason why their competition should be forced to accommodate the problems of others. Charlie Cauchi says the small distance between the Mid-Gippsland clubs is important. The Mid-Gippsland league is a working man's competition. Players can work on Saturday mornings and still get to their match on time. This might not be possible if the league were expanded to include clubs from the Alberton league, which is based over the hills in South Gippsland.

The most vocal member of the discussion is Tony Giardina, who is not on the league's executive, but as a life-long Mid-Gippsland man, he is also part of the furniture. The previous evening, in the warm expanses of the rooms at Boolarra, I had found Tony to be a genial man. But here in the confines of Charlie Cauchi's kitchen he is far more expressive. His main source of frustration is the AFL, which he believes is removed from the people it is meant to serve. It is a refrain I hear from country footy people throughout Victoria, but there is a sharper edge to the frustration of the Mid-Gippsland officials.

Tony Giardina takes me back to the previous night, when we were watching the AFL game between Sydney and Richmond on television. After every goal, a graphic shot up on to the screen to reveal that a particular sponsor was giving $250 to grassroots football.

"But where?" Tony asks.

"Where in grassroots football?"

In 2018, AFL Gippsland is one of twelve regional commissions that operate under the aegis of AFL Victoria Country. Each regional commission is responsible for raising funds as well as running the game.

At the beginning of the 2018 season, each player registration in Gippsland cost $65. In May 2018, about four or five rounds into the season, AFL Gippsland notified all clubs in their region that each senior player must pay an extra $30 and each junior player must pay an extra $5. No explanation was given.

At later meetings, AFL Gippsland officials revealed that their body faced a severe cash shortfall. However, most league and club officials failed to see why the players should have been forced to cover for the regional commission.

In Charlie Cauchi's kitchen in Morwell, Tony Giardiana points out that the AFL is planning to build new headquarters in Melbourne. He struggles to see how new digs for the top administrators is more important than fixing country football.

Another sticking point among the Mid-Gippsland men is stability. Travis Switzer has recently resigned as the chief executive of AFL Gippsland, contributing further to the organisation's reputation for a high turnover of staff. All the officials around the table in Charlie Cauchi's kitchen have served the league for many years; in the case of Rod Lucas, it's almost three decades. "Our league has been going for eighty years," says Charlie. "We've had fewer changes in eighty years than AFL Gippsland has had in five years."

When the Mid-Gippsland officials make these points through official circles, the AFL officials counter by asking them what is likely to happen when they themselves move on. Would the Mid-Gippsland league run so smoothly without its long-serving officials? It is an obvious question. I ask them myself. They have no answer.

The other argument against maintaining the competition's status quo is the decline in junior numbers. While the ten clubs all field senior teams in 2018, only five field teams at the under-seventeen level. Boolarra is among the five clubs that are unable to find enough players to field a thirds team.

Before I go, Laurie Williams presents me with my own copy of *From the Ashes* as well as a copy of his history of the Maryvale footy club, for which I'm very grateful. I thank the Mid-Gippsland men for their hospitality, especially Charlie Cauchi.

On the drive back through the rich, rolling country to the south, I ponder the question of whether the Mid-Gippsland league can remain an island in a sea of volatility. Through my research into league restructures and the workings of football administration, I have learnt that nothing stays the same in country footy because populations always shift. As long as there is a drift from the land into the cities and towns, there will be changes to the structures of competitions.

Unfortunately for the officials from the Mid-Gippsland league, I doubt their many capabilities will be enough to maintain their competition in the format that has endured for so long. In fact, with reference to one of the competition's more curious clubs, I don't think they have a ghost of a chance.

30

Scones Overboard

Given that I'm staying in Mirboo North, I'm keen to see the early part of the senior match at Mirboo North's home ground before making sure I'm at Boolarra for the spread at half-time. As I drive inside the gates at the Walter J. Tuck Reserve on the outskirts of Mirboo North, I'm struck when I learn that the temperature is nine degrees. With the rain falling in intermittent bursts and the wind cutting in off the nearby hills, I figure that the temperature gauge must have overstated the figure by at least half. It's been a long time since I arrived at a footy ground in such bleak conditions.

I'm also shocked when I see the slope of the ground. While I had heard about the rather pronounced gradient from wing to wing, I had not expected a ski run. The temperature would have to drop by only a few degrees and the children would be tempted to bring out toboggans. I can imagine midfielders scrabbling around in the slush while junior players scream past them on their plastic flyers, testing the speed of the run along the half-forward line.

And yet I like it around here. I love the pine trees that stand tall and proud around the edge of the reserve, and I love the all-round footy-ness of going to a game with a few clouds about the place. In these days of little rain and excellent drainage, I quite miss the experience of wet-weather football. Maybe it's nostalgia for my youth, when we struggled to pull our feet out of the mud and thought nothing of it, but that's just the way I feel. I walk through the mist and drizzle to ask the president, Steve Rogers, about his citadel of mud and glory.

Steve Rogers is forty-nine years of age. In his working life, he is the regional manager for roadside assistance with the Royal Automobile Club of Victoria. His wife Angie is the club secretary. While Steve is in his first year as club president, Angie has been the secretary for four years.

Steve Rogers has played almost 500 club games for Mirboo North. Just over a decade ago, in 2007, he was thirty-eight years of age when he enjoyed his most successful year. I sense that he is one to underplay himself when he says that his role during that season was to act as a decoy forward. If he led to the pocket, it left more space for the stars like Tim Traill to work in. Steve is very proud when he says that he and Traill kicked seventeen goals between them in a match against Boolarra in 2007. The fact that Traill kicked fifteen and he kicked two means the decoy plan worked beautifully. At the end of the 2007 season, Steve Rogers enjoyed his reward when he played in his only senior premiership team.

For much of the past decade, Steve has continued to play in the reserves because he simply loves playing footy. He is able to talk to me during the reserves match today because he injured his calf last week. He'll be back on the park next week if they pick him.

Steve Rogers leans on a bench in the social rooms and frowns when I ask about the ski slope masquerading as a footy ground. The slope starts on the wing in front of the social rooms and reaches down to the opposite wing before sliding off into a gully at the bottom of the reserve. Steve tells me that the slope is seventeen feet (almost six metres) from wing to wing. I ask whether it might be time to fix it.

"It's not on my agenda."

He says the club would rather spend money on the entrance to the Walter Tuck Reserve, which I must admit is dangerous. The club would also like to improve the lighting at the ground, and renovate the change rooms to cater better for women players and umpires. He concludes that the club is unlikely to find the money to go cutting into the slope any time soon.

'Besides, I like it."

Why?

"Because it's ours."

Mirboo North started in the Mid-Gippsland league like a shot from a cannon. After entering the competition in 1955, the Tigers lost the Grand Final in their first season to Boolarra by two points. The Mirboo North ruckman, Dave Snell, had a shot for goal after the siren, but hit the post. Mirboo North then won the next two premierships, in 1956 and 1957. A photo on the wall in the social rooms celebrates the 1956 premiership team, which included five brothers from the Snell family. Dave Snell was the captain, but Bill Snell, who was known as "Billo", was the star. Billo Snell had played at centre half-forward in Essendon's VFL premiership team in 1950. Jack Dyer, who was the Richmond coach at the time, remarked that Snell was one of the best centre half-forwards he had seen. During a practice match before the next season, however, Snell was kicked in the head, and he struggled to get over his injury. He returned to the Dons' team late in the season and played in the team that lost the 1951 Grand Final to Geelong. The next season, in 1952, he played eight games before retiring from VFL football.

After taking on captain-coaching roles at Stawell and Thorpdale, Billo Snell returned to Mirboo North for the 1956 season and helped the club break through for a flag. Mirboo North won again the next year, with "Feathers" Peacock, the full-forward, kicking 150 goals for the season. But in 1958 Mirboo North left the Mid-Gippsland league for the South Gippsland league, where they stayed for a decade.

In 1969, they were readmitted back into the Mid-Gippsland league, but they were unable to recapture the supremacy of their earlier stint. The Tigers battled away for almost forty years, until 2006, before they broke through for another senior premiership. In the past decade, they have won five senior flags. Tim Traill, the full-forward who has kicked about 900 goals for the club, is the only player to have played in all five premiership teams. Traill also played in Boolarra's premiership team in

1997, giving him a tally of six premierships in the Mid-Gippsland league over the course of twenty years. A burly character who uses his strength to patrol the goalsquare, he has been a large figure in the competition in all possible ways.

Steve Rogers says the Mirboo North footy club is in a good place. The Tigers have a loyal bunch of players and a stream of teenagers who are keen to break into the senior team. The high school is stable with 300 students. "And we get some good weather," he says.

I introduce myself to the veteran midfielder Clancy Bennett, who was the captain of the Tigers' premiership teams in 2006 and 2007. During a stint in the Wimmera league, he played in Dimboola's breakthrough premiership team in 2013. Back at Mirboo North, he was the playing-coach of the Tigers team that surged to the premiership in 2017.

Today, Clancy has been ruled out of the match against Morwell East because he failed a fitness test. Now thirty-six years of age, he is a gentle-looking man, sensitive and intelligent, but I have been assured of his toughness around the ball and his capacity to make decisions as a leader. He and his wife Laura Poole live in Tyers, which is fifty minutes away, because it is closer to Laura's work as a journalist in the ABC newsroom in Sale. Clancy is a teacher at Kurnai College in Morwell and drives back to Mirboo North to play at his home club. Like Peter Rennie, the eternal footballer, he is lean and wiry, and clearly athletic. He sees no reason to stop playing while the club is winning and he's still enjoying it.

As the senior players warm up before the opening bounce, I notice that the No.8 player for Morwell East, Zach Mangin, is doing lane work while wearing a club-issue beanie. It is that sort of day. And it turns out it is that sort of match. Both teams slug away. Mirboo North look to be handling the conditions a bit better when I leave during the second quarter. According to the Bureau's weather app, the temperature has climbed to double figures when I embark on the fifteen-kilometre journey to Boolarra.

The day clears during the glorious trip along winding roads. The sun peeks out from behind the clouds to turn the rolling hills to a dripping shade of verdant. Just as I park my van beside the Boolarra oval, the players trudge from the field to have a rest during half-time. While the sun is now out, the ground is sodden. Players' jumpers are caked in mud from the centre-wicket area. The stark white of the four-corner fence that traces the circumference of the ground contrasts against the rich greens and browns of the oval and the large gum trees that loom beyond the boundary. To my surprise, the scoreboard reveals that Boolarra are yet to score. The players' faces are ashen.

In the social rooms, a gloomy silence hangs over the brilliant display of cakes and scones. The sandwiches have been cut into quarters. The icing on the cakes is pink and yellow. It is such a shame to see the anticipation of Thursday evening punctured so horribly. Keith Holmes's cheery visage has given way to a pallid acceptance of terrible fortune. Boolarra have been in this position before. But not after such an expectant build-up. The afternoon tea sits largely untouched.

James Holmes, Keith's son, throws himself into the match after the break. He puts his body into the path of opposition players and tries to work the ball out to his teammates. I note the pride of Keith and his wife Lisa as their son tries to push back against the tide of defeat. Jesse Giardina, the coach's son, also throws himself into the match. Mick Cleaver, who has already played in the reserves match, kicks a goal. It is his first day of footy since he played in the victorious team in the 2011 Grand Final. And now he's playing in his second match in one day. He kicks another goal. He is Boolarra's only goalkicker in the senior game. Yarragon defeat the Demons by seventy points, 12.12 (84) to 2.2 (14).

In the rooms after the siren, Tony Giardina lets rip over his players' poor performance. His son Jesse is choked up. Most of the Demons players look non-plussed. Tony Giardina finishes his address on a positive note. "We're finally healthy. We've got a good strong base. The only way is up."

Outside the rooms, Tony gives me an interview in which he expresses frustration over the predicament of his team and the league, and the difficulty of gaining respect when you're mired in a losing streak. Paul Dodds, the president, keeps a brave face, but even he is unable to hide his disappointment. He knows that you can serve the best food imaginable, and generate a warm spirit in the coldest climate, but a footy club is a tough place to be if you can't win a game.

The Boolarra footy club has the will to fight and a strong community, but the town does not have a school like Mirboo North does. I sense there is plenty for the club to chew over.

Map 4: Wedderburn and District

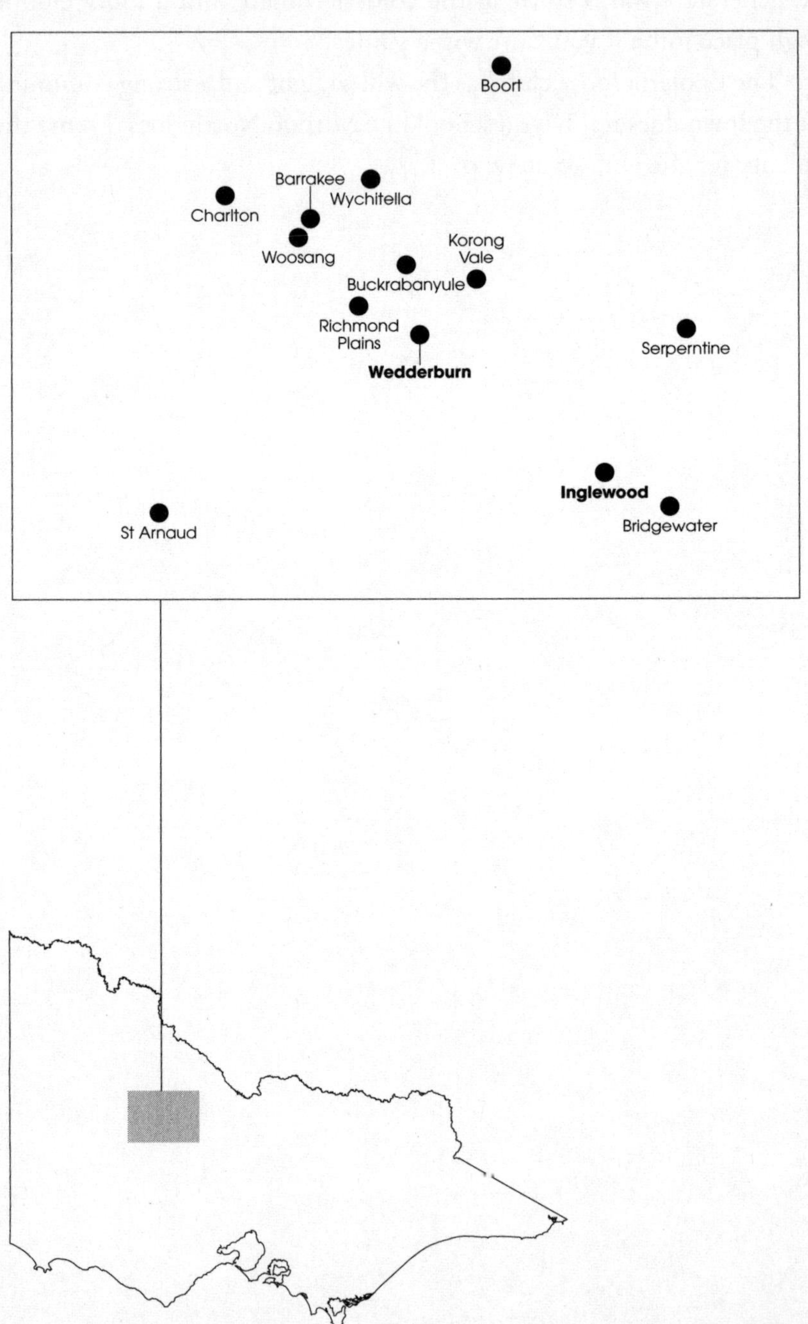

31

Joe Gould's Lament

The list of county football clubs that have folded over the course of the past century stretches into the hundreds. Most of those clubs served farming communities and folded when there were no longer enough young men in the district to field a team. Some of those clubs had wonderfully obscure names. One of those clubs was Woosang.

My path to Woosang began in 2015 when I interviewed Roger Paterson, a former Wedderburn wingman, about his championing of the Woosang Challenge, which was his description for a match between Wedderburn and Charlton in the North Central Football League. Roger had learnt that, in 1928, the Woosang Football Club had won a particularly grand trophy when it defeated Wedderburn in the final match that season. When the Woosang footy club was disbanded, most of the players went to Wedderburn or Charlton. Hence Roger's idea to inaugurate the Woosang Challenge for matches between the two clubs. Roger invited me to check out Woosang's old ground with him if ever I got the chance.

Roger Paterson came to discover the history of the Woosang footy club through the research of Debbie Feeny, from nearby Gooroc. Debbie had grown up listening to stories about Woosang from her father, whose name was Harold McGurk. As a young woman, Debbie married Gerald

Feeny, whose grandfather, J.J. Feeny, was the man after whom the medal for the best and fairest player in the North Central league was named. With plenty of footy talk on both sides of her family, Debbie decided to look into the McGurk family's footy story with Woosang, In doing so, she discovered a story that encompassed the history of the club.

Debbie's great-grandparents, Thomas McGurk and Bridget Costello, were Irish immigrants who met on the Goldfields in Ballarat in 1852. Eventually, they selected land at Woosang, at the lower end of the North Central region, in 1874. Of their eight children, Debbie's grandfather, John, was the youngest. At the age of sixteen, John McGurk began playing football for Foley's Hill. After that club disbanded, the Woosang Football Club was formed from its remnants in 1896. According to his granddaughter, John McGurk was fast, and strong, and a thumping kick. He was captain of Woosang in many matches. He was also captain of Buckrabanyule, Nine Mile and Wedderburn at various times, but he played out his career at Woosang. Debbie says reports in the Wedderburn newspapers reveal that he was among the best players in almost every match. John McGurk never took a backward step. He retired in 1923 at the age of forty-nine.

John McGurk's three sons also played for Woosang. Debbie's father, Harold, was the youngest. She says her father was also an excellent player, and a deadly accurate drop-kick. In 1947, Harold McGurk was injured when a tractor rolled on to him and stretched his knee ligaments. He bandaged the knee and played on, but his capacity was limited. The fortunes of Harold's football club reflected his own fortunes. After the club was hobbled, it folded in 1950.

Harold McGurk's sons, Greg and Alan, went on to play good footy for Charlton. Greg McGurk was a full-forward with a sticky pair of hands. Alan was a quick, versatile on-ball player. The two brothers played in several premiership teams with the Navies, and both represented the North Central league.

Debbie enjoyed watching her brothers play at Charlton, but she always felt a great affinity with her father's stories from Woosang. She began researching the club and the district. When she put out a request to see Woosang photos, local families came up with about twenty from the footy club. One of Debbie's favourites was the photo of a combined team from four local clubs, including Woosang, which ventured down to Bendigo to play a challenge match against the South Bendigo Football Club at the Upper Reserve, now called the Queen Elizabeth Oval, in 1902. In the photo, you can see the brickwork of the grandstand that had just been completed at Bendigo's showpiece ground.

Debbie's photo collection grew to include a picture of Woosang's team in 1909, with John McGurk, her grandfather, holding between his knees a football bearing an inscription of the year. The picture of the 1928 team that won the senior premiership includes Hugh McGurk, her cousin, and Joe Gould, the club's proudest figure. The photos depict a happy time for a thriving district. Debbie says she became especially keen to record matters to do with the Woosang footy club because, while the clubs in the larger towns often had clubrooms in which to house their memorabilia, the clubs based in small farming districts had no such luxury. When these clubs folded, their history tended to vanish.

While researching the Woosang footy club, Debbie discovered that two brothers from Inglewood, the Pappos brothers, who owned a café in the town, had donated a silver-plated football to be awarded to the winner of the 1928 Final in the Korong District Central Football League. In that Final, Woosang defeated Wedderburn. In Woosang's 1928 premiership photo, the club president, Sam Giblett, proudly holds the bulbous trophy.

When the Wedderburn Football Club asked Debbie Feeny to do a bit of research into the clubs's early years, she wrote about Wedderburn, but she also wrote about Woosang. In her writings about Wedderburn and Woosang, she mentioned the silver-plated football that had been donated by the Pappos brothers in 1928. The item pricked the attention of Roger Paterson, a former wingman and official and a Wedderburn life member.

Roger Paterson's family story shares similarities with the story of Debbie Feeny's forebears. Rogers' great-grandfather, James Paterson, emigrated from Scotland during the Gold Rush. He and his wife Isabella tried their luck on the Goldfields around Ballarat and Maryborough before moving to Wedderburn in late 1854. They built a house on the outskirts of town, and James returned to his trade of wheelwright and builder. The Presbyterian Church that he built in Charlton still stands. He also served as the shire president of the Shire of Korong.

In 1872, James Paterson selected a block in the Buckrabanyule district, north of where the McGurk family had settled in Woosang. James Paterson called his property Nardoo Vale, after the nearby Nardoo Hills. Later, he bought a property that he called Glen View, after the region in Scotland in which he had grown up. James and his wife Isabella had seven children. Their oldest son, John Paterson, took over the Glen View property in 1982. After Isabella died, John had another three children by his second wife, Susan. The two farms, Nardoo Vale and Glen View, were passed down through the generations.

Roger Paterson began farming at Glen View when he left school. As a young man, he played tennis for Woosang during summer, but with no Woosang footy club to play for during winter, he played for Wedderburn. As it happened, he joined the Burners on the cusp of a successful era. He played on a wing in the Wedderburn teams that won the premierships in the North Central league in 1968 and 1970. In the latter Grand Final, Wedderburn defeated Charlton by seven goals. Four years later, in 1974, Wedderburn were highly favoured to defeat Charlton in another grand final, but Charlton turned the tables and won that match by five goals. The two clubs enjoyed a fierce rivalry in this era.

Forty years after the 1974 Grand Final, inspired by the writings of Debbie Feeny, Roger Paterson approached the Charlton and Wedderburn footy clubs about playing for what he described as the Woosang Challenge. Neither club was interested at first. Slowly, however, they warmed to the idea, and the challenge was issued under Roger's patronage in 2014. Country footy's ruling body, the Victorian Country Football League, supported the concept by designating a match between the clubs in 2015 as their WorkSafe Match of the Month. I interviewed Roger on radio about the background to the Woosang Challenge. Afterwards, he invited me to check out the Woosang ground with him. Three years later, during the 2018 season, I finally took him up on his offer.

It is a grey and overcast Friday afternoon when I turn off the Calder Highway about halfway between Wedderburn and Charlton to meet Roger Paterson and his dog Scooter at the beginning of the Woosang-Nine Mile Road. We drive about one kilometre south and turn into a paddock that was once the Woosang Recreation Reserve. The paddock features a war memorial and shooting targets for clay shooters. The sole reminder of the paddock's former life as a sports reserve is a tennis umpire's chair, which is surrounded by a scattering of logs.

Roger tells me about the rite of passage for teenaged tennis players. In his day, you had to learn how to be an umpire if you were to be a member of the team. Roger says he learnt many life skills, such as sorting out disputes and getting on with all ages, while sitting in that umpire's chair. He gazes at the chair and gives a wistful smile. It stands tall in a sea of green grass. The branches of the trees on the edge of the reserve rustle in the wind.

On this wintry afternoon, Roger shows me the striking photo of Woosang's 1928 premiership team while he explains the background. After being founded from the remnants of the Foley's Hill footy club in 1896, Woosang spent the years before World War 1 playing mostly against teams from nearby farming districts. Between the two world wars, the club took on rivals from larger towns like Boort, Bridgewater, Inglewood and Wedderburn. In 1928, the farmers from the small district of Woosang defeated the larger clubs to win the premiership in both the senior competition and the junior competition, which these days we would call the reserves. Joe Gould, the Woosang captain, is at the centre of the 1928 photo, keeping a child in check while he cradles the football that bears the premiership inscription. His face looks strong and soulful. Next to him, Sam Giblett, the president, holds the Pappos brothers' silver-plated trophy.

In subsequent seasons, Charlton, Quambatook and Rheola joined the competition while other clubs folded or left or dropped down a grade. In 1939, teams from Boort, Charlton, Wedderburn and Woosang comprised the Korong District Central Football league. The level below was called the Gladstone association. Teams from Borung, Buckrabanyule, Bears Lagoon, Korong Vale and Wychitella played in that competition.

While the Korong league resumed after the war, several clubs from the Gladstone association failed to reappear, and the Gladstone competition was abandoned. Wedderburn and Korong Vale, a team formed largely by railway workers from the local railway junction, won premierships in the Korong league in the years after the war. Before the 1949 season, Quambatook rejoined from the north and Logan, a farming district, fielded a reserves team. Joe Gould was still the Woosang captain twenty years after his club's greatest triumph, but on the eve of the 1949 season, the loyal veteran was angered when a handful of players from the Yeungroon district decided they wanted to leave Woosang to play for Charlton. Joe was furious that the renegade few would leave their local team to play for a team with the might of Charlton. The players left anyway. Boort, another club from a larger town, won the 1949 premiership.

In 1950, Wedderburn's decision to leave the Korong league for a stronger league sounded the death knell for the clubs from farming districts in the region. Woosang managed to field a reserves team in 1950, but the end of the season, the club folded, and the Korong competition folded along with it. All these years later, as we stand in the old recreation reserve, it's hard not to look at Woosang's 1928 team photo and imagine the pain of Joe Gould at the demise of his club.

After the demise of the Woosang footy club, several Woosang players joined Wedderburn while others joined Charlton. Wedderburn won the North Central league's premiership in 1951. The Woosang footballers, however, continued to play cricket and tennis at Woosang, and the local recreation reserve remained the sporting and social focus for the district. The Woosang reserve included a cricket pitch, three asphalt tennis courts and two clay tennis courts. The Woosang hall was the site of morning teas during the week and dances on Saturday nights. By the late 1960s, however, the Woosang reserve was barely in use. In 1970, the hall was sold. The new owner dismantled it and took it away. The sporting clubs fell away with it.

Roger points to the spot where the hall once stood, just a few metres beyond the tennis umpire's chair. I picture footballers spilling out of the hall on the night of the premierships in 1928, the biggest night in the history of the district. They are shouting at the sky about their triumph over the men from the towns. I do not feel sad as I listen to stories about Joe Gould and the turncoats from Yeungroon. I feel a sense of life that once spilt across the grass.

I ask Roger about the Wedderburn teams of his own era. He says the 1969 team was more talented than the team that won the premiership in 1968, but it suffered a blow when it lost the Second Semi-final to Birchip in unusually hot and windy conditions. Wedderburn's rivals in the Preliminary Final were Watchem-Corack, who were led by the former South Melbourne player Bill McGrath. A large identity in the region, McGrath called on all his experience to corral Wedderburn's talent and eke out a victory for his team. "He outsmarted us," Roger says of McGrath.

The next week, Bill McGrath led Watchem-Corack to victory over Birchip in the Grand Final by two goals. McGrath later employed his leadership skills to become a state politician, representing the National Party in the seats of Lowan and Wimmera over the course of twenty years.

Halfway through the 1970 season, Wedderburn were placed sixth of the eight teams in the North Central league. In the paddock at Woosang, I ask Roger how Wedderburn were able to come through and win the flag from so far back. Rogers says Wedderburn had a highly talented team that started slowly and gathered momentum as the season wore on. Unusually for the time, the Burners played under a non-playing coach, Bertie Rowe from Golden Square. Bertie Rowe was an inspiration to his players. His shrewd positional changes turned the fortunes of many games. The club might well have won more flags in that era.

The clubs from the farming districts around Wedderburn had delightfully lyrical names: Wychitella, Barrakee, Buckrabanyule. When Roger Paterson points north, towards the block that his great-grandfather selected, he says Buckrabanyule means "end of the hills" in the local Aboriginal dialect. I later look up the *Victorian Places* website, which is a scholarly site produced by Monash University, in conjunction with Queensland University. The site suggests the name means "the middle hill of three hills".

Roger is unsure of the provenance of "Woosang". He agrees with me that it does sound Chinese, but Debbie Feeny later assures me that, while there were Chinese on the goldfields around St Arnaud, there were none in the farming districts around Wedderburn. She believes Woosang derives from an Aboriginal description like many place names in the region.

To the south of the reserve, a low of range of hills turns blue in the winter sun. I bid Roger Paterson goodbye after an intriguing stopover in Woosang.

32
Roaring Days

I have always held a small flame for Inglewood, the town on the Calder Highway between Bendigo and Wedderburn. My grandmother, who was then called Win O'Shannessy, spent much of her early life there. I liked going there for a meal at the pub and a look-around in the op shops when I lived down the road in Bendigo for a few years. These days, I like the old buildings and the town's peculiar quirks, the link with the roaring days of our golden past.

Early in the 2018 footy season, I took the opportunity to explore the town's past, my family's links with the town and the local footy club. Not a bad combo, in my view.

The impetus was my mother's wish to go to Inglewood to dig around on some family matters. I offered to take her for a weekend in May. My daughter Ellen came along for the ride. We went out to the Kingower cemetery and bumped into distant relatives who just happened to be there at the same time. At the Inglewood cemetery, we found the gravestone for my great-grandmother, who had died as a young woman, leaving my grandmother in the care of her wider family. It was the first time my mother had seen the gravestone. The experience moved her to quiet tears. I felt moved to see my mother so touched by the tragic events of a century ago. We stayed in Bridgewater and watched the royal wedding on the telly.

Of course, as I was away in the country, I was keen to do a little footy research. I arranged to meet Howard Rochester, the former secretary of the Inglewood footy club and the current president of the Inglewood and District Historical Society. Our meeting proved to be a fascinating interlude.

It is a perfect, late autumn morning. Weak sunlight takes the edge off the cold, still air. I sit with Howard next to a woodpile at the back of his house in Brooke Street, which is the main street in Inglewood. Howard is unshaven, and he wears an orange beanie that is perched forward on his head. He is proud to say that he has rescued the chairs on which we are sitting from the tip. The cushions cost $15 at Bunnings. I look across the yard to a sign for an old fish-and-chip menu that is hanging on the far wall in the shed. Howard and his family ran the fish and chip shop in Inglewood for several years. The menu includes whiting, potato cakes, scallops and deep-fried Mars bars. "We sold a few of those," Howard says of the Mars bars.

Howard Rochester, who is now seventy-one years of age, grew up in Inglewood, the son of a boot-maker. As a young man, he spent sixteen years in Melbourne working as a linesman for the old PMG, the Postmaster-General's Department, before he returned to Inglewood with his family of a wife and three children.

Back in Inglewood, he bought land behind the town and built a school camp that he ran for twenty-two years. During this period, he became fascinated by the indications of the Aboriginal past on his property. An archaeological survey confirmed his belief that his land was the site of middens and ceremonial grounds. A local farmer, Roly Barber, showed him around his own property, which once was an Aboriginal mission. Roly showed Howard the site of the old Aboriginal camp in his top paddock. Howard developed a deep interest in the Aboriginal history of the region, which built on his growing interest in Inglewood's golden era.

Victoria's Gold Rush began after the discovery of gold near Ballarat in 1851. Eight years later, in 1859, gold was discovered in Inglewood. The Inglewood rush was the last great rush in Victoria.

The town of Inglewood developed in *ad hoc* fashion because of the primacy of the diggings. The main street, Brooke Street, has a kink in it, even to this day, because it was diverted around a mine shaft. Inglewood is the only town in Victoria without a public building on the main street. During the Gold Rush, the town's burghers had visions of grandeur about the town's expansion. To accommodate the expected filaments of growth, the burghers built the court house, the town hall and the hospital on dispersed sites off the main street. Inglewood's population swelled to 50,000 within months of the discovery of gold, but five years later, in 1864, it was down to 12,000. The burghers' visions of expansion would be unfulfilled.

In 1864, the town's population included 2600 gold miners who were digging a long way underground. But the miners who were sinking shafts to find gold had to stop at a depth of 300 feet (about ninety metres) because they struck water. Many of the miners who had the capacity to sink deep shafts drifted off to the diggings in New Zealand. The town of Reefton on the South Island would come to feature a handful of mines that were named after towns on the goldfields of Central Victoria, such as Dunolly and Inglewood.

In 1899, the population of the town of Inglewood in Victoria was down to about 1200 when forty-six residents joined the Commonwealth forces to fight in the Boer War in South Africa. Frances Hines, a nurse from the Inglewood hospital, became the first Australian woman to die during active service.

After the British had declared war on Germany in 1914, about 300 residents from Inglewood and its surrounding district enlisted to fight in World War 1. Many died. Others never returned. The town of Inglewood struggled to recover from the effects of the war.

According to Australian Census figures, the population of the town of Inglewood in 1921 was just over 1100. Almost a century later, as Howard Rochester and I sit in his backyard on an autumn morning in 2018, the town's population is just over 700.

Howard Rochester's family links to the Australian continent can be traced back to our colonial beginnings. His antecedent Henry Rochester was a convict who arrived in Sydney on the Second Fleet. Henry's son James did well. He bought and sold property in Windsor, which was then a town just to the west of Sydney. During the Gold Rush, James Rochester's son Thomas drifted from Windsor down to Inglewood. Thomas Rochester had sevens sons, four of whom played football for Inglewood: Thomas Junior, Charlie, Windsor and Eric. Windsor had been named after his father's home town.

The family's link with the football club began in 1891, when Charlie and Tom Rochester began to play. Windsor played from 1906 until 1910. Eric played for only a short time before making his mark as an administrator.

In 1903, Eric Rochester opened a business called Rochester Boot Repairs in the town's main street. After the outbreak of World War 1, several of the Rochester brothers enlisted. Tom Junior and Windsor died during the war, while Charlie died from the effects of the war after he had returned home. Eric tried to enlist, but he was disallowed because of the extent of bereavement in his family.

Eric Rochester later expanded his boot repairs business and renamed it the Rochester Emporium. At the football club, Eric was the president when the Blues appointed Carji Greeves, the former Geelong champion who, in 1924, had won the first Brownlow Medal, as Inglewood's captain-coach in 1935. Carji Greeves, then aged thirty-one, was at the helm for only half a season before he fell ill and relinquished his role.

Eric Rochester had two sons, Eddie and Windsor, who were good footballers. The older son, Eddie, took over his father's emporium, while Windsor became a baker. Although Eddie was a promising player, weakening eyesight and the demands of weekend work ended his days on the field. Eddie went on to be a trainer and boot-studder for more than forty years. Every week he posted Inglewood's selected teams on the notice board in the window of his shop. The notice board is now in the Inglewood clubrooms.

While Eddie had to work in his shop on Saturday mornings, Windsor's work as a baker allowed him to finish work in time to get to the footy. After making his senior football debut in his home town in 1936, Windsor was invited to try out with three VFL clubs, Richmond,

Melbourne and Footscray. He remained in Inglewood and became a club legend.

Eric Rochester's other son, Richard, played a little bit of footy before he, too, served the Inglewood footy club as an official for more than forty years. During that time, Richard performed every role from secretary to manning the gate.

My man in Inglewood, Howard Rochester, is the son of Eddie Rochester, the man who ran the Rochester Emporium. Howard himself played in the Inglewood reserves. Later, he served on the committee. From 2002 to 2005, he was the club secretary. Through his interest in the district's history, he has an excellent grasp on the club's history. Before the publication in 2016 of the book to celebrate the 140th anniversary of the Inglewood footy club, Howard helped the author, David Rose, with the research. Throughout the club's long history, less than thirty people have been named life members. Howard Rochester takes great pride in the fact that he is one of them.

Howard also takes great pride in the fact that the Inglewood Football Club was a foundation member of the Victorian Football Association, in 1877. I get a sense of the club's early years through talking to Howard and, later, consulting David Rose's superb club history, which is called *Bothumpian Blues*.

On the formation of the Victorian Football Association in 1877, the five original city clubs were Albert Park, Carlton, Hotham, Melbourne and St Kilda. The seven provincial clubs that joined the VFA in its inaugural season were Geelong, Barwon, Ballarat, Beechworth, Castlemaine, Inglewood and Rochester. Inglewood's delegate to the VFA in 1877 was E.L. Curr, who was the captain of the team for at least one match that season. The club's president in 1877 was Maurice Blackburn, who was the manager of the Inglewood branch of the Bank of Victoria. Later, Blackburn's son Maurice Junior would start the Maurice Blackburn law firm that remains prominent in Melbourne.

In 1877, the first season in which the VFA ran the game, its twelve clubs did not play weekly matches against each other according to a fixture, but they did play each other in challenge matches. In July 1877, a team consisting of players from Inglewood and the surrounding district hosted the Melbourne Football Club in a match at the Inglewood Cricket Ground. The match was made possible by the newly opened railway line between the town of Sandhurst (later renamed Bendigo) and Inglewood. According to a report in the *Inglewood Advertiser*, twelve Melbourne players arrived at the Inglewood station at 10 o'clock on the evening before the scheduled match. Several Inglewood footballers and supporters were at the station to welcome them. The mayor of Inglewood, Thomas Tatchell, who was the publican at the Royal Hotel, declared that the visitors could enjoy "free and full accommodation" at his establishment.

The rest of the team arrived by train at midday on the day of the match. An hour after the arrival of the Melbourne players, both teams gathered at the ground. While the Melbourne players were clearly identifiable by their red caps and hose, the Inglewood players were given white caps in an attempt to create a uniform appearance. However, according to the report, two members of the Inglewood team, players Calvert and Williams, wore "the striking red knickerbockers and striped stockings and shorts adopted by the Wedderburn club". The Inglewood district team took the field with twenty-five players, while Melbourne had only twenty. The Melbourne players, however, were accustomed to playing together, and their greater cohesion enabled them to win two goals to nil.

At 4 o'clock, according to the newspaper report, "a general muster took place at Piggott's Pelican Hotel". Maurice Blackburn, the Inglewood president and chairman, and Bob Sillett, the Melbourne captain, addressed the gathering of sixty. Mayor Tatchell led a deputation to the railway station "to witness the departure of the train conveying our visitors to their homes so far away".

According to *The Footballer*, the leading football publication of the time, Inglewood also played home and away matches against Wedderburn and Serpentine during the 1877 season, with the balance of results favouring Serpentine. Towards the end of the season, a combined team from Inglewood and Serpentine played a match against the Sandhurst Football Club at the Upper Reserve (now the Queen Elizabeth Oval) in

Sandhurst. The home team won five goals to nil. In the return match at Inglewood, neither team could score.

Although Inglewood's performances were raggedy in 1877, the club remains proud that it was a foundation member of the VFA.

33

By Gum

After its early adventures as part of the Victorian Football Association, the Inglewood Football Club played against local rivals in an assortment of competitions until, in 1903, it became a foundation member of the Loddon Valley Football Association, along with Arnold's Bridge, Bridgewater and Newbridge. Today, three of those clubs – Inglewood, Bridgewater and Newbridge – are proud that they continue to play in a competition that they helped to found more than a century ago.

Inglewood wore blue and red guernseys during the inaugural season of the Loddon Valley competition. The club elected Harry Lamprell as captain. Because of trouble arising from early matches between Bridgewater and Inglewood, the association ruled that an umpire from Bendigo was required to officiate in games between the two clubs. When Bridgewater and Inglewood were scheduled to play at Inglewood in the match to decide the 1903 premiership, a VFA umpire was appointed to officiate, while the captains of Arnold's Bridge and Newbridge were appointed as the goal umpires.

Throughout the era before and after the turn of the century, the performances of the Inglewood forward Jack Turpie were so commanding that he was nicknamed "the Thurgood of the North", in reference to the Essendon champion Albert Thurgood. In the final against Bridgewater in the Loddon Valley competition's inaugural season, in 1903, Turpie kicked two goals to set up victory for his team by nineteen points, 3.10 (28) to 1.3 (9).

Inglewood's most notable product in its early years was Percy Martyn, who played for the club as a seventeen-year-old in 1909. The next year, in 1910, Martyn played in Inglewood's premiership team. He then headed down to Melbourne and played in the VFL for St Kilda in 1912 and Richmond in 1913. In his first season at Punt Road, he won Richmond's goalkicking award as well as a reputation as a magnificent exponent of the place kick. In 1915, he transferred to Essendon, where he settled into the backline. He played for Victoria in 1920.

Martyn later coached at Tasmanian clubs North Hobart, North Launceston and Devonport. After returning to Victoria, he coached Bendigo league clubs Eaglehawk and South Bendigo. In 1939, he completed his career circle by coaching Inglewood. He also coached the club after World War 2.

After the war, Inglewood resumed playing at the recreation reserve on the corner of Heales and Morrow streets, to the west of the main street, which is Brooke Street. In 1946, Jim "Noey" Watts, a high-flying forward who had been invited to try out at St Kilda before the war, was happy simply to play football at his home club after surviving a period as a prisoner of war under the Japanese. George Vanston, the Inglewood full-forward, had played in armed services games with the Royal Australian Air Force during the war. Back at their home club, George Vanston and Noey Watts formed a potent combination in attack as Inglewood surged towards success.

On the final day of the 1946 season, football fans in the Loddon Valley region were so pleased with the return of full-scale football that an estimated crowd of 1400 descended on the Newbridge oval to see Inglewood play Bridgewater in the Grand Final. In a tight finish, Bridgewater kicked the only goal of the final quarter, but Inglewood held on to win by two points. George Vanston kicked three goals. Windsor

Rochester, the big ruckman and centre half-back, was best on ground, while Ralph Medcalf, the son of the multiple premiership player Alec Medcalf, was among the best players.

Five years later, in 1951, the Inglewood Football Club moved to a new recreation reserve near the dog leg where the Calder Highway bends into Brooke Street. Brian "Nipper" Dowling, a youngster whose family members had played for the club since the late nineteenth century, kicked the first goal on the new ground. It was a goal that heralded a dominant era.

During the 1951 season, Inglewood assembled one of the greatest goal-to-goal lines in the competition's history, consisting of Charlie Catto (full-back), Windsor Rochester (centre half-back), Ralph Medcalf (centre), Father Jim O'Brien (centre half-forward) and George Vanston at full-forward. Inglewood defeated Bealiba by two goals in the 1951 Grand Final at Newbridge.

Charlie Catto was the captain of the team that won the premiership in 1953. Before the next season, in 1954, the club raised £1100 and built new rooms. In the opening round, the Blues set a club record for a winning margin when they defeated Newbridge by 130 points, 26.15 (171) to 6.5 (41), with Brian Dowling kicking seven goals and Ted Bradley and Tom Prosser kicking five each. On the last day of the season, Charlie Catto, the full-back with the safe hands, was again the captain as Inglewood defeated Bears Lagoon-Serpentine, the club known as the Violets, in the 1954 Grand Final at Bridgewater.

Early in the 1956 season, the Inglewood team bus was held up by flood waters on the road to Mitiamo. After finally arriving at Mitiamo's ground at 3 o'clock, the Inglewood players took the field and edged out the home team by two goals. Graham "Squirty" Roberts, a recruit from Bealiba, kicked four goals for his new club. The Blues then won the next ten games in succession, with the evergreen Ralph Medcalf and Windsor Rochester in good form.

In 1956, a former Inglewood player called Frank Harding made a welcome contribution to his home region. Harding had played for Inglewood before the First World War. After moving to Melbourne, he joined the police force, and later he was appointed the Victorian

Supervisor of Bookmakers. His energetic work for charities included raising thousands of dollars for the Inglewood hospital.

During the 1956 season, Frank Harding donated a trophy to be awarded to the Loddon Valley league's best and fairest player as voted by the umpires. Inglewood's Ralph Medcalf won the inaugural award. Medcalf was then best on ground in the Grand Final as Inglewood defeated Bears Lagoon-Serpentine, once again at Bridgewater.

The Blues' final triumph in this era occurred after the club had enticed the former Carlton and Williamstown player Bill Redmond to cross from South Bendigo before the 1958 season to become the captain-coach. Redmond secured the signatures of fellow recruits such as Max Martin, Des Pearse and Kelvin Thompson. Eddie Harrison, a multiple premiership player in the district, was a tower of strength in the Inglewood backline, having moved up from Bridgewater.

In 1958, Inglewood appeared set for another premiership when they led Bridgewater by thirty-two points at three-quarter time of the Grand Final at Newbridge. The Red and Whites, however, kept Inglewood scoreless in the last quarter, and only just failed to bridge the gap. Inglewood won by one point to earn their fifth premiership for the decade. Five players – Ralph Medcalf, Windsor Rochester, Charlie Catto, Brian Dowling and Ted Bradley – were members of all five premiership teams in the period from 1951 to 1958.

After their triumph in 1958, the Blues fell behind their Loddon Valley opponents for the next decade. Finally, in 1971 they returned to the top after recruiting Ralph Conboy, who had played for Yarrawalla and South Bendigo, to become the captain-coach. The club also netted other recruits from the Bendigo league, including Terry Day (Sandhurst), Dennis Grotto (South Bendigo) and Denis Griffiths (Eaglehawk), but it was the contingent of local players led by the Birthisel boys, Les and Daryl, who were distant cousins, as well as Lindsay Kelly, Bob Grundy, David Vanston, Ian "Barney" Triplett and the veteran rover Squirty Roberts who provided the ballast for success.

The best player for Inglewood in 1971 was the wingman Malcolm Johns. The Blues careered through the season undefeated. In the Grand

Final, which was held at Korong Vale, Malcolm Johns was best on ground as the Blues defeated Calivil. Malcolm Johns's son Nathan would later captain the club. To this day, Malcolm and Nathan Johns comprise the only father-son combination to win Inglewood's senior and junior best and fairest awards.

A decade after their triumph in 1971, Inglewood returned towards the top of the ladder after picking up a slew of recruits from Bendigo. In 1984, under the captain-coach Rod Southon, the Blues recruited the wingman Steve Robinson from Sandhurst. The ruckman Ian Chamberlain played his 150th game for the club, and the full-forward Darrell Billett kicked 100 goals.

In 1984, Inglewood made their first grand final for ten years, only to lose to Bridgewater at Mitiamo. The next year, in 1985, Inglewood again faced Bridgewater in the Grand Final, and again suffered disappointment. In 1986, Inglewood faced Bridgewater in the Grand Final for the third consecutive season, this time at Marong. Inglewood trailed by three goals at half-time. The Blues then kicked eight goals in the third quarter, with the full-forward Kelvin Dows kicking his 100th goal for the season. Under the captain-coach Daryl Canty, Inglewood went to win by fifteen points to earn their first premiership for fifteen years. The defenders Peter Mason and Gary Jacobs were deserved premiership heroes after battling away for the Blues for a decade.

Unfortunately for Inglewood, the flag in 1986 would be the club's last taste of success for a long time. As Howard Rochester and I sit in Howard's backyard in 2018, the Blues are yet to win another flag – and they look a long way from doing so.

Howard tells me that Ralph Medcalf, a ruck-rover who worked for the lands department, is clearly the outstanding player in the club's history. Howard motions towards the house behind his own. Beryl Medcalf, Ralph's widow, lives there, and is still going strong at the age of ninety-two.

Howard says that Windsor Rochester, his uncle, was a big, hard man who could pick up the ball in one hand. Howard brings Windsor Rochester to life by breathing in and out, making the noise of a steam engine.

"They reckon he sounded like a train coming," he says.

"Everyone would get out of the way!

Howard says the Bridgewater footy club, which is based only eight kilometres to the south, remains Inglewood's greatest rival, but the Blues have been unable to keep pace with their neighbours. He notes that, for many decades, the town of Bridgewater was surrounded by small farms. Bridgewater footy teams always featured a strong contingent of players from the farms that were strung out along the Loddon River.

The town of Inglewood, by contrast, has had few farms in its vicinity because the old goldfields were not made available for selection after the Gold Rush.

During the late nineteenth century, Yorkshire boilers and Cornish boilers were used to power jackhammers and other tools in the mine shafts. After the diggings were abandoned, the goldfields were designated as Crown land. The town of Inglewood became home to the eucalyptus oil industry because of all the Mallee gums on the Crown land. The old boilers were deployed to steam the gum leaves and help to create eucalyptus oil. With few farms in the region to feed players into Inglewood footy teams, the Blues fell behind their rivals.

Now, much of the land around Inglewood has been designated as a state park or a nature reserve. As well as the Kooyoora State Park, there is the Kangderaar Bushland Reserve and the Inglewood and Mount Korong nature conservation reserves. None of these reserves produce footballers for Inglewood.

While all clubs in the Loddon Valley league now recruit out of Bendigo, Inglewood's plight is made difficult by the club's lack of success in recent decades, and the extra distance from Bendigo compared to many rivals.

Howard Rochester has been the timekeeper at Inglewood for a dozen years. He invites me to join him for a match in the timekeepers' box. As I take a last, admiring look at the fish-and-chip menu on the wall in the garage, I tell him I might just do so.

Afterwards, I am taken by the newspaper articles on the wall in Cousin Jack's Bakehouse about local strikes. The Hand of Faith, one of the world's biggest gold nuggets, was found behind the Kingower school, just to the west of Inglewood, in 1980. The Hand of Faith is the largest nugget still in existence. It now rests in noisy repose at the Golden Nugget Casino in Las Vegas.

Just this year, on Easter Sunday 2018, a strike on the old Kingower tip revealed nuggets that weighed a total of 300 ounces, or eight and a half kilograms. I thought the days of finding gold in the shallow earth around Inglewood were long gone, but it seems I am wrong. There is much to be explored.

34

Box of Tricks

It is late in the season when I venture to Inglewood to take up Howard Rochester's invitation to join him in the timekeepers' box. Inglewood, known as the Blues, are hosting Marong in their Round 17 match in the Loddon Valley league. Inglewood are last on the ladder. Marong are second last. The Blues have a chance to end the season with a win at home. If they do, it would get them off the bottom of the ladder and lend the club some hope of gaining momentum the following season. As it stands, Inglewood have won eight of the past nine wooden spoons. They need hope of some description.

While many timekeepers' boxes are elevated, allowing the officials to see clearly over the heads of the spectators, this one is not elevated at all. It is not even a box. Instead, it is a room that is tucked between the change rooms for the home team and the away team. You enter by stepping inside the away team's room then opening another door that allows you into the cramped quarters where the timekeepers sweat on the minutes and seconds that define their work.

I will call the Inglewood timekeepers' quarters a box, despite it being a room, because it sounds right. Sometimes, despite all attempts, there is just no getting around tradition. When I enter the Inglewood timekeepers' box, I find a stack of cardboard boxes in a corner and a row of shelves along a wall. Most of the timekeeper's box is taken up with a platform on which there are two tall chairs. Howard Rochester is sitting on one tall chair. The Marong timekeeper, Bill McIlrath, is on the other. The two men lean on a bench and peer out the open window. The elevation provided by the platform allows them to see just over the heads of the spectators who wander along in front of them.

Bill McIlrath is connected to the Marong club through his daughter, who is a netballer. He is new to this timekeeping caper for the football club. When I ask him about the Marong footballers, he says he is still getting to know them. While Marong footy teams wear the old Fitzroy guernseys of orangey-red and blue, Bill wears new-edition Richmond apparel. The yellow and black of his cap and scarf have the sheen of premiership pride.

Howard, meanwhile, is wearing a Carlton scarf that he picked up in an op shop in Hobart. He wears it because Inglewood, like Carlton, are the Blues. They wear navy blue jumpers with a white "V". Unlike his Marong counterpart, Howard himself is well accustomed to this timekeeping caper. A few years ago, he groomed a replacement. For several weeks, he tutored the man in question on the rigmarole of clocking on and clocking off and writing down the scores. But then the potential replacement died. As we sit in the box on this cold winter's day, Howard remains open to offers for anyone who would like his job.

While we keep on eye on the footy, Howard describes with enthusiasm the events of his week as the president of the Inglewood historical society. About 200 turned up at the Inglewood cemetery for the society's commemoration of the Battle of Amiens. Howard had organised the event to commemorate the battle's centenary. One guest, who had written a book on the battle, spoke about the six fallen soldiers who had been laid to rest in the cemetery in unmarked graves. Howard unveiled the plaques that had been inscribed to commemorate the soldiers. Two guests donated $1000 towards the erection of headstones. Howard says he saw faces in the crowd that he had not seen for fifty years.

Howard adds a footy aside to the events at the cemetery. When he was searching for the graves of the six soldiers, he found the grave of his old junior footy coach Archie Keam, or Archibald Carrington Keam, as Howard describes him in full. A.C. Keam took care of the Inglewood under-sixteen team during the 1960s. Many Inglewood people thought he was English, because he spoke in a different way to the rest of the town, but Howard says that Archie had a cleft palate, which led him to speak with a particular diction.

Archie Keam was a handyman who did odd jobs. At the footy club, he was more of a trainer than a coach. He imparted little footy knowledge to the junior players, but he made sure they trained in some fashion, and he made sure they got to the games. Archie drove an Austin A30 ute in which he seated five boys along the front seat and fifteen in the tray at the back. With his speed along the dirt roads, he raised the dust on a dry day and he splashed through the puddles in the wet. Howard says Archie Keam kept the junior team going for a decade. At the commemoration of the Battle of Amiens, seven former Inglewood junior footballers gave him $50 each to put towards a headstone for Archie's grave.

During the second quarter of the Inglewood senior team's match against Marong late in the 2018 season, the Blues' Bailey Evans kicks a good goal against the stiff breeze. Howard says Inglewood have been competitive in every game this season. For their one victory, they saw off Calivil United for the first time in many years. Howards says David Rose, the club's secretary, and the man who did such a thorough job on the club's history, was instrumental in the victory over Calivil with his performance at half-back. David Rose is busy in this match as well. At the age of thirty-three, he is still one of his team's best players. Rose works as a mining engineer with the Fosterville Gold Mine. He loves the area's golden history. He believes the footy club is a vital part of that history.

We watch for a while as the Inglewood players contain Marong with gritty defence. The Inglewood footy club moved to this ground from the old cricket ground in 1951, just as the club was about to embark on its run of five premierships in eight years. Howard says the ground is based on the site of Chinese diggings during the Gold Rush. For several years, the club had a problem with old mine shafts caving in. Only ten years ago, an old mine shaft collapsed, and left a gaping hole in the forward pocket.

The mention of mining prompts Howard to recall his only strike. Well, a strike of sorts. During the 1986 Grand Final between Inglewood and Bridgewater at Marong, he found fourpence on the ground. The unlikeliness of his find led him to believe that the Blues would enjoy luck on this grand occasion. Sure enough, having lost the previous two grand finals to Bridgewater, the Blues triumphed on their third attempt.

Howards adds that one Inglewood supporter, Adam Murphy, recently found twenty-five ounces (800 grams) of gold, worth $46,000, while prospecting close to town. He gave half of his bounty to his father. When Adam Murphy strolls in front of the timekeepers' box, Howard exalts. "There he is! There's the bloke who found the gold!"

Towards the end of the second quarter, the Inglewood president, Andrew Nevins, sticks his head through the window of the box to offer the timekeepers a coffee. Nevins, a bank manager in Bendigo, is from a family that has produced footballers for Inglewood for more than a century. Four of Inglewood's prominent families are recognised with signs around the oval. The four signs have nothing like the scale of the signs that denote the Lockett End and the Coventry End at the Docklands Oval in Melbourne, but they are a great source of pride to the celebrated families.

The scoreboard wing is called the Medcalf Wing. Charlie Medcalf was a member of the first team to take the field for Inglewood, in a match against Wedderburn in 1876 that ended in a goal-less draw. Alec Medcalf was a fiery centreman who played in five premiership teams from 1923 to 1930. Ralph Medcalf, the player considered the best in the club's history, played in six premiership teams between 1946 and 1958, and won the league goalkicking award in 1966 at the age of forty-three.

The wing in front of the social rooms, the Lamprell Wing, recognises the family of Harry Lamprell, the Inglewood captain during the inaugural season of the Loddon Valley competition, in 1903, and Bill Lamprell, who was the captain in 1946. Bill Lamprell's long, driving kicks propelled the Blues towards the premiership that year. Bill's grandson, Leigh Lamprell, is a former senior captain, and has now coached the junior team for almost a decade.

The western end, the Bradley End, is named after the family of Ted Bradley, who, during an era when scoring was low, kicked nineteen goals for the season in 1895. Ted's four sons, Clarrie, Ted Junior, Ern and Jack, all played in the Inglewood premiership teams in 1926 and 1927. Ted Junior's son, also called Ted, played in the club's five premiership teams from 1951 to 1958. Members of the Bradley family have played for the Blues throughout the club's history.

The eastern end, the Rochester End, is named after the family of Howard Rochester, the current timekeeper and excellent host. In 2001, Howard organised for the football club what was considered one of the best reunions ever held in the town. Howard then served as secretary, and he remains the timekeeper, although not for too much longer if all goes to plan.

In the timekeepers' box during the match against Marong, Howard again makes the noise of an oncoming train, hissing and chugging, when he mentions the Rochester family's main contributor to the club, Windsor Rochester, who bore down on opponents with fearsome force for more than twenty years before retiring in 1959.

With the spirit of Windsor Rochester resounding through the box, the two timekeepers sound the siren for half-time with Inglewood ahead by five points, 7.3 (45) to 6.4 (40). The Blues are on track for a win before their home crowd, which, I note, is not a particularly excitable mob. The supporters offer a few cheers and a bit of a clap as the players file in past the timekeepers' box.

During the third quarter, Howard receives a lovely visit from Belinda Hawken, who is the mother of two teenaged footballers, Dylan and Kyle, as well as the club's match-day secretary. Belinda pops her head through the window of the timekeepers' box and offers Howard a beaming smile. She hands him a card in which she thanks Howard for his help throughout the season. I cannot recall ever seeing an official thank another official with a card. I think Howard might stay on as timekeeper for a while yet.

Halfway through the quarter, another Inglewood youngster, Sam Barnes, snaps a goal only for Marong to score a quick reply. Inglewood lead by seventeen points at three-quarter time, 11.5 (71) to 8.6 (54). Howards notes that the scoreboard on the opposite wing is showing the correct score, as it always does. Michael Rose, the father of David Rose as well as the scoreboard attendant, is renowned for his attention to detail. Howard says it must be a cold day because Michael Rose is wearing shoes.

In the huddle, I become intrigued when Sam Barnes walks behind his teammates with his eyes to the ground. He picks up the players' discarded water bottles and fits them into the twelve compartments of the large plastic bottle-holder. His attention to order reminds me of the Japanese fans during the recent soccer World Cup finals. After the Japan team's three group matches, the Japanese fans gained rave reviews by picking up their rubbish in the stands. Their punk tidiness inspired the supporters of other nations to pick up their rubbish as well. I hope Sam Barnes kicks a few goals against the wind in the final quarter.

Rain beats down and the wind picks up as the huddle disperses. I head towards the scoreboard to have a quick chat with Michael Rose. Sure enough, he is wearing shoes. But that's about it. His full ensemble consists of runners with no socks, shorts, and a long-sleeved shirt that is unbuttoned at the sleeves. "I put on my shoes so I could have a kick with the grandkids," he says.

Despite his penchant for minimum clothing, Michael reveals that today has been the coldest day of the season because of the angle of the wind. I relay to him the assertion of Howard Rochester that his scoreboard is never wrong. Michael Rose hesitates. "I don't want to be boastful," he says. "But, yes, I'm pretty attentive."

Unfortunately for Sam Barnes and his Inglewood teammates, the north-westerly that gathers force in the final quarter is an ill wind. The Blues barely get the ball over their centre line. Marong, however, pepper the goals. The Panthers kick 4.3 (27) to no score in the final quarter to win by ten points, 12.9 (81) to 11.5 (71). A rainbow emerges over the ground as the players make their way towards the rooms.

With his duties over, Howard Rochester emerges from the timekeepers' box to conduct a post-mortem with fellow Inglewood supporters. He bumps into Graham "Squirty" Roberts. Now eighty-three years of age.

Squirty played in three senior premiership teams with the Blues, in 1956, 1958 and 1971. Howard says Squirty was best on ground in an interleague match against the Kerang and District competition. After sixty years on the committee, Squirty Roberts continues to serve the club with a smile. He is a link with a golden past.

Map 5: Mornington Peninsula

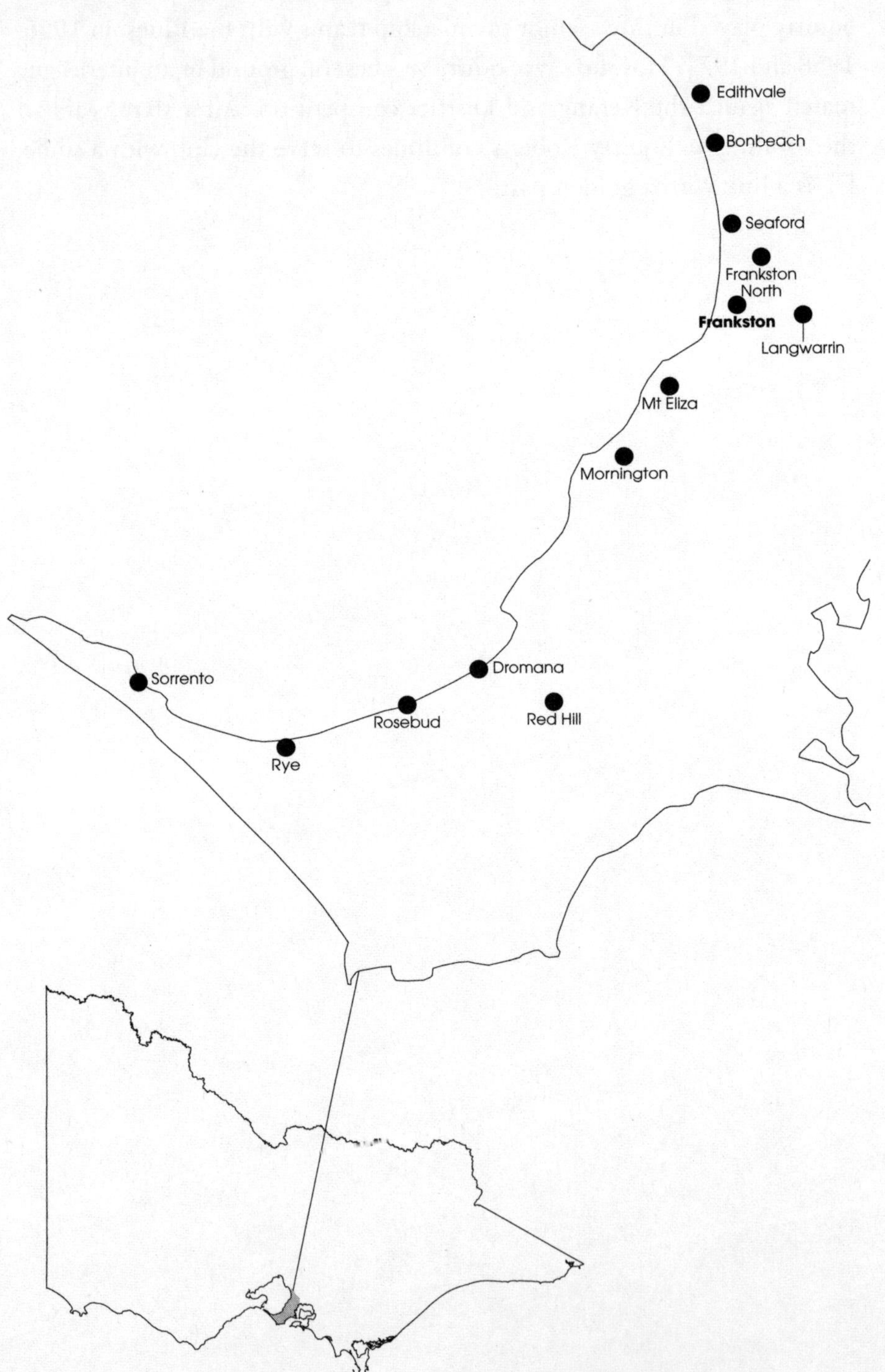

35

Ebbs and Flows

Late in the 2018 season, Neil Custerson, a friend who hosts a footy show on the public radio station in Mornington, asked whether I would head down to Frankston to appear on his wrap-up after the Division 1 Grand Final in the Mornington Peninsula Nepean league. For twenty years, the Peninsula grand final has struck me as one of the great occasions in local footy. Frankston Park, which holds almost 8000, is the perfect venue for the emotional supporters who shout and scream and boo and hiss at the players who go their hardest in the bayside sunshine during the final game of the season. I told Neil I looked forward to heading down his way. As it turned out, my visit would prove one of the most extraordinary experiences in a lifetime of watching footy.

The build-up to the showpiece game of the Peninsula competition in 2018 had everything. The two clubs that had won through to the Division 1 Grand Final in the first season since the reintroduction of a divisional system were Pines and Sorrento, two clubs from opposite ends of the social spectrum. The Pines footy club was a suburban club, from the tough streets of Frankston North; Sorrento were from the moneyed part of the Peninsula, where holiday homes sell for millions. Pines, known as the Pythons, were led by a ruckman who had only ever played for his home club. Sorrento were led by a midfielder who had played in the AFL before making his way to the Peninsula. The events in the days leading up to the match would add further sizzle to this fixture of contrasts.

The Sorrento Football Club is based near the narrow tip of the Mornington Peninsula, the area where the factories and family homes of Rosebud and Rye give way to weatherboard getaways nestled among ti-trees. The front beach in Sorrento is on Port Phillip Bay. The back beach is exposed to the wild seas of Bass Strait. If you head past the Sorrento footy ground towards the end of the Peninsula, you reach Portsea, the playground of the rich and famous, where the grounds of the mansions feature a tennis court for summer hit-ups and a decking for champagne parties. If you go past Portsea, you reach Point Nepean, which was once an army reserve but is now a national park.

The Sorrento footy club resents the perception that it is loaded. But the club's proximity to waterfront real estate tends to colour the notions of rival supporters.

According to the Sorrento footy club's website, the club was formed in 1890. In the early days, the players travelled to their games by paddle steamer. In 1908, Sorrento was among the clubs that formed the Peninsula Football Association. Their opponents during the association's inaugural season were Frankston, Dromana, Hastings, Mornington and Somerville.

In those days, even Frankston was very much a country town, separated from Melbourne in terms of geography and culture. Although Frankston these days is part of Melbourne in terms of geography, it is still separated from the city in terms of culture. People throughout the Peninsula – from the suburbs around Frankston to the hills and dunes at the back of Rosebud and Rye – continue to regard their region as an entity apart. Football on the Peninsula continues to be aligned with country football, reflecting the origins of the game in the region.

In 1934, the two main competitions, the Peninsula Football Association and the Peninsula and District association, combined to form the Mornington Peninsula Football League. The new competition was split into three divisions, with Sorrento in the top division. Twenty-five years later, in 1959, the smaller clubs broke away to form the Nepean league, but Sorrento remained a member of the premier competition, the Mornington Peninsula league.

The Seagulls, as they were known, were successful in this period. From 1952 to 1969, they played in the finals almost every season. About twenty former VFL players were attracted to sign on with the Seagulls during this era, including the former Carlton full-back Harry Caspar and the former Footscray champion Alby Morrison, who both gave several seasons of service. The former St Kilda rover Alan Olle was the Seagulls' playing-coach for almost a decade. Sorrento won three premierships during this period, in 1953, 1964 and 1969.

From 1970, while the clubs in the suburbs around Frankston strengthened as the population grew, Sorrento remained a small club at the end of the Peninsula, with little prospect of growth. While the town of Sorrento was over-run with holiday-makers during summer, it remained a sleepy village during footy season. The Seagulls won successive premierships in 1979 and 1980, largely though the communications skills of the coach, Dennis Le Gassick, who was a former Collingwood player, but by the time of the restructure of Peninsula football in late 1986, the Sorrento footy club was well down the list of influential clubs.

Before the 1987 season, the Mornington Peninsula and Nepean leagues were combined to form the Mornington Peninsula Nepean league, which was split into two divisions based on the strength of the clubs. Sorrento were placed in Division 2. After the next restructure, in 1995, the Seagulls found themselves in Division 3. The club's fortunes continued to decline.

During this period, the Sorrento Football Club was club so low in player numbers and funds that it was in danger of folding. The club began to right itself with the appointment of Don Scott, the former Hawthorn captain, in a junior-coaching role just months after he had galvanised Hawthorn supporters into fighting off the proposed merger with the Melbourne Football Club. Scott took over as coach of the Sorrento under-eighteen team before the 1997 season. His two seasons as the thirds coach enabled the club to bring through enough juniors to provide hope.

In 2000, in pursuit of a renaissance, the Sorrento footy club rebranded itself as the Sharks. The next year, in 2001, two of the players whom Don Scott had coached, Brent Kenyon and Jai Spence, were appointed as co-coaches of the under-eighteen team, and the young coaches led the thirds to the flag.

In 2004, the Mornington Peninsula Nepean league scrapped promotion and relegation and assigned the clubs into two divisions according to geography. According to league officials, the emphasis on the names of the leagues would increase marketing opportunities. The clubs strongly supported the change because they wanted the benefit of local rivalries.

The Peninsula league included the northern clubs, from Chelsea and Edithvale-Aspendale through to Mornington, while the Nepean league included the southern clubs, from Frankston through to Rosebud, Rye and Sorrento. The Casey-Cardinia division included the clubs on the fringe where the Melbourne suburbs meet South West Gippsland, from Keysborough in the suburbs out to Pakenham in the region where housing estates back on to paddocks of grazing stock. This structure would survive for a decade.

Several players from the Sorrento team that had won the thirds premiership a few years previously were entrenched senior footballers. With Tony Blackford as coach, the Sharks broke through to win the 2004 senior premiership in the Nepean league – their first senior flag since the club's triumph under Dennis Le Gassick in 1980, twenty-four years previously.

Three years later, in 2007, the Sharks' fortunes were raised another notch with the appointment of the former St Kilda player Troy Schwarze as the playing-coach. Schwarze enticed his brother Ben to return from the South Australian National Football League club North Adelaide. The Sharks embarked on an unprecedented run of success, playing in seven consecutive grand finals and winning five premierships: in 2008, from 2010 to 2012, and in 2014.

After the 2017 season, Peninsula football was again restructured. Rather than divisions based on geography, the two remaining divisions of the Mornington Peninsula Nepean league were reassigned according to capabilities. Having enjoyed success in the previous decade, the Sorrento footy club was placed in Division 1 for the 2018 season, along with two fellow clubs from the old Nepean league, Rosebud and Frankston Bombers. In all, there were ten clubs in Division 1 and twelve clubs in Division 2 as 2018 season heralded yet another new era in Peninsula football.

While the Sharks' record was powerful for a decade before the 2018 season, the Pines Football Club was only just regaining the strength it had once enjoyed.

The Pines footy club was founded in an area that was once the site of a pine plantation.

In 1910, during an era when the region around Frankston was considered rural, the Frankston Pine Plantation was established just to the north of the town. More than 1 million pine trees were planted in what was described as a state pine forest. Forty years later, the state housing commission was granted permission to build housing there. The pine plantation was cleared, and the first stage of housing on the Pines Forest Housing Estate was completed in 1957. The first street in the estate was called Pine Street. The next streets to be named were Plantation Avenue and Forest Drive. Streets were subsequently named after pine species, including Monterey, Radiata, Corsica, Aleppo and Norfolk streets.

A sports reserve and a technical school were built on a clearing in the housing estate. The Pines Sporting Association was formed in 1963. The next year, in 1964, the Pines Football Club began with a senior team and an under-fifteen team. The senior team played in the Nepean Football League. According to the notes of the late Paul "Bud" Williams on the club's website, the Pines footy club had no clubrooms in in its first season. On match days, club members erected tents that served as the change-rooms and a refreshment booth in which water was heated up on a camp stove to make hot dogs and cups of tea. The senior team played Crib Point in its first game, and lost by 201 points. The Pines senior team went through the 1964 season without a win.

In 1965, the second stage of housing was completed on the Pines housing estate. The population of the area all around Frankston was swelling through the influx of immigrants, mostly from Britain and Ireland. Wearing its distinctive guernsey of green with a red saddle, the

Pines footy club began to improve as junior players graduated to senior ranks. In 1972, the determined wingman Barry Burke was appointed as captain-coach of the club known as the Pythons. Under Burke, the club developed a play-on style. The talented teenagers who emerged through the club's thriving youth program in this era included Russell Greene, who played for Pines' juniors before transferring to Victorian Football Association club Frankston, where he became a member of the Dolphins' under-nineteen team. In Round 1 of the 1974 season, Greene became the first former Pines junior to play a senior game in the Victorian Football League when he made his debut with St Kilda as a sixteen-year-old.

In 1975, the Pines made their first senior grand final, but they lost to Frankston YCW. The next year, still under the coaching of Barry Burke, they turned the tables and defeated Frankston YCW to win the club's first senior premiership. Every member of the team was a local. Pines players were regulars in the Nepean league's interleague team. The Pines won premierships again in 1978 (under the captain-coach Steven Clarke), 1980 (Barry Moore) and 1983 (Andrew "Jack" Norris) before the club's quest for a greater challenge was fulfilled when it was elevated to the Mornington Peninsula league in 1984.

Three years later, in 1987, the Mornington Peninsula league and the Nepean league joined forces to form the divisional competition called the Mornington Peninsula Nepean Football League. Pines by now were entrenched at the top level. In 1988, under the non-playing coach Dale Carpenter, the Pythons defeated Edithvale-Aspendale in the Grand Final to win the club's first premiership in the Mornington Peninsula Nepean competition. For the next few years, the Pythons were never far off the mark. In 1994, under Dale Carpenter's brother Leigh Carpenter, who was also a non-playing coach, the Pythons broke through to win another grand final, this time against Frankston YCW. The midfielder Mark Hustwaite was the Pythons' captain. The team included Patrick "Paddy" Swayn at centre half-back and Gordon Hendry in the ruck.

Twenty-four years later, in 2018, both of those men were still very much part of the club during the feverish build-up to the Pythons' Grand Final against Sorrento.

36

Line in the Sand

In 2018, Paddy Swayn was the coach of Pines, while Gordon "Gordo" Hendry was the club's games record-holder and, even in retirement, the club's inspiration. Beau Hendry, Gordon's elder son, was a co-captain of Pines during the 2018 season, while Luke Tapscott was the playing-coach of Sorrento. Both men were dedicated leaders, inspiring their teams to the top of the ladder. Off the field, both men worked as tradesmen. Hendry was an electrician with a large firm in the city. Tapscott was a builder with a small building firm on the Peninsula.

In 2005, when Beau Hendry made his senior debut, aged seventeen, his father Gordon was still playing in the ruck at the age of thirty-seven. Beau, at 191 centimetres, was not quite as his tall as his father, but he showed his father's willingness to compete. Beau established himself as a key member of the Pythons' backline. When Gordon stepped back to the reserves, Beau succeeded him in the ruck. His relative lack of height led him to develop a style of jumping into opposition ruckmen in an attempt to negate them. Then he would follow up with second and third efforts and try to play the role of an extra onballer.

In 2010, the Pines received another boost from the Hendry family when Gordon's younger son Guy made his senior debut. Gordon was elevated from the reserves to play one game alongside his two sons. He was forty-one years of age. Beau was twenty-two, while Guy was eighteen. Pines defeated Langwarrin by four goals on one of the most celebrated days in the club's history.

By the time of that match in 2010, according to an article in Leader Newspapers' *Frankston Standard*, Gordon Hendry had played 309 senior games and 392 club games. In 2016, at forty-seven years of age, he had two grandchildren when he passed the milestone of 500 club games.

Beau Hendry was twenty-six years of age when he was named Pines' co-captain alongside Jim Messina before the 2015 season. The next year, in 2016, he won his first club best and fairest award. From the outset, he was an aggressive, inspirational leader. Besides the enjoyment of playing alongside lifelong friends, he was motivated by the club's improving fortunes.

In an interview for this book, Beau Hendry said he did not play in the finals for the first ten seasons of his career. The Pines footy club began to change after the appointment of Paddy Swayn, the key defender in the Pines' 1994 premiership team, as the non-playing coach. Swayn had been an assistant coach under Simon Goosey at Frankston in the VFL. Before the 2015 season, he took over as the head coach of his home club, Pines.

After taking over at Pines, Swayn assembled the leadership group, which consisted of Beau Hendry, Jim Messina, Shaun White, Chris Guganovic and Adam "Tassie" Marriner. He told them that, after a decade of up and down performances, the team would only improve if the leaders showed the way. The leaders took on their coach's expectations.

The club also benefited from an injection of leadership in the form of experienced recruits. Luke Potts, a midfielder who had been the captain of Frankston's VFL team, returned before the 2015 season. The powerful key forward Aaron Edwards, who had played ninety-four AFL games over ten seasons at three clubs, West Coast, North Melbourne and Richmond, signed on after meeting Pines players through friends. While injuries had curtailed his AFL career, Edwards enjoyed playing out of the goalsquare at local level. He gave the Pines an avenue to goal as they improved during the 2015 season to make the final five. Edithvale-Aspendale defeated them in the Elimination Final.

Before the next season, in 2016, the Pines' stocks were further strengthened by the recruitment of two highly decorated players, Paul "Chewy" Scanlon and Tim "Bongo" Bongetti, from the Goulburn Valley league club Seymour.

Scanlon's nickname derives from the Scanlen's company that made footy cards and chewing gum. According to an article in the *Frankston Standard*, Scanlon grew up playing at the Bundoora footy club in Melbourne's northern suburbs. A late bloomer, he was nineteen years of age before he played his first senior game with the Bulls in the old Diamond Valley league (now the Northern league). From Bundoora, he went to VFL club Preston Bullants. After five years with the Bullants, he joined the long list of Bullants players who followed Steve Daniel, a former assistant coach at the Preston City Oval, to Seymour. Daniel was the senior coach at Seymour when the Lions embarked on their famous run of three consecutive premierships from 2005 to 2007.

Chewy Scanlon played in two of those premiership teams with Seymour, in 2006 and 2007. In the latter year, he gained the most votes in the count for the Goulburn Valley league's best and fairest award, the Morrison Medal, only to be denied the award because he had been suspended. After Seymour's victory over Shepparton Swans in the Goulburn Valley league's 2007 Grand Final, Scanlon was awarded the two medals for best on ground, the Wilf Cox Medal and the umpires' medal.

Two years later, in 2009, Scanlon won the best and fairest award at the VFL club Bendigo Bombers. A midfielder with the capacity to run all day and an uncanny ability to remove the ball from stoppages, he was a huge factor in Northcote Park's premiership from fifth position in the Northern league in 2012, and he played several seasons with the Tiwi Bombers in the Northern Territory Football League during Wet Season competitions up north. At the end of the 2011-2012 NTFL season in Darwin, Chewy Scanlon and Tim Bongetti were members of the Tiwi Bombers' premiership team.

Tim Bongetti was also a product of Melbourne's northern suburbs, in his case Greensborough. A key forward with a large personality, Bongetti played in the VFL with the Tasmania Devils and Werribee before he returned to his home club, Greensborough, and was a co-captain of the club's winning team in the 2014 Northern league Grand Final. The next year, in 2015, he joined Seymour, where he again played alongside Chewy Scanlon. Pines pulled off a recruiting coup when they landed the experienced pair before the 2016 season.

Pines continued to improve, but in 2016 they were bundled out of the finals series after successive losses. The next year, in 2017, they thrashed Mt Eliza in the Elimination Final but fell short against Bonbeach in their semi-final. Early in the 2018 season, the Pythons looked to be on a path to further disappointment when they lost to Frankston Bombers in Round 5. Some Pines supporters were so angry that they vented their displeasure at players and officials in the social rooms afterwards. The supporters' fear that the improvement of recent seasons would amount to nothing prompted a crisis meeting and a course of action that would change the Pythons' trajectory in 2018.

Luke Tapscott, Sorrento's playing-coach in 2018, grew up nowhere near the fishing boats and bobbing yachts of Port Phillip Bay. Tapscott grew up on an expansive sheep farm – about 6500 acres, or 2600 hectares on the metric scale – near Orroroo, in the Mid-North region of South Australia. Orroroo is to the east of the Flinders Ranges. It is also to the north of Goyder's Line.

In 1865, South Australia's surveyor-general George Goyder drew a line across South Australia that effectively linked all the places with an average rainfall of ten inches (250 millimetres). To the north of the line, the annual rainfall was considered too low for growing crops of wheat. Farmers were therefore advised to concentrate on grazing sheep.

Since the construction of Goyder's Line, it has been used in South Australia to denote what is officially Dry Country. When poets began to describe our sunburnt country, they had places like Orroroo in mind. If you look in any direction to the east or west of the Flinders Ranges, there is red earth and blue sky as far you can see. In an interview for this book, Luke Tapscott said farmers in his home region have always relied on each other. Honesty and trust are two of the values he learnt while growing up on a property near Orroroo.

At fifteen years of age, Tapscott moved to Adelaide to go to boarding school at Prince Alfred College and play footy at North Adelaide. In late 2009, the Melbourne Football Club selected him as their fourth player in the national draft. After the Demons had chosen Tom Scully with selection No.1, they selected Jackson Trengove (2), Jordan Gysberts (11), Luke Tapscott (18), Max Gawn (34) and Jack Fitzpatrick (50). At the time, young Tapscott's ability to kick long to position had earned him comparison with the Brisbane Lions midfielder Daniel Rich, who was renowned for his penetrating kick.

Luke Tapscott was nineteen years of age when he made his AFL debut in Round 1, 2011. The Demons drew with Sydney at the Melbourne Cricket Ground. According to a report in *The Age*, Tapscott was tremendous in defence. He took seven marks, had nineteen touches, and showed composure beyond his years. Although only 180 centimetres tall, he was strongly built. "He is an elite kick, and he relishes the physical contact," the newspaper said.

The report added that Tapscott was unlucky to miss out on the nomination for the AFL Rising Star award after his impressive debut. The player who was nominated after the opening round in 2011, Essendon's Dyson Heppell, would go on to win the award at the end of the season.

Tapscott, however, never quite established himself in Melbourne's senior team. In 2014, he was severely hampered by a back injury. At the end of the season, Melbourne delisted him after he had played forty-eight senior games over five seasons. At twenty-three years of age, he was unsure what to do with his football life or working life, but he did know that he wanted to leave what he described as the "hustle and bustle" of inner Melbourne.

Tapscott's partner, Brittany Drummond, was from Dingley, in Melbourne's outer south-east, where her family was friends with the family of Troy Schwarze, the former St Kilda wingman who was now the playing-coach at Sorrento. Luke Tapscott knew Troy's brother Ben Schwarze through their time together at North Adelaide. Given that Tapscott had two connections to Sorrento, it made sense for him to check out the club. After meeting the Sharks' hierarchy and gaining a sense of the delights of the Peninsula, he signed on for the 2015 season.

Having undergone surgery on his back early in 2015, Luke Tapscott played only four games for the Sharks in his first season. He made great strides, however, off the field. After he had worked at the Sorrento Hotel, the publican, Rob Pitt, was so impressed by Tapscott's work ethic and demeanour that he recommended him to a friend from the Sharks, Rod Layton, as a possible recruit for his building firm. Layton hired Tapscott as a mature-aged apprentice builder. Tapscott, now a qualified builder, has worked for Layton's firm on sites throughout the Peninsula ever since.

In 2016, having recovered from his back injury, Luke Tapscott returned to full fitness and peak form. He also coached Sorrento's under-nineteen team. Players from his thirds team such as Chad Harris, Angus Callaghan and the King brothers, Matt and Ethan, progressed into the senior team. At the end of the 2016 season, while Sorrento's senior team finished outside the top five, in sixth place, the Sharks' under-nineteen team won the thirds Grand Final.

The next year, in 2017, Tapscott let go of the thirds coaching job to become an assistant to the senior coach, Nick Jewell. Despite Jewell's resignation halfway through the season for personal reasons, the Sharks went on to defeat Frankston Bombers in the Grand Final. Tapscott was named best on ground, although he was unsure that he deserved it. His own choice for best on ground was the forward Leigh Poholke, whose attacking play set up the Sharks' victory.

Before the 2018 season, the two divisions of the Mornington Peninsula Nepean competition were restructured so that the strongest clubs would play against each other in Division 1. Sorrento, along with Rosebud and Frankston Bombers, were elevated to play against powerful northern neighbours such as Frankston YCW, Edithvale-Aspendale and Pines. Sorrento gained a huge boost before their new adventure when one of the club's favourite sons, Mitch Hallahan, returned home to play alongside his brother, James Hallahan, who was the Sharks' captain.

In 2013, Mitch Hallahan was a Box Hill Hawks midfielder who had just turned twenty-one years of age when he won the Liston Trophy for the best and fairest player in the VFL, having finished equal at the top of the leaders' board with Steven Clifton of North Ballarat and Jordan

Schroder of Geelong. Hallahan went on to play a total of twenty-six AFL games with Hawthorn and Gold Coast before he returned to Sorrento, aged twenty-five, to play alongside his brother.

Tony Blackford, the coach of Sorrento's premiership team in 2004, returned to the club to coach in 2018. But on the eve of the season, the club president, Bernie Balmer, informed Blackford that his services were no longer required. According to an article in the *Frankston Leader*, Balmer told Blackford that the decision was "nothing personal".

"The club is going to keep it in-house," Balmer told the newspaper. "We need to move on."

Sorrento went on to appoint Luke Tapscott as playing-coach. The Sharks surprised those who doubted the competition's restructure when they motored through the 2018 season. At the end of the home and away rounds, Sorrento were on top of the ladder with fifty-six points from fourteen victories, ahead of Mt Eliza (50), Pines (48), Edithvale-Aspendale (48) and Frankston YCW, the winners of seven of the previous eight grand finals, who rounded out the top five on forty points.

Pines' path to the 2018 finals had begun to gather steam after their loss to Frankston Bombers in Round 5. During the fallout over subsequent days, the club revealed that Dean Laidley, a North Melbourne premiership player and a former Roos coach, would occasionally help out the Pythons as an assistant coach. Laidley had come to the club through his friendship with Aaron Edwards, whom he had coached at North Melbourne, but also through his relationship with a club sponsor. Before long, Laidley committed to helping out at training late in the week and on match days. The Pythons received a further boost when Perry Lewis-Smith, a midfielder who had been playing at Frankston, said he would play out the season with the Pythons.

After the loss to Frankston Bombers, the Pythons also lost their next match, at home to Sorrento, by eleven points. They then fought to a seventeen-point victory in a tight game against Frankston YCW at the Stonecats' home ground. In subsequent matches, Pines built momentum with three victories. In Round 11, they lost at home to Edithvale-Aspendale by one point. The next week, in Round 12, they lost to fellow finals contenders Mt Eliza by three goals. The competition then had a bye round.

On the Thursday night before the bye round, Dean Laidley asked the Pines players to gather in the meeting room after training. He gave the club's 1994 premiership cup to the co-captains, Beau Hendry and Tim Bongetti, and asked them what it felt like to hold the cup. He told them to hold it above their heads, as if they were celebrating on the dais after a grand final. The cup was passed around the room. All the players were invited to hold up the premiership cup.

Laidley reminded the players that twenty-four years was a long time for a club to go without hoisting a premiership cup. Two days later, on the Saturday morning of the bye round, the Pythons enjoyed an energetic training session in perfect winter sunshine. The players felt sharp and focused. The feeling that arose from those two instances under the direction of Dean Laidley set up the Pines for their run home.

The Pythons got back on track with a strong victory over their nemesis in the early rounds, Frankston Bombers, during the resumption after the bye. The next week, they drove an hour down through the Peninsula to Sorrento's home ground, the David McFarlane Reserve, where they scored a victory by three points. Tom McDermott, the Pythons' elusive small forward, kicked five goals against the Sharks. Beau Hendry, the Pines ruckman and co-captain, was best on ground. With the bay just over the hill, the Pythons set sail for the finals.

Under the final-five system, Sorrento, as the minor premiers, enjoyed a break in the first week of the finals. In the Qualifying Final, Pines defeated Mt Eliza by seven goals, with Aaron Edwards kicking six. Guy Hendry and Beau Hendry were named the Pythons' two best players, ahead of Chewy Scanlon.

During the finals series, Scanlon recorded a remarkable feat when, on the eve of his forty-first birthday, he was awarded his second E.V. Shade Medal for the best and fairest player in the Peninsula competition. In his three seasons since he had joined Pines, Scanlon had finished second (2016), first (2017) and first (2018) in the medal count. In an interview with the local newspaper, Scanlon attributed his good form to meticulous preparation. He said he never trained on Tuesday nights, and he trained only rarely on Thursday nights. He went to the gym every day, but his main focus was his recovery session on Sundays.

In the Second Semi-final, Pines got over the top of Sorrento to win by thirteen points, 14.11 (95) to 11.16 (82). Aaron Edwards kicked four goals for the victors, while the midfielders Perry Lewis-Smith and Luke Potts were the Pythons' best players. For the Sharks, the big forward Nick Corp kicked three goals and was named his team's best player, ahead of Luke Tapscott.

The Pythons were through to the Grand Final, their first since their loss to Edithvale-Aspendale in the Grand Final sixteen years earlier, in 2002. But there would be plenty to play out before the match was under way.

37

Pointy End

As the 2018 season progressed in Division 1 of the Mornington Peninsula Nepean league, Sorrento officials became increasingly angry at what they believed were opposition tactics to target their playing-coach and midfielder Luke Tapscott. Late in the season, Sharks officials resolved to train a camera on Tapscott in an attempt to capture any untoward incidents. After Sorrento's loss to Pines in the Second Semi-final at Mornington, the Sharks' film of the match revealed an incident in which the Pines co-captain Beau Hendry appeared to stomp on Tapscott's head. Sorrento officials lodged a request for an investigation into the incident.

In the interim between the opening of the investigation and the hearing, Sorrento took care of the immediate matter at hand when they defeated Mt Eliza by twenty-one points in the Preliminary Final at Frankston Park. Leigh Poholke, the mercurial forward, kicked four goals. The first four players named among Sorrento's best players were the defenders James Brigden and Chad Harris, the vice-captain Nick Marston, and Luke Tapscott. The Sharks suffered a blow during the match when Chris Dawes, the former Collingwood forward, who had played in the Magpies' AFL premiership team in 2010, appeared to strain a calf muscle.

In the footage of the alleged stomping incident during the Second Semi-final, Hendry tackles Tapscott hard to the ground and earns a free kick for holding the ball. Hendry then remonstrates with Tapscott while the Sorrento leader is trapped beneath him. As Hendry makes to get up off the ground, Tapscott entwines Hendry's left leg with his own legs. Hendry, with his left leg entangled, drives his right boot hard towards the ground. After his right foot is planted on the ground, he regains his balance. The umpire is within arm's reach of the incident, but his attention has been diverted towards a player in the opposite direction.

It is not clear from the footage whether Hendry's boot has connected with Tapscott's head. But while Hendry steps back to take his free-kick, Tapscott momentarily holds his head in hands. The ball is relayed back to Hendry as Tapscott gets to his feet. While Hendry handballs to a teammate running past, Tapscott begins to jog as he seeks to regain his composure.

While Beau Hendry would later admit that the footage does not look good, he was adamant that he had not stomped on the head of his opponent. He said his boot had glanced Tapscott's head. If he – a man of 100 kilograms – had meant to stomp on Tapscott, the Sharks leader would not have been able to get up.

In the hearing, the tribunal heard evidence from Hendry and Tapscott. The tribunal members also watched the film of the incident. Beau Hendry was suspended for two matches. He would miss the Grand Final.

The next day, Tapscott's phone erupted. Unwilling to listen to the abuse, the Sorrento midfielder switched off his phone. He would not take a call or look at social media sites throughout the day. Jeff Svigos, the Pines president, took the approach of facing the storm. He took calls from supporters and journalists. He jumped on social media sites to ask everyone to keep their cool. League officials became so alarmed by the frenzy surrounding the decision against Beau Hendry that they organised extra security for the Grand Final.

Pines officials had to decide whether to appeal against Hendry's penalty. To do so would cost the club $5500, with $3000 to be recovered in the event of a finding in the club's favour. Beau Hendry is a much-loved figure at the Pines, from the club's foremost family. When he wears the Pines guernsey, it is with No.34 on his back. Pine supporters began transferring money to the club's bank account to raise funds for the appeal. Usually, the amount that was donated was $34 or a multiple of $34. The funding target was raised within a short time. At Pines training on the Thursday night, the Pythons coach, Paddy Swayn, apologised to Hendry when he said he would be unable to read out his name in the team for Sunday's match. He hoped he would be able to include Hendry's name in the team after the appeal.

The appeals board of AFL Victoria Country scheduled the appeal hearing for the next night, the Friday evening before the Peninsula competition's Grand Final, at the AFL body's headquarters at Princes Park in Carlton. Sorrento players and officials stayed away on the advice of AFL South East, the regional commission that oversees the Mornington Peninsula competition. As no fresh evidence would be heard, Sorrento officials accepted the advice that their presence would not be required. Luke Tapscott, however, was asked to keep his phone on. He went to the MCG to see Melbourne play in a semi-final against Hawthorn, but the events surrounding the hearings sapped his enjoyment of the occasion.

The Pines players all joined Hendry for the journey to Carlton for the hearing. They waited outside the ground while Hendry and Pines officials filed inside.

Beau Hendry was represented by Iain "Fingers" Findlay, the well-known players' advocate at AFL Tribunal hearings. When Findlay opened with the assertion that Hendry's penalty should be overturned because the charge against him had been improperly lodged, the appeals board agreed. Essentially, the paper work had been filled out incorrectly. Hendry's penalty was repealed. He was free to play in the Grand Final. Sorrento officials were disappointed that AFL South East failed to notify the club in writing of the outcome of the appeal.

Although Hendry would have preferred the chance to clear his name, he was nonetheless delighted about the outcome of the hearing. He trained with his Pines teammates the next morning in the knowledge that he was in the team for the Grand Final the following day. Supporters from not only Pines were excited about Hendry's inclusion. Pines were considered the battlers. Sorrento were considered the rich boys. Supporters from throughout the Peninsula filed into Frankston Park on the day of the Grand Final hoping to see the battlers get up.

It is a mild, mid-September day when my son Leo and I enter Frankston Park from the Kars Street end. The ground is packed. Almost 8000 spectators are jammed in wherever they can find space – behind the goals, behind the pockets, in the long, wooden grandstand that runs along the length of the southern wing. Frankston Park on the Peninsula league's final day of the season is a spectacle in any year. This year it is something else again.

I choose the terraced area on the northern wing so that Leo, who is ten years of age, can see the match. We stand among Pines supporters who are mostly cheerful; some of them are nervous. Despite all the security, the atmosphere is tense rather than hostile. Near us, a young Pines supporter has arranged his hair in a mohawk style. The comb of his hairdo has been dyed green and red. Beau Hendry's No.34 has been etched in dye on to the side of the supporter's head.

The crowd is in full voice straight after the opening bounce when Beau Hendry runs over the ball to drive his shoulder into the sternum of James Hallahan, the Sorrento captain, at just the instant when the umpire is about to blow his whistle to signal a ball-up. The umpire maintains his decision. Hallahan, clearly shaken, takes a few seconds to get up. The players arrange themselves around the stoppage. The tone has been set.

The opening five minutes feature a helter-skelter pursuit of the ball from both teams, with the Pines kicking towards the bayside end and Sorrento towards the eastern end, or Kars Street end. Neither team is able to break through for a major score until, on the eight-minute mark, James Hallahan receives a handball from Ryan Williams, the Sorrento ruckman, and kicks a running goal. At the fifteen-minute mark, the Sharks' silver-haired defender, Daniel Grant, is tackled before he has moved off his mark. The umpire awards a fifty-metre penalty. Grant kicks his team's second goal.

Chris Dawes, the Sorrento full-forward, is clearly hobbling. At the other end of the ground, the Sorrento full-back, James Bridgen, wins early contests against Aaron Edwards. The Pines midfielders Luke Potts, Paul Scanlon and Lachlan Marshall are winning a stack of the ball. Potts is playing a superb leader's game, working hard to free the ball from congestion. Scanlon is busy around the stoppages. He always gets his foot to the ball.

The Sharks' strong-marking key forward, Nick Corp, kicks a goal. Leigh Poholke, his fellow forward, marks on the edge of the goalsquare and kicks a goal. The Sharks have four unanswered goals. The Pythons are yet to settle. Beau Hendry continues his fearsome attack on the man and the ball. When he tries to clear the ball out of defence and kicks it out on the full in front of the social club, there is not one Bronx cheer. There is no noise at all. If there are any Sorrento supporters on the northern side of the ground, they are keeping to themselves.

In the shadow of quarter-time, with Pines yet to kick a goal, the Pythons key forward and co-captain Tim Bongetti drifts across in front of a pack to take a one-handed mark. His audacious grab suggests possibility. Sorrento lead by twenty-eight points at quarter-time, 4.6 (30) to 0.2 (2).

Within a minute of the opening of the second quarter, James Hallahan breaks away from a boundary throw-in on the southern side, or grandstand side, and streams towards goal at the bayside end. His long kick finds Leigh Poholke, who takes a good mark and kicks a goal. The Sharks now have unanswered five goals. The Pythons fans are urging a response.

One of the shining lights for the Pines is Guy Hendry, the brother of Beau, who takes a series of marks drifting across the half-back line. At 195 centimetres with a sticky pair of hands, he is a hard player to get past. A few minutes into the second quarter, Guy Hendry takes another mark and receives a clip over the ear from Nick Corp. Beau Hendry bustles in to remonstrate while the umpire signals a fifty metre penalty. Aaron Edwards leads out from the Pines goalsquare and takes a solid mark. He converts from thirty-five metres out to give the Pythons their first goal for the match.

A minute later, at the six-minute mark of the second quarter, Luke Tapscott, the Sorrento coach, receives the ball just inside the centre square and runs forward, seeking to balance before he tries to find a teammate in attack. While he weighs up his options, a hulking figure looms from behind. Beau Hendry's face is etched with intent as he barges towards the Sharks leader. Everyone at the ground can see what is about to happen except Tapscott himself. Hendry bears down like a train in the night. He hurls himself forward to make the tackle. As he does so, his left forearm connects with the cheek of Tapscott before he wraps both arms around the Sorrento player and rides him into the ground on his side. My first instinct is that Tapscott will receive a free-kick for high contact. No one around me agrees. "Ball!" they cry. The umpire penalises Tapscott for holding the ball.

The decision is pivotal. Pines supporters jump and shout. Pines players move to position a little sharper. Beau Hendry holds down Tapscott for a moment and lets him know what he thinks of recent events. Hendry then begins to lift himself to his feet with the ball in his hands. With Tapscott still on the ground beneath him, he raises his foot and makes out to stomp on the figure below. While Hendry is determined and aggressive, he also has an acute sense of theatre. The spectators roar, mixing laughter with bellowing approval. Hendry steps over Tapscott and handballs off to a teammate. The Pythons begin to gather steam.

The ball spills off a pack in the Pines goalsquare and Aaron Edwards kicks a goal. Perry Lewis-Smith, the Pines midfielder, wins a free-kick for holding the ball and he, too, kicks a goal. Daniel Grant, Sorrento's veteran defender, continues to hold out attacks and keep his cool, but some of his teammates are looking unsure. The Sharks do not appear confident when they have the ball.

Luke Tapscott keeps hurling himself into the path of danger. He is heroic, but he is growing frustrated. He gives away a free-kick for a high tackle. Aaron Edwards kicks his third goal for the second quarter. Perry Lewis-Smith kicks his second for the quarter. Scores are level at the twenty-two minute mark.

In the shadow of half-time, Tim Bongetti is awarded a free kick when Ryan Williams, the burly Sorrento ruckman, tries to throw him out of the way in a ruck contest. Bongetti lollops in with his distinctive, bouncy approach and takes a shot from outside the fifty-metre arc. His left boot sends the ball high and long. The crowd's roar increases as the ball begins to descend. It falls over the players' heads and over the goal-line. The roar of the crowd takes off into the sky over Frankston. Pines players converge on their talisman to celebrate. The Pythons have kicked six unanswered goals. They go into half-time with a five-point lead, 6.6 (42) to 5.7 (37).

After half-time, the wretched day of Chris Dawes is confirmed when he fails to reappear on the ground. Just after play resumes, a supporter on the terraces reveals that the beer has run out. Sorrento strike the first blow on the scoreboard, with a goal to the lead-up forward Jayden Tomkins. Two minutes later, Tomkins kicks another. Nick Corp then kicks two goals to put the Sharks three goals head. Now it is the Pythons who are reeling. It is hard to keep up with the fits and surges of this gripping game.

The Pines' Nick Wilcox arrests his team's slide by snapping with his left foot for a goal. James Hallahan replies for Sorrento, showing strength and poise to kick a brilliant goal. Hallahan is leading the way for the Sharks. His brother, Mitch, continues to clear out from packs with his own eye-catching surges. The Sharks look to be in control, but, as has happened throughout the match, the effervescent Tim "Bongo" Bongetti pops up to renew hope for the Pythons. The big No.6 takes a huge mark and kicks a long goal. Pines are back within two goals.

As time-on approaches in the third quarter, Sorrento defender Jackson Grant is penalised for deliberate out of bounds. The free-kick is there. The fallout for the Sharks is calamitous. Tom McDermott, the Pines small forward who has barely been near the ball, leads out and takes the pass. From twenty metres out on an angle, he kicks truly. A few minutes later, McDermott reels backs after a high tackle and receives a free-kick. From twenty-five metres out, he again kicks truly. Another minute later, McDermott again draws the action. He is an old-fashioned half-forward flanker: unsighted for long periods, but capable of turning the game in a burst. He receives another free-kick for a high tackle. This time he's fifty-metres out. A true marksman, he kicks straight again. It's his third goal in a matter of minutes. Pines players converge on him to celebrate as the siren sounds with the Pythons in front by five points, 11.9 (75) to 10.10 (70).

The last quarter is every bit as tense and erratic as its precedents, only more so. Brendan Barfoot, a busy Pines forward with a touch of cheek, takes a strong mark and kicks a goal from forty metres out. As soon the ball goes through the goalposts, he runs to Luke Tapscott to tell him all about it.

Chad Harris, the young Sorrento defender, brings down Pines forward Aaron Ludewig as Ludewig makes towards goal. Harris still has gas in the tank. The big Sorrento forward, Nick Corp, takes a strong mark and finds Leigh Poholke, who kicks a goal. The Sharks are within five points. However, their ambition to overhaul the Pythons is put on hold – because a streaker jumps the fence from behind the bayside goals.

While the officiating umpire stands in the centre with the ball in hand, ready to resume play, the streaker strides through the centre square. The footballers have every right to be filthy. The most intense match of their lives is being halted by a naked fool. But most of them are laughing. They show no sign of ill-feeling. The umpire on the northern wing signals a free-kick against the streaker for dropping the ball. Life intervenes in local footy.

After a two-minute delay, Sorrento strike first when Marcus Gardner kicks a goal under pressure. The Sharks are in front by a point. The Pines midfielder Kyal Jacobson is bumped after he kicks the ball. Shaun White, the Pines veteran, takes the resultant free-kick for downfield and kicks a goal. Pines are back in front, by five points. Luke Tapscott makes a big tackle on Beau Hendry. Both players get up, their brows furrowed with concentration. No remonstration. No pantomime stomp. It's all business now.

Guy Hendry, who has been excellent in the air, sits under a high ball and appears to take the mark, only for his opponent, Nick Corp, to reach over and snatch the ball out of Hendry's hands as the Pines defender brings the ball down. Outrageously, the umpire rules that Hendry was not in control of the mark when Corp took the ball. He calls play on. Corp lumbers clear and kicks long to the unmarked Leigh Poholke on the edge of the goalsquare. Poholke kicks his fourth for the match.

In the crowd, Jeff Svigos, the Pines president, looks up at the faces of the Pythons fans on the northern hill. In his day, Svigos was a forward who played in three premiership teams with his home club during the Pythons' years in the Nepean league. He knows the club inside out. When he looks up at the hill and see so many faces contorted with rage after Nick Corp's apparent act of thievery, he holds fears for what might happen if the Pythons get done in a close one. And he, as the president, would be responsible!

A couple of minutes later, Guy Hendry is still smarting after his disallowed mark. He gives away a free-kick to James Hallahan. Luke Potts, who has been resolute all match, grabs Guy Hendry by the jumper with two hands and demands that he get a hold of himself. Ben Thomas, the Pines defender, takes a strong mark. Sorrento midfielders embark on a chain of handballs that rockets along the wing, through Ryan Williams, James Hallahan, Luke Tapscott and Chad Harris. Back to Luke Tapscott. The Sharks go forward. The Pythons rebound. The Sharks go forward again. Marcus Gardner, quiet early in the match, snaps from a pocket to kick his second goal for the quarter. Sorrento are up by a goal. The clock ticks into time-on of the final quarter.

The ball is on the northern wing, just inside the centre square, when the umpire rules that Marcus Gardner has held Nick Boswell without the ball. Boswell tries to push off. Gardner makes an effort to retard him. His effort is not aggressive, nor is it clumsy. Yet the umpire awards a fifty-metre penalty!

Nick Boswell appears calm as he jogs forward to his mark just inside the fifty-metre arc. He hears the calls of the crowd. He hears the advice of his teammates. He loves this moment. From forty-five metres out, he kicks a drop-punt that sails straight through the goals. Scores are level, 14.11 (95) apiece. Boswell smiles as he jogs back to defence.

From the ball-up in the centre square, Beau Hendry tumbles the ball forward. Ryan Williams passes to Luke Tapscott. Daniel Grant, the Sorrento defender, runs the ball along the wing. Perry Lewis-Smith, the Pines midfielder, latches on to a loose ball. Nick Boswell, the smiling defender, swoops on a loose ball just inside the centre square. Boswell breaks a tackle and handballs to Lachlan Marshall, who finds

Aaron Ludewig, a solid figure wearing No.19, unmarked in a forward pocket. The siren goes.

The siren!

Scores are level!

Ludewig does not smile like Nick Boswell. He looks worried. He goes back to his mark. He does not hear his teammates' advice to take his time. He walks in to take his kick straight away, before nerves and the occasion can get the better of him. The ball spins end on end, through air that is thick with expectation. It proceeds on a straight path, not deviating an inch. It sails through for a behind. It is enough. Pines have won by a point with a kick after the siren.

A sea of green and red envelops Aaron Ludewig and every Pines player. After twenty-four years without a premiership, the Pythons have won a classic, a match that will live in my memory and the memory of everyone who is at Frankston Park. The Pythons have won three of their four matches against the Sharks in 2018, all by narrow margins. In the Grand Final, they answered every challenge. The Sharks were gallant. The players shake hands.

The radio show gets off to a slow start because of technical issues; it's as if the excitement is too much for the cords and wires. Then the show hits a groove. But that is a story for a day that is far less remarkable than this one.

38

The Final Count

Every year, country footy produces its share of dramas during the finals, if not quite on the scale of the events surrounding the Mornington Peninsula Nepean league's 2018 Grand Final. In rounding up the fortunes of the clubs mentioned in previous chapters, I will mention a couple of further dramas before finishing up with a statistic that underpins the triumphs and tribulations in this book. You can check out the fortunes of every club in country Victoria and beyond in the review at the back of the book.

In the Goulburn Valley league in 2018, Shepparton defeated Kyabram in the Grand Final in one of the great upsets of our time. Kyabram, having won sixty-two games in succession, lost to the Bears by two points. In Mildura, the Sunraysia league Grand Final between Irymple and Ouyen United was less dramatic but no less tense. Ouyen United emerged with their noses in front. For the second time in three years, the wheat farmers from the Mallee hoisted the premiership cup after a victory over a rival from the citrus country to the north.

Late in the home and away rounds in the 2018 season, I received a shock when Paul Dodds, the Boolarra president, informed me that he had resigned as the club president just days after my visit to the foot of the

Strzelecki Ranges. During the social function in the rooms after Boolarra's game against Yarragon, Paul and one of the players had become embroiled in a dispute over a club matter. The matter ended up unresolved.

The next morning, Paul Dodds called a meeting of the club's committee, and said the player must be sacked from the club or he himself would resign. The committee members saw Paul's point of view but, ultimately, they disagreed with him. Paul Dodds carried through with his threat to resign. He was replaced as president by Simon Buglisi, who was the captain of Boolarra's 2011 premiership team. Just over a week after Paul Dodds had left Boolarra, he umpired his first match as a member of the Latrobe Valley Umpires Association, a thirds game between Mid-Gippsland league rivals Newborough and Yinnar.

Paul Dodds went on to umpire eleven matches, concluding his season with two junior grand finals at the Ted Summerton Reserve in Moe. The Boolarra footy club, having hoped to find sunshine during the wintry depths of June, finished their season without a win, but the club was confident that it had laid a foundation for improvement.

During the Mid-Gippsland league finals, Mirboo North lost the First Semi-final to Yallourn-Yallourn North. Clancy Bennett shared Mirboo North's best and fairest award with Josh Taylor. And I came to realise the power of the Strzelecki Ranges, which separate the South Gippsland and Mid-Gippsland regions, as a mental barrier as well as a geographic divide.

Late in the season, AFL Victoria Country published its ruling that the Mid-Gippsland league and the Alberton league should merge to form the proposed Central and Southern Gippsland Football League. Mid-Gippsland officials lodged an appeal against the ruling, and won their appeal. The league, however, did experience a measure of change when the Yarragon footy club was cleared to the Ellinbank and District league. Yarragon's departure from the Mid-Gippsland league at the end of the 2018 season marked the first modification to the league's composition of clubs since the Maryvale footy club had folded more than thirty years earlier, in 1987. The Mid-Gippsland league entered the 2019 season with nine clubs, but only four teams in the thirds competition.

The jilted clubs from the Alberton league – six in all – were left to soldier on. After Fish Creek had defeated Foster in the Alberton league Grand Final in 2018, the Roos lost nine of their best players, including two league best and fairest winners, Ethan Park and Tom Cameron, because, in part, those players no longer wanted to play in a six-team competition. AFL Victoria Country was left with a mess as they tried to come up with a viable competition for the clubs in South Gippsland.

Towards the end of the 2018 home and away rounds, I spent a weekend in Kyabram trying to find out just how the Bombers had become unbeatable. Kyabram had not lost since the 2015 Grand Final, in which they went down to Benalla. When I was in Kyabram in 2018, the Bombers were approaching sixty games without loss. During the finals, they passed the Victorian record of the famous suburban club Vermont, who had won sixty-one games in succession from 1988 to 1991.

On the final day of the 2018 season, in a shock to themselves and everyone with even a passing interest in local footy, Kyabram lost the Goulburn Valley league Grand Final to Shepparton by two points. I had planned to write about Kyabram's winning streak but time and space – and, yes, the Grand Final result – have worked against me. No matter the shock of the Grand Final, I want to recognise Kyabram's extraordinary feat in winning sixty-two consecutive games.

In the Loddon Valley league, Inglewood lost their final match of the season to Mitiamo. To the north of Inglewood, Wedderburn finished fifth in the North Central League, just outside the top four, while Sea Lake-Nandaly Tigers made the finals for the first time in just their third year in the competition. The Tigers defeated Donald by three points in their semi-final before losing to Birchip-Watchem in the Preliminary Final.

In the Sunraysia league, Ouyen United continued on their merry way after my Grand Tour with Michael "Boozer" Robertson and the subsequent match at Underbool. In an unforeseen development, a series of photos from a club photographer, Jo Morrish, went viral.

Jo Morrish is a mother of three children – a son and two daughters – who play either footy or netball for Ouyen United. Jo has taken footy and netball photos for the club as a volunteer for several years. In her real job, she described herself as an activities worker at the Ouyen hospital. She also ran a spraying business with her family, and she did a bit of book-keeping for a local company. She was the secretary of the Ouyen Harness Racing Club, and she took photos for the harness racing club in Mildura. “So I keep busy,” she told me.

The particular photos that Jo took that excited so much attention depict a mark from Will Farrer, the Ouyen United full-forward, in a match against Red Cliffs. The *Sunraysia Daily* in Mildura ran a series of photos highlighting Farrer’s mark; the *Sunday Herald-Sun* in Melbourne ran the photo of Farrer at the peak of his ascent. Those most effusive about Will Farrer’s mark in their comments on social media included Martin Flanagan, the former journalist from *The Age* who has a renowned eye for the poetry in footy, and Graham Cornes, the father of Chad and Kane Cornes, and a noted former high-flyer himself.

Josh Gregg, the Ouyen United midfielder, and the grandson of the great Ron Gregg, went on to win the McLeod Medal for the best and fairest player in the Sunraysia league, while his Kangas teammate Tom Morrish won the goalkicking award. In the Sunraysia league Grand Final, which was held at the City Oval in Mildura, the Kangas started slowly in their duel against Irymple. The Swallows looked to have the game in hand before Ouyen United’s Simon Brown, a midfielder from the Brown family of Underbool, kicked a goal on the siren at three-quarter time to bring the Kangas within nine points at the final change.

Ouyen United kicked two goals in the last quarter to take the lead. Nick Mee from Irymple kicked a goal from outside the fifty-metre arc to return the lead to the Swallows, who were now up by a point. Ouyen United won the clearance from the subsequent ball-up. Brad Vallance, the Ouyen United midfielder, won a free-kick between the centre square and the fifty-metre arc. Vallance roosted the ball through the goals and on to the trotting track. Ouyen United were up by five points with five minutes to go. During a finish of almost unbearable tension, neither team could score. In another classic grand final to end the 2018 season, Ouyen United won by five points.

The Kangas’ best players included the co-coach and key defender Andy Jardine as well the midfielders Dean Staunton and Brad Vallance. The team included Travis Latta, who, after his inclusion for the match against Merbein in Round 10, had agreed to play out the season with the seniors. Travis Latta was a member of the Kangas' 2018 premiership team just a few weeks shy of his fortieth birthday.

After the season, I set out to establish just how many clubs had contributed to the family tree of the Ouyen United Football Club. In the State Library of Victoria, I pored over reports and results in Mallee newspapers to work out which clubs were playing where. During this process, I had to decide on a boundary of Ouyen United's catchment area. By my reckoning, that boundary extended north to Hattah, which had a club in the Ouyen District league in the 1920s, and south to Speed and Turriff, which were the foundation clubs of Gorya. Ouyen itself marked the eastern boundary. In the west, I included the clubs aligned with Underbool, which was among the clubs to fold into Ouyen United. Underbool's sphere of influence ended with Linga and Boinka. Both of these clubs played in the Underbool competition in the 1920s.

I left out Murrayville and the clubs that fed into Murrayville in the 1960s, such as Cowangie, Danyo and Tutye. Murrayville still exists as a club in its own right, playing against rivals over the border in South Australia's Mallee league. I also left out the clubs in the old Pier Milan and District competition, to the south-east of Ouyen, because those clubs more or less folded into Nandaly. The Nandaly footy club existed as a club in its own right until 1994, when it merged with Sea Lake to the south.

The clubs that played in the Pier Milan competition in the 1930s included Kulwin, Mittyack and Pier Milan itself. You could argue that there was much traffic of players between those clubs and the clubs around Ouyen. The Ouyen newspapers certainly regarded the Pier Milan competition as being in their readership area. The Mittyack footy club even played in the Ouyen District competition for a short time in the 1950s.

But the three clubs in question, Kulwin, Mittyack and Pier Milan, were at the top of the railway line that extended from the Korong Vale junction, near Wedderburn, up to Kulwin. Many competitions in the early days were based along railway lines. It seemed a bit wrong to include those three clubs in Ouyen United's catchment area when they were more aligned with Nandaly, which was on the same railway line.

So, after all those considerations, I proposed that, over the course of a century, a total of thirty-two clubs had fed into Ouyen United. I felt a bit sheepish when I revealed my figure to Michael "Boozer" Robertson, the man who had inspired me to join him on his Grand Tour of the old Mallee grounds as a means of investigating the forty-three clubs that had fed into Ouyen United.

Boozer thought about my figure for a while. He had forgotten how he had arrived at his own figure. He looked at my list. He worked out that he might have included the clubs that I regarded as being outside Ouyen United's catchment area. If you include those clubs, you get to forty-one. He had also included Gorya, which had played as a club in its own right for fifty years; his uncles, the McLean brothers, had been among Gorya's greatest players. And he had included Tyenna, because his father, the great Ginger Robertson, had taken him to the Tyenna oval on his original tour of the old Mallee grounds in 2003.

I did not come across Tyenna in the newspaper reports, but that is not to say that Ginger Robertson had not played footy on the Tyenna oval. Boozer suspected that Tyenna might have fielded a team during one of the patriotic leagues that were formed as the basis for occasional matches during war-time.

In any case, whether you accept my figure or Boozer's figure, it is undeniable that a lot of clubs have fed into the Ouyen United footy club. Long may the current club continue to thrive as the focus for footy in the north-west of the state.

39

Grand Old Flags

Most country footballers go through their careers battling to win a premiership. Others strike it lucky. Late in the 2018 season, an opportune email led me to look into the phenomenon of just how fortunate some players can be.

Throughout the 2018 season, I co-hosted a weekly country footy show on the Racing Sports Network, better known as RSN, in Melbourne. In September, in the lead-up to the Murray league Grand Final, we interviewed Jason Limbrick, the Nathalia key forward, about the prospect of playing in his eighth premiership team. It was a figure I found astonishing, mostly because it highlighted the turnaround in fortunes for his club.

Nathalia entered the Murray Football League in 1933. For the next seventy years, they won four premierships. Since winning the flag in 2005, however, Nathalia have been unable to stop winning premierships. Jason Limbrick made his senior debut with Nathalia, the club known as the Purples, in 2006, and played in a premiership team in his first season. During our interview in 2018, his easy manner and sense of perspective lent an indication of the reasons behind the club's gold rush in subsequent years.

But I was also astonished by the number itself – eight premierships. I said I could not imagine too many country footballers with a tally to match.

Over the following weekend, Nathalia defeated Barooga, and Jason Limbrick's tally of premierships did rise to eight. In the Wimmera league Grand Final, Horsham defeated the Southern Mallee Giants, and I received an email that referred to Jason's number of premierships.

Laurie Taylor, a former president of the Horsham Football Club, had written to tell me that Brad Hartigan, a Horsham midfielder, had extended his number of premierships far beyond the tally that had so impressed me during my interview with the footballer from Nathalia. Laurie just wanted me to know that, as good as the player from Nathalia might be, he had a little way to go if he were to catch Brad Hartigan, who had just played in his twelfth premiership team.

I craned to check my screen.

Twelve premierships!

For many years, the Wimmera league was among the top country footy leagues in the state. Its standing has fallen in recent years, as families have left the wheat fields, and footy strongholds like Warracknabeal and Stawell have struggled to keep their young players. But even so, the Wimmera league remains a highly respected league. And twelve premierships in any competition is an extraordinary achievement.

I have a local-footy email list. After receiving the note from Horsham's Laurie Taylor, I sent out an email in which I asked simply whether anyone knew of a country footballer who could match Brad Hartigan's tally of flags. Then I repeated the request to my PD Footy page on Facebook. I received several replies about players with eight to ten premierships. These replies were the genesis of what would become my premiership list.

Most of the players listed in the replies came from Wycheproof, Nullawil and Albury. My initial plan was to look into premierships in country Victoria, but the significant presence of Albury on the list posed a problem. Albury is in New South Wales, but it would have been preposterous to rule out any premierships that had been won with Albury given that the competition in which the Tigers play, the Ovens and Murray league, is strongly aligned with Victorian football. So I decided to include premierships with all clubs that play in competitions that straddle the Victorian border. And I decided that the Border Rule would include not only clubs in New South Wales, but those in South Australia as well. Then I broadened the parameters to include all clubs in the southern Riverina, whether or not their competition did straddle the border with Victoria, because the southern Riverina shared a common football history with Victoria.

This expansion of the catchment area to just beyond the Victorian border meant that I discovered long lists of premiership players at the Riverina clubs Osborne and Wagga Tigers – as well as the South Australian clubs Mundulla and South Gambier.

Just after I started compiling my list, I discovered that Bill Traill – in my opinion the most learned man on Gippsland football – had compiled a list of multiple premiership players in Gippsland, and his cut-off mark for inclusion was six flags. So I employed a cut-off mark of six flags as well. Finally, I made the starting point for the list the end of World War 2. It would have just been too unwieldy and time-consuming to go back any further.

Despite all attempts to create a thorough record, I have no doubt there are some deserving players who are absent from the list at the back of this book. I hope to include them in a revised list at a later date.

In the meantime, I'm keen to discover more about Brad Hartigan, the footballer who in 2018 played in his twelfth premiership team. On a balmy night during the pre-season in 2019, I head up the Western Highway to attend the Horsham Football Club's training session at the Horsham City Oval. My trip reveals that there is an element of serendipity in playing in multiple premiership teams: it pays to come of age at a time when your club is about to enter its period of glory. But there is also a huge element of competiveness and durability required if you are hoping to play your part in a string of triumphs.

The Horsham Football Club was originally based at the Horsham showgrounds, just to the north of the Wimmera River, where it began playing after the club's formation in 1885. Eighteen years later, in 1903, the club moved to the Horsham City Oval, and it has been based there ever since.

After I pull up at the Horsham City Oval, I run my eye over the ground and notice that the small grandstand on the northern wing is

The sign that welcome you to the Mallee as you enter the town of Birchip from the south is like a welcome to another world [Mark Daffey]

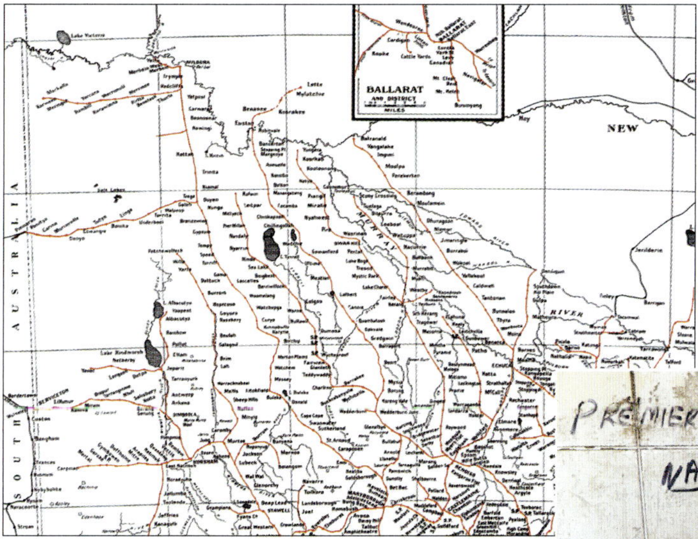

The railway lines of north-west Victoria, as depicted on the 1946 railways map of the state [Australian Railway Historical Society]

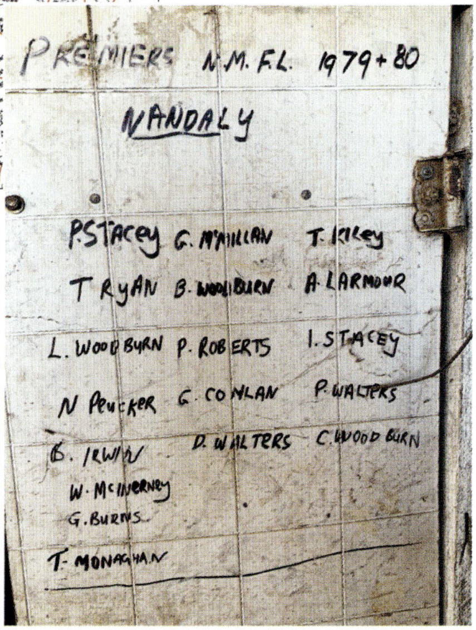

Nandaly's 1979 premiership team, as found on a door in the shearing shed at the Parkinson family's farm [Terrence Kiley]

The totem poles (clockwise from top left) for the Tempy, Gorya, Tempy-Gorya-Patchewollock and Tiega football clubs at Blackburn Park in Ouyen [Paul Daffey]

Fintan Magee's portrait of Nick "Noodle" Hulland, a local farmer and the Ouyen United reserves coach, on the Patchewollock silo is thirty-five metres high [Mark Daffey]

Stony Creek centre half-back Andrew Logan, who nabbed an elusive dog during a match against Toora [Paul Daffey]

The Gloster brothers Ray (left), 91, and Ken, 89, at Underbool. Ray was a timekeeper, Ken a premiership captain [Paul Daffey]

Inglewood's Graham "Squirty" Roberts (left) and Howard Rochester. Squirty, 83, played in three flags with the Blues [Paul Daffey]

Boolarra midfielder James Holmes is splattered but unbowed after a disappointing loss to Yarragon [Paul Daffey]

Michael "Boozer" Robertson takes a minute out of his tour of the old Mallee grounds. The board explains the family tree of Ouyen United in the lead-up to the construction of the totem poles at Blackburn Park in 2009 [Paul Daffey]

Nine totem poles represent the clubs that folded into one during the years after World War 2 to create Ouyen United. The poles represent (from left) Tempy, Gorya, Patchewollock, Tempy-Gorya-Patchewollock, Ouyen United, Ouyen Rovers, Ouyen, Kiamal and Tiega [Paul Daffey]

Ouyen United full-forward Will Farrer soars over the McGlashan brothers Jarrod (left) and Liam, of Red Cliffs, to take a mark for the ages in the Sunraysia league in 2018 [Jo Morrish]

The scoreboard at Patchewollock has been unused since 1999. The ground now hosts sheepdog trials [Paul Daffey]

Greg Vallance mans the scoreboard at Underbool, which depicts a lead to Ouyen United early in the Kangas' match against Merbein in Round 10, 2018 [Paul Daffey]

Wedderburn premiership wingman Roger Paterson and Scooter take a break from reminiscing at the old Woosang Recreation Reserve [Paul Daffey]

Right: Horsham midfielder Brad Hartigan with the twelve premiership medals he earned with his home club during the sixteen seasons from 2003 to 2018 [Paul Daffey]

Below left: One of the wings at the Horsham City Oval is named after Max Burke, who was a Horsham trainer for fifty-five years [Paul Daffey]
Below right: Pines fans filled the terraced area near the social club on the northern wing at Frankston Park during the Mornington Peninsula Nepean league's 2018 Division 1 Grand Final [Paul Daffey]
Bottom: Boolarra's Cameron Dalrymple sizes up play during the Demons' home match against Yarragon in 2018 [Paul Daffey]

unnamed, while the interchange box in front of the stand has a sign across the lip of the roof that says, "Max Burke Wing". On the other side of the oval, the scoreboard is unnamed but the dugout in front of the scoreboard bears a small sign that says, "Hugh Avery Wing". It is unusual for two dugouts to be named after significant figures, while the grandstand, the scoreboard and the pavilion remain unnamed. I head upstairs to meet Demons stalwarts in the social rooms.

In the social rooms, I meet Brian "Mangler" Burke, who is enjoying a quiet drink with half a dozen old teammates while the training night gets under way on the oval outside. Brian, a burly man whose reflective conversation is at odds with his nickname, runs a painting business in Horsham. He is wearing white work pants and a polo shirt that are spattered with paint. Brian is the son of Max Burke, who I've just learnt has an interchange dugout named after him. Brian and his twin brother Greg were the second and third children of the eleven children in the family of Max Burke and his wife Val. Brian explains that his father was a trainer at the footy club for fifty-five years, from 1965 to 2010. Hugh Avery, the man honoured on the scoreboard wing, was a trainer at the club for thirty-five years. The two wings therefore are named after trainers who served the club for a combined total of ninety years.

Brian himself played with Horsham for a decade, from 1972 to 1982; he was the ruckman in the Demons' premiership teams in 1972 and 1974. For the last five years of his playing career, he was one of several Horsham footballers who went out to the Horsham and District league club Laharum, a club based at the northern end of the Grampians. A decade after he had finished as a player, Brian Burke coached Horsham for three years, from 1999 to 2001. He remains heavily involved at the club as a past player and coach. His son Jordyn has been a senior player with the Demons for the past decade.

When I broach the subject of premierships with Brian, he says it was not always the case that Horsham won flag after flag. After winning the premiership in the Wimmera league in 1938, Horsham plugged away for two decades while clubs like Ararat, Stawell and Warracknabeal scooped up the premierships. Horsham's fortunes turned around after the appointment of Col Wilson as captain-coach. Having played at full-back in Melbourne's 1959 VFL premiership team, Col Wilson was appointed captain-coach of Horsham before the next season. The Demons won a breakthrough premiership in Wilson's first year in charge, in 1960, and another premiership in 1962.

Before the 1966 season, Horsham appointed Garry Hamer as captain-coach. Hamer was originally from Lemnos in the Goulburn Valley league. He played fifty games with Geelong from 1961 to 1965 before taking the coach's job at Horsham. During the week, Hamer taught maths and science at Horsham Tech. In the summer, he was a fast bowler for the Horsham Cricket Club. In one season, he and Rex "Wrecker" McKenzie from Dimboola were the opening bowlers for a country Victorian team that hosted a touring England team in a match at the Horsham City Oval.

In the winter, Hamer was a superb leader of his football club. A big, athletic man, he drove his players towards achieving a certain level of fitness. Playing at centre half-forward, Hamer led the Demons to three premierships, in 1967, 1968 and 1970. Brian Burke says Hamer's four years as coach of the Demons marked a significant period. Not only did the club establish a culture of success; it also built the social rooms in which we are now standing, all through voluntary work from players and officials.

Many Horsham footballers would play in multiple premiership teams in the coming years. Many famous stories would arise. In 1972, the diminutive rover Peter Wood kicked 9.3 in the Grand Final, including eight goals from snaps, as Horsham defeated Ararat. In 1982, Peter "Dicky" Morrison, the winner of three medals for the best and fairest player in the league, was a late inclusion in Horsham's team for the Grand Final after hauling himself out of his sick bed. Dicky Morrison was best on ground as Horsham defeated Dimboola.

Horsham continued to figure in premiership calculations for another decade, until an official embezzled the club of many thousands of dollars. During the 1990s, the club's existence was in peril. Officials held merger talks with Horsham United, their co-tenants at the city oval, only to think better of it. The club held a crisis function at which 100 supporters each pledged $100. The $10,000 that was raised helped to ward off the threat of extinction.

Brad Hartigan started playing senior football at just the time when the Demons were emerging from their financial crisis. After rebounding from the hard times, the Demons became the most dominant force in country football. Horsham won ten flags in a row from 2003 to 2012 before stumbling in 2013. The next year, in 2014, Horsham won a flag against all odds. The Demons were also the underdogs in the 2017 and 2018 grand finals, but they won both of those matches as well, bringing their tally of premierships in this era to thirteen in sixteen seasons. Brad Hartigan missed only one of those thirteen winning grand finals, in 2007, because he was playing with North Ballarat in the VFL. He has played alongside his brother Jeremy in five premiership teams.

Brian Burke, leaning on a bench in the social rooms, describes Brad Hartigan as a skilful player with the capacity to play out every match. Brian says the Demons champion is also tough and unselfish, with the capacity to think his way through a game. If an opponent is enjoying a purple patch, Brad assigns himself to the dangerous player.

"He's not a game breaker," Burke says. "He accumulates. He's doing the same at the end of the game as he was at the start."

Brian Burke was especially proud when his son Jordyn Burke and Brad Hartigan were the co-coaches of the victorious team in 2014. The pair were lifelong friends. During the 2014 season, they employed the mantra that if an opposition team kicked two goals in a row, it must not be allowed to kick three. If the opposition kicked successive goals, Brad would become a tagger or a loose man in defence — whatever it took to curb the opposition's momentum. In 2018, Brad Hartigan and Jordyn Burke were no longer the club's coaches, but they still got a kick out of playing alongside each other in another premiership team.

The balcony in front of the bar offers a fine view across the Horsham City Oval on this warm Wimmera evening. When I walk on to the balcony to join half a dozen club luminaries, I am asked by one of the Horsham men whether I recognise the figure who is directing the under-seventeen team's session on the far wing. The figure is wearing the unlikely combination of jeans and footy boots. He has his back to us, and is a fair way off in the distance, but even so, I should have been able to recognise him by his distinctive gait.

"Of course," I say, when I am told that it is Shane Heard. The former Essendon midfielder, who was renowned for his punishing fitness regimen, had such a distinctive gait. Shane is one of four brothers who played tough, creative football for Horsham. Now, at the age of sixty, he still looks fit enough to be a footballer, and he still has his bandy gait. Apparently, Shane still works a speed ball like no one else in the Wimmera. His approach to fitness helps to set the tone for the club.

As the senior players dawdle on to the field to begin their training session, I meet two former club presidents: Laurie Taylor, the man who alerted me of Brad Hartigan's premiership tally, and Bruce Hartigan, who is the father of Brad Hartigan and a club legend himself. Laurie is in his courier gear. He has a contract with Australia Post. Bruce is dressed in jeans and a shirt. He runs a pub. Before long, another former president, Rod Dumesny, wanders on to the balcony. Rod is a businessman and farmer who lives just out of town.

Laurie Taylor is busy comparing the number of premierships overseen by the trio of presidents when he takes a call about the cricket presentation that is to be held in the rooms over the weekend. He shoots off to sort out a few details. Laurie's energy and drive appear to be one reason behind the success of the Horsham Football Club.

As Laurie goes about sorting out the cricket function, Bruce Hartigan and I watch training while he gives me an understated rundown of his family's history with the club. I later augment his rundown with details that I glean from a stained and battered centenary history of the club that Rod Dumesny lends me.

Bruce Hartigan's great-grandfather, Charlie Ward, was a member of the first Horsham teams after the club's formation in 1885. The Horsham Football Club included members of the Ward family through the years. A member of the Ward family, Violet Ward, married a footballer called John Hartigan. The couple had three sons, Jim, Dean and Jack Hartigan, who, in 1945, were all members of Horsham's senior team after the resumption of football following the war. The youngest, Jack, went down to Melbourne, where he played senior VFL football for Hawthorn and St Kilda. Jack was described in the Horsham newspaper as a left-footed midget star. He later returned to Horsham, and coached the club.

Jack Hartigan's sons, Dean and Bruce, were star footballers from a young age. Dean played in Horsham's 1972 premiership team as a seventeen-year-old before heading down to Essendon under the VFL's country zoning laws. He played senior footy with the Bombers before moving on to VFA club Coburg, where he became a VFA representative player.

His brother Bruce Hartigan, with whom I am standing on the balcony, remained in Horsham. A left-footer like his father, he played in the Horsham footy club's 1978 premiership team, and he was in the team that lost the 1981 Grand Final to Nhill in an upset. After that disappointment, Bruce took the job of playing-coach at Taylors Lake in the Horsham and District league. The club struggled in the newly expanded competition. After watching Horsham win that season's Grand Final in the Wimmera league, Bruce returned to his home club and played in the team that defeated Dimboola in the Grand Final the next season, in 1983. He later joined Brian Burke and other Demons teammates who had ventured out to Laharum. Bruce was a member of the Laharum team that won the Horsham and District league's Grand Final in 1987.

He then returned to Horsham and played in the Demons' 1989 and 1990 premiership teams, bringing his tally of senior premierships to five. He also coached Kalkee in the Horsham and District league for three years, but it was in off-field roles back at Horsham that he experienced a different side of football to the pleasure of playing in premiership teams with old mates.

Map 6: Wimmera

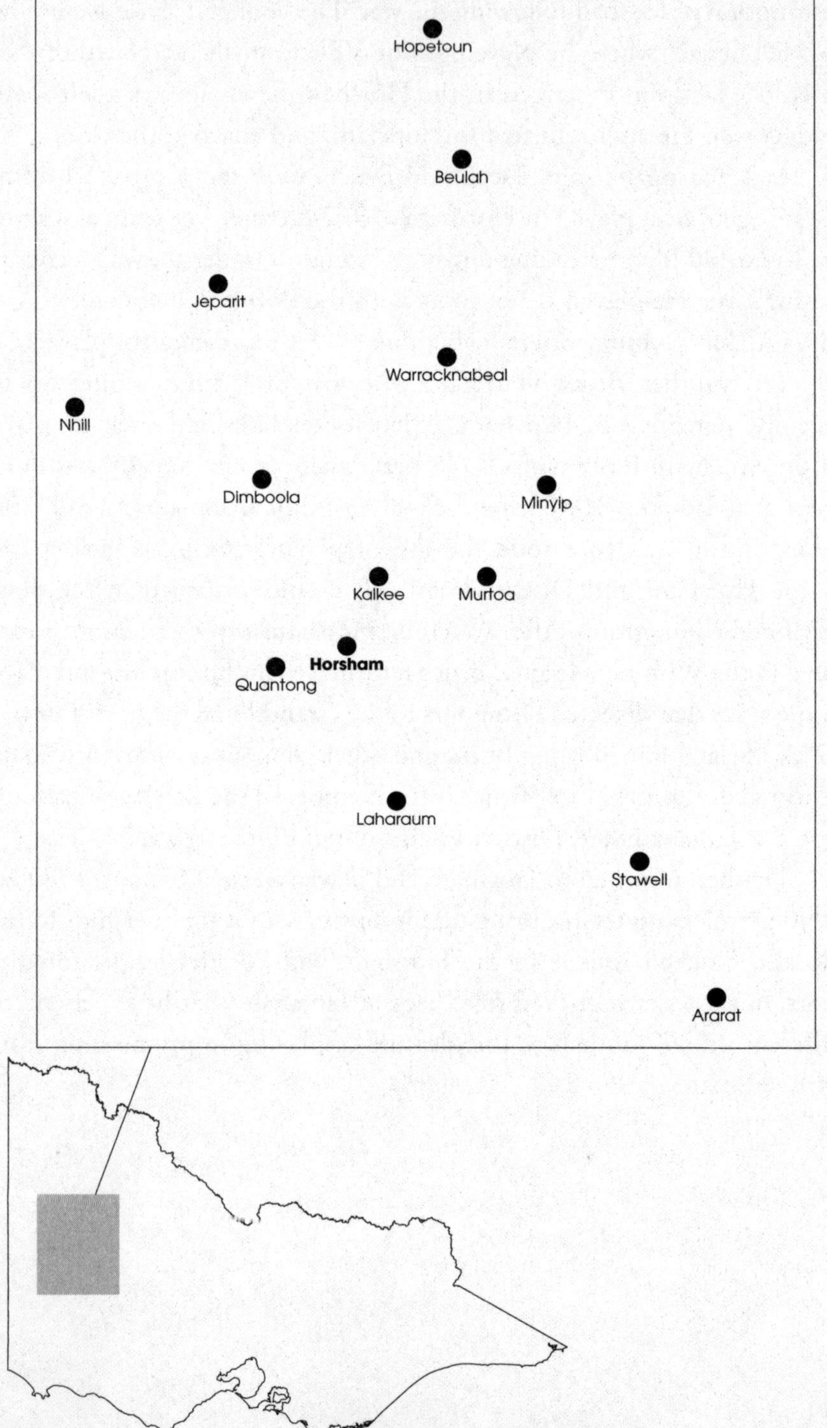

40

Hartigan's Haul

Most footballers believe there could be nothing more consuming than the desire to chase the ball, but Bruce Hartigan, the former Horsham champion, was among those who learnt that off-field matters can become even more consuming, especially during a crisis. Without the efforts of Bruce and others to revive the Horsham Football Club, there is no way that Bruce's son Brad Hartigan would have become one of the most feted footballers in country Victoria.

Bruce Hartigan was Horsham's coach in 1991 when the club spiralled into turmoil brought on by the embezzlement of many thousands of dollars. Amid the turmoil, the club sacked Bruce as coach. He left for Kalkee, the club based in a farming district to the north of Horsham, where he enjoyed coaching a club based in a strong community, but his heart remained with Horsham. The Demons were in disarray. In response to the persistent urgings of Horsham Football Club officials Jeff Both and Graeme O'Connor, Bruce Hartigan agreed to coach the Demons, with Jason Merlo as his co-coach. Before the 1996 season, in their attempt to lift Horsham back up the Wimmera league ladder, the two coaches spoke to 125 prospective recruits.

Under the direction of the well-known country football official Brendan Ryan, the structure of junior football in Horsham was overhauled in this period. Two junior clubs now fed into the Horsham Football Club. The junior clubs produced several talented players. The sons of former players who emerged in this period were also talented. With Bruce Hartigan and Jason Merlo as the co-coaches, the Demons introduced two highly talented teenagers, Luke Carr and Stuart Farr, to senior football. Both were what the club described as "sons of guns". Luke's father, Bruce "Whiskey" Carr, and Stuart's father, Denis "Seal" Farr, had won league and club best and fairest awards, and played in premiership teams. The inclusion of Luke Carr and Stuart Farr in the senior team during the coaching tenure of Bruce Hartigan and Jason Merlo, a tenure which lasted from 1996 to 1998, helped to establish the pattern for growth through talented youth.

By the turn of the century, with Bruce Hartigan now as president, the Horsham Football Club was back on its feet. In 2002, under the coaching of Guy Smith, the Demons rose up to what had been familiar territory until a decade previously; they rose towards the top of the ladder. Their opponents in the Preliminary Final were Warrack Eagles, a star-studded team that was riding a wave of momentum in its first season after the merger of Warracknabeal and the Mallee league club Brim. The Eagles defeated Horsham by one point. According to Guy Smith, the narrow loss in the 2002 Preliminary Final left his young Demons players hungry.

On this night at the Horsham City Oval, Guy Smith is watching training from the boundary line. He is now the club's high performance coach. When I ask the gathering on the balcony about Brad Hartigan's first senior game, which was midway through the 2003 season, the balcony men holler towards Smith about giving the definitive version of events.

Smith is a mechanic who runs a small business in town. He is wearing work boots, shorts and a high-viz shirt, and he still looks fit despite the fact that he retired as a footballer more than a decade ago. He explains that, during the 2003 season, he promoted two players from the under-seventeen team, Jye Smith and Brad Hartigan, because the senior team needed zip. "They made a huge difference from the first game," he says.

Jye Smith and Hartigan were both only sixteen years of age, but they held their spots for the rest of the season. In the final week of the season, they were selected in the team to play against Stawell in the 2003 Grand Final at the Anzac Memorial Oval in Warracknabeal. In that match, Horsham's centre half-back, Damien Skurrie, played one of the best games seen in a Wimmera league grand final. Skurrie took mark after mark, and drove the Demons into attack. Brad Hartigan and Jye Smith played their parts as Horsham won by twenty-five points, earning the club its first premiership for twelve years.

In Guy Smith's final year of his coaching tenure, in 2005, he assigned tagging roles to Brad Hartigan. In that year's Grand Final, against Dimboola, Smith gave Hartigan the job on Carl Lohde, who was a fly-in player from Darwin. Hartigan, still only nineteen years of age, withstood a battering from Dimboola opponents who were eager to break his tag. Hartigan stood his ground and made a strong contribution as the Demons won their third consecutive premiership.

Smith says Hartigan reprised his effort from the 2005 Grand Final more than a decade later, in 2017, when his poise and discipline helped to swing the match the Demons' way in the Grand Final against Minyip-Murtoa at the Horsham City Oval. Smith says Hartigan's performance against the Burras was typically selfless. "He's never been about accolades."

Back on the balcony, the men of Horsham agree that Brad Hartigan's most memorable performance in his twelve victorious grand finals was the victory over the Demons' hometown rivals, the Horsham Saints, in 2014 – despite the fact that he struggled to get the ball. Hartigan went into the game under an injury cloud. His right ankle was so swollen that he could not kick with his right foot. For most of the match, he was on and off the ground. Through a few acts of gritty leadership, he helped to inspire his team to a famous victory.

When I ask the men on the balcony the whereabouts of the Horsham Saints' home ground, Coughlin Park, Bruce Hartigan points north. "You can see the lights from here," he says, as the gathering dusk accentuates the glow over the Saints' ground. On the city oval in front of us, I count about thirty-five players going through their drills with impressive intensity. Brad

Hartigan is especially active, moving with purpose, and willing his teammates to greater effort. All players drip with sweat in the balmy conditions.

As I watch the Horsham session, I imagine there must be a far lesser turnout at the training sessions of rival clubs. With a population of almost 16,000, Horsham is the biggest town in the Wimmera region. According to the 2016 Census, the next biggest town with a club in the Wimmera league is Ararat, with a population of 8300, ahead of Stawell (5500), Warrracknabeal (2300) and Nhill (1800). Dimboola has 1400 people, while the towns that underpin the Minyip-Murtoa footy club, Minyip and Murtoa, have 400 and 750 people respectively. Hopetoun and Beulah, the towns that combined resources in 2015 to form the Southern Mallee Giants, have populations of 540 and 330 respectively.

While the smaller towns would rely almost entirely on agriculture for job opportunities, the opportunities are broader in a larger town like Horsham. On the balcony at the Horsham City Oval, the club's football manager, Terry Arnel, is an example of a footballer from a rural background who has moved to Horsham for work and then joined the Demons. Arnel played in a premiership with his home club, Birchip-Watchem, in 2001. After several years of courting by Horsham officials, he signed with the Demons. He ended up playing in eight premiership teams with his adopted club, mostly at full-back, while the club's greatest player in this era, David Johns, was at full-forward. The pair were the bookends in several premiership teams. Arnel is now the manager of an electrical firm that is one of the largest employers in Horsham.

After a sharp training session, Brad Hartigan joins me in the social rooms upstairs for an interview about his bountiful career. He is medium-sized and lightly framed, with thick, wavy hair. Now thirty-two years of age, he looks fit and trim. While there was a certain hunger to him during the training session, he has an easy manner off the field. He first strikes me as shy, but then I come to believe he's just understated. By not making a fuss, he is conserving energy for the things that count. He fetches a beer each for the two of us from the fridge behind the bar.

Midfielders who enjoy long careers often have strict training regimens, even at country level. Brad says his only extra work is a weekly bike ride during summer; on Saturday mornings, he joins a group that sets out from Horsham for a fifty-kilometre ride through country roads. He avoids running so as to ease the load on his ankles and knees. His job as a plumber means he is active enough. When I mention his intensity during training, he explains that he missed the session on Tuesday for family reasons. "So I was feeling fresh," he says.

Brad and his wife Lucy have two children, Eadie, 6, and Scout, 2. Lucy is an accomplished netballer with Horsham, so their journeys to Ararat, Nhill and elsewhere on winter weekends amount to family excursions. Brad's parents Bruce and Adele still love going to their games, adding to the sense of a family occasion. When I ask Brad whether he is a similar player to his father, he notes that Bruce was a left-footer. "And he was more of a goalkicker than me."

Bruce Hartigan was coaching Kalkee when Brad started playing footy in the Kees' junior team. According to Bruce, his son was so young that he spent his first match building sandcastles in the goalsquare. When I run this detail past Brad, he almost rolls his eyes, only to resist the urge and conserve his energy. "Dad likes that story," he says.

I would argue that most footballers have a clear recollection of their first senior game. Brad, however, is one of those who has no recollection at all. When I ask whether he at least remembers the feeling surrounding his first game, he thinks for a moment then says: "Being intimidated."

When Brad Hartigan was sixteen to twenty years of age, opponents often targeted him. When I ask whether any particular teams sought to punish him, he surprises me. Most footballers give a general answer to such a question, fearing a backlash if they nominate a rival. Brad sees no reason to be anything other than honest. He says Stawell and Dimboola were very physical.

"They tried to rough me up," he says.

Why?

"I don't know."

Brad remembers playing the last seven or eight games in the 2003 season before becoming a premiership player at sixteen years of age. He was too young to realise the scale of his achievement. He just played his heart out and was pleased with the rewards. In the coming years, he continued to play his heart out. The rewards continued to come.

Brad Hartigan wore No.9 in his first season but later swapped to No.20, which was the number worn by his father. His brother Jeremy, who has a larger build, played mostly at centre half-back.

Horsham teams in the early years of their premiership run were notable for their superior spines, with players like Terry Arnel and David Johns just too good for lesser opponents. As the years wore on, the club's emphasis switched to running power. The Demons achieved most of their premiership success during this era under the coaching of Stuart Farr. Brad Hartigan says Farr deserves huge credit for guiding his team through the club's greatest era.

As a player, Stuart Farr was renowned for his toughness and diligence. Before the 2006 season, he became a co-coach along with Damien Bunworth. After a few seasons of shared duties, Farr took the job on his own. In all, he played in nine premiership teams with Horsham, from 2003 to 2011, and he coached seven premiership teams, from 2006 to 2012. Brad Hartigan says he especially remembers Farr's performance in his last grand final as a player.

It was in 2011. Farr's ankle by then was shot. In the final quarter of the Grand Final against Warrack Eagles at Dimboola, the Eagles looked likely to finish over the top of Horsham. Stuart Farr, however, put the pain of his ankle injury to one side and willed himself to sprint past an Eagles defender. He pounced on the ball in the goalsquare and kicked a goal. It was the game's turning point. Horsham went on to win by twelve points and earn their ninth consecutive premiership.

Stuart Farr coached Horsham for one more season, in 2012, but he was unable to play in that season's Grand Final. He then went out to Dimboola before the 2013 season, and coached the Roos to victory over the Horsham Saints in the 2013 Grand Final.

In 2013, Brad Hartigan was twenty-six years of age when he took on the joint coaching role at Horsham with his childhood friend, Jordyn Burke. Brad says he enjoyed the challenge of leading the club while still trying to get a kick himself. In his first season as a co-coach, Horsham's premiership sequence ended at ten in a row, from 2003 to 2012, when they lost the 2013 Preliminary Final to Horsham Saints. The next year, in 2014, the Demons rediscovered their triumphant ways.

After defeating Warrack Eagles by two points in the 2014 Preliminary Final at Dimboola, the Horsham players returned to their clubrooms in Horsham to eat pizzas together. Brad Hartigan had badly rolled his ankle and could barely walk. He looked around the social rooms and saw a series of feet and legs immersed in ice buckets or encased in ice wraps. He wondered how his teammates were going to come up for their challenge against their hungry opponents, Horsham Saints. Since entering the competition twenty years earlier, the Saints had played in seven grand finals without success. The 2014 Grand Final at Stawell provided a golden chance for the Saints to break through.

Brad Hartigan was severely hampered throughout the game. In the last quarter, he planted himself at full-forward with a plan to simply soak up the attention of a key defender. His performance was redolent of Stuart Farr's effort in willing his team to victory in the Grand Final three years earlier, in 2011.

In the last quarter of the 2014 Grand Final, Horsham Saints had the wind, but they failed to finish off their attacks. The Demons got up to score an improbable victory by six points. While Brad Hartigan might have been unknowing during the early years of his premiership run, he savoured every second in the aftermath of the 2014 Grand Final.

In our interview in the social rooms after training, he nominates the 2014 premiership as his favorite in large part because he was one of the coaches, but also because the Demons were given little chance before the Grand Final. He says he also felt great satisfaction after the 2017 and 2018 grand finals because the victories in both games were also achieved against the odds. "And you don't know when it's going to be the last one."

During the course of our interview, Brad tells me that his brother Jeremy has moved to Echuca for work reasons, and now plays with Echuca United. Brad accepts a copy of my premiership list and raises his eye towards the top of the page. When he sees his name on the second line, he almost frowns. I am forced to admit that recently I have been alerted of a man from Omeo, high up in the hills in East Gippsland, in the opposite corner of the state, who has exceeded his tally of twelve premierships by one. I tell him about the late John Crisp, who was a great worker for his club long after he had finished playing. Brad withholds comment. I sense he'll be pushing hard for his thirteenth flag.

After the interview, Rod Dumesny, one of the former presidents, fetches out of his car his copy of the club's 1985 centenary book to help me clear up some of my questions. The book looks like it's been a beer coaster at every premiership celebration since its publication. I love it immediately.

I proceed along Firebrace Street towards my accommodation at the White Hart Hotel, the pub that Brad Hartigan's parents, Bruce and Adele, run in the town's main street. Adele is full of life. She expresses herself with a hearty joy to the same degree that Brad expresses himself with quiet confidence. Adele brings me out a bowl of risotto. Her hospitality is as warm as the evening outside.

While Bruce grew up in Horsham, Adele grew up on a farm near Quantong, just to the west of the town. The pair met as teenagers. As well as raising three children, they've been up to their neck in country footy throughout their lives. If not for the work of the Hartigan couple and a handful of others, the Horsham Football Club would have struggled to survive the stricken years of the 1990s.

The Hartigans' love for the Demons shines through in their stories about footballers. They tell me about Gary Chequer, a tough ruckman who compensated for his lack of height with application and vigour. They describe the talents of David "Legs" Burke, a brother of Brian "Mangler" Burke, whose long limbs gave rise to his nickname. Bruce says Legs was not much of a footballer until he reached eighteen years of age, after which he was a star. He left Horsham and headed down to Essendon, where he kicked five goals in his senior debut in 1980. Legs played only two more games with the Bombers, and returned home.

Their most affectionate stories revolve around the two trainers who have been honoured on the interchange boxes on the wings at the city oval. Adele brings out photos to show me Hugh Avery, whom everyone called Hughy, or "Ughy", in recognition of his habit of keeping the letter "h" to himself. Hughy also had a tendency to pronounce the letter "r" as "w". After one particular night of premiership celebrations, he began to ride his bike home along the path beside the Wimmera River. A player later found him asleep in the grass by the path.

The player asked the trainer what he was doing.

Hughy shook himself and looked up.

"Just having a west."

Bruce extricates himself from our table to return to the bar. On the television screen above our heads, the former Sydney champion Adam Goodes appears on the screen. Goodes has been in the news since the booing controversy that preceded his retirement. An overweight drinker with plenty of opinions but no sense of place declares that Goodes was all right until he lost his way. Bruce goes quiet. He continues to wipe down the bar. Adam Goodes ran the boundary for the Horsham senior team as a teenager. He showed promise when he made his senior debut. Then he joined the North Ballarat Rebels in the elite under-eighteen competition and his AFL journey was under way. Bruce says Goodes has never forgotten his roots.

"He still comes back here," he says. "And he always says hello – every time."

Bruce and Adele Hartigan continue working towards midnight. In their late fifties, an age when their peers are beginning to wind down, they are putting in seventy-hour weeks in an attempt to revive the fortunes of the pub. They believe that if you take something on, you do it to the best of your ability. You keep going until you can give no more. As Bruce bustles around the bar, I see why his son Brad has played in twelve premierships, and remains motivated to win more.

The next day, I head north for the purposes of research. I head to Kalkee, where I stop to look at the home ground of one of the few remaining clubs in Victoria to be based in a farming district. I head through Hopetoun, the original stronghold of Mallee football, before I reach Patchewollock, where Bryce the publican has done me the great honour of setting aside the honeymoon suite. I enjoy the banter around the horseshoe bar as Boozer Robertson, my tour guide from Tempy, beguiles visitors with his colourful tales. Simon Grigg, the former champ from Patchewollock, gives a speech of wandering charm before drawing the raffle. I'm not the winner. But of course I'm the winner. I've been on a wonderful journey into the heart of country footy. It's time for a Wyperfeld steak.

Acknowledgements

I would like to thank all members of my family for their support, especially Mum and Dad (Marie and Terry), and the children, Michael, Ellen and Leo. Also my brothers Mark, Luke and Phil, especially Mark, whose brilliant photos feature in the second photo insert.

I would like to think my proofreaders Andrew "Gigs" Gigacz and Vin Maskell, both of whom have been great friends and sounding boards on writing matters over the years.

The two main sounding boards on the Ouyen United chapters were Michael "Boozer" Robertson and Gerald "Gerry" Leach, both of whom are natural storytellers with wonderful eyes for detail. Their proofing work was significant.

I would like to thank Peter Healy, Bernie Kelly and Boozer Robertson for providing the impetus for this project, although none of them realised it at the time. Geoff van Wyngaarden offered advice on the project from beginning to end.

Peter Healy, Chris Brown, Mary Collins and Des "Speedie" Robertson were wonderfully generous in supplying photos, as well as a bank of stories during the handover of photos. Chris Brown, besides telling many stories and giving full access to his extensive collection of photos and memorabilia, was a great help with the appendices.

I would like to thank my friends Rod "Rocket" Gillett and Richard Jones. Our three-way chats about country footy never fail to enlighten and entertain. Rocket's influence on the draft for the book was profound, especially the early chapters. I cannot thank Rocket enough for his input in this regard.

I would also like to thank:

Merle Pole, the president of the Ouyen District History and Genealogy Centre, for her work at the centre and her encouragement of the book

Tim Brain from Beulah for helping out with the timeline of Mallee footy

Glenn McMahon, from countryfootyscores.com, for collating the best and fairest winners from each competition

Tom Mullane-Grant, the veteran full-forward as well as the sales and marketing director from the Bright Brewery, for helping out with supplies for the launch at short notice

Robin Letts from the *Buloke Times* for being one of the great men of country newspapers, but also for supplying the North Central league team for the 1974 country championships final.

I would like to thank the following for interviews and/or their help with the proofing of chapters:

Ouyen United: Chris Brown, Michael Brown, Max Crow, Jock Gibbins, Des Healy, Peter Healy, Laurie Kalms, Richie Kalms, Bernie Kelly, Jamie Latta, Gerry Leach, Donald McGregor, Bill Morrish, Nerida Morrish, Jarrod Munro, Brian O'Callaghan, Denis O'Callaghan, Michael Robertson, Lorraine Shaddock

Nathalia: Terry Kiley

Boolarra: Ann Carter, Paul Dodds, Tony Giardina, Keith Holmes

Mirboo North: Clancy Bennett, Steve Rogers

Mid-Gippsland league: Charlie Cauchi, Stan Kerrigan

Woosang and Wedderburn: Debbie Feeny, Roger Paterson

Inglewood: Howard Rochester, David Rose

Pines: Beau Hendry, Jeff Svigos

Sorrento: Bernie Balmer, Luke Tapscott

Horsham: Rod Dumesny, Brad Hartigan, Bruce and Adele Hartigan, Laurie Taylor.

I would like to thank the following for their help in compiling the premiership list:

Matt Ahern (Pakenham), Brent Alexander (Osborne), Sonya Alexander (Narre Warren), Troy Auld (Bridgewater), John Bance (Wagga Tigers), Darren Barker (Nullawil), Lauren Bills (Bairnsdale), Tony Blohm (Swan Hill), Tracey Boyce (Redan), Brendan Brooks (Cobram), Paul Busuttil (Frankston YCW), Mick Butler (Barooga), Bruce Calder (Chiltern), Tom Carroll (Ganmain), Jack Cedelland (Ganmain), Tracey Hinton (Orbost), Ron Cole (Warrnambool), Arthur Doddrell (Bairnsdale),

Craig Farrell (North Geelong), Travis Fursland (Bell Post Hill), Murray Frew (Bairnsdale), Raymond Gallagher (Swifts Creek), Merv Gaylor (Wycheproof-Narraport), Andy Gray (Kerang), Jason Harding (Fish Creek), Neil Hawkins (Simpson), Tony Hickey (Mildura Imperials), Jan Hickmott (Tyntynder), Kevin Hill (Wangaratta Rovers), Travis Hole (East Gambier), Stephen Hoy (Koroit), Lew Humphreys (Waaia), Terry Hunter (Traralgon), Frank Johnson (Cranbourne), Andrew Kelly (Sorrento), Ashley Lambert (Coleraine), John "Rowdy" Lappin (Chiltern), Nathan Lawless (Tungamah), Lisa Lee (Omeo), Andrew Livingstone (Traralgon), Don Livingstone (Fish Creek), Trevor Ludeman (Northern United), Anthony Lyons (Wagga Tigers), Tracey Mark (Nathalia), Bill McCann (South Barwon), Shawn McCormick (Golden Square), David McNamara (Mt Pleasant), Ian McTaggart (Ocean Grove), Jon Mock (Mundulla), Ken Moore (Ellinbank), Robert Newnham (Border-Walwa), Melissa Nihill (Mt Pleasant), Michael O'Beirne (Carngham-Linton), Brad Overend (Wy Yung), Tavis Perry (Rushworth), Dale Purcell (North Shore), Stanley "Digger" Roberts (North Ballarat), Wayne Robbins (Minyip), Adam Salmon (South Gambier), Glen Scholtes (Calivil United), Jarad Smith (Caliivil United), Michael Spalding (Ararat), Andrew Stuart (Jindera), Laurie Taylor (Horsham), Ken Townrow (Nullawil), Bill Traill (Maffra), Graham Treloar (Pakenham), Ashley Walpole (Woodside), Eric Walpole (Woodside), Craig Waters (Upwey-Tecoma), Kathy Wittingham (Lindenow South).

Bibliography

Country footy books

Danny Lannen (editor), *Wheatbelt Warriors: A Tribute to the Wimmera Football League*, Wimmera Mail-Times, 2001

Adam McNicol, *Marching On: 85 Years of Football in the Manangatang District, 1914-1999*, Manangatang Football Club Back-to Committee, 2000

Peter Lines, *South Australian Country Football Digest: Volume 2*, Peter Lines, 2017

David Rose, *Bothumpian Blues: 140 Years of the Inglewood Football Netball Club*, Inglewood Football Netball Club, 2016

Laurie Williams and Cliff Greenwood, *From the Ashes: A History of the Mid Gippsland Football League 1935-1985*, Mid Gippsland Football League, 1985

Country footy booklets

Simon Grigg (club president), *TGP: Tempy-Gorya-Patchewollock 1971-1996*, Tempy-Gorya-Patchewollock Football Club, 2014

Bill Morrish and Jock Gibbins (editors), *Tiega Football Club: 1910-1981*, Tiega Football Club, 1981

Howard Rochester (editor), *Inglewood Football Club 1876-2001: 125th Anniversary and Team of the Century*, Inglewood and District Historical Society, 2001

Frank C. Simpson (committee chairman), *Horsham Football Club Centenary* 1885-1985, Horsham Football Club Centenary Committee, 1985

Greg Vallance (club president), *20 Year Reunion: 1982-2002*, Walpeup-Underbool Football Netball Club, 2002

Footy books

Geoffrey Blainey, *A Game of Our Own: The Origins of Australian Football*, Black Inc, 2004

Ashley Browne (editor), *Grand Finals, Volume 1: 1897-1938*, Slattery Media Group, 2011

Ashley Browne (editor), *Grand Finals, Volume 2: 1939-1978*, Slattery Media Group, 2012

Rob Hess and Bob Stewart (editors), *More Than a Game: An Unauthorised History of Australian Rules Football*, Melbourne University Press, 1998

Robert Pascoe, *The Winter Game: The Complete History of Australian Football*, Text Publishing, 1995

Other books

Geoffrey Blainey, *Our Other Side of the Country: The Story of Victoria*, Methuen Haynes, 1984

Hugh Carroll, *Mallee Roots to Vanilla Slices: Ouyen – One Hundred Years*, Ouyen Centenary Book Committee, 2009

Alfred S. Kenyon, *The Story of the Mallee*, Victorian Historical Magazine, Volume IV, 1914-1915

Robert Lee, *The Railways of Victoria: 1854-2004*, Melbourne University Publishing, 2007

Jocelyn Lindner, *Murrayville 1910-2007: A History of the Development of Murrayville and District*, Murrayville Liaison Committee, 2007

Jennifer McLennan, *Time, Tide and the Tyrrell: A History of the Shire of Wycheproof*, Hargreen Publishing Company, 1994

Winifred M. Nixon, *While the Mallee Roots Blaze: The Story of Berriwillock*, Back-to Berriwillock Committee, 1965

John Pickard, *Victorian Historical Journal*, Volume 90, Number 1, "The Victorian Mallee Fence", Royal Historical Society of Victoria, 2019

Ian J. Wemyss, *A Brief History of Inglewood*, Inglewood and District Historical Society, 1973

Appendix 1

1.1 Ouyen United

At the game

Sunraysia FL, Round 10, 2018

Ouyen United 18.19 (127) d Merbein 7.6 (48)

Underbool Recreation Reserve

Goals – Ouyen United: T. Morrish 5; Aron Morrish 4; Jamar, Latta, Healy, Palmer 2; J. Mead; **Merbein:** Harradine 2; Dorman, Wilson, Holmes, Mazza, Sedgman.

Best – Ouyen United: Gregg, Grigg, T. Morrish, Aron Morrish, J. Mead, Jardine. **Merbein:** Rogers, Frankel, Bregeut, Andrews, Sedgman, Cavallo

Premiership teams

North West Mallee FL, 1946 Grand Final

Underbool 10.12 (72) d Danyo 5.9 (39)

Tutye Recreation Reserve

Underbool, 1946 premiership team

B: R. Lewis, L. Whisson, A. Pryse

HB: D. Pryse, W. Kilpatrick, L. Stone

C: J. Klyne, L. Robinson, W. Aikman

HF: E. Stone, L. Zibell, E. Elliott

F: J. Mossop, I. Renkin, L. Wandell

Foll: R. Brown, T. Jackson, K. Renkin

Ouyen District FL, 1947 Grand Final

Ouyen 10.10 (70) d Tempy 6.7 (43)

Ouyen Recreation Reserve

Ouyen, 1947 premiership team

B: R. Chisholm, A. Eldridge, K. Vallance

HB: P. Floyd, J. Floyd, G. Cameron

C: M. Emmett, C. Smith, W. Kemp

HF: J. Clark, W. Golding, R. McKay

F: A. Leiper, K. Floyd, H. Sporn

Foll: J. Mills, I. Johnston,. J. Baker

19th: W. Emmett; 20th: W. Steele

Mallee FL, 1960 Grand Final
Walpeup 14.20 (104) d Ouyen 9.7 (61)
Blackburn Park, Ouyen
Walpeup, 1960 premiership team
B: A. Kruss, D. Zanker, A. Munro
HB: B. Woodall, B. Sheahan, L. Latta
C: N. Latta, R. Gregg, G. Raeck
HF: K. Logan, D. Bell, T. Blandthorn
F: A. Mann, H. Woodall, N. Stone
Foll: K. McSwain, A. Wakefield
Rover: C. Tuohey
19th: R. Schubert, 20th: W. Woodall

Mallee FL, 1967 Grand Final
Tiega d Murrayville, scores unavailable
Blackburn Park, Ouyen
Tiega, 1967 premiership team
B: A. Bennett, J. Pengelly, R. Drendel
HB: T. Monaghan, H. Shaddock, M. Gibbins
C: E. Shaddock, W. Morrish, K. Shaddock
HF: W. Morrish, D. O'Callaghan, B. O'Callaghan
F: B. Weir, M. McKay, B. Phelan
Foll: K. Karpavicius, J. Gibbins, R. Parsons.
19th: B. McIntyre; 20th: W. Scott

Mallee FL, 1968 Grand Final
Walpeup 19.17 (131) d Tiega 7.16 (58)
Blackburn Park, Ouyen
Walpeup, 1968 premiership team
B: N. Blandthorn, G. Wakefield, D. Alger
HB: A. Lee, G. Pengelly, G. Williams
C: T. Fraser, D. Pohlner, J. Logan
HF: D. Gniel, B. Gniel, D. Blandthorn
F: S. Stone, R. Latta, H. Ferguson
Foll: K. McSwain, M. Ferguson, N. Latta
19th: R. Raeck; 20th: R. Billing

Mallee FL, 1971 Grand Final
Kiamal 14.9 (93) d Tiega 8.16 (64)
Blackburn Park, Ouyen

Kiamal, 1971 premiership team
B: R. Hickmott, D. Thompson, R. Marks
HB: R. Pohlner, W. Munro, F. O'Callaghan
C: K. Munro, P. Munro, L. Christie
HF: R. Perry, L. O'Callaghan, D. Pohlner
F: S. Thompson, G. Kay, P. Kay
Foll: S. McArthur, R. Dixon, B. Loxton
19th: L. Finch; 20th: P. McDougall

Mallee FL, 1975 Grand Final
Underbool 22.20 (152) d TGP 21.16 (142)
Blackburn Park, Ouyen
Underbool, 1975 premiership team
B: R. Gloster, K. Brown, K. Stone
HB: P. McDermott, G. Crow, J. Morrison
C: D. Aikman, W. Morrish, M. Brown
HF: G. Hayter, M. Crow, W. Aldous
F: R. Stone, C. Brown, R. Cummings
Foll: D. Brown, P. Stone, S. Stone
19th: R. Elliott; 20th: P. Aikman

Mallee FL, 1978 Grand Final
Walpeup 23.11 (149) d d Ouyen 22.14 (146)
Blackburn Park, Ouyen
Walpeup, 1978 premiership team
B: L. Stone, G. Pryse, R. O'Shannessy
HB: B. Kotch, B. Gniel, R. Lester
C: K. Stone, Bob Latta, G. Leach
HF: H. Bell, M. Ferguson, P. Greenham
F: D. Blandthorn, Roy Latta, N. Blandthorn
Foll: J. Pryse, M. Woodall, S. Stone
19th: G. Stratford, 20th: W. Matthews

Northern Mallee FL, 1987 Grand Final
Ouyen Rovers 11.13 (79) d TGP 8.19 (67)
Blackburn Park, Ouyen
Ouyen Rovers, 1987 premiership team
B: N. Warren, P. Young, D. Maw
HB: J. Plozza, I. Clark, P. Morrish
C: D. Briggs, M. Donaghy, D. Ryan

HF: R. Hahnel, R. Marks, G. Murphy
F: K. Maginness, A. Manley, P. Taylor
Ruck: T. Cook, M. Steele, S. Locke
Inter: M. Pohlner, I. Stacey

Northern Mallee FL, 1993 Grand Final
Ouyen Rovers 13.12 (90) d Beulah 12.11 (83)
Blackburn Park, Ouyen
Ouyen Rovers, 1993 premiership team
B: M. Donaghy, R. Morrish, C. Shaddock
HB: A. Munro, R. Marks, I. Stacey
C: D. O'Callaghan, S. Manley, C. O'Callaghan
HF: C. McLeish, T. Cook, M. Bursill
F: B. Hahnel, M. Peterson, R. O'Connor
Ruck: L. Mason, M. Mellington, J. Cresp
Inter: J. Scott, R. O'Callaghan

Mallee FL, 1998 Grand Final
Ouyen United 21.16 (142) d Beulah 13.12 (90)
Woomelang Recreation Reserve
Ouyen United, 1998 premiership team
B: G. Munro, S. Whitty, S. Anderson
HB: J. Kay, D. Smith, A. Robertson
C: H. Bell, J. Munro, W. Grace
HF: S. Robertson, D. Munro, D. Burns
F: L. Monaghan, R. O'Callaghan, C. McKay
Ruck: T. Mellington, M. Mellington, T. White
Inter: K. Curran, J. Shean

Mallee FL, 2001 Grand Final Rematch
Walpeup-Underbool 13.10 (88) d Berri-Culgoa 10.12 (72)
Hopetoun Recreation Reserve
Walpeup-Underbool, 2001 premiership team
B: Marcus Brown, J. Wakefield, M. Baker
HB: A. Willsmore, T. Latta, K. Munro
C: T. Brown, S. Munro, D. Boseley
HF: B. Kelly, D. O'Shannessy, L. Crow
F: R. Willsmore, J. Brown, Matt Brown
Ruck: M. Pole, D. Latta, B. Montgomery
Inter: S. Ovenden, C. Wandel, S. Brown

Mallee FL, 2007 Grand Final
Walpeup-Underbool 13.10 (88) d Ouyen United 10.18 (78)
Beulah Recreation Reserve
Walpeup-Underbool, 2007 premiership team
B: A. Willsmore, V. Noonan, J. Wakefield
HB: D. Brown, P. Brown, C. Lynch
C: T. Latta, L. Nathan, D. Latta
HF: T. Vallance, D. O'Shannessy, M. Palmer
F: J. Charles, M. Brown, C. Vorwerk
Ruck: M. Pole, J. Stone, S. Munro
Inter: R. Stone, M. Lynch, A. Brown

Mallee FL, 2011 Grand Final
Ouyen United 17.14 (116) d Sea Lake-Nandaly Tigers 8.12 (60)
Woomelang Recreation Reserve
Ouyen United, 2011 premiership team
B: J. Coates, B. Jardine, J. Langdon
HB: D. Jardine, A. Jardine, A. O'Callaghan
C: B. Mole, G. Joyce, K. O'Shannessy
HF: D. Healy, B. Vallance, B. Knowles
F: W. Grace, R. Lindsey, R. O'Callaghan
Ruck: C. Deckert, M. Hahnel, P. Caldow
Inter: T. Barker, D. Leach, Alex Morrish

Sunraysia FL, 2016 Grand Final
Ouyen United 16.10 (106) d Mildura 11.11 (77)
City Oval, Mildura Recreation Reserve
Ouyen United, 2016 premiership team
B: Z. McGlynn, K. Barker, Alex Morrish
HB: M. Palmer, A. Jardine, D. Jardine
C: D. Fishwick, M. Hahnel, T. Morrish
HF: J. Farrer, B. Vallance, Kane Munro
F: M. Healy, W. Farrer, D. Staunton
Ruck: L. Brandy, H. Armour, J. Roe-Duggan
Inter: Aron Morrish, B. Summerhayes, J. McGlynn

Sunraysia FL, 2018 Grand Final
Ouyen United 10.11 (71) d Irymple 10.6 (66)
City Oval, Mildura Recreation Reserve

Ouyen United, 2018 premiership team
B: R. Monaghan, K. Barker, M. Taylor
HB: J. Grigg, A. Jardine, Alex Morrish
C: S. Mead, B. Vallance, M. Palmer
HF: J. Farrer, T. Latta, T. Morrish
F: D. Gregory, M. Healy, W. Farrer
Ruck: M. Jamar, J. Gregg, D. Staunton
Inter: T. Barker, Aron Morrish, S. Brown

Interleague teams

Ouyen District FL 14.16 (100) d North Central 11.7 (73)
Donald Recreation Reserve, July 1947
Ouyen District FL, 1947 team
B: P. Monaghan (Kiamal), A. Eldridge (Ouyen), J. Healy (Tiega)
HB: G. Burns (Tempy), G. Wakefield (Walpeup), R. Burns (Tempy)
C: W. Hickmott (Kiamal), C. Smith (Ouyen), D. Lynch (Patchewollock)
HF: K. McMahon (Tiega), J. Moylan (Kiamal), S. Healy (Walpeup)
F: M. Young (Patchewollock), H. Robertson (Tempy), L. Newell (Goyra)
Foll: J. Mills (Ouyen), S. Lynch (Gorya), J. Baker (Ouyen)
19th: J. Vallance (Walpeup); 20th: K. Johnson (Gorya)

Mallee FL 6.12 (48) d Sunraysia FL [2] 5.10 (40)
No.1 Oval, Mildura, July 1973
Mallee FL, 1973 team
B: D. Brown (Underbool), J. Chant (Tiega), W. Matthews (Ouyen)
HB: F. O'Callaghan (Kiamal), W. Munro (Kiamal), D. Healy (Tiega)
C: E. Shaddock (Tiega), D. Pohlner (Kiamal), A. Peters (TGP)
HF: G. Hosking (Kiamal), P. Chitty (Kiamal), G. Robertson (TGP)
F: N. Blandthorn (Walpeup), G. John (Tiega), K. Sleep (Tiega)
Foll: S. Thompson (Kiamal), P. Short (Ouyen), B. O'Callaghan (Tiega)
19th: W. Morrish (Tiega), L. Morrish (Tiega)

VCFL Championships Final, 1974
North Central FL 14.5 (89) d Hampden FL 10.10 (70)
Reid Oval, Warrnambool
North Central FL, 1974 championship team
B: L. Grose (Charlton, North Central FL), J. Connelly (Birchip, North Central FL), K. Andrews (St Arnaud, North Central FL)
HB: J. Forster (Wedderburn, North Central FL), M. Gilmour (Donald, North Central FL), J. White (Ouyen, Mallee FL)

C: A. Wills (Wedderburn, North Central FL), J. Vallance (Watchem-Corack, North Central FL), R. Evans (Charlton, North Central FL)
HF: M. Wood (St Arnaud, North Central FL), H. Delahunty (Donald, North Central FL), B. Gniel (Walpeup, Mallee FL)
F: K. Rayner (Wedderburn, North Central FL), J. Jess (St Arnaud, North Central FL), G. Robertson (Tempy-Gorya-Patchewollock, Mallee FL)
Foll: R. Green (Donald, North Central FL), D. Hindson (Charlton, North Central FL), K. Sait (Charlton, North Central FL)
19th: R. Latta (Walpeup, Mallee FL); 20th: C. Brown (Kiamal, Mallee FL)

Southern Mallee FL 22.17 (149) d Mallee FL 22.10 (142)
Blackburn Park, Ouyen, July 1978
Mallee FL, 1978 team
B: K. Jolly (TGP), B. Gniel (Walpeup), G. Barker (Kiamal)
HB: M. Ferguson (Walpeup), J. White (Ouyen), K. Brown (Underbool)
C: P. Caldow (Ouyen), R. Vallance (Ouyen), A. Peters (TGP)
HF: R. Latta (Walpeup), R. Dixon (Ouyen), M. Robertson (TGP)
F: N. Blandthorn (Walpeup), C. Brown (TGP), D. Brown (Ouyen)
Foll: P. Short (Ouyen), C. Lockett (Underbool), R. Payne (Underbool)
19th man: C. Young (TGP); 20th: I. Bloomfield (Ouyen)

Southern Mallee FL 12.18 (90) d Northern Mallee FL 12.9 (81)
Lord Nelson Park, St Arnaud, May 1979
Northern Mallee FL, 1979 team
B: K. Jolly (TGP), K. Giddings (Sea Lake), G. Barker (Kiamal)
HB: K. Brown (Underbool), K. Curran (Manangatang), S. Mallet (Kiamal)
C: L. Morris (Manangatang), W. Carmichael (Tiega), I. Stacey (Nandaly)
HF: G. McMillan (Nandaly), B. Gniel (Walpeup), P. Roberts (Nandaly)
F: P. Louttit (Sea Lake), C. Brown (TGP), J. Burns (TGP)
Ruck: J. Pryse (Walpeup), S. Grigg (TGP), M. Burns (TGP)
Inter: G. Young (TGP), D. Ryan (Tiega)

Canberra AFL 21.24 (150) d VCFL 14.10 (94)
Manuka Oval, Canberra, June 1980
Victorian Country Football League, 1980 team
B: P. Sheen (Warrnambool, Hampden FL), B. Symes (Benalla, Ovens & Murray FL), P. Brown (North Ballarat, Ballarat FL)
HB: K. Adams (Swan Hill, Mid-Murray FL), I. Salmon (Leongatha, Latrobe Valley FL), V. Hugo (Narrandera, South West District FL)

C: C. Walker (Shepparton, Goulburn Valley FL), J. Gieschen (Maffra. Latrobe Valley FL), M. Robertson (Woomelang-Lascelles, Southern Mallee FL)
HF: G. Mountjoy (Golen Square, Bendigo FL), M. Delahunty (Murtoa, Wimmera FL), R. Ballingall (Warragul. Latrobe Valley FL)
F: J. Wright (East Gambier. Western Border FL), R. Best (Golden Square, Bendigo FL), R. Haring (Rochester, Goulburn Valley FL)
Ruck: A. Southcombe (Golden Square, Bendigo FL), G. Moyle (Hamilton, Western Border FL), R. Weightman (South Mildura, Sunraysia FL)
Inter: G. Nichols (Turvey Park, South West District FL), R. Rendell (Kerang, Northern District FL), D. Gilmour (Donald, North Central FL)

VFL/AFL players

Gorya
Jim Jones, **Carlton:** 1939-1940, 1945-1946, 15 games, 1 goal

Kattyoong
Hugh Carroll, **North Melbourne:** 1932, 9 games, 1 goal

Kulwin
Kevin Curran, **Richmond:** 1943-1945, 16 games, 28 goals

Murrayville
Dave Duff, **Melbourne:** 1926, 11 games, 26 goals
Kieran Sporn, **Essendon:** 1989-1993, 72 games, 65 goals; **Fitzroy:** 1994, 12 games, 6 goals; Total: 1989-1994, 84 games, 71 goals
Trent Sporn, **Carlton:** 2002-2006, 50 games, 8 goals

Ouyen
Ron McDonald, **Richmond:** 1955-1960, 92 games, 84 goals

Ouyen Imperials
Jack Clements, **Hawthorn:** 1936-1937, 7 games, 6 goals

Ouyen Rovers I
Bill Blair, **Geelong:** 1935, 2 games, 0 goals

Ouyen Rovers II
Wayne Campbell, **Richmond:** 1991-2005, 297 games, 172 goals
Paul Morrish, **Richmond:** 1986, 1989: 4 games, 0 goals; **Essendon:** 1991, 7 games, 0 goals; **Fitzroy:** 1992-1993, 20 games, 1 goal; Total: 31 games, 1 goal

Patchewollock

Hugh Torney, **Essendon:** 1933-1943, 173 games, 81 goals

Pier Milan

Bill Ford, **Richmond:** 1927, 1 game, 1 goal; **Hawthorn:** 1934-1937, 56 games, 38 goals; Total: 1927, 1934-1937, 57 games, 39 goals

Frank Ford, **Richmond:** 1931, 16 games, 11 goals; **Essendon:** 1932-1933, 21 games, 26 goals; Total: 37 games, 37 goals

Tempy

George Archibald, **Melbourne:** 1941-1945, 47 games, 5 goals

Keith Robertson, **North Melbourne:** 1957-1958, 1960-1963, 69 games, 9 goals

Tempy-Gorya

Gordon Casey Junior, **Carlton:** 1968, 1 game, 1 goal; **Footscray:** 1969-1975, 125 games, 5 goals; Total: 1968-1975, 126 games, 6 goals

Tempy-Gorya-Patchewollock

Trevor Poole, **Richmond:** 1984-1989, 99 games, 56 goals; **Geelong:** 1990-1993, 54 games, 34 goals; Total: 1984-1993, 153 games, 90 goals

Tiega

Ernst Nunn, **Footscray:** 1929-1931, 26 games, 19 goals; **Collingwood:** 1932, 5 games, 1 goal; Total: 1929-1932, 31 games, 20 goals

Denis O'Callaghan, **Collingwood:** 1968-1973, 1975, 129 games, 3 goals

Torrita

Jack Logan, **Footscray:** 1946-1948, 31 games, 14 goals

Tutye

Wally Kelly, **Footscray:** 1933-1935, 1938, 22 games, 3 goals

Walpeup

Dennis Bell, **Collingwood:** 1961, 2 games, 1 goal

John Bell, **Collingwood:** 1969, 2 games, 0 goals

Walpeup-Underbool

Kane Munro, **West Coast:** 2000-2003, 18 games, 11 goals

Dallas Willsmore, **Hawthorn:** 2017, 2 games, 0 goals

Underbool

Max Crow, **Essendon:** 1974, 1976-1982, 136 games, 139 goals; **St Kilda:** 1983-1985, 40 games, 53 goals; **Footscray:** 1986, 12 games, 18 goals; Total: 1974, 1976-1986, 188 games, 210 goals

1.2 Nandaly

Premiership team

Northern Mallee FL, 1979 Grand Final

Nandaly 18.12 (120) d Manangatang 14.13 (97)

Blackburn Park, Ouyen

Nandaly, 1979 premiership team

B: P. Stacey, G. McMillan, T. Kiley

HB: T. Ryan, B. Woodburn, A. Larmour

C: L. Woodburn, P. Roberts, I. Stacey

HF: N. Peucker, G. Conlan, P. Walters

F: B. Irwin, D. Walters, C. Woodburn

Foll: W. McInerney, G. Burns, T. Monaghan

Inter: M. Kiley, P. Kiley

VFL/AFL players

Nandaly

Geoff McMillan, **Richmond:** 1978-1979, 11 games, 5 goals

Greg Conlan, **Richmond:** 1983-84, 6 games, 3 goals

1.3 Boolarra, Mirboo North

At the games

Mid-Gippsland FL, Round 12, 2018

Mirboo North 11.12 (78) d Morwell East 3.9 (27)

Walter Tuck Reserve, Mirboo North

Goals – Mirboo North: J. Robertson 3; L. Palmer, L. Powell, B. Wilson 2; Z. Kilgower, J. Taylor; **Morwell East:** F. Marks, P. Henry, S. Lambert.

Best – Mirboo North: J. Brooks, H. Kerr, J. Taylor, J. Blackford, M. Wightman, L. Powell; **Morwell East:** F. Marks, B, Francis, R Michaelides, D. Field, A. Brown, J. Lont.

Boolarra 2.2 (14) lt **Yarragon** 12.12 (84)

Boolarra Recreation Reserve

Goals – Yarragon: M. Jolly, S, Smith, B. Wolfe, P. Carmody 2; B. Neve, P. Harvey, M. Whyte, T. Follet; **Boolarra:** M. Cleaver 2.
Best – Yarragon: M. Whyte, A. Budge, B. Wolfe, P. Carmody, S. Smith, B. Neve; **Boolarra:** M. Windsor, J. Holmes, S. Mazou, J. Giardina, T. Beamish, D. Wilson.

Premiership teams

Mid Gippsland FL, 1997 Grand Final
Boolarra 20.10 (130) d Newborough 16.13 (109)
Ronald Reserve, Morwell
Boolarra, 1997 premiership team
B: T Evans, D. Smith, D. Thomas
HB: P. Gridley, B. Richards, S. Mayer
C: Z. Lutton, M. Kaser, B. Stoops
HF: D. Luff, T. Traill, A. Marino
F: J. Harry, S. Julin, J. Mayer
Ruck: H. Forbes, R. Arranz, S, Rutjens
Inter: C. Flanagan, D. Reiske, S. Gourley

Mid-Gippsland FL, 2007 Grand Final
Mirboo North 11.18 (84) d Yinnar 11.7 (73)
Ted Summerton Reserve, Moe
Mirboo North, 2007 premiership team
B: R. Kelly, D. Gardener, B. Dalliston
HB: C. Bennett, S. Keel, S. Wallace
C: D. Turner, P. Mongta, H. Schaeche
HF: D. Pinneri, K. Berchtold, S. Renwick
F: B. Palmer, T. Traill, T. Hamilton
Ruck: D. Webb, S. Busuttil, N. Bickerton
Inter: P. Magyar, D. Banks, S. Rogers

Mid Gippsland FL, 2011 Grand Final
Boolarra 13.4 (82) d Trafalgar 8.5 (53)
Ted Summerton Reserve, Moe
Boolarra, 2011 premiership team
B: S. Fox, J. Cargill, R. Kelly
HB: J. Dyer. V. Corbett, D. Metcalf
C: C. Sheriff, J. McFarlane, C. Risely
HF: D. Wilson, S. Boddy, R. Fox
F: B. Appleby, K. Towt, A. Thorpe
Ruck: T. Leys, M. Dyer, M. Cleaver
Inter: S. Buglisi, J. Holmes, T. Salerno

Mid-Gippsland FL, 2017 Grand Final
Mirboo North 5.12 (42) d Yinnar 5.10 (40)
Morwell Recreation Reserve
Mirboo North, 2017 premiership team
B: L. Palmer, P. Taylor, B. Richards
HB: C. Bennett, J. Blackford, J. Blair
C: H. Kerr, J. Nash, D. Turner
HF: R. Oddy, Z. Kilgower, J. Robertson
F: J. Taylor, T. Traill, B. Wilson
Ruck: J. Brooks, D. Pinneri, D. Mayman
Inter: B. Ridgway, D. Taylor, M. Wightman

VFL/AFL players

Boolarra
Danny Morgan, **Essendon:** 1995-1997, 16 games, 2 goals

Mirboo North
Leo Dobrigh, **Melbourne:** 1920, 1 game, 0 goals; **Richmond:** 1923, 2 games, 0 goals: Total: 1920, 1923, 3 games, 0 goals
Roy Farmer, **St Kilda:** 1914, 8 games, 2 goals
Daniel Harris, **North Melbourne:** 2001-2009, 149 games, 44 goals; **Gold Coast:** 2011, 11 games, 2 goals; Total: 2001-2009, 2011, 160 games, 46 goals
Jack Mathews, **North Melbourne:** 1941, 3 games, 1 goal
Michael Patterson, **Richmond:** 1959-1969, 152 games, 73 goals
Ted Shiels, **Fitzroy:** 1929, 3 games, 0 goals
Bill Snell, **Essendon:** 1950-1952, 36 games, 16 goals
Percy Watson, **Essendon:** 1920, 1 game, 0 goals
Jason Winderlich, **Essendon:** 2003-2015, 129 games, 83 goals

1.4 Woosang, Wedderburn

Premiership teams

North Central FL, 1968 Grand Final
Wedderburn 16.10 (106) d Watchem-Corack 14.11 (95)
Lord Nelson Park, St Arnaud
Wedderburn, 1968 premiership team
B: M. Jackson, F. Kelly, R. Steel
HB: H. Jackson, L. Gould, M. Bradley
C: R. Connelly, S. Monti, R. Paterson
HF: M. Gould, R. Jackson, R. Anderson
F: T. Kirk, L. Chalmers, C. Smith

Foll: R. Galvin, J. Plim, G. Allen
19th: R. Sutton; 20th: I. Jackson

North Central FL, 1970 Grand Final
Wedderburn 17.10 (112) d Charlton 11.5 (71)
Lord Nelson Park, St Arnaud
Wedderburn, 1970 premiership team
B: S. Monti, L. Judd, L. Rowe
HB: R. Jones, L. Gould, B. Taylor
C: L. Learmonth, J. Rohan, R. Paterson
HF: M. Gould, R. Steel, R. Jackson
F: L. Astbury, A. Jackson, R. Connelly
Foll: R. Galvin, D. Maxwell, R. Sutton
19th: B. Andrews; 20th: T. Kirk

VFL/AFL players

Wedderburn
Creswell "Mickey" Crisp, **Carlton:** 1931-1941, 183 games, 281 goals
Gordon Crisp, **Carlton:** 1936, 1938: 8 games, 3 goals
Percy Jackson, **Footscray:** 1934, 3 games, 0 goals
Dudley Probyn, **St Kilda:** 1942, 9 games, 18 goals
Malcolm Smith, **South Melbourne,** 1958, 5 games, 6 goals
Gordon Waters, **Hawthorn:** 1937-1941, 32 games, 0 goals

1.5 Inglewood

At the game

Loddon Valley FL, Round 17
Inglewood 11.5 (71) lt **Marong** 12.9 (81)
Inglewood Community Sports Centre
Goals – Marong: T. Wilson 3; J. Fitzpatrick, Z. Turnbull, B. Franzini 2; P. Ryan, C. Ross, C. Fleming; **Inglewood:** P. McKay 3; N. Leach, L. Drummond, B. Evans, S. Barnes, J. Essex, N. Wharton, R. McNish.
Best – Marong: Z. Turnbull, B Franzini, P. Ryan, C. Williamson, P. Gretgrix, B. Pollock; **Inglewood:** T. Milka, B. Evans, R. McNish, D. Rose, S. Harris, N. Leach.

Premiership teams

Loddon Valley FL, 1971 Grand Final
Inglewood 13.10 (88) d Calivil 7.9 (51)

Korong Vale Recreation Reserve

Inglewood, 1971 premiership team

B: L. Kelly, J. Summers, D. Grotto
HB: D. Birthisel, D. Vanston, G. Fuller
C: K. Rowley, W. Robins, M. Johns
HF: I. Chamberlain, R. Conboy, J. Richardson
F: G. Roberts, D. Griffiths, B. Grundy
Foll: L. Birthisel, I. Triplett, R. Campbell
19th: R Norton; 20th: N. Mitchell

Loddon Valley FL, 1986 Grand Final

Inglewood 17.13 (115) d Bridgewater 13.12 (90)
Malone Park, Marong

Inglewood, 1986 premiership team

B: S. Phillips, N. Wellington, P. Mason
HB: R. Cartledge, G. Billett, G. Jacobs
C: I. Ladiges, M. Starr, S. Robinson
HF: M. Dempsey, D. Canty, S. Leech
F: R. Earl, D. Billett, L. McKenzie
Foll: M. Gilmore, K. Dows, D. Cashin
Inter: K. Patterson, J. Starr

VFL/AFL players

Inglewood

Val Marchesi, **Geelong:** 1922, 15 games, 4 goals; **Essendon:** 1923-1924, 8 games, 0 goals; Total: 1922-1924, 23 games, 4 goals

Percy Martyn: **St Kilda**, 1912, 9 games, 11 goals; **Richmond,** 1913-15, 21 games, 50 goals; **Essendon,** 1915, 1918-21, 45 games, 7 goals; Total: 1912-1915, 1918-1921, 75 games, 68 goals

1.6 Pines, Sorrento

At the game

Mornington Peninsula Nepean FL, 2018 Division 1 Grand Final

Pines 14.12 (96) d Sorrento 14.11 (95)

Goals – Pines: A. Edwards, T. McDermott 3; P. Lewis-Smith, T. Bongetti 2; N. Wilcox, N. Boswell, S. White, B. Barfoot; **Sorrento:** L. Poholke 4; N. Corp 3; M. Gardner, J. Tonkins, J. Hallahan 2; D. Grant

Best – Pines: P. Lewis-Smith, L Potts, T. Bongetti, B. Hendry, N. Boswell; **Sorrento:** D. Grant, C. Harris, M. Hallahan J. Tomkins, J. Hallahan, L. Poholke

Premiership teams

Nepean FL, 1976 Grand Final
Pines 14.10 (94) d Frankston YCW 10.16 (76)
Olympic Park Recreation Reserve, Rosebud
Pines, 1976 premiership team
B: D. Saunders, K. McLaren, R. Mallett
HB: P. Watson, L. Gay, C. Saunders
C: B. Burke, C. Lewis, G. Abblitt
HF: G. McDonald, J. Bloom, C. Moorhouse
F: T. Verity, K. Greenough, W. Mills
Foll: M. Nodgen, M. Simic, P. Clarke
19th: I. Goodman; 20th: W. Hunt

Nepean FL, 1983 Grand Final
Pines 20.10 (130) d Crib Point 8.15 (63)
Olympic Park Recreation Reserve, Rosebud
Pines, 1983 premiership team
B: S. Stark, G. Tedge, M. Simic
HB: P. Plane, S. Gay, J. Smith
C: C. Saunders, A. Norris, R. Jackson
HF: S. Jackson, M. Rowley, C. McPherson
F: B. McIlwraith, J. Svigos, J. Merriner
Ruck: S. Andrew, K. Sutton, A. Tedge
Inter: D. Goodman, I. Marsh

Mornington Peninsula Nepean FL, 1988 Division 1 Grand Final
Pines 14.10 (94) d Edithvale-Aspendale 12.13 (85)
Frankston Park
Pines, 1988 premiership team
B: D. Howard, S. Johnson, S. Stark
HB: I. Marsh, M. Rowley, L. Vaughan
C: M. Hamling, S. Jackson, R. Jackson
HF: M. Hustwaite, P. Housden, C. McPherson
F: M. Greene, C. Neal, A. Tedge
Ruck: P. Williams, K. Sutton, S. Osborne
Inter: F. D'Agostino, M. Remy

Mornington Peninsula Nepean FL, 2018 Division 1 Grand Final
Pines 14.12 (96) d Sorrento 14.11 (95)
Frankston Park

Pines, 2018 premiership team
B: B. Thomas, J. Fisher, D. John
HB: N. Boswell, G. Hendry, L Potts
C: N. Wilcox, P. Scanlon, J. Boyle
HF: H. Parker, T. Bongetti, T. McDermott
F: B. Barfoot, A. Edwards, K. Jacobson
Ruck: B. Hendry, P. Lewis-Smith, L. Marshall
Inter: A. Ludewig, S. White, J. Hughes, B. Lewis

VFL/AFL players

Pines
Nathan Burke, **St Kilda:** 1987-2003, 323 games, 124 goals
Mark Greene, **St Kilda:** 1976-1977, 7 games, 0 goals
Russell Greene: **St Kilda:** 1974-1980, 120 games, 52 goals; **Hawthorn:** 1980–1988, 184 games, 82 goals; Total: 1974-1988, 304 games, 134 goals
Brendan Moore, **Essendon:** 1987-1988, 1990, 7 games, 1 goal
Steve Newman, **Fitzroy:** 1988, 1 game, 0 goals

Sorrento
Mitch Hallahan, **Hawthorn:** 2014, 6 games, 2 goals; **Gold Coast:** 2015-2017, 20 games, 5 goals; Total: 2014-2017, 26 games, 7 goals
* Tom Lynch, **Gold Coast:** 2011-2018, 131 games, 254 goals
John McCarthy, **Collingwood:** 2008-2011, 18 games, 10 goals; **Port Adelaide:** 2012, 21 games, 5 goals; Total: 2008-2012, 39 games, 15 goals
* Myles Poholke, **Adelaide:** 2018, 9 games, 3 goals
Andrew Scott, **Hawthorn:** 1972-1973, 6 games, 4 goals

* still playing

1.7 Horsham

Premiership teams

Wimmera FL, 1972 Grand Final
Horsham 24.22 (166) d Ararat 13.14 (92)
Anzac Memorial Park, Warracknabeal
Horsham, 1972 premiership team
B: G. Young, C. Dorrington, R. Downdell
HB: B. Hopper, G. Chequer, N. Brown
C: B. Carr, D. Farr, G. Burdett

HF: D. Hartigan, P. Burke, T. Jenkins
F: S. Cramer, J. Carr, P. Wood
Foll: R. Young, P. Glare, G. Wood
19th: B. Burke; 20th: B. Thomson

Wimmera FL, 1979 Grand Final
Horsham 24.14 (158) d Murtoa 18.16 (124)
Dimboola Recreation Reserve
Horsham, 1979 premiership team
B: M. Hickmott, T. Heath, D. Heard
HB: G. Smart, S. Holmes, M. Munn
C: B. Hartigan, P. Morrison, P. Taylor
HF: B. Thomson, J. Jordan, D. Lavithis
F: P. Creek, P. Bunn, R. Wood
Ruck: P. O'Brien, G. Chequer, P. Wood
Inter: E. Pekin, B. Burke

Wimmera FL, 1983 Grand Final
Horsham 24.14 (158) d Dimboola 11.8 (74)
Anzac Memorial Park, Warracknabeal
Horsham, 1983 premiership team
B: M. Williams, J. O'Callaghan, K. Duncan
HB: P. O'Beirne, S. Holmes, M. Fry
C: D. Eastwell, P. Morrison, R. Wood
HF: B. Hartigan, G. Parish, S. Smith
F: D. Hair, G. Driscoll, A. Pope
Ruck: A. Light, P. Light, D. Lavithis
Inter: B. Kennedy, D. Patterson

Wimmera FL, 2003 Grand Final
Horsham 14.16 (100) d Stawell 11.9 (75)
Anzac Memorial Park, Warracknabeal
Horsham, 2003 premiership team
B: S. Both, D. Richardson, B. Askew
HB; G. Faux, D. Skurrie, R. Lennon
C: Q. Rethus, D. Bunworth, J. Wright
HF: G. Smith, S. Dumesny, B. Tepper
F: C. Walsh, D. Johns, J. Smith
Ruck: W. Frost, S. Farr, A. Carter
Inter: **B. Hartigan**, M. Hallan, L. Spasic

Wimmera FL, 2004 Grand Final
Horsham 20.17 (137) d Horsham Saints 11.5 (71)
Horsham City Oval
Horsham, 2004 premiership team
B: S. Both, G. Faux, D. Richardson
HB: R. Lennon, D. Skurrie, G. Smith
C: N. Ryan, D. Bunworth, J. Wright
HF: S. Dalziel, A. Perkins, D. Johns
F: S. Batchelor, L. Carr, A. Barnett
Ruck: S. Dumesny, S. Farr, A. Carter
Inter: **B. Hartigan**, J. Hamilton, B. Askew

Wimmera FL, 2005 Grand Final
Horsham 18.10 (118) d Dimboola 12.15 (87),
Anzac Memorial Park, Warracknabeal
Horsham, 2005 premiership team
B: S. Both, T. Arnel, B. Askew
HB: L. Carr, D. Skurrie, J. Rentsch
C: J. Wright, D. Bunworth, T. Pickett
HF: S. Dumesny, A. Perkins, C. Penny
F: G. Smith, D. Johns, **B. Hartigan**
Ruck: Z. Holmes, S. Farr, S. Batchelor
Inter: J. Geue. L. Spasic, A. Emmerson

Wimmera FL, 2006 Grand Final
Horsham 27.9 (171) d Dimboola 20.6 (126)
Central Park, Stawell
Horsham, 2006 premiership team
B: S. Both, M. Leeming, J. Williams
HB: B. Askew, T. Arnel, J. Rentsch
C: A. Seer, S. Farr, T. Pickert
HF: L. Carr, C. Penny, A. Thomson
F: J. Ross, D. Johns, J. Geue
Ruck: G. Liston, **B. Hartigan**, S. Batchelor
Inter: Z. Holmes, A. Emmerson, D. Bunworth

Wimmera FL, 2007 Grand Final
Horsham 20.13 (133) d Stawell 13.12 (90)
Anzac Memorial Park, Warracknabeal

Horsham, 2007 premiership team
B: L. Spasic, T. Arnel, J. Williams
HB: J. Hartigan, L. Woodward, J. Rentsch
C: B. Durack, S. Farr, A. Seers
HF: A. Thomson, L. Carr, J. Wright
F: A. Barnett, D. Johns, N. Pekin
Ruck: G. Liston, P. Adlington, S. Batchelor
Inter: D. Bunworth, L. Smith, J. Geue

Wimmera FL, 2008 Grand Final
Horsham 19.14 (128) d Horsham Saints 9.8 (62)
Alexandra Oval, Ararat
Horsham, 2008 premiership team
B: L. Spasic, M. Arnel, J. Pekin
HB: **B. Hartigan**, J. Wright, T. Arnel
C: B. Durack, S. Farr, C. Heath
HF: D. Johns, J. Burke, J. Hamilton
F: A. Barnett, L. Carr, D. Parish
Ruck: G. Liston, M. Anson, S. Batchelor
Inter: K. Obst, J. Geue, N. Kelly

Wimmera FL, 2009 Grand Final
Horsham 16.14 (110) d Warrack Eagles 13.8 (86)
Dimboola Recreation Reserve
Horsham, 2009 premiership team
B: L. Sodermann, T. Arnel, R. McRae
HB: B. Durack, J. Hartigan, A. Pekin
C: J. Kerr, S. Farr, N. Kelly
HF: A. Barnett, J. Burke, L. Carr
F: J. Lloyd, D. Johns, S. Batchelor
Ruck: J. Ward M. Anson, **B. Hartigan**
Inter: G. Liston, J. Geue, M. O'Callaghan

Wimmera FL, 2010 Grand Final
Horsham 17.16 (118) d Nhill 8.12 (60)
Central Park, Stawell
Horsham, 2010 premiership team
B: N. Kelly, T. Arnel, J. Pekin
HB: M. O'Callaghan, J. Hartigan, B. Durack
C: B. Nelson, **B. Hartigan**, J. Kerr

HF: J. Lloyd, J. Burke, S. Farr
F: D. Johns, D. Parish, S. Batchelor
Ruck: G. Liston, M. Anson, A. Barnett
Inter: A. Pekin, S. Christopher, T. Hasse

Wimmera FL, 2011 Grand Final
Horsham 15.7 (97) d Warrack Eagles 12.13 (85),
Dimboola Recreation Reserve
Horsham, 2011 premiership team
B: S. Christopher, T. Arnel, C. Walsh
HB: J. Duncan, J. Hartigan, J. Lloyd
C: J. Bennett, N. Pekin, L. Spasic
HF: **B. Hartigan**, D. Skurrie, J. Wood
F: S. Farr, D. Parish, A. Thomson
Ruck: M. O'Callaghan, J. Rentsch, D. Taylor
Inter: B. Nelson, R. O'Connor, J. Pekin

Wimmera FL, 2012 Grand Final
Horsham 21.11 (137) d Warrack Eagles 13.12 (90)
Central Park, Stawell
Horsham, 2012 premiership team
B: C. Walsh, S. Christopher, T. Arnel
HB: J. Thompson, J. Hartigan, J. Duncan
C: B. Nelson, N. Pekin, J. Wood
HF: S. Gilbert, J. Burke, D. Parish
F: J. Geue, D. Skurrie, A. Thomson
Ruck: M. O'Callaghan, P. Adlington, **B. Hartigan**
Inter: T. Blake, J. Lloyd, R. Stacey

Wimmera FL, 2014 Grand Final
Horsham 12.10 (82) d Horsham Saints 9.8 (62)
Central Park, Stawell
Horsham, 2014 premiership team
B: D. Taylor, R. Conboy, J. Schmidt
HB: N. Kelly, J. Hartigan, H. Young
C: J. Mentha, T. Eldridge, B. Nelson
HF: B. Lakin, J. Burke, B. Lloyd
F: S. Hobbs, J. Geue, M. O'Callaghan
Ruck: S. Christopher, **B. Hartigan**, N. Pekin
Inter: A. Thomson, B. Batchelor, R. O'Connor

Wimmera FL, 2017 Grand Final
Horsham 7.19 (61) d Minyip-Murtoa 5.7 (37)
Horsham City Oval
Horsham, 2017 premiership team
B: J. Hartigan, L. Carr, A. Harfield
HB: S. Hobbs, J. Mibus, B. Lakin
C: R. Kemp, **B. Hartigan**, B. Cross
HF: J. Wood, T. Blake, B. Lloyd
F: D. Roberts, B. Carberry, J. Geue
Ruck: T. Wade, R. Conboy, J. Mentha
Inter: M Lloyd, S. Hernon, D. Taylor

Wimmera FL, 2018 Grand Final
Horsham 11.10 (76) d Southern Mallee Giants 9.3 (57)
Anzac Memorial Oval, Warracknabeal
Horsham, 2018 premiership team
B: D. Taylor, D. Cross, W. Deayton
HB: C. Williams, A. Harfield, B. Lakin
C: B. Cross, **B. Hartigan**, R. Williams
HF: B. Mines, J. Burke, B. Patterson
F: B. Hobbs, J. Mibus, J. Wood
Foll: B. Carberry, R. Conboy, R. Kemp
Inter: S. Hernon, K. King, S. Bigham

VFL/AFL players

Horsham
Robert Amos, **Essendon:** 1973-1976, 1978-1979, 54 games, 15 goals
George "Ginger" Bell, **Essendon:** 1933-1942, 120 games, 4 goals
Des Bethke, **South Melbourne:** 1963-1968, 56 games, 43 goals
Luke Brennan, **Hawthorn:** 2004-2006, 19 games, 11 goals; **Sydney:** 2007-2008, 9 games, 1 goal; Total: 2004-2008, 28 games, 12 goals
David Burke, **Essendon:** 1980, 3 games, 6 goals
Gil "George" Curran, **South Melbourne:** 1906-1907, 5 games, 1 goal
Kevin Dellar, **Essendon:** 1959, 5 games, 0 goals
Alex Doyle, **Carlton:** 1929-1931, 53 games, 32 goals
Adam Goodes, **Sydney:** 1999-2015, 372 games, 464 goals
Ray Harrip, **Geelong:** 1957, 4 games, 0 goals
Dean Hartigan, **Essendon:** 1974-1977, 36 games, 1 goal
Jack Hartigan, **Hawthorn:** 1951-1952, 15 games, 8 goals; **St Kilda:** 1952-1953, 7 games, 6 goals; Total: 1951-1953, 22 games, 14 goals

Shane Heard, **Essendon:** 1977-1987, 1991, 168 games, 39 goals
Adrian Hickmott, **Geelong:** 1992-1995, 50 games, 24 goals; **Carlton:** 1996-1997, 1999-2003, 134 games, 107 goals; Total: 1992-1997, 1999-2003, 184 games, 131 goals
Peter Hickmott, **Essendon:** 1972-1977, 58 games, 18 goals; **Footscray:** 1980, 11 games, 4 goals; Total: 1982-1977, 1980, 69 games, 22 goals
Alex Lee, **Hawthorn:** 1933-1935, 31 games, 1 goal
Peter Light, **Essendon:** 1980, 2 games, 0 goals
* Jake Lloyd, **Sydney:** 2014-2018, 115 games, 26 goals
Godfrey McRae, **Hawthorn:** 1927, 1 game, 0 goals
Bob Miller, **Melbourne:** 1961-1965, 69 games, 3 goals
Bob Norman, **Collingwood:** 1957, 9 games, 9 goals; **Geelong:** 1961, 11 games, 10 goals; Total: 1957, 1961, 20 games, 19 goals
Jim "Jake" Norman, **Geelong:** 1950-1952, 37 games, 15 goals
Bryan Pirouet, **Essendon:** 1970-1971, 14 games, 0 goals
Evan "Dasher" Rees, **Footscray:** 1946-1950, 80 games, 2 goals
* Sebastian Ross, **St Kilda:** 2012-2018, 102 games, 16 goals
Gerald Ryan, **Essendon:** 1906, 1909, 18 games, 3 goals
Darryl Schwarz, **Melbourne:** 1968-1969, 12 games, 0 goals
Jim Shanahan, **Collingwood:** 1924-1926, 42 games, 0 goals; **Carlton:** 1927, 2 games, 1 goal; **Fitzroy:** 1928-1929, 27 games, 3 goals; Total: 1924-1929, 71 games, 4 goals
Michael Sheldon, **Essendon:** 1978-1980, 11 games, 3 goals
Brad Sholl, **North Melbourne:** 1993-1994, 2 games, 0 goals; **Geelong:** 1995–2002, 169 games, 46 goals; Total: 1993-2002, 171 games, 46 goals
Craig Sholl, **North Melbourne:** 1987, 1989-2000, 235 games, 165 goals
Colin Sleep, **Fitzroy:** 1962-1964, 17 games, 5 goals
Sid "Boots" Smith, **Geelong:** 1952-1953, 23 games, 0 goals
Howard Staehr, **Essendon:** 1974, 1976, 5 games, 0 goals
Bob Strachan, **South Melbourne:** 1963-1965, 7 games, 0 goals
Doug Wade, **Geelong:** 1961-1972, 208 games, 834 goals; **North Melbourne:** 1973-1975, 59 games, 223 goals; Total: 1961-1975, 267 games, 1057 goals
Wally Wollerman, **Essendon:** 1933, 9 games, 2 goals
* still playing

Appendix 2

2.1 Clubs and Competitions Around Ouyen and District

Legend
FA = Football Association
FL = Football League

1910

Ouyen District FA: Box Tank, Ouyen, Tiega, Walpeup
Woomelang & District FA: Lascelles, Speed, Watchupga, Woomelang

1911

Ouyen District FA: Box Tank, Ouyen, Tiega, Walpeup
Woomelang & District FA: Minapre, Speed, Watchupga, Woomelang

1912

Ouyen District FA: Ouyen, Tiega, Walpeup
Woomelang & District FA: Lascelles, Speed, Turriff, Woomelang

1913

Northern FA: Lascelles, Speed, Tempy, Turriff
Ouyen District FA: East Rovers, Nunga, Tiega, Walpeup
Underbool & District FA: Boinka, Linga, Nyang, Tutye, Underbool

1914

Ouyen District FA: Nunga, Ouyen, Tiega, Timberoo, Walpeup
North Western FA: Gorya, Lascelles, Tempy, Watchupga, Woomelang
Underbool & District FA: Boinka, Linga, Nyang, Tutye, Underbool

1915

Ouyen District FA: Nunga, Ouyen, Tiega, Walpeup (season abandoned halfway)

1916

In recess, World War 1

1917

In recess, World War 1

1918

In recess, World War 1

1919

Ouyen District FA: Nunga, Ouyen, Tiega, Walpeup
Murrayville & Cowangie FA: Cowangie, Duddo, Murrayville, Ngallo, Tutye, Underbool
North Western FA: Gorya, Lascelles, Tempy, Watchupga, Woomelang

1920

Murrayville & Cowangie FA: Cowangie, Duddo, Murrayville, Ngallo, Tutye, Underbool
North Western FA: Gorya, Lascelles, Tempy, Watchupga, Woomelang
Ouyen District FA: Kiamal, Nunga, Ouyen, Tiega, Walpeup

1921

Boinka & District FA: Boinka, Linga, Nyang, Tutye
North West Mallee District FA: Cowangie, Murrayville, Ouyen, Underbool, Walpeup
North Western FA: Gorya, Lascelles, Tempy, Watchupga, Woomelang
Ouyen District FA: Kiamal, Nunga, Ouyen Wanderers, Tiega

1922

North West Mallee District FA: Boinka, Cowangie, Murrayville, Ouyen, Tiega, Tutye, Underbool, Walpeup
North Western FA: Gorya, Lascelles, Tempy, Watchupga, Woomelang
Ouyen District FA: Kiamal, Nunga, Ouyen Wanderers

1923

North West Mallee District FA: Boinka, Cowangie, Murrayville, Ouyen, Tutye, Underbool, Walpeup
North Western FA: Gorya, Lascelles, Tempy, Watchupga, Woomelang
Ouyen District FA: Kiamal, Nunga, Ouyen North West, Ouyen Rovers, Tiega, Woornack
Mittyack & District FA: Daytrap, Kulwin, Mittyack, Pier Milan

1924

North West Mallee District FA: Boinka, Cowangie, Murrayville, Ouyen, Tiega, Tutye, Underbool, Walpeup
North Western FA: Gorya, Lascelles, Tempy, Watchupga, Woomelang
Ouyen District FA: Kiamal, Nunga, Ouyen North West, Ouyen Rovers, Woornack

1925

North West Mallee District FA: Boinka, Cowangie, Murrayville, Ouyen, Tiega, Tutye, Underbool, Walpeup
North Western FA: Gorya, Lascelles, Tempy, Woomelang
Ouyen District FA: Kiamal, Nunga, Ouyen North West, Ouyen Rovers, Woornack
Mittyack & District FA: Daytrap, Kulwin, Mittyack, Pier Milan

1926

Mallee FA: Beulah, Brim, Hopetoun, Patchewollock, Warracknabeal Seconds
Mittyack & District FA: Daytrap, Kulwin, Mittyack, Pier Milan
North West Mallee District FA: Cowangie, Murrayville, Tiega, Tutye, Walpeup
North West Mallee FL: Boinka, Linga, Tyalla, Underbool
North Western FA: Gorya, Lascelles, Ouyen, Tempy, Woomelang
Ouyen District FA: Bronzewing, Kiamal, Nunga, Ouyen Juniors, Ouyen North West, Woornack

1927

Mallee FA: Beulah, Brim, Hopetoun, Patchewollock
North West Mallee FL: Boinka, Linga, Tutye, Tyalla, Underbool
North Western FA: Gorya, Lascelles, Ouyen, Woomelang
Ouyen District FA: Bronzewing, Kiamal, Nunga, Ouyen North West, Ouyen Rovers, Woornack
Mittyack & District FA: Daytrap, Kulwin, Mittyack, Pier Milan
Western Mallee FA: Tempy, Tiega, Walpeup, Yellumjip

1928

North West Mallee FL: Boinka, Linga, Tyalla, Tutye, Underbool
Ouyen District FA: Bronzewing, Hattah, Kiamal, Nunga, Ouyen North West, Ouyen Rovers
Patchewollock & District FA: Baring, Dering, Patchewollock, Wathe
Walpeup & District FA: Kattyoong, Torrita, Wymlet, Yellumjip
Western Mallee FA: Gorya, Lascelles, Ouyen, Tempy, Tiega, Walpeup

1929

Central Mallee FL: Pirro, Speed, Tempy, Turriff,
Mallee FA: Beulah, Brim, Hopetoun, Lascelles, Rainbow, Yaapeet
North West Mallee FL: Boinka, Linga, Tyalla, Tutye, Underbool
Ouyen District FA: Bronzewing, Hattah, Kiamal, Nunga, Ouyen, Ouyen North West, Ouyen Rovers
Patchewollock & District FA: Baring, Dering, Patchewollock, Wathe
Walpeup & District FA: Kattyoong, Tiega, Torrita, Walpeup, Wymlet, Yellimjup

1930

Mallee FA: Beulah, Brim, Gorya, Hopetoun, Lascelles, Woomelang
North West Mallee FL: Boinka, Cowangie, Kattyoong, Linga, Tutye, Underbool, Walpeup
Ouyen District FA: Bronzewing, Kiamal, Ouyen, Ouyen Rovers, Tempy, Tiega
Patchewollock & District FA: Baring, Dering, Patchewollock, Wathe

1931

Mallee FA: Beulah, Brim, Gorya, Hopetoun, Patchewollock
North West Mallee FL: Boinka, Cowangie, Kattyoong, Linga, Murrayville, Tutye, Underbool, Walpeup
Ouyen District FA: Bronzewing, Kiamal, Ouyen, Ouyen Imperials, Ouyen Rovers, Tempy, Tiega
Pier Milan & District FA: Kulwin, Mittyack, Nandaly, Pier Milan, Pirro

1932

Mallee FA: Gorya, Hopetoun, Lascelles, Watchupga, Woomelang
North West Mallee FL: Boinka, Cowangie, Kattyoong, Linga, Murrayville, Tutye, Underbool
Ouyen District FA: Bronzewing, Kiamal, Ouyen Imperials, Ouyen Rovers, Patchewollock, Tempy, Tiega, Walpeup
Pier Milan & District FA: Kulwin, Mittyack, Myall, Nandaly, Pier Milan, Pirro

1933

Mallee FA: Gorya, Hopetoun, Lascelles, Watchupga, Woomelang
North West Mallee FL: Boinka, Cowangie, Linga, Torrita, Tutye, Underbool
Ouyen District FA: Bronzewing, Kiamal, Ouyen Imperials, Ouyen Rovers, Patchewollock, Tempy, Tiega, Walpeup
Pier Milan & District FA: Kulwin, Mittyack, Myall, Nandaly, Pier Milan, Sea Lake Rovers

1934

Mallee FA: Gorya, Hopetoun, Lascelles, Watchupga, Woomelang
North West Mallee FL: Boinka, Cowangie, Linga, Torrita, Tutye, Underbool
Ouyen District FA: Bronzewing, Kiamal, Ouyen Imperials, Ouyen Rovers, Patchewollock, Tempy, Tiega, Walpeup
Pier Milan & District FA: Kulwin, Mittyack, Myall, Nandaly, Pier Milan

1935

North West Mallee FL: Centrals, Cowangie, Torrita, Tutye, Underbool
Ouyen District FL: Gorya, Kiamal, Ouyen Imperials, Ouyen Rovers, Patchewollock, Tempy, Tiega, Walpeup
Pier Milan & District FA: Kulwin, Lascelles, Mittyack, Myall, Nandaly, Pier Milan

1936

North West Mallee FL: Centrals, Cowangie, Torrita, Tutye, Underbool
Ouyen District FL: Gorya, Ouyen Imperials, Ouyen Rovers, Patchewollock, Tempy, Tiega, Walpeup
Pier Milan & District FA: Kulwin, Lascelles, Mittyack, Myall, Nandaly, Pier Milan

1937

Ouyen District FL: Gorya, Lascelles, Ouyen, Patchewollock, Tempy, Tiega, Walpeup
Ouyen Junior FL: Bronzewing, Kiamal, Ouyen Juniors, Wymlet
North West Mallee FL: Centrals, Cowangie, Danyo, Murrayville, Torrita, Tutye, Underbool
Pier Milan & District FA: Kulwin, Mittyack, Myall, Nandaly, Pier Milan, Sea Lake Imperials

1938

Ouyen District FL: Gorya, Lascelles, Ouyen, Patchewollock, Tempy, Tiega, Walpeup
Ouyen Junior FL: Bronzewing, Kiamal, Ouyen Juniors, Wymlet
North West Mallee FL: Centrals, Cowangie, Danyo, Murrayville, Torrita, Tutye, Underbool
Pier Milan & District FA: Kulwin, Mittyack, Myall, Nandaly, Pier Milan, Sea Lake Imperials

1939

North West Mallee FL: Centrals, Cowangie, Danyo, Murrayville, Torrita, Tutye, Underbool
Ouyen District FL: Gorya, Lascelles, Ouyen, Patchewollock, Tempy, Tiega, Walpeup
Ouyen Junior FL: Bronzewing, Kiamal, Ouyen Juniors, Walpeup
Pier Milan & District FL: Kulwin, Mittyack, Myall, Nandaly, Pier Milan, Sea Lake Imperials

1940

Ouyen District FL: Gorya, Ouyen, Patchewollock, Tempy, Tiega, Walpeup
Ouyen Junior FL: Bronzewing, Kiamal, Ouyen Juniors, Walpeup
North West Mallee FL: Centrals, Cowangie, Danyo, Murrayville, Torrita, Tutye, Underbool
Pier Milan & District FL: Kulwin, Mittyack, Myall, Nandaly, Pier Milan

1941

Ouyen District FL: Kiamal, Ouyen, Patchewollock, Tempy, Tiega, Walpeup
North West Mallee FL: Centrals, Cowangie, Danyo, Murrayville, Torrita, Tutye, Underbool
Pier Milan & District FL: Kulwin, Mittyack, Myall, Nandaly, Pier Milan

1942

In recess, World War 2

1943

In recess, World War 2

1944

Nandaly-Bolton FL: Chinkapook, Manangatang, Mittyack, Nandaly
Ouyen District FL: Kiamal, Ouyen, Tiega, Walpeup

1945

Gorya & District FL: Gorya, Lascelles, Patchewollock, Tempy
Nandaly-Bolton FL: Chinkapook, Imperials, Mittyack, Nandaly
North West Mallee FL: Centrals, Cowangie, Danyo, Murrayville, Torrita, Tutye, Underbool
Ouyen District FL: Kiamal, Ouyen, Tiega, Walpeup

1946

Nandaly-Bolton FL: Annuello, Chillingollah, Chinkapook, Imperials, Mittyack, Nandaly, Waitchie
North West Mallee FL: Centrals, Cowangie, Danyo, Murrayville, Torrita, Tutye, Underbool
Ouyen District FL: Gorya, Kiamal, Ouyen, Patchewollock, Tempy, Tiega, Walpeup

1947

Nandaly-Bolton FL: Annuello, Chillingollah, Chinkapook, Imperials, Kooloonong, Mittyack, Nandaly, Waitchie

North West Mallee FL: Centrals, Cowangie, Danyo, Murrayville, Torrita, Tutye, Underbool

Ouyen District FL: Gorya, Kiamal, Ouyen, Patchewollock, Tempy, Tiega, Walpeup

1948

Nandaly-Bolton FL: Annuello, Chillingollah, Chinkapook, Imperials, Kooloonong, Kulwin, Mittyack, Nandaly

North West Mallee FL: Centrals, Danyo, Murrayville, Torrita, Tutye, Underbool

Ouyen District FL: Gorya, Kiamal, Ouyen, Patchewollock, Tempy, Tiega, Walpeup

1949

Nandaly-Bolton FL: Annuello, Chillingollah, Chinkapook, Imperials, Kooloonong, Kulwin, Mittyack, Nandaly

North West Mallee FL: Centrals, Danyo, Imperials, Murrayville, Torrita, Underbool

Ouyen District FL: Gorya, Kiamal, Ouyen, Patchewollock, Tempy, Tiega, Walpeup

1950

Nandaly-Bolton FL: Annuello, Chillingollah, Chinkapook, Imperials, Kooloonong, Kulwin, Mittyack, Nandaly

North West Mallee FL: Centrals, Cowangie, Danyo, Murrayville, Torrita, Tutye, Underbool

Ouyen District FL: Gorya, Kiamal, Ouyen, Patchewollock, Tempy, Tiega, Walpeup

1951

Nandaly-Bolton FL: Annuello, Chillingollah, Chinkapook, Kooloonong, Kulwin, Manangatang, Mittyack, Nandaly

North West Mallee FL: Centrals, Danyo, Imperials, Murrayville, Torrita, Underbool

Ouyen District FL: Gorya, Kiamal, Ouyen, Patchewollock, Tempy, Tiega, Walpeup

1952

Nandaly-Bolton FL: Annuello, Chillingollah, Chinkapook, Kooloonong, Kulwin, Manangatang, Mittyack

North West Mallee FL: Centrals, Danyo, Imperials, Murrayville, Torrita, Underbool

Ouyen District FL: Gorya, Kiamal, Ouyen, Patchewollock, Tempy, Tiega, Walpeup

1953

North West Mallee FL: Centrals, Danyo, Imperials, Murrayville, Torrita, Underbool

Ouyen District FL: Gorya, Kiamal, Mittyack, Ouyen, Patchewollock, Tempy, Tiega, Walpeup

1954

North West Mallee FL: Centrals, Danyo, Imperials, Murrayville, Torrita, Underbool

Ouyen District FL: Gorya, Kiamal, Mittyack, Ouyen, Patchewollock, Tempy, Tiega, Walpeup

1955

Mallee FL: Gorya, Kiamal, Ouyen, Patchewollock, Tempy, Tiega, Walpeup

North West Mallee FL: Centrals, Danyo, Imperials, Murrayville, Torrita, Underbool

1956

Mallee FL: Gorya, Kiamal, Ouyen, Patchewollock, Tempy, Tiega, Walpeup

North West Mallee FL: Centrals, Danyo, Imperials, Murrayville, Underbool

1957

Mallee FL: Gorya, Kiamal, Ouyen, Patchewollock, Tempy, Tiega, Underbool, Walpeup

North West Mallee FL: Danyo, Imperials Blue, Imperials Red, Murrayville

1958

Mallee FL: Gorya, Kiamal, Ouyen, Patchewollock, Tempy, Tiega, Underbool, Walpeup

North West Mallee FL: Danyo, Imperials, Murrayville, Veterans

1959

Mallee FL: Gorya, Kiamal, Ouyen, Patchewollock, Tempy, Tiega, Underbool, Walpeup

1960

Mallee FL: Gorya, Kiamal, Murrayville, Ouyen, Patchewollock, Tempy, Tiega, Underbool, Walpeup

1961

Mallee FL: Gorya, Kiamal, Murrayville, Ouyen, Patchewollock, Tempy, Tiega, Underbool, Walpeup

1962

Mallee FL: Gorya, Kiamal, Murrayville, Ouyen, Patchewollock, Tempy, Tiega, Underbool, Walpeup

1963

Mallee FL: Gorya, Kiamal, Murrayville, Ouyen, Patchewollock, Tempy, Tiega, Underbool, Walpeup

1964

Mallee FL: Gorya, Kiamal, Murrayville, Ouyen, Patchewollock, Tempy, Tiega, Underbool, Walpeup

1965

Mallee FL: Kiamal, Murrayville, Ouyen, Patchewollock, Tempy-Gorya, Tiega, Underbool, Walpeup

1966

Mallee FL: Kiamal, Murrayville, Ouyen, Patchewollock, Tempy-Gorya, Tiega, Underbool, Walpeup

1967

Mallee FL: Kiamal, Murrayville, Ouyen, Patchewollock, Tempy-Gorya, Tiega, Underbool, Walpeup

1968

Mallee FL: Kiamal, Murrayville, Ouyen, Patchewollock, Tempy-Gorya, Tiega, Underbool, Walpeup

1969

Mallee FL: Kiamal, Murrayville, Ouyen, Patchewollock, Tempy-Gorya, Tiega, Underbool, Walpeup

1970

Mallee FL: Kiamal, Murrayville, Ouyen, Tempy-Gorya, Tiega, Underbool, Walpeup

1971

Mallee FL: Kiamal, Murrayville, Ouyen, Tempy-Gorya-Patchewollock, Tiega, Underbool, Walpeup

1972

Mallee FL: Kiamal, Murrayville, Ouyen, Tempy-Gorya-Patchewollock, Tiega, Underbool, Walpeup

1973

Mallee FL: Kiamal, Murrayville, Ouyen, Tempy-Gorya-Patchewollock, Tiega, Underbool, Walpeup

1974

Mallee FL: Kiamal, Murrayville, Ouyen, Tempy-Gorya-Patchewollock, Tiega, Underbool, Walpeup

1975

Mallee FL: Kiamal, Murrayville, Ouyen, Tempy-Gorya-Patchewollock, Tiega, Underbool, Walpeup

1976

Mallee FL: Kiamal, Murrayville, Ouyen, Tempy-Gorya-Patchewollock, Tiega, Underbool, Walpeup

1977

Mallee FL: Kiamal, Murrayville, Ouyen, Tempy-Gorya-Patchewollock, Tiega, Underbool, Walpeup

1978

Mallee FL: Kiamal, Ouyen, Tempy-Gorya-Patchewollock, Tiega, Underbool, Walpeup

1979

Northern Mallee FL: Kiamal, Manangatang, Nandaly, Sea Lake, Tempy-Gorya-Patchewollock, Tiega, Underbool, Walpeup

Sunraysia FL: Irymple, Merbein, Mildura, Mildura Imperials, Ouyen, Red Cliffs, Robinvale, South Mildura, Wentworth Districts

1980

Northern Mallee FL: Kiamal, Manangatang, Nandaly, Sea Lake, Tempy-Gorya-Patchewollock, Tiega, Underbool, Walpeup

Sunraysia FL: Irymple, Merbein, Mildura, Mildura Imperials, Ouyen, Red Cliffs, Robinvale, South Mildura, Wentworth Districts

1981

Northern Mallee FL: Kiamal, Manangatang, Nandaly, Sea Lake, Tempy-Gorya-Patchewollock, Tiega, Underbool, Walpeup

Sunraysia FL: Irymple, Merbein, Mildura, Mildura Imperials, Ouyen, Red Cliffs, Robinvale, South Mildura, Wentworth Districts

1982

Northern Mallee FL: Manangatang, Nandaly, Ouyen Rovers, Sea Lake, Tempy-Gorya-Patchewollock, Walpeup-Underbool

Sunraysia FL: Irymple, Merbein, Mildura, Mildura Imperials, Ouyen, Red Cliffs, Robinvale, South Mildura, Wentworth Districts

1983

Northern Mallee FL: Manangatang, Nandaly, Ouyen, Ouyen Rovers, Sea Lake, Tempy-Gorya-Patchewollock, Walpeup-Underbool

1984

Northern Mallee FL: Manangatang, Nandaly, Ouyen, Ouyen Rovers, Sea Lake, Tempy-Gorya-Patchewollock, Walpeup-Underbool

1985

Northern Mallee FL: Manangatang, Nandaly, Ouyen Rovers, Sea Lake, Tempy-Gorya-Patchewollock, Walpeup-Underbool

1986

Northern Mallee FL: Manangatang, Nandaly, Ouyen Rovers, Sea Lake, Tempy-Gorya-Patchewollock, Walpeup-Underbool

1987

Northern Mallee FL: Manangatang, Nandaly, Ouyen Rovers, Sea Lake, Tempy-Gorya-Patchewollock, Walpeup-Underbool

1988

Northern Mallee FL: Manangatang, Nandaly, Ouyen Rovers, Sea Lake, Tempy-Gorya-Patchewollock, Walpeup-Underbool

1989

Northern Mallee FL: Manangatang, Nandaly, Ouyen Rovers, Sea Lake, Tempy-Gorya-Patchewollock, Walpeup-Underbool

1990

Northern Mallee FL: Manangatang, Nandaly, Ouyen Rovers, Sea Lake, Tempy-Gorya-Patchewollock, Walpeup-Underbool

1991

Northern Mallee FL: Manangatang, Nandaly, Ouyen Rovers, Sea Lake, Tempy-Gorya-Patchewollock, Walpeup-Underbool

1992

Northern Mallee FL: Manangatang, Nandaly, Ouyen Rovers, Sea Lake, Tempy-Gorya-Patchewollock, Walpeup-Underbool

1993

Northern Mallee FL: Manangatang, Nandaly, Ouyen Rovers, Sea Lake, Tempy-Gorya-Patchewollock, Walpeup-Underbool

1994

Northern Mallee FL: Manangatang, Ouyen Rovers, Sea Lake-Nandaly, Tempy-Gorya-Patchewollock, Walpeup-Underbool

1995

Northern Mallee FL: Manangatang, Ouyen Rovers, Sea Lake-Nandaly, Tempy-Gorya-Patchewollock, Walpeup-Underbool

1996

Northern Mallee FL: Manangatang, Ouyen Rovers, Sea Lake-Nandaly, Tempy-Gorya-Patchewollock, Walpeup-Underbool

1997

Mallee FL: Berriwillock-Culgoa, Beulah, Brim, Hopetoun, Jeparit-Rainbow, Manangatang, Nullawil, Ouyen United, Sea Lake-Nandaly, Walpeup-Underbool, Woomelang-Lascelles, Yaapeet

1998

Mallee FL: Berriwillock-Culgoa, Beulah, Brim, Hopetoun, Jeparit-Rainbow, Manangatang, Ouyen United, Sea Lake-Nandaly, Walpeup-Underbool, Woomelang-Lascelles, Yaapeet

1999

Mallee FL: Berriwillock-Culgoa, Beulah, Brim, Hopetoun, Jeparit-Rainbow, Manangatang, Ouyen United, Sea Lake-Nandaly, Walpeup-Underbool, Woomelang-Lascelles, Yaapeet

2000

Mallee FL: Berriwillock-Culgoa, Beulah, Brim, Hopetoun, Jeparit-Rainbow, Manangatang, Ouyen United, Sea Lake-Nandaly, Walpeup-Underbool, Woomelang-Lascelles

2001

Mallee FL: Berriwillock-Culgoa, Beulah, Hopetoun, Jeparit-Rainbow, Manangatang, Ouyen United, Sea Lake-Nandaly, Walpeup-Underbool, Woomelang-Lascelles

2002

Mallee FL: Berriwillock-Culgoa, Beulah, Hopetoun, Jeparit-Rainbow, Manangatang, Ouyen United, Sea Lake-Nandaly, Walpeup-Underbool, Woomelang-Lascelles

2003

Mallee FL: Beulah, Hopetoun, Jeparit-Rainbow, Manangatang, Ouyen United, Sea Lake-Nandaly Tigers, Walpeup-Underbool, Woomelang-Lascelles

2004

Mallee FL: Beulah, Hopetoun, Jeparit-Rainbow, Ouyen United, Sea Lake-Nandaly Tigers, Walpeup-Underbool, Woomelang-Lascelles

2005

Mallee FL: Beulah, Hopetoun, Jeparit-Rainbow, Ouyen United, Sea Lake-Nandaly Tigers, Walpeup-Underbool, Woomelang-Lascelles

2006

Mallee FL: Beulah, Hopetoun, Jeparit-Rainbow, Ouyen United, Sea Lake-Nandaly Tigers, Walpeup-Underbool, Woomelang-Lascelles

2007

Mallee FL: Beulah, Hopetoun, Jeparit-Rainbow, Ouyen United, Sea Lake-Nandaly Tigers, Walpeup-Underbool, Woomelang-Lascelles

2008

Mallee FL: Beulah, Hopetoun, Jeparit-Rainbow, Ouyen United, Sea Lake-Nandaly Tigers, Walpeup-Underbool, Woomelang-Lascelles

2009

Mallee FL: Beulah, Hopetoun, Jeparit-Rainbow, Ouyen United, Sea Lake-Nandaly Tigers, Walpeup-Underbool, Woomelang-Lascelles

2010

Mallee FL: Beulah, Hopetoun, Jeparit-Rainbow, Ouyen United, Sea Lake-Nandaly Tigers, Walpeup-Underbool, Woomelang-Lascelles

2011

Mallee FL: Beulah, Hopetoun, Jeparit-Rainbow, Ouyen United, Sea Lake-Nandaly Tigers, Walpeup-Underbool, Woomelang-Lascelles

2012

Mallee FL: Beulah, Hopetoun, Jeparit-Rainbow, Ouyen United, Sea Lake-Nandaly Tigers, Walpeup-Underbool, Woomelang-Lascelles

2013

Mallee FL: Beulah, Hopetoun, Jeparit-Rainbow, Ouyen United, Sea Lake-Nandaly Tigers, Walpeup-Underbool, Woomelang-Lascelles

2014

Mallee FL: Beulah, Hopetoun, Jeparit-Rainbow, Ouyen United, Sea Lake-Nandaly Tigers, Walpeup-Underbool, Woomelang-Lascelles

2015

Mallee FL: Ouyen United, Sea Lake-Nandaly Tigers, Southern Mallee Giants, Walpeup-Underbool, Woomelang-Lascelles

2016

Sunraysia FL: Irymple, Merbein, Mildura, Mildura Imperials, Ouyen United, Red Cliffs, Robinvale-Euston, South Mildura, Wentworth Districts

2017

Sunraysia FL: Irymple, Merbein, Mildura, Mildura Imperials, Ouyen United, Red Cliffs, Robinvale-Euston, South Mildura, Wentworth Districts

2018

Sunraysia FL: Irymple, Merbein, Mildura, Mildura Imperials, Ouyen United, Red Cliffs, Robinvale-Euston, South Mildura, Wentworth Districts

2.2 The Foundation Clubs of Ouyen United

Baring	1928-1930
Boinka	1912-1914, 1921-1934
Box Tank	1910-1911
Bronzewing	1926-1934, 1937-1940
Dering	1928-1930
East Rovers	1913
Hattah	1928-1929
Kattyoong	1928-1932
Kiamal	1920-1935, 1937-1941, 1944-1981
Linga	1912-1914, 1921-1934
Nunga	1913-1915, 1919-1929
Nyang	1913-1914, 1921
Ouyen	1910-1915, 1919-1931, 1937-1941, 1944-1984
Ouyen Imperials	1931-1936
Ouyen Juniors	1926, 1937-1938
Ouyen North West	1923-1929
Ouyen Rovers	1923-1925, 1927-1936
Ouyen Wanderers	1921-1922
Patchewollock	1926-1941, 1945-1969
Pirro	1929-1930, 1932
Speed	1910-1913, 1929
Tempy	1913-1914, 1919-1941, 1946-1964
Tiega	1910-1915, 1919-1941, 1944-1981
Timberoo	1914
Torrita	1928-1929, 1933-1940, 1945-1955
Turriff	1912-1913, 1929
Underbool	1913-1915, 1919-1940, 1945-1981
Walpeup	1910-1915, 1919-1941, 1944-1981
Wathe	1928-1930
Woornack	1923-1927
Wymlet	1928-1929, 1937-1938
Yellumjip	1927-1929

The clubs on the fringe of Ouyen United's catchment area

Cowangie	1919-1941, 1945-1948
Danyo	1937-1941, 1945-1958
Kulwin	1923-1927, 1931-1941, 1948-1957
Mittyack	1923-1927, 1931-1941, 1944-1954
* Murrayville	1913-1915, 1919-1941, 1945-1958, 1967-2018
Nandaly	1919-1941, 1944-1993
Pier Milan	1923-1927, 1931-1941
Tutye	1912-1914, 1919-1940, 1945-1948
Tyalla	1926-1929

Merged clubs

Centrals (Boinka & Linga)	1935-1941, 1945-1956
Gorya (Speed & Turriff)	1914, 1919-1928, 1930-1941, 1945-1964
Imperials (Cowangie & Tutye)	1949-1958
Ouyen Rovers (Kiamal & Tiega)	1982-1996
Ouyen United (Ouyen Rovers & Tempy-Gorya-Patchewollock)	1997-2015
* Ouyen United (Ouyen United & Walpeup-Underbool)	2016-2018
Tempy-Gorya	1965-1970
Tempy-Gorya-Patchewollock	1971-1996
United (Danyo, Imperials & Murrayville)	1960-1966
Walpeup-Underbool	1982-2015

* Still playing

2.3 League Chiefs

Ouyen District Football League

	President	Secretary
1946	L. Goudie	A. Leiper
1947	L. Goudie	A. Leiper
1948	L. Goudie	A. Leiper
1949	L. Goudie	G. Mentiplay
1950	L. Goudie	G. Mentiplay
1951	L. Goudie	H. Carroll
1952	L. Goudie	K. Vallance
1953	L. Goudie	K. Vallance
1954	L. Goudie	K. Vallance

Mallee Football League

	President	Secretary
1955	J. Burns	P. Williams
1956	J. Burns	P. Williams
1957	J. Burns	P. Williams
1958	J. Burns	P. Williams
1959	J. Burns	P. Williams
1960	J. Burns	P. Williams
1961	J. Burns	P. Williams
1962	J. Burns	K. Craddock
1963	J. Burns	A. Vincent
1964	J. Burns	A. Vincent
1965	J. Burns	K. Robson
1966	J. Burns	K. Robson
1967	J. Burns	K. Robson
1968	M. Young	K. Robson
1969	M. Young	K. Robson
1970	M. Young	K. Robson
1971	M. Young	B. Appleby
1972	M. Young	B. Appleby
1973	M. Young	R. Wareham
1974	M. Young	R. Wareham
1975	M. Young	R. Wareham
1976	B. Brown	R. Wareham
1977	B. Brown	R. Wareham
1978	B. Brown	B. Kelly

Northern Mallee Football League

	President	Secretary
1979	B. Brown	B. Kelly
1980	B. Brown	B. Kelly
1981	F. Healy	B. Kelly
1982	K. Robinson	L. Casey
1983	K. Robinson	L. Casey
1984	K. Robinson	L. Casey
1985	K. Robinson	L. Lynch
1986	H. Crothers	L. Lynch
1987	H. Crothers	L. Lynch
1988	H. Crothers	L. Lynch
1989	H. Crothers	L. Lynch
1990	H. Crothers	L. Lynch
1991	H. Crothers	L. Lynch
1992	H. Crothers	L. Lynch
1993	H. Crothers	F. Lynch
1994	A. Hall	L. Rogers
1995	A. Hall	L. Rogers
1996	C. Brown	R. Walton

	President	Secretary
Mallee Football League		
1997	L. Fuller	R. Gravestocks
1998	L. Fuller	R. Gravestocks
1999	L. Fuller	R. Gravestocks
2000	C. Brown	J. McFarlane
2001	C. Brown	J. McFarlane
2002	C. Brown	J. McFarlane
2003	C. Brown	J. McFarlane
2004	T. Kiley	J. McFarlane
2005	T. Kiley	J. McFarlane
2006	J. Hallam	J. McFarlane
2007	J. Hallam	J. McFarlane
2008	J. Hallam	J. McFarlane
2009	A. Malcolm	J. McFarlane
2010	A. Malcolm	J. McFarlane
2011	A. Malcolm	J. McFarlane
2012	A. Malcolm	J. McFarlane
2013	A. Malcolm	J. McFarlane
2014	R. Turnbull	J. McFarlane
2015	M. Brown	A. McFarlane

2.4 League Best and Fairest Award-winners

Year	Player	Club
Ouyen District Football League		
1948	D. Lynch	Patchewollock
1949	J. Jones	Gorya
1950	F. Nicol	Kiamal
1951	J. Jones	Gorya
1952	F. Nicol	Kiamal
1953	G. Casey	Gorya
1954	R. Martin	Tempy
Mallee Football League		
1955	R. Gregg	Ouyen
1956	K. McLean	Gorya
1957	N. Evans	Gorya
1958	L. Smale	Patchewollock
1959	L. Smale	Patchewollock
1960	K. Cramp	Gorya
1961	R. Gregg	Ouyen
1962	N. Lillis	Walpeup
1963	R. Lanyon	Patchewollock
1964	R. Kalms	Murrayville
1965	D. Pohlner	Kiamal
1966	T. Speedie	Ouyen
1967	G. Sporn	Murrayville
1968	R. Smith	Kiamal
1969	R. Kalms	Murrayville
1970	R. Kalms	Murrayville
1971	R. Latta	Walpeup
1972	D. Sporn	Murrayville
1973	D. Sporn	Murrayville
1974	J. Hosking	Kiamal
1975	R. Latta	Walpeup
1976	R. Latta	Walpeup
1977	R. Vallance	Ouyen
1978	R. Vallance	Ouyen

Year	Player	Club
Sunraysia Football League		
1979	G. Lucas	Mildura
	G. Robinson	Red Cliffs
	J. White	Ouyen
1980	P. Nash	Mildura Imperials
1981	T. Fitzgerald	Mildura
1982	J. Cleary	Red Cliffs
Northern Mallee Football League		
1979	G. McMillan	Nandaly
1980	W. Carmichael	Tiega
1981	G. Fitzgerald	Sea Lake
1982	P. Scarrott	Sea Lake
1983	A. Lorincz	Ouyen Rovers
1984	A. Lorincz	Ouyen Rovers
1985	G. Daniels	Sea Lake
1986	L. Morris	Manangatang
1987	C. Baker	Nandaly
1988	G. Burns	TGP
	N. Vallance	Walpeup-Underbool
1989	C. Browne	Manangatang
1990	S. Hadland	Manangatang
1991	J. Angus	Sea Lake
	C. Uchtmann	Manangatang
1992	L. Morris	Manangatang
	W. Stone	Walpeup-Underbool
1993	B. Gaylor	Nandaly
1994	S. Manley	Ouyen Rovers
1995	S. Hulland	TGP
1996	T. Mellington	Ouyen Rovers

Year	Player	Club
Mallee Football League		
1997	C. Powell	Manangatang
1998	G. Allen	Berri-Culgoa
	F. Quick	Brim
1999	H. Bell	Ouyen United
2000	L. Wellington	Hopetoun
2001	C. Durie	Berri-Culgoa
2002	D. Schumann	Jeparit-Rainbow
2003	A. Hiscock	Jeparit-Rainbow
	S. Saunders	Beulah
	D. Schumann	Jeparit-Rainbow
2004	C. Robins	Woomelang-Lascelles
2005	J. Clarke	Beulah
2006	M. Dedini	Woomelang-Lascelles
2007	L. Hutchinson	Hopetoun
2008	J. Clarke	Beulah
2009	S. Weekley	Sea Lake-Nandaly Tigers
2010	S. Smith	Beulah
2011	C. Durie	Sea Lake-Nandaly Tigers
	K. Robins	Walpeup-Underbool
	D. Shannon	Beulah
2012	C. Durie	Sea Lake-Nandaly Tigers
2013	T. Donnan	Woomelang-Lascelles
2014	T. Lehmann	Beulah
2015	T. Donnan	Woomelang-Lascelles
Sunraysia Football League		
2016	N. Hamence	Irymple
	A. Rowe	Merbein
	D. Smith	Wentworth
2017	J. Martin	Mildura
2018	J. Gregg	Ouyen United

2.5 Premiers

Legend
FA = Football Association
FL = Football League

Year	Club
Ouyen District FA	
1910	Ouyen
1911	Ouyen
1912	Walpeup
1913	Walpeup
1914	Ouyen
1915	season abandoned
1916	WW1, in recess
1917	WW1, in recess
1918	WW1, in recess
1919	Walpeup
1920	Walpeup
1921	Nunga
1922	Kiamal
1923	Nunga
1924	Ouyen Rovers
1925	Nunga
1926	Bronzewing
1927	Bronzewing
1928	Ouyen Rovers
1929	Ouyen
1930	Ouyen
1931	Ouyen Rovers
1932	Patchewollock
1933	Ouyen Imperials
1934	Tempy
North West Mallee District FA	
1921	Walpeup
1922	Murrayville
1923	Ouyen
1924	Murrayville
1925	Cowangie
1926	Cowangie
Western Mallee FA	
1927	Tempy
1928	Lascelles
Walpeup & District FA	
1928	Torrita
1929	Tiega
Central Mallee FL	
1929	Speed
Patchewollock & District FA	
1928	Patchewollock
1929	Patchewollock
1930	Baring
Pier Milan & District FA	
1931	Pier Milan
1932	Mittyack
1933	Myall
1934	Myall
1935	Pier Milan
1936	Pier Milan
1937	Pier Milan
1938	Pier Milan
1939	Pier Milan
1940	Nandaly
1941	Kulwin

Year	Club
North West Mallee FL	
1931	Kattyoong
1932	Cowangie
1933	Underbool
1934	Underbool
1935	Underbool
1936	Underbool
1937	Cowangie
1938	Centrals
1939	Cowangie
1940	Murrayville
1941	WW2, in recess
1942	WW2, in recess
1943	WW2, in recess
1944	WW2, in recess
1945	Murrayville
1946	Underbool
1947	Danyo
1948	Murrayville
1949	Imperials
1950	Murrayville
1951	Imperials
1952	Imperials
1953	Murrayville
1954	Murrayville
1955	Underbool
1956	Murrayville
1957	Murrayville
1958	Imperials
Ouyen Junior FL	
1937	Ouyen Juniors
1938	Kiamal
1939	Ouyen Juniors
1940	Bronzewing
Ouyen District FL	
1935	Gorya
1936	Gorya
1937	Ouyen
1938	Ouyen
1939	Tempy
1940	Ouyen
1941	Tempy
1942	WW2, in recess
1943	WW2, in recess
1944	Ouyen
1945	Tiega
1946	Ouyen
1947	Ouyen
1948	Tempy
1949	Tempy
1950	Tempy
1951	Patchewollock
1952	Tempy
1953	Tempy
1954	Ouyen
Mallee FL	
1955	Ouyen
1956	Patchewollock
1957	Patchewollock
1958	Gorya
1959	Gorya
1960	Walpeup
1961	Ouyen
1962	Murrayville

Year	Club
1963	Murrayville
1964	Tiega
1965	Tempy-Gorya
1966	Tempy-Gorya
1967	Tiega
1968	Walpeup
1969	Tiega
1970	Tiega
1971	Kiamal
1972	Tiega
1973	Tiega
1974	Tempy-Gorya-Patchewollock
1975	Underbool
1976	Tiega
1977	Tempy-Gorya-Patchewollock
1978	Walpeup
Sunraysia FL	
1979	Robinvale
1980	Red Cliffs
1981	Red Cliffs
1982	Mildura
Northern Mallee FL	
1979	Nandaly
1980	Tempy-Gorya-Patchewollock
1981	Tempy-Gorya-Patchewollock
1982	Sea Lake
1983	Tempy-Gorya-Patchewollock
1984	Tempy-Gorya-Patchewollock
1985	Ouyen Rovers
1986	Ouyen Rovers
1987	Ouyen Rovers
1988	Sea Lake

Year	Club
1989	Manangatang
1990	Ouyen Rovers
1991	Sea Lake
1992	Sea Lake
1993	Ouyen Rovers
1994	Manangatang
1995	Sea Lake-Nandaly
1996	Manangatang
Mallee FL	
1997	Jeparit-Rainbow
1998	Ouyen United
1999	Berri-Culgoa
2000	Beulah
2001	Walpeup-Underbool
2002	Manangatang
2003	Beulah
2004	Beulah
2005	Beulah
2006	Ouyen United
2007	Walpeup-Underbool
2008	Walpeup-Underbool
2009	Sea Lake-Nandaly Tigers
2010	Beulah
2011	Ouyen United
2012	Walpeup-Underbool
2013	Sea Lake-Nandaly Tigers
2014	Woomelang-Lascelles
2015	Sea Lake-Nandaly Tigers
Sunraysia FL	
2016	Ouyen United
2017	Irymple
2018	Ouyen United

Appendix 3

The Premiership List

Country footballers who have played in six or more senior flags in country Victoria and beyond (since World War 2)

13

John Crisp, **Wy Yung**: 1961; **Omeo**: 1962-1967, 1970-1972, 1975-1977

12

Brad Hartigan, **Horsham**: 2003-2005, 2007-2012, 2014, 2017-2018

Brett Staude, **Mundulla**: 1988-1989, 1991, 1994-2000, 2002, 2004

11

Scott Batchelor, **Horsham**: 1990, 2004-2010; **Horsham Homers**: 1992; **Warracknabeal**: 1994; **Kalkee**: 2000

Ian Clarke, **Mundulla**: 1988-1989, 1991, 1995-2000, 2002, 2004

Ric Hoeben, **Traralgon**: 1980, 1987, 1990-1992, 1994; **Glengarry**: 1983; **Heyfield**: 1997-2000

Andy Kerr, **Fish Creek**: 1955-1956, 1958-1961, 1963-1967

Dick O'Bree, **Lake Boga**: 1953-1954; **Euroa**: 1957-1958, 1963-1965, 1967, 1969-1971

Shane Palmer, **Birchip**: 1986; **Brim**: 1987; **Balranald**: 1989-1990; **Woorinen**: 1993; **Berriwillock-Culgoa**: 1994-1996, 1999; **Tyntynder**: 1997-1998

Mick Ryan, **Edenhope**: 1988; **South Gambier**: 1992, 1994, 1996-2000, 2002, 2005, 2009

Jack Vagg, **Fish Creek**: 1946-1948, 1950, 1952, 1955-1956, 1958-1961

10

Stan Bath, **Fish Creek**: 1947-1948, 1950, 1952, 1955-1956, 1958-1961

Stephen Clarke, **Osborne**: 1991-1992, 1998-2001, 2005; **Albury**: 1995-1997

Tony Hickey, **Mildura Imperials**: 1987-1988, 1990, 1992-1995, 1999, 2004-2005

Shane Hogan, **Nullawil**: 1966, 1971-1973, 1975-1980

Darren Howard, **Osborne**: 1991-1992, 1994, 1998-2001, 2005-2006; **Albury**: 1995

Michael Hunt, **Mundulla**: 1988-1989, 1991, 1994-2000

Roger Hunt, **Mundulla**: 1988, 1991, 1994-2000, 2002

Ben Kenna, **Kolora**: 1995-1996, 2001; **Terang-Mortlake**: 2004-2005, 2008; **Kolora-Noorat**: 2009-2011, 2017

Chris King, **Mundulla**: 1989, 1991, 1994-2000, 2002

Matt O'Toole, **Ultima**: 1996, 2002-2004; **Tyntynder**: 1999; **Golden Square**: 2009-2013

Gerald Pieper, **Wagga Tigers**: 1977-1978, 1980-1981, 1985, 1993-1995, 1997-1998

Adam Salmon, **Glencoe**: 1991-1992; **South Gambier**: 1994, 1996-2000, 2002, 2005

Nick Williams, **Mundulla**: 1989, 1994-2000, 2002, 2004

Ian Wright, **West End**: 1951-1955; **Warrnambool**: 1957, 1959-1960,1962-1963

9

Anthony Armstrong, **Mangoplah-Cookardinia United**: 1993; **Osborne**: 1998-2001, 2005-2006, 2009, 2012

Terry Arnel, **Birchip-Watchem**: 2001; **Horsham**: 2005-2012

Leigh Capewell, **South Gambier**: 1992, 1994, 1996-1998, 2002, 2005, 2009; **Nangwarry**: 1999

Steve Dean, **South Bendigo**: 1990-1991, 1993, **Calivil United**: 2003-2008

Stuart Farr, **Horsham**: 2003-2011

Hayden Gleeson, **Osborne**: 1998-2001, 2005-2006, 2009, 2012, 2017

Keith "Chow" Harvey, **Chiltern**: 1945, 1947-1951, 1953, 1957-1958

Alan "Max" Kennedy, **Mt Pleasant**: 1979-1981, 1983-1984, 1990, 1993-1994, 1997

Michael King, **Mundulla**: 1994-2000, 2002, 2004

Peter Morrison, **Nullawil**: 1971-1973, 1975-1980

John Orr, **North Ballarat**: 1983-1986, 1991-1992, 1994-1996

Joe O'Brien, **Carngham-Linton**: 1982-1985, 1989-1990, 1995, 1997-1998

John Peake, **Chiltern**: 1945, 1947-1951, 1953, 1957-1958

Ron Pollington, **Yarra Junction**: 1954-1955; **Jerilderie**: 1963; **Nullawil**: 1964, 1966, 1971-1973, 1975

Robin Poole, **Berriwillock**: 1954-1956; **Swan Hill**: 1961-1962, 1968-1970, 1972

Keith Poyner, **Nullawil**: 1971-1973, 1975-1980

Trevor Ryan, **Birchip**: 1986; **Brim**: 1987; **Balranald**: 1989-1990; **Woorinen**: 1993; **Tyntynder**: 1997-1999; **Birchip-Watchem**: 2001

Huk Scown, **Mundulla**: 1983, 1988-1989, 1991, 1994-1998

Tony Southcombe, **Golden Square**: 1972, 1975-1976, 1979; **Boort**: 1982; **Northern United**, 1984-1987

Ken Townrow, **Nullawil**: 1964, 1966, 1971-1972, 1976-1980

Joe Talbot, **Fish Creek**: 1958-1961, 1963-1967

Trevor Trewin, **Wycheproof-Narraport**: 1972, 1975-1977, 1981, 1983-1985, 1991

8

Brad Aiken, **Collingullie-Ashmont-Kapooka**: 1999, 2002-2003, 2008-2010, 2014; **Collingullie-Glenfield Park**: 2015

Wayne Billings, **Warrnambool**: 1984, 1986-1989, 1992, 2001-2002

Paul Bills, **Bairnsdale**: 2000-2002, 2006-2007, 2009-2010; **Maffra**: 2004

Josh Bray, **Murrabit**: 1999, 2005, 2007; **Kerang**: 2010, 2013-2016

Michael Brenia, **Wangaratta Rovers**: 1964-1965, 1971; **Beechworth**: 1974, 1979; **Tarrawingee**: 1975; **Glenrowan**: 1980-1981

Len Brill, **Ganmain**: 1946, 1948-1951, 1953, 1956-1957

Neville Buckland, **Fish Creek**: 1959-1961, 1963-1967

William Caldow, **Carngham-Linton**: 1985, 1987, 1989-1990, 1995, 1997-1998, 2000

Don "Dumpy" Calvert, **Bairnsdale Rovers**: 1946; **Bairnsdale**: 1951-1952, 1954, 1956; **Lucknow**: 1959; **Lindenow South**: 1962, 1964

Stewart Carr, **Mildura Imperials**: 1992-1995, 1999, 2004; **Wentworth**: 2001; **Manangatang**: 2002

Bill Carroll, **Ganmain**: 1946, 1948-1951, 1953, 1956-1957

John "Digger" Carroll, **Ganmain**: 1946, 1948-1951, 1953, 1956-1957

David Chant, **Kongorong**: 1988; **South Gambier**: 1992, 1994, 1996-2000

Damian Clark, **Ocean Grove**: 1994-1997, 2000-2003

Ron Clifford, **North Geelong**: 1949-1955, 1958

Bill Couch, **Terang**: 1979, 1981; **Warrnambool**: 1984, 1986-1989, 1992

Mathew Davidson, **Bairnsdale**: 2002, 2004, 2006-2007, 2009-2010; **Romsey**: 2011-2012

Matt Davies, **Nathalia**: 2007-2008, 2012, 2015-2017; **Shepparton United**: 2010-2011

Jack Dean, **North Geelong**: 1949-1955, 1958

Kevin Delaney, **Upwey-Tecoma**: 1978-1980, 1989-1991, 1993-1994

Aaron Demeo, **Calivil**: 1996; **Calivil United**: 1998, 2003-2008

Col Durie, **Berriwillock-Culgoa**: 1994-1996, 1999; **Echuca**: 2002; **Sea Lake-Nandaly Tigers**: 2009, 2014-2015

Frank Fopiani, **North Shore**: 1993, 1995-2000; **St Mary's**: 2004

Matt Fowler, **Albury**: 1995-1997, 2009-2011; **Thurgoona**: 2016-2017

Andrew Freemantle, **Calivil**: 1996; **Golden Square**: 2001; **Calivil United**: 2003-2008

Justin Gee, **Mt Pleasant**: 1993-1995, 1997, 2000-2001, 2005-2006

Nathan Gemmill, **Rochester**: 1999; **Nathalia**: 2005-2008, 2012; **Shepparton United**: 2010-2011

Ben Goodall, **Koroit**: 2003, 2007, 2009, 2014-2018

Brady Herdman, **Eaglehawk**: 2007-2008; **Wedderburn**: 2011-2014; **North Bendigo**: 2015-2016

Greg Hixon, **Waaia**: 1989-1992, 1994-1995, 2002, 2005

Brendan "Joe" Hogan, **Nullawil**: 1971-1973, 1975, 1977-1980

Colin Hunt, **North Ballarat**: 1982-1986, 1991-1992, 1996

David Johns, **Horsham**: 2003-2010

Jason Limbrick, **Nathalia**: 2006-2008, 2012, 2015-2018

Wes Lewis, **Torquay**: 1987, 1989; **North Ballarat**: 1991-1992, 1994; **Tyntynder**: 1998-1999; **Woorinen**: 2002

Joel Mackie, **Jindera**: 2008; **Albury**: 2009-2011, 2014-2016, 2018

Wayne Mayne, **Mildura Imperials**: 1986, 1988, 1990, 1992-1995, 1999

Cliff McGannon, **Fish Creek**: 1952, 1955-1956, 1958, 1960-1961, 1963-1964

Mark McLennan, **Wycheproof-Narraport**: 1981, 1983-1985, 1991, 1995-1997

Christen McPherson, **Ganmain-Grong Grong-Matong**: 1996, 2004-2006, 2008-2011

Greg "Googa" Morley, **Traralgon**: 1990-1992, 1994, 1998-2000, 2005
Paul Mullen, **South Gambier**: 1994, 1996-2000; 2002, 2005
Craig Nankervis, **Frankston YCW**: 2003, 2010-2012, 2014-2017
Robert "Ninga" O'Connell, **Golden Square**: 1975-1976, 1979; **Eaglehawk**: 1980, 1982; **Mt Pleasant**: 1990, 1993-1994
Luke O'Toole, **Ultima**: 1996, 2002-2003, 2006, 2014-2015; **Tyntynder**: 1999, 2002
Matt "Chicken" Palmer, **Ultima**: 2002-2003; **Swan Hill**: 2005; **Walpeup-Underbool**: 2007-2008, 2012; **Ouyen United**: 2016, 2018
Irvine Park, **Fish Creek**: 1948, 1952, 1955-1956, 1958-1960, 1963
Steven Priest, **Wagga Tigers**: 1993-1995, 1997-1999, 2001, 2007
Simon Riddoch, **North Shore**: 1990, 1993, 1995-2000
Tim Robb, **North Albury**: 1955; **Wagga Tigers**: 1957-1959, 1961-1962; **Collingullie**: 1963-1964
Brad Rohde, **Bridgewater**: 2010-2016; **Strathfieldsaye**: 2017
Steven Schultz, **Culcairn**: 1990; **Wagga Tigers**: 1993-1995, 1997-1999, 2001
Eric Smith, **Fish Creek**: 1946-1948, 1950, 1952, 1955-1956, 1958
Troy "Snowy" Thamm, **Kerang**: 2004, 2010, 2012-2017
Danny Verbeek, **Wycheproof-Narraport**: 1983, 1985, 1991, 1995, 1997;
Nullawil: 1998, 2000-2001
Scott Waarsdorp, **Waaia**: 1989-1992, 1994-1995; **Kyabram**: 1996; **Rushworth**: 2004
Danny Warren, **North Shore**: 1993, 1995-2000; **Belmont Lions**: 2007
Clinton Wells, **South Barwon**: 2001, 2005-2007, 2009-2010, 2012-2013

7

John Albon, **North Shore**: 1974, 1976-1977, 1980-1981, 1983, 1990
Trent Anderson, **Heyfield**: 1997-2000, 2005, 2007, 2009
Greg Andrews, **Mundulla**: 1988-1989, 1991, 1994-1997
Greg Atkins, **Pakenham**: 1973-1974, 1982, 1987-1990
Drew Barnes, **Nathalia**: 2005-2008, 2018; **Yarrawonga**: 2012-2013
Sam Barnes: **Wedderburn**: 2007, 2011-2014; **North Bendigo**: 2015-2016
Byron Barry, **Frankston YCW**: 2010-2012, 2014-2017
Ash Bennett, **Nullawil**: 1986; **Wycheproof-Narraport**: 1991, 1995-1997, 2000; **Minyip**: 1992
Allan Bish, **Wycheproof-Narraport**: 1983-1985, 1991, 1995-1997
Denis Brooks, **Waaia**: 1989-1992, 1994-1995, 2002
Peter Brown, **North Ballarat**: 1978-1979, 1982-1986
Scott Brown, **Swan Hill**: 1991, 2005, 2008; **Minyip**: 1992-1993; **Minyip-Murtoa**: 1996-1997
John Brunner, **Benalla All Blacks**: 1981; **Yarrawonga**: 1989; **Barooga**: 1992-1994, 1997; **Devenish**: 2005
Milne "Spud" Bryant, **Walwa**: 1948-1950, 1955-1958

Hayden Burgiel, **Maffra**: 2002-2004, 2006-2007, 2009-2010
Ryan "Rizza" Butler, **Nathalia**: 2005-2008, 2018; **Shepparton United**: 2010- 2011
Wilfred Carter, **Lindenow South**: 1997-1998, 2013, 2015-2016; **Wy Yung**: 2005, 2008
Col Campbell, **Woodside**: 1947-1952, 1957
Luke Carr, **Horsham**: 2004-2009, 2017
Laurie "Dooley" Carroll, **Ganmain**: 1946, 1949-1951, 1953, 1956-1957
Russell Christy, **Orbost**: 1981, 1990, 1996, 1998-1999; **Buchan**: 2004-2005
Trevor Clarke, **Osborne**: 1994-1995, 1998-2001; **Griffith**: 2003
Darren Clutton, **Bridgewater**: 2010-2016
Troy Coates, **Kerang**: 2004, 2012-2017
Jie Coghlan, **Frankston YCW**: 2010-2012, 2014-2017
Ray "Flex" Colvin, **Wagga Tigers**: 1985, 1993-1995, 1997-1999
Warren Coles, **Wycheproof-Narraport**: 1975-1977, 1981, 1983-1985
Arthur "Dookie" Crozier, **Ganmain**: 1946, 1948-1951, 1953, 1956
Andrew Dalgleish, **Cranbourne**: 1985-1987, 1989-1991, 1995
Greg Dinning, **Mundulla**: 1989, 1995-2000
John Drummond, **Walwa**: 1948-1950, 1955-1958
Ash Eames, **Frankston YCW**: 2010-2012, 2014-2017
Adrian Fantella, **Bell Post Hill**: 2010-2012, 2014-2017
Dave Foat, **Woodside**: 1947-1952, 1957
George Foat, **Woodside**: 1947-1952, 1957
James Garvey, **South Barwon**: 2005-2007, 2009-2010, 2012-2013
Joel Geue, **Horsham**: 2005-2009, 2014, 2017
John "Jock" Gibbins, **Tiega**: 1964, 1967, 1969-1970, 1972-1973, 1976
Ryan "Woody" Gillingham, **Kerang**: 2010, 2012-2017
Owen Gooden, **Osborne**: 1998-2001, 2005-2006; **Turvey Park**: 2002
Drew Haebich, **Devenish**: 2003, 2005; **Tungamah**: 2008-2009, 2013-2015
Scott Hamblin, **Ganmain-Grong Grong-Matong**: 1991-1992, 1996, 2004-2006, 2008
Irving "Bubbles" Hanna, **Walwa**: 1948-1950, 1955-1958
Jason Hillier, **Mundulla**: 1995-2000, 2004
Bill Hocking, **West End**: 1954-1955, 1962; **Warrnambool**: 1957, 1959-1960, 1966
Merv Holmes, **Milawa**: 1969; **Wangaratta Rovers**: 1972, 1974-1975, 1977-1979
Ron Howes, **Chiltern**: 1945, 1947-1948, 1950-1951, 1953, 1957
Kevin Hunt, **Border-Walwa**: 1984, 1990-1992, 1996-1998
Kyle Hutchison, **Frankston YCW**: 2010-2012, 2014-2017
Chris Hyde, **Albury**: 2009-2011, 2014-16, 2018

Norm Jackson, **Pakenham**: 1947-1948, 1951-1952, 1955-1957

Deon Jones, **Bridgewater**: 2010-2016

Glenn Keast, **North Gambier**: 1987; **North Shore**: 1995-2000

Max Kerr, **Woodside**: 1947-1952, 1957

Cecil Kidgal, **Pakenham**: 1947-1948, 1951-1952, 1955-1957

Tony Lane, **Traralgon**: 1987, 1990-1992, 1994, 1998-1999

Alan Lowe, **Traralgon**: 1978, 1980; **Morwell**: 1983, 1985, 1988; **Yarram**: 1986; **Won Wron-Woodside**: 1994

Mark Lloyd, **Golden Square**: 2009-2013; **Wedderburn**: 2014; **Kerang**: 2016

Shane Lymer, **Bell Post Hill**: 2010-2012, 2014-2017

Terry Mackin, **Fish Creek**: 1946-1948, 1950, 1952, 1955-1956

Bob Mason, **Sale**: 1949-1950, 1953-1955, 1957, 1959

Travis Matheson, **Kerang**: 2010, 2012-2017

Ross Maxted, **South Bendigo**, 1994; **Calivil United**: 2003-2008

Bill McConnell, **West End**: 1954-1955; **Warrnambool**: 1957, 1959-1960, 1962-1963

Lee McCorkell, **Warrnambool**: 1977-1978, 1884, 1986-1989

Ray McGannon, **Fish Creek**: 1955-1956, 1958-1961, 1963

Eddie McNicol, **Wycheproof-Narraport**: 1981, 1983-1985, 1991, 1995, 1997

Josh Mibus, **Donald**: 2006; **Kalkee**: 2009-2012; **Horsham**: 2017-2018

Tim Milsome, **North Shore**: 1990, 1995-2000

Pat Monckton, **Pakenham**: 1951-1952, 1955-1957, 1961-1962

Phillip "Toot" Morgan, **Shepparton United**: 1988-1989; **Colbinabbin**: 1991, 1998-1999, 2002-2003

Garry Mountjoy, **Golden Square**: 1975-1976, 1979; **Northern United**: 1984-1987

Daniel Nalder, **Bridgewater**: 2010-2016

Terry Ness, **Turvey Park**: 1980, 1987-1990; **Marrar**: 1995-1996

Steve Norman, **Wangaratta Rovers**: 1971-1972, 1974-1975, 1977-1979

Russell Northe, **Traralgon**: 1990-1992, 1994, 1998-2000

Luke Packer, **Albury**: 2009-2011, 2014-2016, 2018

Matthew Patzel, **South Gambier**: 1996-2000, 2002; **Glencoe:** 2008

Brad Pay, **Kerang**: 2010, 2012-2017

Alan Peake, **Chiltern**: 1945, 1948-1950, 1953, 1957-1958

Ray Pincott, **Bairnsdale**: 1947, 1951-1952, 1954, 1956, 1958-1959

Anthony Pisano, **St Mary's**: 2004; **Bell Post Hill**: 2010-2012, 2014-2016

Hayden Polglase, **Calivil United**: 2003-2004; **Wedderburn**: 2007, 2011-2014

Russell "Wally" Pratt: **Ellinbank**: 1974-1975, 1983-1984, 1988, 1995; **Buln Buln**: 1981

Michael Preston, **Bairnsdale**: 2001-2002, 2006, 2009-2010; **Lindenow**: 2016-2017

Andrew Priest, **Wagga Tigers**: 1994-1995, 1997-1999, 2001, 2007

Jack Purse, **Walwa**: 1948-1950, 1955-1958
Ash Quinn, **Nathalia**: 2006-2008, 2012, 2015-2016, 2018
Glenn Richards, **Calivil**: 1990, 1996; **Calivil United**: 1998, 2003-2006
Wes Richardson, **Darley**: 1954, 1956; **Nhill**: 1964-1965, 1969; **Horsham**: 1970, 1974
Darren Ryan, **North Shore**: 1993, 1995-1996, 1998-2000; **Bannockburn**: 2003
John Ryan, **Fish Creek**: 1956, 1958, 1963, 1965-1967; **Rupanyup**: 1961
Leo Ryan, **Nullawil**: 1975-1980, 1986
Steve Saynor, **Upwey-Tecoma**: 1978-1980, 1989-1991; **Won Wron-Woodside**: 1994
Darren Scott, **Waaia**: 1989-1992, 1994-1995, 2002
Darren Sims, **South Gambier**: 1992, 1994, 1996-1997, 1999-2000, 2002
Mitchell Steele, **Ganmain-Grong Grong-Matong**: 2004-2006, 2008-2011
Guy Stringer, **Pines**: 1994; **Sorrento**: 2004, 2008, 2010-2012, 2014
Len "Spot" Taylor, **Walwa**: 1948-1950, 1955-1958
Isaac Templeton, **Koroit**: 2007, 2009, 2014-2017; **Nirranda**: 2018
Michael Thompson, **Albury**: 2009-2011, 2014-2016, 2018
Bruce Tompkins, **North Geelong**: 1949-1955, 1958
Damien Tubb, **Bairnsdale**: 2000-2002, 2004; **Swifts Creek**: 2008, 2010-2011
Frank Tuohey, **Mt Pleasant**: 1968, 1971, 1979-1981, 1983-1984
Brett Vallender, **Nathalia**: 2005, 2007-2008, 2012, 2015-2017
Luke Walsh, **Ganmain-Grong Grong-Matong**: 2004-2006, 2008-2011
Clive "Wonder" Waugh, **North Geelong**: 1949-1953, 1955, 1958
John White, **Wycheproof-Narraport**: 1972, 1976-1977, 1981, 1983-1985
Paul White, **Wycheproof-Narraport**: 1975-1977, 1981, 1984-1985, 1991
Paul Williams, **North Shore**: 1993, 1995-2000
Adam Wiseman, **Geelong Amateurs**: 2004; **South Barwon**: 2006-2007, 2009-2010, 2012-2013

6

Cameron Addie, **Bell Post Hill**: 2011-2012, 2014-2017
Graeme D. Allan, **Wycheproof-Narraport**: 1965, 1967, 1972, 1975-1977
Caleb Bacely, **Bell Post Hill**: 2010-2012, 2014-2015, 2017
Geoffrey Balderas, **Lorne**: 1974, 1976, 1980-1983
Ash Barker, **Redan**: 2002-2003, 2006-2007, 2009, 2011
Anthony Barry, **Frankston YCW**: 2010-2012, 2014-2015, 2017
Tim Barton, **Bell Post Hill**: 2010, 2012, 2014-2017
Graeme Bates, **Traralgon**: 1963-1965, 1968-1969, 1972
Mark Berenger, **Frankston YCW**: 1989, 1991-1993, 1997, 2003
David Bodley, **Frankston YCW**: 2010-2012, 2014-2016
Brian Bourke, **Pakenham**: 1951-1952, 1955-1957, 1961

Hugh Bourke, **Pakenham**: 1952, 1955-1957, 1961-1962
Des Brisbane, **Shepparton**: 1963-1966, 1968-1969
Sam Bristow, **Maffra**: 2003-2004, 2006-2007, 2009-2010
David Brooks, **Barooga**: 1981, 1986-1987, 1992-1993; **Cobram**: 1984
Kevin Brooks, **Barooga**: 1986-1987; 1992-1994, 1997
Arthur Buckland, **Fish Creek**: 1961, 1963-1967
Damien Bunworth, **Laharum**: 1995; **Horsham**: 2003-2007
Jordyn Burke, **Horsham**: 2008-2010, 2012, 2014, 2018
Norm Bussell, **Wangaratta Rovers**: 1964-1965, 1974-1975; **Whorouly**: 1977-1978
Doug Cail, **Northern United**: 1967, 1972-1973, 1975, 1978-1979
Anthony "George" Carroll, **Ganmain-Grong Grong-Matong**: 1996, 2004-2006, 2008; **Rivcoll**: 2001
Brian "Mick" Carroll, **Ganmain**: 1949-1951, 1953, 1956-1957
Garry "Curly" Carroll, **Ganmain**: 1953, 1956-1957, 1964-1965, 1969
Joe Carroll, **Ganmain**: 1946, 1948-1951, 1953
Gary Chequer, **Horsham**: 1968, 1970, 1972, 1974, 1976, 1979
Graeme "Yank" Clark, **Minyip**: 1991-93; **Minyip-Murtoa**: 1996-98
Jesse Clark, **Kerang**: 2010, 2012, 2014-2017
Matthew Coates, **Kerang**: 2010, 2012-2016
Michael Collins, **Narre Warren**: 2006-2008, 2010, 2012-2013
Barry Cook, **Wangaratta Rovers**: 1974-1975, 1977-1979; **Milawa**: 1985
Alistair Corry, **Nathalia**: 2008, 2012, 2015-2018
John Craig, **Mt Pleasant**: 1984, 1990, 1993-1995, 1997
Luke Daly, **Albury**: 2010-2011, 2014-2016, 2018
Greg Excell, **Mundulla**: 1996-2000, 2002
Denis Farr, **Horsham**: 1967-1968, 1970, 1972, 1974; **Kalkee**: 1978
Maurie "Bumper" Farrell, **Moyhu**: 1959-1960, 1962; **Greta**: 1965-1967
Matthew Fear, **South Gambier**: 1992, 1994, 1996-1998, 2000
Derrick Filo, **Castlemaine**: 1992; **Balranald**: 1994; **Kyneton**: 1995, 1997; **Eaglehawk**: 2007-2008
Eddie Flynn, **North Wangaratta**: 1973; **Wangaratta Rovers**: 1974-1975, 1977-1979
Ray Foat, **Woodside**: 1947-1952
Kevin French, **Wangaratta**: 1946, 1949-1952; **Tarrawingee**: 1953
Travis Fursland, **Bell Post Hill**: 2010-2012, 2014-2016
Murray Gall, **Euroa**: 1964-1965, 1967, 1969-1971
Raymond Gallagher, **Swifts Creek**: 1980-1982, 1993, 1997, 2002
Pat Garrett, **Cranbourne**: 1986-1987, 1989-1991, 1993
Marty Gleeson, **North Ballarat**: 1978-1979, 1982-1984, 1986
Paul Gleeson, **Osborne**: 1991-1992, 1995, 1998, 2000-2001
Wayne Glynn, **South Gambier**: 1992, 1994, 1996-1999

Luke Gooden, **Osborne**: 1992, 1994-1995, 1999, 2005-2006
Bill Gordon, **Wycheproof**: 1951-1952, 1957; **Wycheproof-Narraport**: 1964-1965, 1967
Keith "Swampy" Gumbleton, **Ganmain**: 1946, 1948-1951, 1953
Brian Hammond, **Traralgon**: 1963-1965, 1968-1969, 1972
Jim Hart, **Sale**: 1950, 1953-1955, 1957, 1959
Tom Hart, **Sale**: 1950, 1953-1955, 1957, 1959
Jeremy Hartigan, **Horsham**: 2007, 2009-2012, 2014
John Haynes, **Swifts Creek**: 1993, 1997, 2001-2002, 2010-2011
Peter Hickey, **Mildura Imperials**: 1990, 1992-1995, 1999
Neville Hogan, **Wangaratta Rovers**: 1964-1965, 1971-1972, 1974-1975
Peter Hogan, **Nullawil**: 1976-1980, 1986
Nick Horsford, **Maffra**: 2002-2004, 2006, 2009-2010
Justin Hosie, **Osborne**: 1992, 1995, 1998-2001
Victor Hugo, **Narrandera**: 1972, 1974, 1979, 1981, 1986; **Coleambally**: 1977
Wayne "Radish" Hulands, **Simpson**: 1970, 1975-1976, 1979, 1981-1982
Terry Hunter, **Traralgon**: 1963-1965, 1969, 1972, 1978
Grant Johnson, **Sorrento**: 2004, 2008, 2010-2012, 2014
Allan Jones, **Wycheproof-Narraport**: 1964-1965, 1967, 1972, 1975-1976
Gary Jones, **Maffra**: 2002-2004, 2006-2007, 2010
Jason Kerby, **South Barwon**: 2006-2007, 2009-2010, 2012-2013
Jason Kimball, **Border-Walwa**: 1990-1992, 1996-1998
Ben Lappin, **Chiltern**: 1945, 1947-1951
Wes Lappin, **Chiltern**: 1947-1951, 1953
Tony Lester, **Frankston YCW**: 2003, 2011, 2014-2017
Anthony Lowe, **Mundulla**: 1989, 1991, 1994-1996, 1998
Tim Lowe, **Wangaratta**: 1949-1952, **Beechworth**: 1956; **Moyhu**: 1960
Linsey Lucas, **Woodside**: 1947-1952
David Ludeman, **Northern United**: 1978-1979, 1984-1987
Kevin Lylak, **Frankston YCW**: 2011-2012, 2014-2017
Peter Lynch, **Yarram**: 1972, 1977, 1986; **Leongatha**: 1979, 1985; **Devon-Welshpool**: 1995
Wayne Lynch, **Yarram**: 1972, 1977, 1986; **Leongatha**: 1979, 1982; **Devon**: 1987
Kevin Mack, **Tyntynder**: 1955; **Wangaratta**: 1957, 1961; **Corryong**: 1968-1969, 1972
Daniel Maher, **Albury**: 2009-2011, 2014-2016
Seamus Maloney, **Mildura Imperials**: 1992-1993, 1995, 2004-2005, 2008
Roly Marklew, **Wangaratta Rovers:** 1960, 1971-1972; **Tarrawingee**: 1963-1964; **North Wangaratta**: 1976
Rob Masters, **Lake Boga**: 1975; **Tyntynder**: 1980, 1983-1984, 1986-1987
Trevor Mattison, **Sorrento**: 2004, 2008, 2010-2012, 2014

Lloyd Maxted, **Calivil**: 1996; **Calivil United**: 1998, 2005-2008.
Josh McCann, **South Barwon**: 2005-2007, 2009-2010, 2012
Ben McCormack, **Sorrento**: 2004, 2008, 2010-2012, 2014
Steven McCormack, **Border-Walwa**: 1990-1992, 1996-1998
Jason McGowan, **North Shore**: 1990, 1993, 1995-1997; **Torquay**: 1988
John McGrath, **Jindera**: 1956-1957, 1960-1961, 1963-1964
Mick McKay, **Tiega**: 1967, 1969-1970, 1972-1973, 1976
Chris McLaren, **Koroit**: 2003, 2007, 2009, 2014-2015, 2017
Joe McLaren, **Koroit**: 2007, 2009, 2014-2017
Neil "Ninga" McLennan, **Nullawil**: 1973, 1975-1977; **Tyntynder**: 1980, 1983
David McNamara, **Mt Pleasant**: 1990, 1993, 1995, 1997, 2000-2001
Les McPherson, **Ganmain**: 1946, 1948-1951, 1953
Kevin McVilly, **Simpson**: 1975, 1979, 1981-1982, 1991, 1993
Ralph Medcalf, **Inglewood**: 1946, 1951, 1953-1954, 1956, 1958
Peter "Dicky" Morrison, **Horsham**: 1967-1968, 1970, 1979, 1982-1983
Kevin Mills, **Kalkee**: 2000, 2008-2012
Norm Minns, **Chiltern**: 1947; **Wangaratta**: 1949-1952; **Benalla**: 1953
Jon Mock, **Mundulla**: 1997-2000, 2002, 2004
Doug Monckton, **Pakenham**: 1948, 1951-1952, 1955-1957
Bill Morrish, **Tiega**: 1967, 1969-1970, 1972-1973; **Underbool**: 1975
Lindsay Morrish, **Tiega**: 1964, 1967, 1969-1970, 1972-1973
Michael Mullan, **South Gambier**: 1996-2000, 2002
Justin Munro, **South Gambier**: 1996; **Coleraine**: 2005, 2007-2010
Gary Murnane, **Lorne**: 1974, 1976, 1980-1983
Robert Newnham, **Border-Walwa**: 1984, 1990, 1992, 1996-1998
Paul Nihill, **Mt Pleasant**: 1994-1995, 1997, 2000, 2005-2006
Brian Noonan, **Shepparton**: 1963-1966, 1968-1969
Gerard O'Neill, **Chiltern**: 1947-1951, 1953
Vin O'Neill, **Kiewa-Sandy Creek**: 1972, 1976-1977, 1981, 1983-1984
Bill Peake, **Chiltern**: 1957-1958, 1968, 1971-1972; **Wangaratta**: 1961
Frank Peake, **Chiltern**: 1947-1951, 1957
Anthony Perkins, **Jeparit-Rainbow**: 1997; **Kalkee**: 2000, 2008-2009; **Horsham**: 2004-2005
Barry Phelan, **Tiega**: 1964, 1967, 1969-1970, 1972-1973
Stephen Pratt, **Ellinbank**: 1983-1984, 1987-1988, 1995; **Nyora**: 1993
David Preston, **Bairnsdale**: 2000-2002, 2004, 2006-2007
Lachie Ralphs, **Calivil United**: 2003-2008
Matt Rava, **Ganmain-Grong Grong-Matong**: 2006, 2008-2011; **Osborne**: 2017
Chris Redenbach, **Bairnsdale**: 1981; **Lindenow**: 1986, 1989, 1991; **Lucknow**: 1993, 1997
Tim Robinson, **Wandella**: 2008-2011, 2017; **Kerang**: 2014

Windsor Rochester, **Inglewood**: 1946, 1951, 1953-1954, 1956, 1958
Arthur Roy, **Ganmain**: 1949-1951, 1953, 1956-1957
Mark Sandilands, **Upwey-Tecoma**: 1989-1991, 1993-1994, 1999
Nick Scanlon, **Narre Warren**: 2006-2008, 2010, 2012-2013
Troy Schwarze, **Sorrento**: 2008, 2010-2012, 2014, 2017
Eddie Shaddock, **Tiega**: 1964, 1967, 1969-1970, 1972-1973
Harry Shaddock, **Tiega**, 1964, 1967, 1969-1970, 1972-1973
Bob Sharman, **Chiltern**: 1947-1951; **Barnawatha**: 1956
Blake Shay, **Kerang**: 2012-2017
Steve Sherwell, **Ocean Grove**: 1994-1997, 2000, 2003
Heath Sims, **South Gambier**: 1998-2000, 2002, 2005, 2009
Craig Smith, **Bairnsdale**: 2000-2002, 2004, 2006-2007
Darryl Smith, **Wangaratta Rovers**: 1972, 1974-1975, 1977-1979
Jarad Smith, **Calivil United**: 1998, 2003-2007
Rob Soulsby, **Bairnsdale**: 2000-2002, 2004, 2006-2007
Ron Standfield, **Fish Creek**: 1958-1961, 1963, 1967
Adrian Stapleton, **Ocean Grove**: 1995, 1997, 2000-2003
Craig Staude, **Mundulla**: 1988-1989, 1991, 1994, 1996-1997
Ben Tellis, **Frankston YCW**: 2003, 2010-2012, 2014-2015
Bill Toleman, **Warrnambool**: 1957, 1959-1960, 1962-1963, 1966
Neil Tompkins, **North Geelong**: 1949-1954
Craig Tosetti, **Coleraine**: 2005, 2007-2010, 2013
Tim Traill, **Boolarra**: 1997; **Mirboo North**: 2006-2007, 2013-2014, 2017
Des Trotter, **Horsham**: 1970; **East Gambier**: 1972-1973, 1975-1976; **Warracknabeal**: 1977
Barney Tuohey, **Mt Pleasant**: 1971, 1979-1981, 1983-1984
Nigel Van Der Veer, **North Ballarat**: 1978-1979, 1982-1984, 1986
Tom Wallace, **Ellinbank**: 1946, 1952-1955, 1961
Eric Walpole, **Woodside**: 1948-1952, 1957
Mark Walter, **Hamilton**: 2004; **Kerang**: 2012-2016
Robert Waterson, **Nullawil**: 1975-1976, 1978-1979; **Gunbower**: 1980; **Swan Hill**: 1985
David Watts, **Nullawil**: 1979-80, 1986, 1998, 2000-2001
Kevin White, **Lorne**: 1974, 1976, 1980-1983
Brenton Wiese, **Mundulla**: 1983, 1988-1989, 1991, 1994-1995
Graham Wood, **Horsham**: 1970, 1972; **Quantong**: 1973, 1976-1977; **Kalkee**: 1978
Peter Wood, **Horsham**: 1972, 1974, 1976, 1979, 1982; **Laharum**: 1987
Bill Young, **Warrnambool**. 1957, 1959-1960, 1962-1963, 1966
Harry Young, **Kalkee**: 2008-2012; **Horsham**: 2014

Appendix 4

2018 Season Review

Legend

FL = Football League
LEAGUE B&F MEDAL = league best-and-fairest medal
BOG AWARD = best-on-ground award in Grand Final

ALBERTON FL

Fish Creek	**56**
Stony Creek	**44**
Foster	**36**
Toora	**32**
Tarwin	24
Meeniyan-Dumbalk United	0

LEAGUE B&F MEDAL
Ethan Park, **Fish Creek**
Jesse Manton, **Toora**

LEADING GOALKICKER
Kael Bergles, **Stony Creek** 89

GRAND FINAL
Fish Creek 14.11 (95) d Foster 6.6 (42)

VENUE
Meeniyan Recreation Reserve

BOG MEDALS
Ethan Park, **Fish Creek**
Tom Cameron, **Fish Creek**

BALLARAT FL

East Point	**60**
North Ballarat City	**52**
Melton	**52**
Darley	**52**
Bacchus Marsh	**48**
Lake Wendouree	**44**
Sebastopol	40
Sunbury	40
Redan	20
Ballarat	20
Melton South	12

LEAGUE B&F MEDAL
Daniel Burton, **Bacchus Marsh**

LEADING GOALKICKER
Aaron Witts, **Bacchus Marsh** 51

GRAND FINAL
Melton 14.11 (95) lt **East Point** 15.7 (97)

VENUE
Mars Stadium, North Ballarat

BOG MEDAL
Paul Kodorenko, **East Point**

BELLARINE FL

Barwon Heads	**64**
Anglesea	**48**
Modewarre	**44**
Geelong Amateur	**44**
Queenscliff	**44**

Ocean Grove	40
Torquay	36
Drysdale	20
Portarlington	12
Newcomb	8

LEAGUE B&F MEDAL
Jackson Bews, **Anglesea**
Matthew Dyer, **Barwon Heads**

LEADING GOALKICKER
Jordan Erskine, **Anglesea** 83

GRAND FINAL
Barwon Heads 5.16 (46) lt **Modewarre** 14.9 (93)

VENUE
Mortimer Oval, Drysdale

BOG MEDAL
John Meesen, **Modewarre**

BENDIGO FL

Strathfieldsaye	**64**
Eaglehawk	**60**
Kyneton	**50**
Sandhurst	**48**
Gisborne	**44**
Golden Square	40
South Bendigo	30
Kangaroo Flat	16
Maryborough	4
Castlemaine	4

LEAGUE B&F MEDAL
Jack Geary, **Golden Square**

LEADING GOALKICKER
Kaiden Antonowicz, **South Bendigo** 76

GRAND FINAL
Eaglehawk 19.8 (122) d Strathfieldsaye 11.7 (73)

VENUE
Queen Elizabeth Oval, Bendigo

BOG MEDALS
Jonty Neaves, **Eaglehawk**
Brodie Collins, **Eaglehawk**

CENTRAL HIGHLANDS FL

Waubra	**64**
Beaufort	**60**
Gordon	**56**
Buninyong	**52**
Springbank	**52**
Hepburn	**48**
Newlyn	**44**
Dunnstown	**42**
Bungaree	40
Learmonth	34
Ballan	28
Skipton	28
Creswick	20
Rokewood-Corindhap	16
Daylesford	12
Clunes	8
Carngham-Linton	8

LEAGUE B&F MEDAL
Joel Mahar, **Bungaree**

LEADING GOALKICKER
Jack Duke, **Beaufort** 49

GRAND FINAL
Beaufort 15.9 (99) d Buninyong 9.7 (61)

VENUE
Mars Stadium, North Ballarat

BOG MEDAL
Jack Duke, **Beaufort**

CENTRAL MURRAY FL

Woorinen	**56**
Mallee Eagles	**52**
Swan Hill	**50**
Kerang	**40**
Cohuna Kangas	**36**
Balranald	34
Koondrook-Barham	24
Tooleybuc-Manangatang	22
Tyntynder	16
Lake Boga	14
Nyah-Nyah West United	8

LEAGUE B&F MEDAL
Joel Helman, **Cohuna Kangas**

LEADING GOALKICKER
Glenn Boyd, **Woorinen** 57

GRAND FINAL
Woorinen 15.7 (97) d Mallee Eagles 11.10 (76)

VENUE
Swan Hill Recreation Reserve

BOG MEDAL
Jose Milado, **Woorinen**

COLAC & DISTRICT FL

Birregurra	**66**
Lorne	**60**
South Colac	**56**
Simpson	**46**
Alvie	**44**
Apollo Bay	40
Otway Districts	24
Colac Imperials	18
Irrewarra-Beeac	10
Western Eagles	4

LEAGUE B&F MEDAL
Mark McCormack, **Lorne**

LEADING GOALKICKER
Thomas Mullane-Grant,
Otway Districts 76

GRAND FINAL
Birregurra 5.7 (37) lt **Lorne** 8.10 (58)

VENUE
Central Reserve, Colac

BOG MEDAL
Steven Oliver, **Lorne**

EAST GIPPSLAND FL

Stratford	**54**
Lakes Entrance	**54**
Wy Yung	**46**
Lindenow	**40**
Boisdale-Briagolong	40
Lucknow	38
Paynesville	12
Orbost-Snowy Rovers	4

LEAGUE B&F MEDAL
Lachlan Heywood, **Stratford**

LEADING GOALKICKER
Darren Allen, **Lindenow** 57

GRAND FINAL
Stratford 8.10 (58) d Lakes Entrance 7.6 (48)

VENUE
Bairnsdale Recreation Reserve

BOG MEDAL
Josh Kiss, **Stratford**

ELLINBANK & DISTRICT FL

Nyora	**64**
Longwarry	**56**
Warragul Industrials	**50**
Catani	**46**
Poowong	**44**
Ellinbank	36
Buln Buln	28
Nilma-Darnum	18
Neerim-Neerim South	12
Lang Lang	6

LEAGUE B&F MEDAL
Russell Lehman, **Longwarry**
Jack Hazendonk, **Poowong**

LEADING GOALKICKER
Daniel Fry, **Longwarry** 76

GRAND FINAL
Nyora 3.4 (22) d Longwarry 2.6 (18)

VENUE
Western Park, Warragul

BOG MEDAL
Russell Lehman, **Longwarry**

FARRER FL (NSW)

Marrar	**68**
North Wagga	**64**
Temora	**52**
East Wagga-Kooringal	**48**
Charles Sturt University	**44**
Northern Jets	28
The Rock-Yerong Creek	24
Barellan	20
Coleambally	12

LEAGUE B&F MEDAL
Nick Hull, **East Wagga-Kooringal**

LEADING GOALKICKER
Daniel Jordan, **North Wagga** 71

GRAND FINAL
Marrar 8.8 (56) d North Wagga 6.8 (44)

VENUE
Robertson Oval, Wagga Wagga

BOG MEDAL
Jack Reynolds, **Marrar**

GEELONG FL

Leopold	**68**
St Mary's	**60**
St Joseph's	**56**
South Barwon	**48**
Colac	**48**
Newtown & Chilwell	44
Bell Park	40
Grovedale	24
North Shore	16
Geelong West Giants	12
St Albans	12
Lara	4

LEAGUE B&F MEDAL
Matt McMahon, **Newtown & Chilwell**

LEADING GOALKICKER
Aiden Grace, **St Mary's** 59

GRAND FINAL
St Mary's 11.11 (77) lt **St Joseph's** 13.8 (86)

VENUE
GMHBA Stadium, Geelong

BOG MEDAL
Joe Macula, **St Joseph's**

GEELONG & DISTRICT FL

Inverleigh	**64**
Thomson	**60**
Bell Post Hill	**52**
Geelong West Giants	**48**
Bannockburn	**44**
Winchelsea	44
Werribee Central	42
North Geelong	24
Belmont Lions	20
Anakie	18
East Geelong	16
Corio	0

LEAGUE B&F MEDAL
Matthew James, **Bell Post Hill**

LEADING GOALKICKER
Jayden Ettridge, **Bell Post Hill** 60

GRAND FINAL
Inverleigh 5.13 (43) lt **Thomson** 10.13 (73)

VENUE
Gordon TAFE Oval, St Albans

BOG MEDAL
Reece Holwell, **Thomson**

GIPPSLAND FL

Maffra	**60**
Leongatha	**60**
Sale	**56**
Moe	**40**
Traralgon	**40**
Warragul	36
Bairnsdale	26
Drouin	18
Morwell	16
Wonthaggi	8

LEAGUE B&F MEDAL
Tom Marriott, **Leongatha**

LEADING GOALKICKER
Chris Dunne, **Leongatha** 76

GRAND FINAL
Leongatha 10.13 (73) d Maffra 10.4 (64)

VENUE
Morwell Recreation Reserve

BOG MEDALS
Col Sanbrook, **Leongatha**
Cade Maskell, **Leongatha**

GOLDEN RIVERS FL

Nullawil	**60**
Ultima	**56**
Wandella	**52**
Hay	**40**
Murrabit	28

Moulamein 28
Quambatook 12
Macorna 12
Wakool 0

LEAGUE B&F MEDAL
Andrew Oberdorfer, **Nullawil**

LEADING GOALKICKER
Arnold Kirby, **Ultima** 84

GRAND FINAL
Nullawil 12.16 (88) d Ultima 6.10 (46)

VENUE
Moulamein Recreation Reserve

BOG MEDAL
Kyle Doran, **Nullawil**

GOULBURN VALLEY FL

Kyabram **72**
Shepparton **56**
Benalla **52**
Echuca **52**
Tatura **46**
Mansfield **38**
Euroa 36
Rochester 32
Seymour 28
Shepparton United 16
Mooroopna 4
Shepparton Swans 0

LEAGUE B&F MEDAL
Sam Martyn, **Benalla**
Nik Rokahr, **Shepparton**

LEADING GOALKICKER
Kayne Pettifer, **Kyabram** 106

GRAND FINAL
Kyabram 8.13 (61) lt **Shepparton** 9.9 (63)

VENUE
Deakin Reserve, Shepparton

BOG MEDAL
Ashley Holland, **Shepparton**

HAMPDEN FL

Koroit **64**
Port Fairy **48**
Camperdown **48**
South Warrnambool **40**
Warrnambool **38**
Terang-Mortlake 28
Hamilton Kangaroos 26
Cobden 24
Portland 24
North Warrnambool 20

LEAGUE B&F MEDAL
Brett Harrington, **Koroit**

LEADING GOALKICKER
Jarrod Korewha, **Koroit** 72

GRAND FINAL
Camperdown 6.10 (46) lt **Koroit** 8.9 (57)

VENUE
Reid Oval, Warrnambool

BOG MEDALS
Liam Hoy, **Koroit**
Jeremy Hausler, **Koroit**

HEATHCOTE & DISTRICT FL

North Bendigo	**56**
Leitchville-Gunbower	**56**
Huntly	**48**
Colbinabbin	**40**
Lockington-Bamawm United	**40**
Mount Pleasant	20
White Hills	12
Heathcote	12
Elmore	4

LEAGUE B&F MEDAL
Ryan Semmel, **Huntly**

LEADING GOALKICKER
Matthew Perri, **Leitchville-Gunbower** 78

GRAND FINAL
Leitchville-Gunbower 14.10 (94) d North Bendigo 12.13 (85)

VENUE
Specialist Breeders Australia Oval, Huntly

BOG MEDAL
Jordan Ford, North **Bendigo**

HORSHAM & DISTRICT FL

Harrow-Balmoral	**68**
Kalkee	**64**
Jeparit-Rainbow	**56**
Edenhope-Apsley	**48**
Stawell Swifts	**46**
Natimuk United	**38**
Laharum	36
Noradjuha-Quantong	32
Rupanyup	32
Pimpinio	12
Taylors Lake	8

LEAGUE B&F MEDAL
Nick Pekin, **Harrow-Balmoral**

LEADING GOALKICKER
Jayden Kuhne, **Kalkee** 64

GRAND FINAL
Harrow-Balmoral 11.10 (76) d Kalkee 6.15 (51)

VENUE
Horsham City Oval

BOG MEDAL
Anthony Close, **Harrow-Balmoral**

HUME FL (NSW)

Henty	**64**
Brock-Burrum Saints	**60**
Holbrook	**50**
Osborne	**48**
Jindera	**48**
Culcairn	**40**
Rand-Walbundrie-Walla	30
Howlong	28
Coreen-Daysdale-Hopefield-Buraja United	24
Billabong Crows	16
Lockhart	12
Murray Magpies	12

LEAGUE B&F MEDAL
Steven Jolliffe, **Howlong**

LEADING GOALKICKER
Trent Castles, **Jindera** 111

GRAND FINAL
Brock-Burrum Saints 15.19 (109) d Jindera 8.11 (59)

VENUE
Walbundrie Recreation Reserve

BOG MEDAL
Matt Seiter, **Brock-Burrum Saints**

KOWREE-NARACOORTE-TATIARA FL (SA)

Kaniva-Leeor United	**60**
Penola	**52**
Keith	**48**
Mundulla	**48**
Lucindale	**40**
Naracoorte	24
Border Districts	20
Kybybolite	20
Padthaway	16
Kingston	16
Bordertown	8

LEAGUE B&F MEDAL
George Tiring, **Keith**
Tim McIntyre, **Mundulla**

LEADING GOALKICKER
Nicholas Murphy, **Kaniva-Leeor United** 74

GRAND FINAL
Keith 8.5 (53) lt **Mundulla** 8.8 (56)

VENUE
Keith Recreation Reserve

BOG MEDAL
Jake McGrice, **Mundulla**

KYABRAM & DISTRICT FL

Tallygaroopna	**70**
Stanhope	**66**
Nagambie	**60**
Lancaster	**56**
Dookie United	**48**
Avenel	**40**
Merrigum	40
Girgarre	36
Murchison-Toolamba	28
Undera	26
Violet Town	16
Longwood	8
Rushworth	8
Ardmona	2

LEAGUE B&F MEDAL
Kaine Herbert, **Undera**

LEADING GOALKICKER
Mathew Waterson, **Nagambie** 78

GRAND FINAL
Tallygaroopna 11.15 (81) d Nagambie 9.6 (60)

VENUE
Mooroopna Recreation Reserve

BOG MEDAL
Tim Karolidis, **Tallygaroopna**

LODDON VALLEY FL

Newbridge	**56**
Maiden Gully-YCW	**48**
Pyramid Hill	**40**
Bears Lagoon-Serpentine	**36**
Mitiamo	**36**
Calivil United	28
Bridgewater	28
Marong	12
Inglewood	4

LEAGUE B&F MEDAL
Chris Down, **Calivil United**

LEADING GOALKICKER
Jordan Gilboy, **Newbridge** 74

GRAND FINAL
Newbridge 11.11 (77) d Mitiamo 4.9 (33)

VENUE
Laser Plumbing Bendigo Oval, Bridgewater

BOG MEDAL
Alex Code, **Newbridge**

MALLEE FL (SA)

Border Downs-Tintinara	**30**
Karoonda	**23**
Peake	**19**
Pinnaroo	**10**
Lameroo	8
Murrayville	0

LEAGUE B&F MEDAL
Alex Stidiford, **Border Downs-Tintinara**

LEADING GOALKICKER
Sam Janetzki, **Peake** 63

GRAND FINAL
Border Downs-Tintinara 14.17 (101) d Karoonda 6.7 (43)

VENUE
Coonalpyn Oval

BOG MEDAL
Nathan Stark, **Border Downs-Tintinara**

MARYBOROUGH-CASTLEMAINE DISTRICT FL

Carisbrook	**60**
Natte Bealiba	**60**
Talbot	**50**
Harcourt	**46**
Trentham	**40**
Navarre	**36**
Royal Park	**32**
Maldon	**28**
Lexton	28
Avoca	28
Maryborough Rovers	24
Newstead	12
Campbells Creek	4
Dunolly	0

LEAGUE B&F MEDAL
Matthew Bilton, **Carisbrook**

LEADING GOALKICKER
Ashley Munari, **Carisbrook** 105

GRAND FINAL
Carisbrook 14.11 (95) d Natte Bealiba 3.5 (23)

VENUE
Princes Park, Maryborough

BOG MEDAL
Jackson Bowen, **Carisbrook**

MID-GIPPSLAND FL

Trafalgar	**68**
Yallourn-Yallourn North	**56**
Yinnar	**54**
Mirboo North	**46**
Thorpdale	**40**
Morwell East	32

Yarragon	26
Newborough	26
Hill End	12
Boolara	0

LEAGUE B&F MEDAL
Jared Risol, **Newborough**

LEADING GOALKICKER
Dean Macdonald, **Yallourn-Yallourn North** 101

GRAND FINAL
Trafalgar 12.12 (84) d Yinnar 9.14 (68)

VENUE
Morwell Recreation Reserve

BOG MEDALS
Klay Butler, **Trafalgar**
Matt van Schajik, **Trafalgar**

MININERA & DISTRICT FL

Wickliffe-Lake Bolac	**68**
Penshurst	**52**
Glenthompson-Dunkeld	**50**
Lismore-Derrinallum	**44**
Tatyoon	**44**
Moyston-Willaura	36
Streatham-Mininera-Westmere Rovers	32
Woorndoo-Mortlake	28
Great Western	20
Hawkesdale-Macarthur	18
Ararat Eagles	12
Caramut	0

LEAGUE B&F MEDAL
Michael Lockyer, **Lismore-Derrinallum**

LEADING GOALKICKER
William Slattery, **Wickliffe-Lake Bolac** 77

GRAND FINAL
Wickliffe-Lake Bolac 17.16 (118) d Tatyoon 4.4 (28)

VENUE
Alexandra Oval, Ararat

BOG MEDALS
Brad Keilar, **Wickliffe-Lake Bolac**
Tas Clingan, **Wickliffe-Lake Bolac**

MORNINGTON PENINSULA NEPEAN FL

Division 1

Sorrento	**56**
Mt Eliza	**50**
Pines	**48**
Edithvale-Aspendale	**48**
Frankston YCW	**40**
Frankston Bombers	36
Bonbeach	32
Mornington	20
Rosebud	18
Seaford	12

LEAGUE B&F MEDAL
Paul Scanlon, **Pines**

LEADING GOALKICKER
Aaron Edwards, **Pines** 72

GRAND FINAL
Pines 14.12 (96) d Sorrento 14.11 (95)

VENUE
Frankston Park

BOG MEDAL
Perry Lewis-Smith, **Pines**

Division 2

Dromana	**68**
Red Hill	**54**
Karingal	**52**
Chelsea	**50**
Langwarrin	**42**
Hastings	40
Pearcedale	26
Somerville	24
Rye	24
Devon Meadows	24
Tyabb	24
Crib Point	4

LEAGUE B&F MEDAL
Adam Kirkwood, **Rye**

LEADING GOALKICKER
Jesse Murphy, **Langwarrin** 74

GRAND FINAL
Red Hill 9.5 (59) lt **Dromana** 10.7 (67)

VENUE
Frankston Park

BOG MEDAL
Josh Bateman, **Dromana**

MURRAY FL

Nathalia	**68**
Barooga	**64**
Finley	**52**
Cobram	**52**
Numurkah	**48**
Rumbalara	**48**
Mulwala	**40**
Echuca United	**32**
Moama	32
Shepparton East	24
Congupna	20
Tungamah	20
Tongala	20
Katandra	12
Deniliquin	8

LEAGUE B&F MEDAL
Brodie A'Vard, **Barooga**

LEADING GOALKICKER
Brodie Ross, **Nathalia** 69

GRAND FINAL
Nathalia 13.8 (86) d Barooga 7.6 (48)

VENUE
Mercury Sports Complex, Shepparton

BOG MEDAL
Jarrod Maskell, **Nathalia**

NORTH CENTRAL FL

Birchip-Watchem	**56**
Wycheproof-Narraport	**56**
Sea Lake-Nandaly Tigers	**32**
Donald	**32**
Wedderburn	26
St Arnaud	26
Charlton	20
Boort	8

LEAGUE B&F MEDAL
Lochlan Sirett, **Birchip-Watchem**

LEADING GOALKICKER
Stephen Paulke, **Birchip-Watchem** 68

GRAND FINAL
Wycheproof-Narraport 8.8 (56) d Birchip-Watchem 2.10 (22)

VENUE
Charlton Park

BOG MEDALS
Boe Bish, **Wycheproof-Narraport**
Ricky Allan, **Wycheproof-Narraport**

NORTH GIPPSLAND FL

Yarram	**68**
Traralgon-Tyers United	**60**
Churchill	**52**
Rosedale	**44**
Sale City	**40**
Woodside	40
Heyfield	28
Gormandale	16
Cowwarr	8
Glengarry	4

LEAGUE B&F MEDAL
Griffin Underwood, **Yarram**

LEADING GOALKICKER
Stuart Buckley, **Sale City** 54

GRAND FINAL
Yarram 8.17 (65) d Churchill 5.3 (33)

VENUE
Traralgon Recreation Reserve

BOG MEDAL
Jesse Field, **Yarram**

NORTHERN RIVERINA FL (NSW)

Tulligibeal	**60**
Hillston	**40**
Lake Cargelligo	**36**
West Wyalong-Girral	**32**
Ungarie	8
Condobolin-Milby	4

LEAGUE B&F MEDAL
Aaron Hart, **Lake Cargelligo**

LEADING GOALKICKER
Brant Frankel, **Tulligibeal** 56

GRAND FINAL
Tullibigbeal 15.5 (95) d Lake Cargelligo 9.14 (68)

VENUE
West Wyalong Recreation Ground

BOG MEDAL
Kieran Fair, **Tullibigeal**

OMEO DISTRICT FL

Bruthen	**52**
Lindenow South	**40**
Swifts Creek	**40**
Omeo-Benambra	**36**
Buchan	6
Swan Reach	6

LEAGUE B&F MEDAL
Harley Kenner, **Bruthen**

LEADING GOALKICKER
Max Solomon, **Lindenow South** 81

GRAND FINAL
Bruthen 14.11 (95) d Swifts Creek 10.9 (69)

VENUE
Swan Reach Recreation Reserve

BOG MEDAL
Craig Taylor, **Bruthen**

OVENS & KING FL

Milawa	**64**
Tarrawingee	**64**
Benalla All Blacks	**56**
Glenrowan	**56**
King Valley	**48**
Bright	**40**
Greta	40
Whorouly	24
Moyhu	24
Goorambat	12
North Wangaratta	4
Bonnie Doon	0

LEAGUE B&F MEDAL
Chris Dube, **Greta**

LEADING GOALKICKER
James McClounan, **Milawa** 94

GRAND FINAL
Tarrawingee 9.7 (61) d Milawa 5.4 (34)

VENUE
W.J. Findlay Oval, Wangaratta

BOG MEDAL
Daine Porter, **Tarrawingee**

OVENS & MURRAY FL

Albury	72
Wodonga Raiders	**60**
Wangaratta	**56**
Yarrawonga	**52**
Lavington	**38**
North Albury	30
Wodonga	24
Myrtleford	16
Corowa-Rutherglen	12
Wangaratta Rovers	0

LEAGUE B&F MEDAL
Brodie Filo, **Wodonga Raiders**

LEADING GOALKICKER
Michael Newton, **Wangaratta** 81

GRAND FINAL
Albury 11.12 (78) d Wangaratta 10.10 (70)

VENUE
Norm Minns Oval, Wangaratta

BOG MEDAL
Dean Polo, **Albury**

PICOLA & DISTRICT FL

Waaia	72
Picola United	**60**
Deniliquin Rovers	**56**
Blighty	**52**
Strathmerton	**44**
Rennie	**44**
Berrigan	44
Katunga	32
Katamatite	28
Tocumwal	12
Mathoura	12

Yarroweyah	8
Jerilderie	4

LEAGUE B&F MEDAL
Mark Ryan, **Picola United**
Ashley Thompson, **Waaia**

LEADING GOALKICKER
Charlie Burrows, **Waaia** 51

GRAND FINAL
Picola United 3.6 (24) lt **Rennie** 9.8 (62)

VENUE
Jerilderie Recreation Reserve

BOG MEDAL
Nic O'Bryan, **Rennie**

RIDDELL DFL

Rupertswood	**56**
Riddell	**52**
Diggers Rest	**48**
Wallan	**48**
Macedon	**44**
Romsey	**36**
Woodend-Hesket	32
Sunbury Kangaroos	24
Melton Centrals	24
Lancefield	12
Broadford	4
Rockbank	4

LEAGUE B&F MEDAL
Jesse Davies, **Wallan**

LEADING GOALKICKER
Haydn Ross, **Riddell** 74

GRAND FINAL
Riddell 6.9 (45) lt **Diggers Rest** 9.12 (66)

VENUE
Clarke Oval, Sunbury

BOG MEDALS
Tom Gleeson, **Diggers Rest**
Tommy Taylor, **Diggers Rest**

RIVERINA FL (NSW)

Griffith	**72**
Collingullie-Glenfield Park	**60**
Ganmain-Grong Grong-Matong	**52**
Mangoplah-Cookardinia United-Eastlake	**46**
Leeton-Whitton	**38**
Coolamon Rovers	36
Turvey Park	30
Wagga Tigers	18
Narrandera	8

LEAGUE B&F MEDAL
Jarred Lane, **Narrandera**

LEADING GOALKICKER
Riley Corbett, **Ganmain-Grong Grong-Matong** 70

GRAND FINAL
Collingullie-Glenfield Park 12.8 (80) d Griffith 12.6 (78)

VENUE
Narrandera Sportsground

BOG MEDAL
Daniel Kennedy, **Collingullie-Glenfield Park**

AFL SOUTH EAST

Narre Warren	**56**
Berwick	**52**
Cranbourne	**44**
Beaconsfield	**36**
Officer	**26**
Tooradin-Dalmore	22
Pakenham	20
Doveton	0

LEAGUE B&F MEDAL
Madison Andrews, **Berwick**

LEADING GOALKICKER
Harrison Money, **Berwick** 56
Marc Holt, **Cranbourne** 56

GRAND FINAL
Berwick 8.25 (73) d Narre Warren 2.10 (22)

VENUE
Edwin Flack Reserve, Berwick

BOG MEDAL
Travis Tuck, **Berwick**

SOUTH WEST DISTRICT FL

Heywood	**60**
Heathmere	**56**
Dartmoor	**40**
Westerns	**36**
Coleraine	**28**
Tyrendarra	28
Branxholme-Wallacedale	8
Cavendish	0

LEAGUE B&F MEDAL
Tyson Hogan, **Coleraine**

LEADING GOALKICKER
Mick Wilson, **Heathmere** 83

GRAND FINAL
Heathmere 8.6 (54) lt **Heywood** 11.18 (84)

VENUE
Dartmoor Recreation Reserve

BOG MEDAL
Nick Johnstone, **Heywood**

SUNRAYSIA FL

Ouyen United	**56**
Red Cliffs	**52**
Robinvale-Euston	**48**
Irymple	**40**
South Mildura	20
Wentworth	16
Mildura	12
Merbein	4

LEAGUE B&F MEDAL
Josh Gregg, **Ouyen United**

LEADING GOALKICKER
Tom Morrish, **Ouyen United** 48

GRAND FINAL
Ouyen United 10.11 (71) d Irymple 10.6 (66)

VENUE
City Oval, Mildura

BOG MEDAL
Brad Vallance, **Ouyen United**

TALLANGATTA & DISTRICT FL

Kiewa-Sandy Creek	**64**
Barnawatha	**60**
Thurgoona	**60**
Tallangatta	**56**
Mitta United	**44**
Dederang-Mt Beauty	36
Rutherglen	32
Beechworth	32
Yackandandah	16
Chiltern	16
Wahgunyah	16
Wodonga Saints	0

LEAGUE B&F MEDAL
Cameron McNeill, **Barnawatha**

LEADING GOALKICKER
Guy Telford, **Kiewa-Sandy Creek** 87

GRAND FINAL
Kiewa-Sandy Creek 14.16 (100) d Thurgoona 9.8 (62)

VENUE
Sandy Creek Recreation Reserve

BOG MEDAL
Jack Di Mizio, **Kiewa-Sandy Creek**

UPPER MURRAY FL

Bullioh	**60**
Federal	**44**
Cudgewa	**36**
Corryong	**28**
Border-Walwa	8
Tumbarumba	4

LEAGUE B&F MEDAL
Zac Burhop, **Bullioh**

LEADING GOALKICKER
Hamish Clark, **Bullioh** 63

GRAND FINAL
Bullioh 12.18 (90) d Federal 9.8 (62)

VENUE
Tallangatta Valley Recreation Reserve

BOG MEDAL
Hamish Clark, **Bullioh**

WARRNAMBOOL & DISTRICT FL

Nirranda	**64**
Old Collegians	**64**
Kolora-Noorat	**56**
Timboon Demons	**52**
South Rovers	**48**
Merrivale	40
Allansford	32
Dennington	28
Russells Creek	24
East Warrnambool	20
Panmure	12

LEAGUE B&F MEDAL
Andrew McMeel, **Russells Creek**

LEADING GOALKICKER
Jason Rowan, **Merrivale** 72

GRAND FINAL
Nirranda 10.11 (71) d Old Collegians 5.10 (40)

VENUE
Reid Oval, Warrnambool

BOG MEDAL
John Paulin, **Nirranda**

WEST GIPPSLAND FL

Phillip Island	**56**
Nar Nar Goon	**56**
Koo Wee Rup	**56**
Inverloch-Kongwak	**56**
Cora Lynn	**44**
Garfield	40
Korumburra-Bena	20
Bunyip	16
Kilcunda-Bass	8
Dalyston	8

LEAGUE B&F MEDAL
Brendan Kimber, **Phillip Island**

LEADING GOALKICKER
Jason Wells, **Koo Wee Rup** 88

GRAND FINAL
Phillip Island 14.18 (102) d Koo Wee Rup 0.3 (3)

VENUE
Garfield Recreation Reserve

BOG MEDAL
Aaron Edwards, **Phillip Island**

WESTERN BORDER FL (SA)

Casterton-Sandford	**25**
Millicent	**25**
West Gambier	**18**
East Gambier	**18**
North Gambier	6
South Gambier	4

LEAGUE B&F MEDAL
Tom Hutchesson, **Millicent**

LEADING GOALKICKER
Brayden Kain, **South Gambier** 51

GRAND FINAL
Millicent 11.10 (76) d East Gambier 11.6 (72)

VENUE
McDonald Park, Mt Gambier

BOG MEDAL
Tom Hutchesson, **Millicent**

WIMMERA FL

Horsham	**64**
Southern Mallee Giants	**56**
Ararat	**52**
Horsham Saints	**48**
Warrack Eagles	**44**
Minyip-Murtoa	36
Stawell	36
Nhill	16
Dimboola	8

LEAGUE B&F MEDAL
Ryan Kemp, **Horsham**
Dan Mendes, **Ararat**
Nick Peters, **Warrack Eagles**

LEADING GOALKICKER
Ryan Kemp, **Horsham** 79

GRAND FINAL
Southern Mallee Giants 9.3 (57) lt **Horsham** 11.10 (76)

VENUE
Anzac Memorial Park, Warracknabeal

BOG MEDAL
Ben Lakin, **Horsham**

AFL YARRA RANGES

Division 1

Woori Yallock	**56**
Olinda-Ferny Creek	**52**
Wandin	**52**
Upwey-Tecoma	**52**
Healesville	**40**
Mount Evelyn	36
Monbulk	36
Emerald	20
Belgrave	8
Warburton-Millgrove	8

LEAGUE B&F MEDAL
Marcus Hottes, **Olinda-Ferny Creek**

LEADING GOALKICKER
Justin Van Unen, **Wandin** 96

GRAND FINAL
Wandin 16.11 (107) d Woori Yallock 9.16 (70)

VENUE
Yarra Glen Football Ground

BOG MEDAL
Robbie Ross, **Wandin**

Division 2

Seville	**68**
Yarra Glen	**64**
Yarra Junction	**52**
Gembrook-Cockatoo	**48**
Alexandra	**32**
Yea	32
Powelltown	32
Kinglake	24
Thornton-Eildon	8

LEAGUE B&F MEDAL
Mark Cecere, **Seville**

LEADING GOALKICKER
Nathan O'Keefe, **Seville** 82

GRAND FINAL
Yarra Junction 20.17 (137) d Seville 6.5 (41)

VENUE
Healesville Football Ground

BOG MEDAL
Troy Armstrong, **Yarra Junction**